WOMEN'S STUDIES INTERNATIONAL

WOMEN'S STUDIES INTERNATIONAL
Nairobi and Beyond

Edited by Aruna Rao

The Feminist Press
at The City University of New York
New York

All rights reserved. Published 1991 by The Feminist Press at The City University of New York, 311 East 94th Street, New York, NY 10128.
Distributed by The Talman Company, 150 Fifth Avenue, New York, NY 10011.

94 93 92 91 6 5 4 3 2 1

Library of Congress Cataloging-in-Publication Data
Women's studies international: Nairobi and beyond / edited by Aruna Rao.
    p. cm.
  Includes bibliographical references.
  ISBN 1-55861-031-6 (alk. paper) : $35.00 —
  ISBN 1-55861-032-4 (pbk. : alk. paper) : $15.95
  1. Women's studies. 2. Women in development. 3. Women's studies—
Directories. I. Rao, Aruna.
HQ1180.W684 1991
305.4'07—dc20   90-48653
                                                       CIP

This publication is made possible, in part, by a major contribution from the Ford Foundation and by funds from the L. J. Skaggs and Mary C. Skaggs Foundation.

Cover and text design: Paula Martinac

Cover photos: top and bottom left: panelists and participants at the Nairobi NGO United Nations Forum, July 1985, courtesy of Florence Howe; *right:* member of the Self Employed Women's Association, courtesy of Martha Stuart Communications

Typeset by Rachel's Wife, North Creek, New York 12853.
Printed in the United States of America on acid-free paper by McNaughton & Gunn, Inc., Saline, Michigan.

To my parents, Susheela and P. J. Rao

CONTENTS

ACKNOWLEDGMENTS

This volume is the product of cooperative efforts on the part of many. I would like to take this opportunity to thank our authors for their creativity and hard work; our Advisory Board for their helpful suggestions and comments; the Ford Foundation whose support enabled us to publish this volume; my friend and colleague in this venture, Florence Howe, one of the founders of The Feminist Press and publisher of *Women's Studies International: Nairobi and Beyond;* and the staff of The Feminist Press, particularly Susannah Driver, Kathy Casto, Rebecca Rozanski, Donna Weir, and Nataly Jones, for their valuable editorial and production assistance. Lastly, I would like to thank my husband, Reidar Kvam, who helped pull together this volume for publication.

FOREWORD

The complexity of the issues and challenges facing women's studies internationally is succinctly illustrated in this volume of collected articles and program descriptions. The book is also a testimony to the remarkable growth of the field within a relatively short period of two decades. Research, writing, and teaching on women's issues received a new life globally in the 1970s, largely due to the international women's movement and the United Nations Decade for Women and Development (1975–1985). More important, this upsurge of interest was sustained even after the Decade was over. As some of the articles in this volume point out, research and teaching on gender issues have been institutionalized in a number of places around the world, although the institutional foothold often remains tenuous and marginal. Women's concerns have also been institutionalized in governments (in women's ministries, women's bureaus, and women's units) and in international organizations—multilateral and bilateral development agencies, private foundations, and nongovernmental organizations (NGOs). Indeed, it is this coalition of diverse forces—researchers, activists, governments, NGOs, and international development agencies—that has kept women on the global agenda for the last twenty years.

The multifaceted objectives of this diverse constituency, in part, explain the various themes of this volume. Women's studies does not aim merely to make a contribution to theory and learning; it has the more immediate objective of influencing policy and action. Linking research, policy, and action as an integrated and interactive process is one of the major goals of women's studies internationally. Several articles in this volume describe how this connection was accomplished in concrete situations.

It is difficult to evaluate the contributions and impact of a relatively new field such as women's studies. This book highlights some of the fundamental questions raised by practitioners regarding goals, contents, and methods of learning. It demonstrates how a focus on gender results in changing established concepts and methods of data collection, social analysis, and policy planning. It identifies priority areas that deserve attention in the future. It also provides a resource list and a guide to selected women's research and training centers on several continents. The book is, thus, a valuable source of information for a variety of audiences: researchers, activists, and policy makers in national and international organizations.

This volume also points toward new directions for women's studies throughout the world. With limited resources and within a short time frame, research and teaching on gender issues have made a good beginning internationally but face an even more challenging future. One major challenge voiced by several authors is alternative conceptualization of theoretical models of analysis. Research up to now has focused more often on demonstrating the limitations of existing theories, models, and methodologies, but formulation of alternatives has not received equal attention. This remains a major weakness of women's studies which needs to be addressed in the future. A related problem is lack of wide dissemination and use of existing research findings. Alternative conceptual frameworks and methodologies developed in micro surveys and special studies are rarely used by nonfeminist researchers or specialists unacquainted with women in development (WID) writings, programs, and projects.

Macro-micro linkage is yet another challenge facing women's studies internationally. Researchers have generated substantial amounts of data at the community and project levels but have yet to explore how changes in women's lives at these micro levels are affected by changes in overall social and economic policies. In fact, policies not aimed specifically at women but at promoting economic growth, engineering social change, or altering the distribution of natural resources such as land, water, and forest often have a far greater impact in changing gender roles and status than do more limited efforts of women-specific programs and projects. The process through which gender-blind macro policies yield gender-differentiated results at the micro level needs to be analyzed further so that the social and economic policy instruments that support women's status and well-being can be identified and advocated.

Finally, creating a vision of an alternative world order remains a continuing challenge for women's studies. From the beginning, feminists have asserted the need for a different vision of the future; but the elements of this future order at the local, national, regional, and international levels have not been adequately spelled out. In the absence of such an elaboration there is a misperception that women's studies is only concerned about the conditions and fate of women and not of people. Future research and teaching need to highlight the message that a feminist perspective on development connotes not only women's self-development; it also implies redefinition of all the issues that confront humanity.

Rounaq Jahan

WOMEN'S STUDIES INTERNATIONAL

INTRODUCTION

Aruna Rao

This volume contains an international portrait of feminist research, teaching strategies, policy, and action. It grew out of the Women's Studies International (WSI) meetings at the Nairobi NGO (nongovernmental organization) United Nations Forum in 1985—four panels and thirteen workshops in which practitioners from all over the world shared insights on theoretical debates and dilemmas, institutions and program strategies, methodological approaches, practical problems, and needed resources.

Though the Nairobi conference is half a decade behind us, requests for the papers produced for the meetings and for other related and updated information still come in from all quarters. In response, we present here an overview of the discussions held at Nairobi as well as a series of papers, some of which originate from the Nairobi WSI sessions and some which reflect contemporary thinking since the conference. Most important, in response to requests from our colleagues at Nairobi, we also highlight model programs in women's studies, women in development, and gender studies from around the world, and include an annotated listing of organizations engaged in feminist research and teaching.

HISTORY AND DEVELOPMENT OF WOMEN'S STUDIES INTERNATIONAL

WSI came into being in July 1980 at the Copenhagen NGO Forum, a part of the mid-decade meeting of the UN Decade for Women. There, The Feminist Press in collaboration with two institutions—the Simone de Beauvoir Institute of Concordia University, Montreal, and the Research

1

Center for Women's Studies, SNDT Women's University, Bombay—as well as the U.S. National Women's Studies Association, organized a series of well-attended panels and workshops on a variety of subjects ranging from women's studies research methodologies to links with theory. At those sessions, it became clear that what people wanted most was a "network," beginning with the compilation, maintenance, and sharing of a mailing list to enable participants to communicate on a regular basis. On the last day of the Copenhagen conference, the core participants of the WSI sessions formed the WSI Network, coordinated by Florence Howe (The Feminist Press) and Vina Mazumdar (Center for Women's Development Studies, New Delhi), and housed at The Feminist Press. The network functioned well in the five years between Copenhagen and Nairobi and facilitated the planning of the WSI sessions in 1985.

The Nairobi WSI, however, differed vastly from its predecessor. Four times as many people attended the Nairobi sessions as those in Copenhagen. WSI Nairobi also reflected the growth of the international network started at Copenhagen. It was sponsored by twenty-four institutions from fourteen countries ranging from Canada to Argentina to Japan. Planning for the conference took place in stages beginning at the UNESCO-sponsored international conference on women's studies held at The Hague in the spring of 1985. The program was finalized that summer in New York by the WSI planning committee—Gloria Bonder (Argentina), Mariam Chamberlain (U.S.), Florence Howe (U.S.), Vina Mazumdar (India), and Aruna Rao (India).

A large percentage of the Nairobi WSI participants were from Africa, Asia, and Latin America, while those at Copenhagen came predominantly from Europe and the U.S. No doubt, this was in part a function of the conference's location, but it also reflected the growing interest and achievements in this field among practitioners in the non-Western world.

WSI NAIROBI: THEMES, SHARED CONCERNS, AND ENDURING DIFFERENCES

WSI Nairobi sessions were held over a period of seven days. Panel topics focused on: Women's Studies as a Strategy for Educational Change; New Developments in Research on Women; Integrating Gender into Development Training; and Women's Centers as Agents of Change. Workshop sessions dealt with such issues as theoretical perspectives in women's studies; institutionalization; participatory research methodologies; teaching methods; links between research, action, and public policy; integration of race and class/caste into women's studies; women's studies, law, and civil rights; new developments in women's history; the "new" women's literature: autobiographies, diaries, and letters; and women's studies: linkages and future development.

The WSI Nairobi experience reconfirmed that questioning and change remained fundamental characteristics of feminist research, teaching strategies, and action. Women's studies questions philosophical and political traditions, and aims to change cultural values and attitudes and their ideological and institutional manifestations. In the first instance that involves making the invisible visible. In the Nairobi workshop on theoretical perspectives in women's studies, Florence Howe emphasized the importance of "naming," pointing out that "to have an identity, you must have a history." In the United States, women's studies in the early seventies grew out of the women's movement. Vina Mazumdar stated that in India, women's studies grew out of a need to examine the impact of development processes on women. In these two countries as elsewhere, women's studies also tends to be multidisciplinary, cognizant of its political nature; it also aims to be integrative of class, caste, and/or race.

Second, in the course of making the invisible visible, feminist scholars and activists question objective knowledge and the inviolability of scientific truths that are assumed to be outside human intervention. This involves analyzing language and the processes by which meaning has been acquired, and analyzing what these processes reveal about how power is constituted and operates.[1] It also involves analyzing difference, "deconstructing binary oppositions," and determining how they are operating in specific contexts (Scott, 1988). At the same time, feminist scholars and practitioners are attempting to legitimize research methodologies and teaching strategies, and to use new sources of information on women's lives that previously were considered academically illegitimate. Many researchers and activists talked about the participatory research methods they are using to generate information by involving the research subjects as active partners. The aim of this process is to bring about a two-way communication between the researcher and the researched, and at the same time to increase their awareness of their own situation and the possibilities for collective action. As Adriana Santa Cruz (Chile), who directs a regional information network in Latin America, pointed out, "It is not enough to research; we must also communicate."

However, some scholars at Nairobi cautioned about the limitations of participatory research methods and about making generalizations based on small samples. "Participatory research cannot be a substitute for economic surveys," pointed out K. Saradamoni (India), while Norma Shorey-Brian (Barbados) suggested that "we do not need to legitimize action-oriented research in terms of traditional, formal methodologies since the aims of both are very different." Teaching methods in women's studies are similarly concerned with breaking down hierarchical barriers between the teacher and the taught, and in probing new sources for information on women's lives. These sources include diaries, letters, and poems written by women in various places and times, ranging from Meiji Japan to the turn of the century in Bangladesh to contemporary southern black communities in the

United States. In many countries, feminist researchers are also investigating areas previously untouched, such as family violence in India and female sexuality in Brazil.

Third, the research and teaching methods newly in use in women's studies implicitly involve broadening the base of power, where knowledge is power. Empowerment is also fundamentally entwined with legal education and the implementation of legal and civil rights. How do women in the fields and factories get information on their legal rights? In what areas are women still discriminated against? Where is new legislation needed? What is the responsibility of women's studies practitioners vis-à-vis the enactment and enforcement of laws supporting women? These were some of the issues debated at the WSI Nairobi workshop, Women, Law, and Civil Rights.

Empowering women is a key aim of women's centers around the world. At Nairobi, WSI session participants also discussed the role of women's centers and women's studies/women in development programs in generating and disseminating information on and to women, providing services to women, and lobbying for policy and program changes. Women's studies programs in Brazil, for example, include sex-education and literacy programs for poor women in urban slums, while women in development programs in Zimbabwe conduct literacy and training in income-generation skills for poor rural women; campus-based women's centers in the U.S. provide both university and local community women with a sheltered place to share experiences and learn from each other, just as do women's centers in the Third World, such as Saheli in India, which acts as a community support group for battered women. Both the Women in Nigeria group and the Equity Policy Center in Washington conduct policy research that they use to lobby their respective governments. And though many of these centers and programs are small, they represent a voice and provide both hitherto unavailable laboratories for experimentation and vehicles for engineering social change. Collectively, they make a difference.

The Nairobi WSI sessions also highlighted enduring tensions and points of difference in orientation, terminology, and priorities among feminist researchers, teachers, policy makers, and activists. One of these tensions is between academic research and theory generation on the one hand and activism on the other. Speaking to this issue, Fulvia Rosenberg (Brazil) pointed to the necessity of distinguishing the "needs of scientific knowledge from the objectives of political practice." By "putting knowledge [solely] at the service of a changing practice," women's studies researchers in Brazil, she believes, at first neglected theoretical reflection, which is indispensable to action. But the discussions at Nairobi (and elsewhere) indicate that the attempt to separate knowledge generation from activism remains controversial because to some it implies a return to the kinds of academic hierarchies and control over knowledge and power that feminist practice in its broadest sense aims to break.

Another tension is the difference implied in some contexts between women's studies and women in development studies. In the U.S. context, the two have usually been separated. But in a developing country's context, because women's studies necessarily looks at women's experience in the context of poverty as well as in relation to development policies and programs, there is no such separation. At one meeting on women's studies in Asia, participants agreed that "women's studies was aimed at balancing our understanding of social reality with information on women's contribution to that process, women's perceptions (of their own lives, struggles, aspirations), and on the roots and structures of inequality that exclude women from the frameworks of intellectual inquiry and social action."[2] In Europe as well, women's studies and women in development studies are integrated. Within certain disciplines, feminist studies focus on Western societies, and in other disciplines such studies have a non-Western orientation.

More important, over the decade there has been a shift in emphasis from a specific focus on women as a group to an analysis of gender differences among women and between women and men. Partly this shift reflects a growing emphasis on the differences among women of various races, classes, and castes. Partly too, it reflects the importance for knowledge generation as well as program and policy change of analyzing female/male differences within and across classes: what specific groups of women and men do, why, and with what resources, and within what cultural, political, economic, and familial contexts.

How do we choose what is most appropriate for our own contexts? How do we recognize and use notions of gender difference and yet make arguments for equality? What is the effect of our choice on our ability to build a political constituency? And what is the relationship between theory/knowledge building and political practice?

In analyzing a parallel debate on conflicting feminist positions and political strategies characterized as "equality versus difference," Joan W. Scott suggests that "the critical feminist position must always involve ... the systematic criticism of the operations of categorical difference, the exposure of the kinds of exclusions and inclusions—the hierarchies—it constructs, and a refusal of their ultimate 'truth.'" "However," she states, this refusal should not be "in the name of an equality that implies sameness or identity, but rather in the name of an equality that rests on differences—differences that confound, disrupt, and render ambiguous the meaning of any fixed binary opposition . . . To do anything else is to buy into the political argument that sameness is a requirement for equality, an untenable position for feminists . . . who know that power is constructed on and so must be challenged from the ground of difference" (Scott, 1988).

ORGANIZATION OF THIS VOLUME

In the pages that follow, some of these debates and others are explored in depth. However, it should be noted that many important issues and topics are not dealt with here nor does this volume claim global coverage on the issues discussed. The gaps are circumstantial, not intentional.

In the volume's opening section, "Theory and Learning," Scott specifies in her article, "Gender: A Useful Category of Historical Analysis," how one can think about the effects of gender in social and institutional relationships. Scott develops a two-part definition of gender (each with several subsets), whose elements are interrelated but analytically distinct. "The core of the definition rests on an integral connection between two propositions: gender is a constitutive element of social relationships based on perceived differences between the sexes, and gender is a primary way of signifying relationships of power."

Next, in her article on education and rural women in the Indian context, Mazumdar picks up on the potential of educators and educational institutions in finding answers and building new minds through research and teaching. She places the responsibility for learning to unlearn our misconceptions about women's lives squarely on the educational system. "Modern education has blinded us to the reality of women's lives in the villages," she asserts. Thus, it is the duty of educational institutions to generate more accurate information by investigating the past and contemporary histories of rural women. Therein, Mazumdar believes, is the key to understanding "the origin of women's subordination" and "changing the present iniquitous and destructive path of development."

The third article in this section illustrates a key alternative to traditional theoretical conceptualizations. In it, Bruce challenges the traditional conceptualization of the "household" in economic theory. "Since men's and women's access to and control of resources differ systematically in the wider world—the world of income relations," she argues, "why would their personal economies be served by a common ground plan in the internal world of income relations?" Drawing on empirical evidence from many countries, Bruce argues that "men and women have distinct self-interests within the family," which are "pursued not through playing out cooperative plans, but rather through institutionalized inequalities." How is this concept relevant to policy? Simply and most importantly, it underscores that "individuals rather than households should be the recipients of economic outlays, whether in the form of cash outlays, valued goods, or wage-earning opportunities, with women being more appropriate recipients when certain ends are desired."

The following section, "Teaching and Strategies for Change," illustrates both a macrocosmic view and a micro, on-the-ground perspective. In the first article, Barroso discusses the role of women's studies as a strategy for social change. She outlines a two-fold strategy for the women's studies community: first, to keep close ties to the women's movement; and second, to keep an open and flexible approach in institution building, substantive analysis, methodological choices, and styles of expression. Echoing Fulvia Rosenberg's concern, Barroso argues for a sharing of responsibilities among women's studies practitioners "so that each one of us does not have to be on permanent duty for every protest, for every campaign. Thus, we simultaneously accord legitimacy to the systematic study that is so much needed and that is our special contribution both to the movement and to the social sciences."

The second article in this section presents an illustration of a nontraditional teaching/training situation. In it, Stuart describes the use of video as a tool in the grassroots training and organizing of women. Focusing on the use of video by the Self Employed Women's Association (SEWA) in India, Stuart points to the flexibility and adaptability of video with regard to training at the local level. "Video puts illiterate viewers as well as illiterate producers on par with their literate counterparts. This levelling or equalizing element can transform relationships, encourage a high degree of participation, and have great impact."

The third section of the volume focuses on policy making: utilizing research findings and existing data in lobbying for policy change. In the first of the two articles in this section, McKee analyzes a case in Nepal—the Status of Women study—where successful linkages were made between research on gender issues in agriculture and government policy. What were the factors that contributed to the study's use for policy purposes? McKee suggests several, including the facts that the study focused on a "strategic topic ... that was of high priority to the target audience," it "compared men and women," "it combined both quantitative and qualitative data," and it tailored the "project design and dissemination of results to [its] policy audience."

The second article, by Thomson, describes and analyzes a recent, innovative project to integrate gender issues in development research and policy in Thailand. Housed at the Thailand Research Development Institute, a high-level think tank on national development issues, the project forged effective ways of utilizing information to convince key decision makers of the significance of women's roles to the achievement of national development goals, informal networking to build the ranks of its allies, and participatory teamwork in responding to needs of key actors in the policy arena as those needs arose. Thomson stresses the important and unique role women play as grassroots leaders in challenging stereotypic attitudes about the skills and interests of poor rural women. In taking responsibility for rural and community development work, they themselves are often their most effective advocates.

The issue of institutionalization is addressed by two articles in the fourth section of this volume, "Institutionalization." Howe examines the growth and institutionalization of women's studies in the United States. The role of educational institutions in generating new knowledge was a paramount goal in the minds of academics in the U.S. context as is indicated in the manifestos of women's studies programs in the 1970s. Howe points out that throughout that decade, women's studies programs spread rapidly because of both student demand and the existence of a sizeable percentage of female faculty. As of 1989, Howe counted 504 women's studies programs in the United States, and her article goes on to identify the factors that promoted this institutionalization.

What are some of the ways in which new knowledge generated about women is used? What are some effective ways of mainstreaming gender issues in development in, for example, training? My article addresses these questions. In it, I analyze five training experiments drawn from around the world that attempt to "integrate gender into a mainstream planning framework and equip managers of major economic and social development schemes to effectively meet women's needs, enhance their productivity, and ensure their access to development benefits." These programs share similar goals but differ in terms of theoretical perspectives, institutionalization strategies, training styles, the materials they use, and the levels of personnel they reach. I examine the implications of these differences, discuss the problems they face, and indicate future directions.

"Research on Women: New Models and Priorities," the fifth section in this volume, contains three reviews of research on women and gender issues. Bonder reviews past research in women's studies in Latin America, while Karim and Reddock deal with Southeast Asia and the Commonwealth Caribbean respectively. All three authors delineate priority topics for future research in their area of concern.

The section that follows, "Program Descriptions," highlights in considerable detail ten programs from around the world, primarily university based, that engage in research and teaching on women and gender issues. The programs included here are: the Women, Men and Development Course at the Institute of Development Studies, University of Sussex; the Centre for Women's Studies in Education at the Ontario Institute for Studies in Education; the Center for Women's Studies at Ohio State University; the Women and Development Program at the Institute of Social Studies, The Hague; the Institute for Women's Studies in the Arab World, Beirut University College; the Center for Women's Studies in Buenos Aires; the Interdisciplinary Program on Women's Studies at the Colegio de Mexico; the Research Center for Women's Studies at the SNDT Women's University in Bombay; and the Women in Development Consortium in Thailand and Canada.

The final section of this volume consists of a listing of more than two hundred centers that are involved in research, teaching, publishing, information dissemination, networking, and program planning and implementation on issues concerning women worldwide.

CONCLUSION

The Women's Studies International Network, which was born in Copenhagen and grew in Nairobi, has now expanded to encompass still more feminist scholars and practitioners around the world engaged in productive and innovative work. Some are just beginning while others have made tremendous progress. In sharing insights and information on theory, methods, research priorities, teaching strategies, institutionalization, and policy making and programs, this volume hopes to broaden the knowledge base in the field. But it represents only one part of a process of sharing and strengthening, which we hope will continue among feminists worldwide.

In conclusion, I share a few words sent from Julinda Abu Nasr, director of the Institute for Women's Studies in the Arab World in Beirut and a member of the Advisory Board for this volume. Julinda reminds us how basic are the challenges facing some of us and how important it is for all of us to remember each other.

> ... You may know that we do not have any mail service now in Lebanon due to the horrible situation here. Occasionally we have a pouch from New York that may come through Cyprus ... We need all the help we can get to promote peace ... You can't imagine what a nightmare we are living through. Peace, peace, peace—that is all we long for. We spend most of our days in bomb shelters, shivering and worrying about our lives, our loved ones, our homes and friends. We have no electricity, no water, no communication with the rest of the world. No words can describe the state of misery we are living in. May God have mercy and grant decision makers, wherever they are, some mercy, wisdom, and compassion for the suffering of the people of Lebanon. What you see and hear is generally distorted and not factual. Politicians and news media people can bluff everybody by their presentations and rhetoric. Justice—where is it? How can we reach it? Is it fair that a whole nation be sacrificed for the interest of a few who are greedy and malicious?

Julinda Abu Nasr
Beirut, September 1989

NOTES

1. Joan Scott, "Deconstructing Equality-Versus-Difference: Or, the Uses of Poststructuralist Theory for Feminism," *Feminist Studies* 14, no. 1 (Spring 1988).

2. *Report of the Expert Meeting on Women's Studies and Social Sciences in Asia,* UNESCO, Bangkok, 1983.

I

THEORY
AND LEARNING

GENDER: A USEFUL CATEGORY OF HISTORICAL ANALYSIS

Joan W. Scott

Gender. n. a grammatical term only. To talk of persons or creatures of the masculine or feminine gender, meaning of the male or female sex, is either a jocularity (permissible or not according to context) or a blunder.—Fowler's *Dictionary of Modern English Usage*, (Oxford, 1940).

Those who would codify the meanings of words fight a losing battle, for words, like the ideas and things they are meant to signify, have a history. Neither Oxford dons nor the Academie Française have been entirely able to stem the tide, to capture and fix meanings free of the play of human invention and imagination. Mary Wortley Montagu added bite to her witty denunciation "of the fair sex" ("my only consolation for being of that gender has been the assurance of never being married to any one among them") by deliberately misusing the grammatical reference.[1] Through the ages, people have made figurative allusions by employing grammatical terms to evoke traits of character or sexuality. For example, the usage offered by the *Dictionnaire de la langue française* in 1876 was, "On ne sait de quel genre il est, s'il est mâle ou femelle, se dit d'un homme très-caché, dont on ne connait pas les sentiments."[2] And Gladstone made this distinction in 1878: "Athene has nothing of sex except the gender, nothing of the woman except the form."[3] Most recently—too recently to find its way into dictionaries or the *Encyclopedia of the Social Sciences*—feminists have in a more literal and serious vein begun to use "gender" as a way of referring to the social organization of the relationship between the sexes. The connection to grammar is both explicit and full of unexamined possibilities. Explicit because the grammatical usage involves formal rules that follow from the masculine or feminine designation; full of unexamined possibilities because in many Indo-Euro-

13

pean languages there is a third category—unsexed or neuter.

In its most recent usage, "gender" seems to have first appeared among American feminists who wanted to insist on the fundamentally social quality of distinctions based on sex. The word denoted a rejection of the biological determinism implicit in the use of such terms as "sex" or "sexual difference." "Gender" also stressed the relational aspect of normative definitions of femininity. Those who worried that women's studies scholarship focused too narrowly and separately on women used the term "gender" to introduce a relational notion into our analytic vocabulary. According to this view, women and men were defined in terms of one another, and no understanding of either could be achieved by entirely separate study. Thus Natalie Davis suggested in 1975, "It seems to me that we should be interested in the history of both women and men, that we should not be working only on the subjected sex any more than a historian of class can focus entirely on peasants. Our goal is to understand the significance of the *sexes*, of gender groups in the historical past. Our goal is to discover the range in sex roles and in sexual symbolism in different societies and periods, to find out what meaning they had and how they functioned to maintain the social order or to promote its change."[4]

In addition, and perhaps most important, "gender" was a term offered by those who claimed that women's scholarship would fundamentally transform disciplinary paradigms. Feminist scholars pointed out early on that the study of women would not only add new subject matter but would also force a critical reexamination of the premises and standards of existing scholarly work. "We are learning," wrote three feminist historians, "that the writing of women into history necessarily involves redefining and enlarging traditional notions of historical significance, to encompass personal, subjective experience as well as public and political activities. It is not too much to suggest that however hesitant the actual beginnings, such a methodology implies not only a new history of women, but also a new history."[5] The way in which this new history would both include and account for women's experience rested on the extent to which gender could be developed as a category of analysis. Here the analogies to class (and race) were explicit; indeed, the most politically inclusive of scholars of women's studies regularly invoked all three categories as crucial to the writing of a new history.[6] An interest in class, race, and gender signaled first, a scholar's commitment to a history that included stories of the oppressed and an analysis of the meaning and nature of their oppression and, second, scholarly understanding that inequalities of power are organized along at least three axes.

The litany of class, race, and gender suggests a parity for each term, but, in fact, that is not at all the case. While "class" most often rests on Marx's elaborate (and since elaborated) theory of economic determination and historical change, "race" and "gender" carry no such associations. No unanimity exists among those who employ concepts of class. Some scholars employ Weberian notions, others use class as a temporary heuristic device. Still, when we invoke class, we are working with or against a set of definitions that, in the case of Marxism, involve an idea of economic causality and a vision of the path along which history has moved dialectically. There is no such clarity or coherence for either race or gender. In the case of gender, the usage has involved a range of theoretical positions as well as simple descriptive references to the relationships between the sexes.

Feminist historians, trained as most historians are to be more comfortable with description than theory, have nonetheless increasingly looked for usable theoretical formulations. They have done so for at least two reasons. First, the proliferation of case studies in women's history seems to call for some synthesizing perspective that can explain continuities and discontinuities and account for persisting inequalities as well as radically different social experiences. Second, the discrepancy between the high quality of recent work in women's history and its continuing marginal status in the field as a whole (as measured by textbooks, syllabi, and monographic work) points up the limits of descriptive approaches that do not address dominant disciplinary concepts, or at least that do not address these concepts in terms that can shake their power and perhaps transform them. It has not been enough for historians of women to prove either that women had a history or that women participated in the major political upheavals of Western civilization. In the case of women's history, the response of most non-feminist historians has been acknowledgment and then separation or dismissal ("women had a history separate from men's, therefore let feminists do women's history, which need not concern us"; or "women's history is about sex and the family and should be done separately from political and economic history"). In the case of women's participation, the response has been minimal interest at best ("my understanding of the French Revolution is not changed by knowing that women participated in it"). The challenge posed by these responses is, in the end, a theoretical one. It requires analysis not only of the relationship between male and female experience in the past but also of the connection between past history and current historical practice. How does gender work in human social relationships? How does gender give meaning to the organization and perception of historical knowledge? The answers depend on gender as an analytic category.

For the most part, the attempts of historians to theorize about gender have remained within traditional social scientific frameworks, using longstanding formulations that provide universal causal explanations. These theories have been limited at best because they tend to contain reductive or overly simple generalizations that undercut not only history's disciplinary sense of the complexity of social causation but also feminist commitments to analyses that will lead to change. A review of these theories will expose their limits and make it possible to propose an alternative approach.[7]

The approaches used by most historians fall into two distinct categories.

The first is essentially descriptive; that is, it refers to the existence of phenomena or realities without interpreting, explaining, or attributing causality. The second usage is causal; it theorizes about the nature of phenomena or realities, seeking an understanding of how and why these take the form they do.

In its simplest recent usage, "gender" is a synonym for "women." Any number of books and articles whose subject is women's history have, in the past few years, substituted "gender" for "women" in their titles. In some cases, this usage, though vaguely referring to certain analytic concepts, is actually about the political acceptability of the field. In these instances, the use of "gender" is meant to denote the scholarly seriousness of a work, for "gender" has a more neutral and objective sound than does "women." "Gender" seems to fit within the scientific terminology of social science and thus dissociates itself from the (supposedly strident) politics of feminism. In this usage, "gender" does not carry with it a necessary statement about inequality or power nor does it name the aggrieved (and hitherto invisible) party. Whereas the term "women's history" proclaims its politics by asserting (contrary to customary practice) that women are valid historical subjects, "gender" includes but does not name women and so seems to pose no critical threat. This use of "gender" is one facet of what might be called the quest of feminist scholarship for academic legitimacy in the 1980s.

But only one facet. "Gender" as a substitute for "women" is also used to suggest that information about women is necessarily information about men, that one implies the study of the other. This usage insists that the world of women is part of the world of men, created in and by it. This usage rejects the interpretive utility of the idea of separate spheres, maintaining that to study women in isolation perpetuates the fiction that one sphere, the experience of one sex, has little or nothing to do with the other. In addition, gender is also used to designate social relations between the sexes. Its use explicitly rejects biological explanations, such as those that find a common denominator for diverse forms of female subordination in the facts that women have the capacity to give birth and men have greater muscular strength. Instead, gender becomes a way of denoting "cultural constructions"—the entirely social creation of ideas about appropriate roles for women and men. It is a way of referring to the exclusively social origins of the subjective identities of men and women. Gender is, in this definition, a social category imposed on a sexed body.[8] Gender seems to have become a particularly useful word as studies of sex and sexuality have proliferated, for it offers a way of differentiating sexual practice from the social roles assigned to women and men. Although scholars acknowledge the connection between sex and (what the sociologists of the family called) "sex roles," these scholars do not assume a simple or direct linkage. The use of gender emphasizes an entire system of relationships that may include sex, but is not directly determined by sex or directly determining of sexuality.

These descriptive usages of gender have been employed by historians most often to map out a new terrain. As social historians turned to new objects of study, gender was relevant for such topics as women, children, families, and gender ideologies. This usage of gender, in other words, refers only to those areas—both structural and ideological—involving relations between the sexes. Because, on the face of it, war, diplomacy, and high politics have not been explicitly about those relationships, gender seems not to apply and so continues to be irrelevant to the thinking of historians concerned with issues of politics and power. The effect is to endorse a certain functionalist view ultimately rooted in biology and to perpetuate the idea of separate spheres (sex or politics, family or nation, women or men) in the writing of history. Although gender in this usage asserts that relationships between the sexes are social, it says nothing about why these relationships are constructed as they are, how they work, or how they change. In its descriptive usage, then, gender is a concept associated with the study of things related to women. Gender is a new topic, a new department of historical investigation, but it does not have the analytic power to address (and change) existing historical paradigms.

Some historians, were, of course, aware of this problem, hence the efforts to employ theories that might explain the concept of gender and account for historical change. Indeed, the challenge was to reconcile theory, which was framed in general or universal terms, and history, which was committed to the study of contextual specificity and fundamental change. The result has been extremely eclectic: partial borrowings that vitiate the analytic power of a particular theory or, worse, employ its precepts without awareness of their implications; or accounts of change that, because they embed universal theories, only illustrate unchanging themes; or wonderfully imaginative studies in which theory is nonetheless so hidden that these studies cannot serve as models for other investigations. Because the theories on which historians have drawn are often not spelled out in all their implications, it seems worthwhile to spend some time doing that. Only through such an exercise can we evaluate the usefulness of these theories and, perhaps, articulate a more powerful theoretical approach.

Feminist historians have employed a variety of approaches to the analysis of gender, but they come down to a choice between three theoretical positions.[9] The first, an entirely feminist effort, attempts to explain the origins of patriarchy. The second locates itself within a Marxian tradition and seeks there an accommodation with feminist critiques. The third, fundamentally divided between French post-structuralist and Anglo-American object-relations theorists, draws on these different schools of psychoanalysis to explain the production and reproduction of the subject's gendered identity.

Theorists of patriarchy have directed their attention to the subordination of women and found their explanation for it in the male "need" to dominate the female. In Mary O'Brien's ingenious adaptation of Hegel, she defined male domination as the effect of men's desire to transcend their alienation

from the means of the reproduction of the species. The principle of genera-
tional continuity restores the primacy of paternity and obscures the real
labor and the social reality of women's work in childbirth. The source of
women's liberation lies in "an adequate understanding of the process of
reproduction," an appreciation of the contradiction between the nature of
women's reproductive labor and (male) ideological mystifications of it.[10]
For Shulamith Firestone, reproduction was also the "bitter trap" for women.
In her more materialist analysis, however, liberation would come with
transformations in reproductive technology, which might in some not too
distant future eliminate the need for women's bodies as the agents of species
reproduction.[11]

If reproduction was the key to patriarchy for some, sexuality itself was the
answer for others. Catherine MacKinnon's bold formulations were at once
her own and characteristic of a certain approach: "Sexuality is to feminism
what work is to marxism: that which is most one's own, yet most taken
away." "Sexual objectification is the primary process of the subjection of
women. It unites act with word, construction with expression, perception
with enforcement, myth with reality. Man fucks woman; subject verb
object."[12] Continuing her analogy to Marx, MacKinnon offered, in the place
of dialectical materialism, consciousness-raising as feminism's method of
analysis. By expressing the shared experience of objectification, she argued,
women come to understand their common identity and so are moved to
political action. For MacKinnon, sexuality thus stood outside ideology,
discoverable as the unmediated, experienced fact. Although sexual relations are defined in MacKinnon's analysis as social, there is nothing except
the inherent inequality of the sexual relation itself to explain why the system
of power operates as it does. The source of unequal relations between the
sexes is, in the end, unequal relations between the sexes. Although the
inequality of which sexuality is the source is said to be embodied in a "whole
system of social relationships," how this system works is not explained.[13]

Theorists of patriarchy have addressed the inequality of males and
females in important ways, but, for historians, their theories pose problems.
First, while they offer an analysis internal to the gender system itself, they
also assert the primacy of that system in all social organization. But theories
of patriarchy do not show how gender inequality structures all other
inequalities or, indeed, *how* gender affects those areas of life that do not seem
to be connected to it. Second, whether domination comes in the form of the
male appropriation of the females' reproductive labor or in the sexual
objectification of women by men, the analysis rests on physical difference.
Any physical difference takes on a universal and unchanging aspect, even
if theorists of patriarchy take into account the existence of changing forms
and systems of gender inequality. A theory that rests on the single variable
of physical difference poses problems for historians: it assumes a consistent
or inherent meaning for the human body—outside social or cultural construction—and thus the ahistoricity of gender itself. History becomes, in a

sense, epiphenomenal, providing endless variations on the unchanging theme of a fixed gender inequality.

Marxist feminists have a more historical approach, guided as they are by a theory of history. But, whatever the variations and adaptations have been, the self-imposed requirement that there be a "material" explanation for gender has limited or at least slowed the development of new lines of analysis. Whether a so-called dual-systems solution is proffered (one that posits the separate but interacting realms of capitalism and patriarchy) or an analysis based more firmly in orthodox Marxist discussions of modes of production is developed, the explanation for the origins of and changes in gender systems is found outside the sexual division of labor. Families, households, and sexuality are all, finally, products of changing modes of production. That is how Engels concluded his explorations of the *Origins of the Family*;[15] that is where economist Heidi Hartmann's analysis ultimately rests. Hartmann insisted on the importance of taking into account patriarchy and capitalism as separate but interacting systems. Yet, as her argument unfolds, economic causality takes precedence, and patriarchy always develops and changes as a function of relations of production. When she suggested that "it is necessary to eradicate the sexual division of labor itself to end male domination," she meant ending job segregation by sex.[16]

Early discussions among Marxist feminists circled around the same set of problems: a rejection of the essentialism of those who would argue that the "exigencies of biological reproduction" determine the sexual division of labor under capitalism; the futility of inserting "modes of reproduction" into discussions of modes of production (it remains an oppositional category and does not assume equal status with modes of production); the recognition that economic systems do not directly determine gender relationships, indeed, that the subordination of women pre-dates capitalism and continues under socialism; the search nonetheless for a materialist explanation that excludes natural physical differences.[17] An important attempt to break out of this circle of problems came from Joan Kelly in her essay, "The Doubled Vision of Feminist Theory," where she argued that economic and gender systems interacted to produce social and historical experiences; that neither system was causal, but both "operate simultaneously to reproduce the socioeconomic and male-dominant structures of [a] particular social order." Kelly's suggestion that gender systems had an independent existence provided a crucial conceptual opening, but her commitment to remain within a Marxist framework led her to emphasize the causal role of economic factors even in the determination of the gender system: "The relation of the sexes operates in accordance with, and through, socioeconomic structures, as well as sex/gender ones."[18] Kelly introduced the idea of a "sexually based social reality," but she tended to emphasize the social rather than the sexual nature of that reality, and, most often, "social," in her usage, was conceived in terms of economic relations of production.

The most far-reaching exploration of sexuality by American Marxist feminists is in *Powers of Desire,* a volume of essays published in 1983.[19] Influenced by increasing attention to sexuality among political activists and scholars, by French philosopher Michel Foucault's insistence that sexuality is produced in historical contexts, and by the conviction that the current "sexual revolution" required serious analysis, the authors made "sexual politics" the focus of their inquiry. In so doing, they opened the question of causality and offered a variety of solutions to it; indeed, the real excitement of this volume is its lack of analytic unanimity, its sense of analytic tension. If individual authors tend to stress the causality of social (by which is often meant "economic") contexts, they nonetheless include suggestions about the importance of studying "the psychic structuring of gender identity." If "gender ideology" is sometimes said to "reflect" economic and social structures, there is also a crucial recognition of the need to understand the complex "link between society and enduring psychic structure."[20] On the one hand, the editors endorse Jessica Benjamin's point that politics must include attention to "the erotic, fantastic components of human life," but, on the other, no essays besides Benjamin's deal fully or seriously with the theoretical issues she raises.[21] Instead, a tacit assumption runs through the volume that Marxism can be expanded to include discussions of ideology, culture, and psychology and that this expansion will happen through the kind of concrete examination of evidence undertaken in most of the articles. The advantage of such an approach lies in its avoidance of sharp differences of position, the disadvantage in its leaving in place an already fully articulated theory that leads back from relations of the sexes based to relations of production.

A comparison of American Marxist-feminist efforts, exploratory and relatively wide-ranging, to those of their English counterparts, tied more closely to the politics of a strong and viable Marxist tradition, reveals that the English have had greater difficulty in challenging the constraints of strictly determinist explanations. This difficulty can be seen most dramatically in the recent debates in the *New Left Review* between Michèle Barrett and her critics, who charged her with abandoning a materialist analysis of the sexual division of labor under capitalism.[22] It can be seen as well in the replacement of an initial feminist attempt to reconcile psychoanalysis and Marxism with a choice of one or another of these theoretical positions by scholars who earlier insisted that some fusion of the two was possible.[23] The difficulty for both English and American feminists working within Marxism is apparent in the works I have mentioned here. The problem they face is the opposite of the one posed by patriarchal theory. Within Marxism, the concept of gender has long been treated as the by-product of changing economic structures; gender has had no independent analytic status of its own.

A review of psychoanalytic theory requires a specification of schools, since the various approaches have tended to be classified by the national origins of the founders and the majority of the practitioners. There is the Anglo-American school, working within the terms of theories of object-relations. In the U.S., Nancy Chodorow is the name most readily associated with this approach. In addition, the work of Carol Gilligan has had a far-reaching impact on American scholarship, including history. Gilligan's work draws on Chodorow's, although it is concerned less with the construction of the subject than with moral development and behavior. In contrast to the Anglo-American school, the French school is based on structuralist and post-structuralist readings of Freud in terms of theories of language (for feminists, the key figure in Jacques Lacan).

Both schools are concerned with the processes by which the subject's identity is created; both focus on the early stages of child development for clues to the formation of gender identity. Object-relations theorists stress the influence of actual experience (the child sees, hears, relates to those who care for it, particularly, of course, to its parents), while the post-structuralists emphasize the centrality of language in communicating, interpreting, and representing gender. (By "language," post-structuralists do not mean words but systems of meaning—symbolic orders—that precede the actual mastery of speech, reading, and writing.) Another difference between the two schools of thought focuses on the unconscious, which for Chodorow is ultimately subject to conscious understanding and for Lacan is not. For Lacanians, the unconscious is a critical factor in the construction of the subject; it is the location, moreover, of sexual division and, for that reason, of continuing instability for the gendered subject.

In recent years, feminist historians have been drawn to these theories either because they serve to endorse specific findings with general observations or because they seem to offer an important theoretical formulation about gender. Increasingly, those historians working with a concept of "women's culture" cite Chodorow's or Gilligan's work as both proof of and explanation for their interpretations; those wrestling with feminist theory look to Lacan. In the end, neither of these theories seems to me entirely workable for historians; a closer look at each may help explain why.

My reservation about object-relations theory concerns its literalism, its reliance on relatively small structures of interaction to produce gender identity and to generate change. Both the family division of labor and the actual assignment of tasks to each parent play a crucial role in Chodorow's theory. The outcome of prevailing Western systems is a clear division between male and female: "The basic feminine sense of self is connected to the world, the basic masculine sense of self is separate."[24] According to Chodorow, if fathers were more involved in parenting and present more often in domestic situations, the outcome of the oedipal drama might be different.[25]

This interpretation limits the concept of gender to family and household experience and, for the historian, leaves no way to connect the concept (or the individual) to other social systems of economy, politics, or power. Of course, it is implicit that social arrangements requiring fathers to work and mothers to perform most child-rearing tasks structure family organization. Where such arrangements come from and why they are articulated in terms of a sexual division of labor is not clear. Neither is the issue of inequality, as opposed to that of assymmetry, addressed. How can we account within this theory for persistent associations of masculinity with power, for the higher value placed on manhood than on womanhood, for the way children seem to learn these associations and evaluations even when they live outside nuclear households or in households where parenting is equally divided between husband and wife? I do not think we can without some attention to symbolic systems, that is, to the ways societies represent gender, use it to articulate the rules of social relationships, or construct the meaning of experience. Without meaning, there is no experience; without processes of signification, there is no meaning (which is not to say that language is everything, but a theory that does not take it into account misses the powerful roles that symbols, metaphors, and concepts play in the definition of human personality and human history).

Language is the center of Lacanian theory; it is the key to the child's induction into the symbolic order. Through language, gendered identity is constructed. According to Lacan, the phallus is the central signifier of sexual difference. But the meaning of the phallus must be read metaphorically. For the child, the oedipal drama sets forth the terms of cultural interaction, since the threat of castration embodies the power, the rules of (the father's) law. The child's relationship to the law depends on sexual difference, on its imaginative (or fantastic) identification with masculinity or femininity. The imposition, in other words, of the rules of social interaction are inherently and specifically gendered, for the female necessarily has a different relationship to the phallus than the male does. But gender identification, although it always appears coherent and fixed, is, in fact, highly unstable. Like words themselves, subjective identities are processes of differentiation and distinction, requiring the suppression of ambiguities and opposite elements in order to assure (and create the illusion of) coherence and common understanding. The idea of masculinity rests on the necessary repression of feminine aspects—of the subject's potential for bisexuality—and introduces conflict into the opposition of masculine and feminine. Repressed desires are present in the unconscious and are constantly a threat to the stability of gender identification, denying its unity, subverting its need for security. In addition, conscious ideas of masculine or feminine are not fixed, since they vary according to contextual usage. Conflict always exists, then, between the subject's need for the appearance of wholeness and the imprecision of terminology, its relative meaning, its dependence on repression.[26] This kind of interpretation makes the categories of "man" and "woman" problematic by suggesting that masculine and feminine are not inherent characteristics but subjective (or fictional) constructs. This interpretation also implies that the subject is in a constant process of construction, and it offers a systematic way of interpreting conscious and unconscious desire by pointing to language as the appropriate place for analysis. As such, I find it instructive.

I am troubled, nonetheless, by the exclusive fixation on questions of "the subject" and by the tendency to reify subjectively originating antagonisms between males and females as the central fact of gender. In addition, although there is openness in the concept of how "the subject" is constructed, the theory tends to universalize the categories and relationship of male and female. The outcome for historians is a reductive reading of evidence from the past. Even though this theory takes social relationships into account by linking castration to prohibition and law, it does not permit the introduction of a notion of historical specificity and variability. The phallus is the only signifier; the process of constructing the gendered subject is, in the end, predictable because always the same. If, as film theorist Teresa de Lauretis suggests, we need to think in terms of the construction of subjectivity in social and historical contexts, there is no way to specify those contexts within the terms offered by Lacan. Indeed, even in de Lauretis's attempt, social reality (that is, "material, economic and interpersonal [relations] which are in fact social, and in a larger perspective historical") seems to lie outside, apart from the subject.[27] A way to conceive of "social reality" in terms of gender is lacking.

The problem of sexual antagonism in this theory has two aspects. First, it projects a certain timeless quality, even when it is historicized as well as it has been by Sally Alexander. Alexander's reading of Lacan led her to conclude that "antagonism between the sexes is an unavoidable aspect of the acquisition of sexual identity . . . If antagonism is always latent, it is possible that history offers no final resolution, only the constant reshaping, reorganizing of the symbolization of difference, and the sexual division of labor."[28] It may be my hopeless utopianism that gives me pause before this formulation, or it may be that I have not yet shed the episteme of what Foucault called the Classical Age. Whatever the explanation, Alexander's formulation contributes to the fixing of the binary opposition of male and female as the only possible relationship and as a permanent aspect of the human condition. It perpetuates rather than questions what Denise Riley refers to as "the dreadful air of constancy of sexual polarity." She writes: "The historically constructed nature of the opposition [between male and female] produces as one of its effects just that air of an invariant and monotonous men/women opposition."[29]

It is precisely that opposition, in all its tedium and monotony, that (to return to the Anglo-American side) Carol Gilligan's work has promoted. Gilligan explained the divergent paths of moral development followed by boys and girls in terms of differences of "experience" (lived reality). It is not surprising that historians of women have picked up her ideas and used them to explain the "different voices" their work has enabled them to hear. The problems with these borrowings are manifold, and they are logically connected.[30] The first is a slippage that often happens in the attribution of causality: the argument moves from a statement such as "women's experience leads them to make moral choices contingent on contexts and relationships" to "women think and choose this way because they are women." Implied in this line of reasoning is the ahistorical, if not essentialist, notion of woman. Gilligan and others have extrapolated her description, based on a small sample of late twentieth-century American schoolchildren, into a statement about all women. This extrapolation is evident especially, but not exclusively, in the discussions by some historians of "women's culture" that take evidence from early saints to modern militant labor activists and reduce it to proof of Gilligan's hypothesis about a universal female preference for relatedness.[31] This use of Gilligan's ideas provides sharp contrast to the more complicated and historicized conceptions of "women's culture" evident in the *Feminist Studies* 1980 symposium.[32] Indeed a comparison of that set of articles with Gilligan's formulations reveals the extent to which her notion is ahistorical, defining woman/man as a universal, self-reproducing binary opposition—fixed always in the same way. By insisting on fixed differences (in Gilligan's case, by simplifying data with more mixed results about sex and moral reasoning to underscore sexual difference), feminists contribute to the kind of thinking they want to oppose. Although they insist on the revaluation of the category "female" (Gilligan suggests that women's moral choices may be more humane than men's), they do not examine the binary opposition itself.

We need a refusal of the fixed and permanent quality of the binary opposition, a genuine historicization and deconstruction of the terms of sexual difference. We must become more self-conscious about distinguishing between our analytic vocabulary and the material we want to analyze. We must find ways (however imperfect) to continually subject our categories to criticism, our analyses to self-criticism. If we employ Jacques Derrida's definition of deconstruction, this criticism means analyzing in context the way any binary opposition operates, reversing and displacing its hierarchical construction, rather than accepting it as real or self-evident or in the nature of things.[33] In a sense, of course, feminists have been doing this for years. The history of feminist thought is a history of the refusal of the hierarchical construction of the relationship between male and female in its specific contexts and an attempt to reverse or displace its operations. Feminist historians are now in a position to theorize their practice and to develop gender as an analytic category.

Concern with gender as an analytic category has emerged only in the late twentieth century. It is absent from the major bodies of social theory articulated from the eighteenth to the early twentieth centuries. To be sure, some of those theories built their logic on analogies to the opposition of male and female, others acknowledged a "woman question," still others addressed the formation of subjective sexual identity, but gender as a way of talking about systems of social or sexual relations did not appear. This neglect may in part explain the difficulty that contemporary feminists have had incorporating the term gender into existing bodies of theory and convincing adherents of one or another theoretical school that gender belongs in their vocabulary. The term gender is part of the attempt by contemporary feminists to stake claim to a certain definitional ground, to insist on the inadequacy of existing bodies of theory for explaining persistent inequalities between women and men. It seems to me significant that the use of the word gender has emerged at a moment of great epistemological turmoil that takes the form, in some cases, of a shift from scientific to literary paradigms among social scientists (from an emphasis on cause to one on meaning, blurring genres of inquiry in anthropologist Clifford Geertz's phrase),[34] and, in other cases, the form of debates about theory between those who assert the transparency of facts and those who insist that all reality is construed or constructed, between those who defend and those who question the idea that "man" is the rational master of his own destiny. In the space opened by this debate and on the side of the critique of science developed by the humanities, and of empiricism and humanism by post-structuralists, feminists have not only begun to find a theoretical voice of their own but have found scholarly and political allies as well. It is within this space that we must articulate gender as an analytic category.

What should be done by historians who, after all, have seen their discipline dismissed by some recent theorists as a relic of humanist thought? I do not think we should quit the archives or abandon the study of the past, but we do have to change some of the ways we have gone about working, some of the questions we have asked. We need to scrutinize our methods of analysis, clarify our operative assumptions, and explain how we think change occurs. Instead of a search for single origins, we have to conceive of processes so interconnected that they cannot be disentangled. Of course, we identify problems to study, and these constitute beginnings or points of entry into complex processes. But it is the processes we must continually keep in mind. We must ask more often how things happened in order to find out why they happened; in anthropologist Michelle Rosaldo's formulation, we must pursue not universal, general causality but meaningful explanation: "It now appears to me that woman's place in human social life is not in any direct sense a product of the things she does, but of the meaning her activities acquire through concrete social interaction."[35] To pursue meaning, we need to deal with the individual subject as well as social organization and to articulate the nature of their interrelationships, for both are crucial to understanding how gender works, how change occurs. Finally, we need to replace the notion that social power is unified, coherent, and centralized with something like Foucault's concept of power as dispersed constellations of unequal relationships, discursively constituted in social "fields of force."[36] Within these processes and structures, there is room for a concept of human agency as the attempt (at least partially rational) to construct an identity, a life, a set of relationships, a society with certain limits and with language—conceptual language that at once sets boundaries and contains the possibility for negation, resistance, reinterpretation, the play of metaphoric invention and imagination.

My definition of gender has two parts and several subsets. They are interrelated but must be analytically distinct. The core of the definition rests on an integral connection between two propositions: gender is a constitutive element of social relationships based on perceived differences between the sexes, and gender is a primary way of signifying relationships of power. Changes in the organization of social relationships always correspond to changes in representations of power, but the direction of change is not necessarily one way. As a constitutive element of social relationships based on perceived differences between the sexes, gender involves four interrelated elements: first, culturally available symbols that evoke multiple (and often contradictory) representations—Eve and Mary as symbols of woman, for example, in the Western Christian tradition—but also, myths of light and dark, purification and pollution, innocence and corruption. For historians, the interesting questions are, which symbolic representations are invoked, how, and in what contexts? Second, normative concepts that set forth interpretations of the meanings of the symbols, that attempt to limit and contain their metaphoric possibilities. These concepts are expressed in religious, educational, scientific, legal, and political doctrines and typically take the form of a fixed binary opposition, categorically and unequivocally asserting the meaning of male and female, masculine and feminine. In fact, these normative statements depend on the refusal or repression of alternative possibilities, and, sometimes, overt contests about them take place (at what moments and under what circumstances ought to be a concern of historians). The position that emerges as dominant, however, is stated as the only possible one. Subsequent history is written as if these normative positions were the product of social consensus rather than of conflict. An example of this kind of history is the treatment of the Victorian ideology of domesticity as if it were created whole and only afterwards reacted to instead of being the constant subject of great differences of opinion. Another kind of example comes from contemporary fundamentalist religious groups that have forcibly linked their practice to a restoration of women's supposedly more authentic "traditional" role, when, in fact, there is little historical precedent for the unquestioned performance of such a role. The point of new historical investigation is to disrupt the notion of fixity, to discover the nature of the debate or repression that leads to the appearance of timeless permanence in binary gender representation. This kind of analysis must include a notion of politics as well as reference to social institutions and organizations—the third aspect of gender relationships.

Some scholars, notably anthropologists, have restricted the use of gender to the kinship system (focusing on household and family as the basis for social organization). We need a broader view that includes not only kinship but also (especially for complex, modern societies) the labor market (a sex-segregated labor market is a part of the process of gender construction), education (all-male, single-sex, or coeducational institutions are part of the same process), and the polity (universal male suffrage is part of the process of gender construction). It makes little sense to force these institutions back to functional utility in the kinship system, or to argue that contemporary relationships between men and women are artifacts of older kinship systems based on the exchange of women.[37] Gender is constructed through kinship, but not exclusively; it is constructed as well in the economy and the polity, which, in our society at least, now operate largely independently of kinship.

The fourth aspect of gender is subjective identity. I agree with anthropologist Gayle Rubin's formulation that psychoanalysis offers an important theory about the reproduction of gender, a description of the "transformation of the biological sexuality of individuals as they are enculturated." But the universal claim of psychoanalysis gives me pause. Even though Lacanian theory may be helpful for thinking about the construction of gendered identity, historians need to work in a more historical way. If gender identity is based only and universally on fear of castration, the point of historical inquiry is denied. Moreover, real men and women do not always or literally fulfill the terms of their society's prescriptions or of our analytic categories. Historians need instead to examine the ways in which gendered identities are substantively constructed and relate their findings to a range of activities, social organizations, and historically specific cultural representations. The best efforts in this area so far have been, not surprisingly, biographies: Biddy Martin's interpretation of Lou Andreas Salomé, Kathryn Sklar's depiction of Catharine Beecher, Jacqueline Hall's life of Jessie Daniel Ames, and Mary Hill's discussion of Charlotte Perkins Gilman.[39] But collective treatments are also possible, as Mrinalini Sinha and Lou Ratté have shown in their respective studies of the terms of construction of gender identity for British colonial administrators in India and British-educated Indians who emerged as anti-imperialist, nationalist leaders.[40]

The first part of my definition of gender consists, then, of all four of these elements, and no one of them operates without the others. Yet they do not operate simultaneously, with one simply reflecting the others. A question for historical research is, in fact, what the relationships among the four aspects are. The sketch I have offered of the process of constructing gender relationships could be used to discuss class, race, ethnicity, or, for that matter, any social process. My point was to clarify and specify how one needs to think about the effect of gender in social and institutional relationships, because this thinking is often not done precisely or systematically. The theorizing of gender, however, is developed in my second proposition: gender is a primary way of signifying relationships of power. It might be better to say, gender is a primary field within which or by means of which power is articulated. Gender is not the only field, but it seems to have been a persistent and recurrent way of enabling the signification of power in the West, in Judeo-Christian as well as Islamic traditions. As such, this part of the definition might seem to belong in the normative section of the argument, yet it does not, for concepts of power, though they may build on gender, are not always literally about gender itself. French sociologist Pierre Bourdieu has written about how the "di-vision du monde," based on references to "biological differences and notably those that refer to the division of the labor of procreation and reproduction," operates as "the best-founded of collective illusions." Established as an objective set of references, concepts of gender structure perception and the concrete and symbolic organization of all social life.[41] To the extent that these references establish distributions of power (differential control over or access to material and symbolic resources), gender becomes implicated in the conception and construction of power itself. The French anthropologist Maurice Godelier has put it this way: "It is not sexuality which haunts society, but society which haunts the body's sexuality. Sex-related differences between bodies are continually summoned as testimony to social relations and phenomena that have nothing to do with sexuality. Not only as testimony to, but also testimony for—in other words, as legitimation."[42]

The legitimizing function of gender works in many ways. Bourdieu, for example, showed how, in certain cultures, agricultural exploitation was organized according to concepts of time and season that rested on specific definitions of the opposition between masculine and feminine. Gayatri Spivak has done a pointed analysis of the uses of gender in certain texts of British and American women writers.[43] Natalie Davis has shown how concepts of masculine and feminine related to understandings and criticisms of rules of social order in early modern France.[44] Historian Caroline Bynum has thrown new light on medieval spirituality through her attention to the relationships between concepts of masculine and feminine and religious behavior. Her work gives us important insight into the ways in which these concepts informed the politics of monastic institutions as well as of individual believers.[45] Art historians have opened a new territory by reading social implications from literal depictions of women and men.[46] These interpretations are based on the idea that conceptual languages employ differentiation to establish meaning and that sexual difference is a primary way of signifying differentiation.[47] Gender, then, provides a way to decode meaning and to understand the complex connections among various forms of human interaction. When historians look for the ways in which the concept of gender legitimizes and constructs social relationships, they develop insight into the reciprocal nature of gender and society and into the particular and contextually specific ways in which politics constructs gender and gender constructs politics.

Politics is only one of the areas in which gender can be used for historical analysis. I have chosen the following examples relating to politics and power in their most traditionally construed sense, that is, as they pertain to government and the nation-state, for two reasons. First, the territory is virtually uncharted, since gender has been seen as antithetical to the real business of politics. Second, political history—still the dominant mode of historical inquiry—has been the stronghold of resistance to the inclusion of material or even questions about women and gender.

Gender has been employed literally or analogically in political theory to justify or criticize the reign of monarchs and to express the relationship between ruler and ruled. One might have expected that the debates of contemporaries over the reigns of Elizabeth I in England and Catherine de Medici in France would dwell on the issue of women's suitability for political rule, but, in the period when kinship and kingship were integrally related, discussions about male kings were equally preoccupied with masculinity and femininity.[48] Analogies to the marital relationship provide structure for the arguments of Jean Bodin, Robert Filmer, and John Locke. Edmund Burke's attack on the French Revolution is built around a contrast between ugly, murderous *sans-culottes* hags ("the furies of hell, in the abused shape of the vilest of women") and the soft femininity of Marie Antoinette, who escaped the crowd to "seek refuge at the feet of a king and husband" and whose beauty once inspired national pride. (It was in reference to the appropriate role for the feminine in the political order that Burke wrote, "To make us love our country, our country ought to be lovely.")[49] But the analogy is not always to marriage or even to heterosexuality. In medieval Islamic political theory, the symbols of political power alluded most often to sex between man and boy, suggesting not only forms of acceptable sexuality akin to those that Foucault's last work described in classical Greece but also the irrelevance of women to any notion of politics and public life.[50]

Lest this last comment suggest that political theory simply reflects social organization, it seems important to note that changes in gender relationships can be set off by views of the needs of the state. A striking example is Louis de Bonald's argument in 1816 about why the divorce legislation of the French Revolution had to be repealed:

> Just as political democracy "allows the people, the weak part of political society, to rise against the established power," so divorce, "veritable domestic democracy," allows the wife, "the weak part, to rebel against marital authority ... In order to keep the state out of the hands of the people, it is necessary to keep the family out of the hands of wives and children."[51]

Bonald begins with an analogy and then establishes a direct correspondence between divorce and democracy. Harking back to much earlier arguments about the well-ordered family as the foundation of the well-ordered state, the legislation that implemented this view redefined the limits of the marital relationship. Similarly, in our own time, conservative political ideologues would like to pass a series of laws about the organization and behavior of the family that would alter current practices. The connection between authoritarian regimes and the control of women has been noted but not thoroughly studied. Whether at a crucial moment for Jacobin hegemony in the French Revolution, at the point of Stalin's bid for controlling authority, the implementation of Nazi policy in Germany, or the triumph in Iran of the Ayatollah Khomeni, emergent rulers have legitimized domination, strength, central authority, and ruling power as masculine (enemies, outsiders, subversives, weakness as feminine) and made that code literal in laws (forbidding women's political participation, outlawing abortion, prohibiting wage-earning by mothers, imposing female dress codes) that put women in their place.[52] These actions and their timing make little sense in themselves; in most instances, the state had nothing immediate or material to gain from the control of women. The actions can only be made sense of as part of an analysis of the construction and consolidation of power. An assertion of control or strength was given form as a policy about women. In these examples, sexual difference was conceived in terms of the domination or control of women. These examples provide some insight into the kinds of power relationships being constructed in modern history, but this particular type of relationship is not a universal political theme. In different ways, for example, the democratic regimes of the twentieth century have also constructed their political ideologies with gendered concepts and translated them into policy; the welfare state, for example, demonstrated its protective paternalism in laws directed at women and children.[53] Historically, some socialist and anarchist movements have refused metaphors of domination entirely, imaginatively presenting their critiques of particular regimes or social organizations in terms of transformations of gender identities. Utopian socialists in France and England in the 1830s and 1840s conceived their dreams for a harmonious future in terms of the complementary natures of individuals as exemplified in the union of man and women, "the social individual."[54] European anarchists were long known not only for refusing the conventions of bourgeois marriage but also for their visions of a world in which sexual difference did not imply hierarchy.

These examples are of explicit connections between gender and power, but they are only a part of my definition of gender as a primary way of signifying relationships of power. Attention to gender is often not explicit, but it is nonetheless a crucial part of the organization of equality or inequality. Hierarchical structures rely on generalized understandings of the so-called natural relationship between male and female. The concept of class in the nineteenth century relied on gender for its articulation. When middle-class reformers in France, for example, depicted workers in terms coded as feminine (subordinated, weak, sexually exploited like prostitutes), labor and socialist leaders replied by insisting on the masculine position of the working class (producers, strong, protectors of their women and children). The terms of this discourse were not explicitly about gender, but they relied on references to it, the gendered "coding" of certain terms, to establish their meanings. In the process, historically specific, normative definitions of gender (which were taken as givens) were reproduced and embedded in the culture of the French working class.[55]

The subject of war, diplomacy, and high politics frequently comes up when traditional political historians question the utility of gender in their work. But here, too, we need to look beyond the actors and the literal import of their words. Power relations among nations and the status of colonial subjects have been made comprehensible (and thus legitimate) in terms of relations between male and female. The legitimizing of war—of expending young lives to protect the state—has variously taken the forms of explicit appeals to manhood (to the need to defend otherwise vulnerable women and children), of implicit reliance on belief in the duty of sons to serve their leaders or their (father the) king, and of associations between masculinity and national strength.[56] High politics itself is a gendered concept, for it establishes its crucial importance and public power, the reasons for and the fact of its highest authority, precisely in its exclusion of women from its work. Gender is one of the recurrent references by which political power has been conceived, legitimated, and criticized. It refers to but also establishes the meaning of the male/female opposition. To vindicate political power, the reference must seem sure and fixed, outside human construction, part of the natural or divine order. In that way, the binary opposition and the social process of gender relationships both become part of the meaning of power itself; to question or alter any aspect threatens the entire system.

If significations of gender and power construct one another, how do things change? The answer in a general sense is that change may be initiated in many places. Massive political upheavals that throw old orders into chaos and bring new ones into being may revise the terms (and so the organization) of gender in the search for new forms of legitimation. But they may not: old notions of gender have also served to validate new regimes.[57] Demographic crises, occasioned by food shortages, plagues, or wars, may have called into question normative visions of heterosexual marriage (as happened in some circles, in some countries in the 1920s), but they have also spawned pro-natalist policies that insist on the exclusive importance of women's maternal and reproductive functions.[58] Shifting patterns of employment may lead to altered marital strategies and to different possibilities for the construction of subjectivity, but they can also be experienced as new arenas of activity for dutiful daughters and wives.[59] The emergence of new kinds of cultural symbols may make possible the reinterpreting or, indeed, rewriting of the oedipal story, but it can also serve to reinscribe that terrible drama in even more telling terms. Political processes will determine which outcome prevails—political in the sense that different actors and different meanings are contending with one another for control. The nature of that process, of the actors and their actions, can only be determined specifically, in the context of time and place. We can write the history of that process only if we recognize that "man" and "woman" are at once empty and overflowing categories. Empty because thay have no ultimate, transcendent meaning. Overflowing because even when they appear to be fixed, they still contain within them alternative, denied, or suppressed definitions.

Political history has, in a sense, been enacted on the field of gender. It is a field that seems fixed yet whose meaning is contested and in flux. If we treat the opposition between male and female as problematic rather than known, as something contextually defined, repeatedly constructed, then we must constantly ask not only what is at stake in proclamations or debates that invoke gender to explain or justify their positions but also how implicit understandings of gender are being invoked and reinscribed. What is the relationship between laws about women and the power of the state? Why (and since when) have women been invisible as historical subjects, when we know they participated in the great and small events of human history? Has gender legitimated the emergence of professional careers?[60] Is (to quote the title of a recent article by French feminist Luce Irigaray) the subject of science sexed?[61] What is the relationship between state politics and the discovery of the "crime" of homosexuality?[62] How have social institutions incorporated gender into their assumptions and organizations? Have there ever been genuinely egalitarian concepts of gender in terms of which political systems were projected, if not built?

Investigations of these issues will yield a history that will provide new perspectives on old questions (about how, for example, political rule is imposed, or what the impact of war on society is), redefine the old questions in new terms (introducing considerations of family and sexuality, for example, in the study of economics or war), make women visible as active participants, and create analytic distance between the seemingly fixed language of the past and our own terminology. In addition, this new history will leave open possibilities for thinking about current feminist political strategies and the (utopian) future, for it suggests that gender must be redefined and restructured in conjunction with a vision of political and social equality that includes not only sex, but class and race.

NOTES

1. *Oxford English Dictionary* (1961 edn.), vol. 4.

2. Littré, *Dictionnaire de la langue française* (Paris, 1876).

3. Raymond Williams, *Keywords* (New York, 1983), 285.

4. Natalie Zemon Davis, "Women's History in Transition: The European Case," *Feminist Studies*, 3 (Winter 1975–76): 90.

5. Ann D. Gordon, Mari Jo Buhle, and Nancy Shrom Dye, "The Problem of Women's History," in Berenice Carroll, ed., *Liberating Women's History* (Urbana, Ill., 1976), 89.

6. The best and most subtle example is from Joan Kelly, "The Doubled Vision of Feminist Theory," in her *Women, History and Theory* (Chicago, 1984), 51–64, expecially 61.

7. For a review of recent work on women's history, see Joan W. Scott, "Women's

History: The Modern Period," *Past and Present*, 101 (1983): 141–57.

8. For an argument against the use of gender to emphasize the social aspect of sexual difference, see Moira Gatens, "A Critique of the Sex/Gender Distinction," in J. Allen and P. Patton, eds., *Beyond Marxism? Interventions after Marx* (Sydney, 1983), 143–60.

9. For a somewhat different approach to feminist analysis, see Linda J. Nicholson, *Gender and History: The Limits of Social Theory in the Age of the Family* (New York, 1986).

10. Mary O'Brien, *The Politics of Reproduction* (London, 1981), 8–15, 46.

11. Shulamith Firestone, *The Dialectic of Sex* (New York, 1970). The phrase "bitter trap" is O'Brien's, *Politics of Reproduction*, 8.

12. Catherine MacKinnon, "Feminism, Marxism, Method, and the State: An Agenda for Theory," *Signs*, 7 (Spring 1982): 515, 541.

13. Ibid., 541, 543.

14. For an interesting discussion of the strengths and limits of the term "patriarchy," see the exchange between historians Sheila Rowbotham, Sally Alexander, and Barbara Taylor in Raphael Samuel, ed., *People's History and Socialist Theory* (London, 1981), 363–73.

15. Frederick Engels, *The Origins of the Family, Private Property, and the State* (1884: reprint edn., New York, 1972).

16. Heidi Hartmann, "Capitalism, Patriarchy, and Job Segregation by Sex," *Signs*, 1 (Spring 1976): 168. See also "The Unhappy Marriage of Marxism and Feminism: Toward a More Progressive Union," *Capital and Class*, 8 (Summer 1979): 1–33; "The Family as the Locus of Gender, Class, and Political Struggle: The Example of Housework," *Signs*, 6 (Spring 1981): 366–94.

17. Discussions of Marxist feminism include Zillah Eisenstein, *Capitalist Patriarchy and the Case for Socialist Feminism* (New York, 1979); A. Kuhn, "Structures of Patriarchy and Capital in the Family," in A. Kuhn and A. Wolpe, eds., *Feminism and Materialism* (London, 1978); Rosalind Coward, *Patriarchal Precedents* (London, 1983); Hilda Scott, *Does Socialism Liberate Women?* (Boston, 1974); Jane Humphries, "Working Class Family, Women's Liberation and Class Struggles: The Case of Nineteenth-Century British History," *Review of Radical Political Economics*, 9 (1977): 25–41; Jane Humphries, "Class Struggle and the Persistence of the Working Class Family," *Cambridge Journal of Economics*, 1 (1971): 241–58; and see the debate on Humphries's work in *Review of Radical Political Economics*, 12 (Summer 1980): 76–94.

18. Kelly, "Doubled Vision of Feminist Theory," 61.

19. Ann Snitow, Christine Stansell, and Sharon Thompson, eds., *Powers of Desire: The Politics of Sexuality* (New York, 1983).

20. Ellen Ross and Rayna Rapp, "Sex and Society: A Research Note from Social History and Anthropology," in *Powers of Desire*, 53.

21. "Introduction," *Powers of Desire*, 12; and Jessica Benjamin, "Master and Slave: The Fantasy of Erotic Domination," *Powers of Desire*, 297.

22. Johanna Brenner and Maria Ramas, "Rethinking Women's Oppression," *New Left Review*, 144 (March–April 1984): 33–71; Michèle Barrett, "Rethinking Women's Oppression: A Reply to Brenner and Ramas," *New Left Review*, 146 (July–August 1984): 123–28; Angela Weir and Elizabeth Wilson, "The British Women's Movement," *New Left Review*, 148 (November–December 1984): 74–103; Michèle Barrett, "A Response to Weir and Wilson," *New Left Review*, 150 (March–April 1985): 143–47; Jane Lewis, "The Debate on Sex and Class," *New Left Review*, 149 (January–February 1985): 108–20. See also Hugh Armstrong and Pat Armstrong, "Beyond Sexless Class

and Classless Sex: Towards Feminist Marxism," *Studies in Political Economy*, 10 (Winter 1983): 7–44; Hugh Armstrong and Pat Armstrong, "Comments: More on Marxist Feminism," *Studies in Political Economy*, 15 (Fall 1984): 179–84; and Jane Jenson, "Gender and Reproduction; or, Babies and the State," unpublished paper, June 1985, pp. 1–7.

23. For early theoretical formulations, see *Papers on Patriarchy: Conference, London 76* (London, 1976). I am grateful to Jane Caplan for telling me of the existence of this publication and for her willingness to share with me her copy and her ideas about it. For the psychoanalytic position, see Sally Alexander, "Women, Class and Sexual Difference," *History Workshop*, 17 (Spring 1984): 125–35. In seminars at Princeton University in early 1986, Juliet Mitchell seemed to be returning to an emphasis on the priority of materialist analyses of gender. For an attempt to get beyond the theoretical impasse of Marxist feminism, see Coward, *Patriarchal Precedents*. See also the brilliant American effort in this direction by anthropologist Gayle Rubin, "The Traffic in Women: Notes on the 'Political Economy' of Sex," in Rayna R. Reiter, ed., *Towards an Anthropology of Women* (New York, 1975): 167–68.

24. Nancy Chodorow, *The Reproduction of Mothering: Psychoanalysis and the Sociology of Gender* (Berkeley, Calif., 1978), 169.

25. "My account suggests that these gender-related issues may be influenced during the period of the oedipus complex, but they are not its only focus or outcome. The negotiation of these issues occurs in the context of broader object-relational and ego processes. These broader processes have equal influence on psychic structure formation, and psychic life and relational modes in men and women. They account for differing modes of identification and orientation to heterosexual objects, for the more asymmetrical oedipal issues psychoanalysts describe. These outcomes, like more traditional oedipal outcomes, arise from the asymmetrical organization of parenting, with the mother's role as primary parent and the father's typically greater remoteness and his investment in socialization especially in areas concerned with gender-typing." Chodorow, *Reproduction of Mothering*, 166. It is important to note that there are differences in interpretation and approach between Chodorow and British object-relations theorists who follow the work of D. W. Winicott and Melanie Klein. Chodorow's approach is best characterized as a more sociological or sociologized theory, but it is the dominant lens through which object-relations theory has been viewed by American feminists. On the history of British object-relations theory in relation to social policy, see Denise Riley, *War in the Nursery* (London, 1984).

26. Juliet Mitchell and Jacqueline Rose, eds., *Jacques Lacan and the Ecole Freudienne* (London, 1983); Alexander, "Women, Class and Sexual Difference."

27. Teresa de Lauretis, *Alice Doesn't: Feminism, Semiotics, Cinema* (Bloomington, Ind., 1984), 159.

28. Alexander, "Women, Class and Sexual Difference," 135.

29. Denise Riley, "Summary of Preamble to Interwar Feminist History Work," unpublished paper, presented to the Pembroke Center Seminar, May 1985, p. 11.

30. Carol Gilligan, *In a Different Voice: Psychological Theory and Women's Development* (Cambridge, Mass., 1982).

31. Useful critiques of Gilligan's book are: J. Auerbach et al., "Commentary on Gilligan's *In a Different Voice*," *Feminist Studies*, 11 (Spring 1985); and "Women and Morality," a special issue of *Social Research*, 50 (Autumn 1983). My comments on the tendency of historians to cite Gilligan come from reading unpublished manuscripts and grant proposals, and it seems unfair to cite those here. I have kept track of the

references for over five years, and they are many and increasing.

32. *Feminist Studies*, 6 (Spring 1980): 26–64.

33. By "deconstruction," I mean to evoke Derrida's discussion, which, though it surely did not invent the procedure of analysis it describes, has the virtue of theorizing it so that it can constitute a useful method. For a succinct and accessible discussion of Derrida, see Jonathan Culler, *On Deconstruction: Theory and Criticism after Structuralism* (Ithaca, N.Y., 1982), especially 156–79. See also Jacques Derrida, *Of Grammatology* (Baltimore, 1976); Jacques Derrida, *Spurs* (Chicago, 1979); and a transcription of Pembroke Center Seminar, 1983, in *Subjects/Objects* (Fall 1984).

34. Clifford Geertz, "Blurred Genres," *American Scholar*, 49 (October 1980): 165–79.

35. Michelle Zimbalist Rosaldo, "The Uses and Abuses of Anthropology: Reflections on Feminism and Cross-Cultural Understanding," *Signs*, 5 (Spring 1980): 400.

36. Michel Foucault, *The History of Sexuality*, vol. 1, *An Introduction* (New York, 1980); Michel Foucault, *Power/Knowledge: Selected Interviews and Other Writings, 1972–77* (New York, 1980).

37. For this argument, see Rubin, "Traffic in Women," 199.

38. Rubin, "Traffic in Women," 189.

39. Biddy Martin, "Feminism, Criticism and Foucault," *New German Critique*, 27 (Fall 1982): 3–30; Kathryn Kish Sklar, *Catharine Beecher: A Study in American Domesticity* (New Haven, Conn., 1973); Mary A. Hill, *Charlotte Perkins Gilman: The Making of a Radical Feminist, 1860–1896* (Philadelphia, 1980).

40. Lou Ratté, "Gender Ambivalence in the Indian Nationalist Movement," unpublished paper, Pembroke Center Seminar, Spring 1983; and Mrinalini Sinha, "Manliness: A Victorian Ideal and the British Imperial Elite in India," unpublished paper, Department of History, State University of New York, Stony Brook, 1984.

41. Pierre Bourdieu, *Le Sens Pratique* (Paris, 1980), 246–47, 333–461, especially 366.

42. Maurice Godelier, "The Origins of Male Domination," *New Left Review*, 127 (May–June 1981): 17.

43. Gayatri Chakravorty Spivak, "Three Women's Texts and a Critique of Imperialism," *Critical Inquiry*, 12 (Autumn 1985): 243–46. See also Kate Millett, *Sexual Politics* (New York, 1969). An examination of how feminine references work in major texts of Western philosophy is carried out by Luce Irigaray in *Speculum of the Other Woman* (Ithaca, N.Y., 1985).

44. Natalie Zemon Davis, "Women on Top," in her *Society and Culture in Early Modern France* (Stanford, Calif., 1975), 124–51.

45. Caroline Walker Bynum, *Jesus as Mother: Studies in the Spirituality of the High Middle Ages* (Berkeley, Calif., 1982); Caroline Walker Bynum, "Fast, Feast, and Flesh: The Religious Significance of Food to Medieval Women," *Representations*, 11 (Summer 1985): 1–25; Caroline Walker Bynum, "Introduction," *Gender and Religion: On the Complexity of Symbols* (Boston: Beacon Press, 1986).

46. See, for example, T. J. Clarke, *The Painting of Modern Life* (New York, 1985).

47. The difference between structuralist and post-structuralist theorists on this question rests on how open or closed they view the categories of difference. To the extent that post-structuralists do not fix a universal meaning for the categories or the relationship between them, their approach seems conducive to the kind of historical analysis I am advocating.

48. Rachel Weil, "The Crown Has Fallen to the Distaff: Gender and Politics in the Age of Catharine de Medici," *Critical Matrix* (Princeton Working Papers in Women's Studies), 1 (1985). See also Louis Montrose, "Shaping Fantasies: Figurations of

Gender and Power in Elizabethan Culture," *Representations*, 2 (Spring 1983): 61–94; and Lynn Hunt, "Hercules and the Radical Image in the French Revolution," *Representations*, 2 (Spring 1983): 95–117.

49. Edmund Burke, *Reflections on the French Revolution* (1892: reprint edn., New York, 1909), 208–09, 214. See Jean Bodin, *Six Books of the Commonwealth* (1606; reprint edn., New York, 1967); Robert Filmer *Patriarcha and Other Political Works*, ed. Peter Laslett (Oxford, 1949); and John Locke, *Two Treatises of Government* (1690; reprint edn., Cambridge, 1970). See also Elizabeth Fox-Genovese, "Property and Patriarchy in Classical Bourgeois Political Theory," *Radical History Review*, 4 (Spring–Summer 1977): 36–59; and Mary Lyndon Shanley, "Marriage Contract and Social Contract in Seventeenth Century English Political Thought," *Western Political Quarterly*, 32 (March 1979): 79–91.

50. I am grateful to Bernard Lewis for the reference to Islam. Michel Foucault, *Historie de la Sexualité*, vol. 2, *L'Usage des plaisirs* (Paris, 1984). One wonders in situations of this kind what the terms of the subject's gender identity are and whether Freudian theory is sufficient to describe the process of its construction. On women in classical Athens, see Marilyn Arthur, "'Liberated Woman': The Classical Era," in Renate Bridenthal and Claudia Koonz, eds., *Becoming Visible* (Boston, 1976), 75–78.

51. Cited in Roderick Phillips, "Women and Family Breakdown in Eighteenth Century France: Rouen 1780–1800," *Social History*, 2 (May 1976): 217.

52. On the French Revolution, see Darlene Gay Levy, Harriet Applewhite, and Mary Johnson, eds., *Women in Revolutionary Paris, 1789–1795* (Urbana, Ill., 1979), 209–20; on Soviet legislation, see the documents in Rudolph Schlesinger, *The Family in the USSR: Documents and Readings* (London, 1949), 62–71, 251–54; on Nazi policy, see Tim Mason, "Women in Nazi Germany," *History Workshop*, 1 (Spring 1976): 74–113, and Tim Mason, "Women in Germany, 1925–40: Family, Welfare and Work," *History Workshop*, 2 (Autumn 1976): 5–32.

53. Elizabeth Wilson, *Women and the Welfare State* (London, 1977); Jane Jenson, "Gender and Reproduction"; Jane Lewis, *The Politics of Motherhood: Child and Maternal Welfare in England 1900–1939* (Montreal, 1980); Mary Lynn McDougall, "Protecting Infants: The French Campaign for Maternity Leaves, 1890s–1913," *French Historical Studies*, 13 (1983): 79–105.

54. On English utopians, see Barbara Taylor, *Eve and the New Jerusalem* (New York, 1983); on France, Joan W. Scott, "Men and Women in the Parisian Garment Trades: Discussions of Family and Work in the 1830s and 40s," in Pat Thane et al., eds., *The Power of the Past: Essays for Eric Hobsbawm* (Cambridge, 1984), 67–94.

55. Louis Devance, "Femme, famille, travail et morale sexuelle dans l'idéologie de 1848," in *Mythes et représentations de la femme au XIXe siècle* (Paris, 1976); Jacques Rancière and Pierre Vauday, "En allant à l'expo: l'ouvrier, sa femme et les machines," *Les Révoltes Logiques*, 1 (Winter 1975): 5–22.

56. Gayatri Chakravorty Spivak, "'Draupadi' by Mahasveta Devi," *Critical Inquiry*, 8 (Winter 1981): 381–402; Homi Bhabha, "Of Mimicry and Man: The Ambivalence of Colonial Discourse," *October*, 28 (Spring 1984): 125–33; Karin Hausen, "The Nation's Obligations to the Heroes' Widows of World War I," in Margaret R. Higonnet et al., eds., *Women, War and History* (New Haven, Conn., 1986). See also Ken Inglis, "The Representation of Gender on Australian War Memorials," unpublished paper presented at the Bellagio Conference on Gender, Technology and Education, October 1985.

57. On the French Revolution, see Levy, *Women in Revolutionary Paris;* on the American Revolution, see Mary Beth Norton, *Liberty's Daughters: The Revolutionary Experience of American Women* (Boston, 1980); Linda Kerber, *Women of the Republic* (Chapel Hill, N.C., 1980); Joan Hoff-Wilson, "The Illusion of Change: Women and the American Revolution," in Alfred Young, ed., *The American Revolution: Explorations in the History of American Radicalism* (DeKalb, Ill., 1976), 383–446. On the French Third Republic, see Steven Hause, *Women's Suffrage and Social Politics in the French Third Republic* (Princeton, N.J., 1984). An extremely interesting treatment of a recent case is Maxine Molyneux, "Mobilization without Emancipation? Women's Interests, the State and Revolution in Nicaragua," *Feminist Studies,* 11 (Summer 1985): 227–54.

58. On pro-natalism, see Riley, *War in the Nursery;* and Jenson, "Gender and Reproduction." On the 1920s, see the essays in *Strategies des Femmes* (Paris, 1984).

59. For various interpretations of the impact of new work on women, see Louise A. Tilly and Joan W. Scott, *Women, Work and Family* (New York, 1978); Thomas Dublin, *Women at Work: The Transformation of Work and Community in Lowell, Massachusetts, 1826–1860* (New York, 1979); and Edward Shorter, *The Making of the Modern Family* (New York, 1975).

60. See, for example, Margaret Rossiter, *Women Scientists in America: Struggles and Strategies to 1914* (Baltimore, Md., 1982).

61. Luce Irigaray, "Is the Subject of Science Sexed?" *Cultural Critique,* 1 (Fall 1985): 73–88.

62. Louis Crompton, *Byron and Greek Love: Homophobia in Nineteenth-Century England* (Berkeley, Calif., 1985). This question is touched on in Jeffrey Weeks, *Sex, Politics and Society* (New York, 1983).

EDUCATION AND RURAL WOMEN: TOWARD AN ALTERNATIVE PERSPECTIVE

Vina Mazumdar

INTRODUCTION

Feminist scholarship has been challenging the androcentric biases of knowledge establishments all over the world. Critics of the patterns and theories of development that have dominated the global scene since the end of the Second World War have thrown up many denunciations of the urban bias in development planning. Neither group, however, viewed rural women as a significant group for investigation until Ester Boserup's classic study[1] drew attention to this majority. The process of our formal educational institutions has put blinkers on the eyes of even those who came from rural families, making them blind to the women in their own families, villages, and communities.

Let me illustrate this lack of recognition from a real life incident. I and my colleagues at the Center for Women's Development Studies (CWDS) in New Delhi have been involved for the last eight years in an action-research project of employment generation for poor rural women through their own organizations. At the inception of this project, we were discussing possibilities with sixty-four women, landless agricultural laborers, who had identified repeated seasonal migration for agricultural work to other districts as their biggest enemy. Every one of them was a highly skilled agriculturist. But their own region—which was drought prone, unirrigated, and mono-

This is a shorter and revised version of the paper prepared for the Mount Holyoke College 150th Anniversary International Conference on Women and Worldwide Education, November 1987. It elaborates some ideas presented at Women's Studies International at Nairobi in 1985.

cropped—could not provide them work for more than six to eight weeks per year. Earlier generations had supported themselves during the lean seasons by gathering forest produce for food, fodder, and fuel and earning some livelihood through processing minor forest produce. They made ropes, mats, and oil from seeds, brewed liquor, spun yarn from a wild silk worm,[2] sold medicinal herbs, fruits, and seeds to peripatetic traders, and so on. But the forests had disappeared, and they had now become increasingly dependent on seasonal migration to the "green revolution" districts.[3] The younger women, deprived of the forest from their childhoods and forced to shuttle to and fro with their mothers on these recurring treks, never acquired the knowledge of the forest or the skills to process forest produce that their mothers and grandmothers had possessed. Instead, they had acquired skills in paddy cultivation while working alongside their mothers.

The women decided that the price they paid for recurring seasonal migration was too high—50 percent infant mortality, recurring abortions, loss of health and longevity, sexual harassment by labor contractors and employers, and perpetual indebtedness. They wanted work in their own area so that they could send their children to school, maintain and improve their homes, and perhaps get some chance to improve their own lot— maybe learn something new that could help them to earn a better living and protect their own and the children's health a bit more. To achieve these goals, they were ready to form their own organization.

The meeting to form this organization was also attended by local leaders—the chairman of the block-level council[4] and a schoolmaster—who came from the same tribal community as the women. Both had been active peasant leaders. The schoolmaster suggested to us, "Why don't you teach them to make shoulder bags?"[5] My counter question was, "Would you suggest the same for the men of these families?" The prompt reply was, "Of course not; they [the men] are agricultural workers." When I asked whether the women were not also agricultural workers, there was a chorus of protest from the sixty-four women. "Ask him if we have not worked on his fields and many others in the village!"

The chairman of the council turned to the women and admitted that, though a peasant's son by birth, he, too, had been a victim of this blindness. "When the government asked me to plan some income-generating activity for women, I, too, thought of sewing classes and tailoring shops, and forgot that most of you had joined actively in our movements for land reform and fair prices for forest products. I, too, didn't see you primarily as peasants and workers. I have learned my lesson."

In the next few months, he assisted us in forming more such groups[6] and used his substantial influence on the local peasantry to give privately owned plots of uncultivated wasteland to the women's groups. With government funding to meet their wage costs, the women transformed these plots into sericulture plantations, thus reviving an old forest-based industry[7] that had died out in the area.[8]

This story can be replicated from any part of the developing world. These two men were not anti-women nor hostile to the idea of these women earning a living. But their contact with "modern" education had blinded them to the reality of women's lives in their own villages.

UNLEARNING AND RETHINKING

Is the relationship between education and rural women to be a one-way process of us, the educated, providing knowledge to rural women? Or is it to be a two-way process of correcting our errors and removing our blinkers first by learning from them about the reality of their lives, their store of skills and knowledge, and their extraordinary capacity to survive on so little and keep up their courage in the face of problems that would drive most of us to lunatic asylums or suicide?[9] These questions are being raised not only by women and development specialists, but by one of the most renowned agricultural scientists in the world, M. S. Swaminathan: "The greatest challenge before R & D [research and development] institutions lies in motivating scientists and technologists to undertake a process of listening and learning through collaboration with poor (rural) women while developing their research priorities and strategies. This will call for a *learning revolution*.[10]

One of the most difficult and radical challenges that faces education systems all over the world today is how to incorporate the women's dimension into the educational process. As feminists we asked for this integration as a method of achieving gender equality or equity. As a recent critic of development who began nearly three decades ago as a critic of the educational system in my own country—desperately seeking ways to prevent the separation of education from socially relevant issues[11]—I have found the answer from rural women.

As an educational planner I was unaware of women's issues. As a product of an urban middle-class family and a hybrid education at institutions (all urban) in India and Britain, I was even less aware of rural women. As a first generation beneficiary of the equality clauses of the Indian Constitution, I accepted the facile theory that education and equal political rights would remove inequality for all women in time. I didn't realize that the educational process itself was strengthening the hold of patriarchy and introducing new forces for inequality and the subordination and marginalization of women.

For nearly a decade when I was preoccupied with *discovering* rural women in order to identify their problems and needs, my colleagues and I found ourselves increasingly lapsing back from our researcher and teacher status to that of students and learners. Our experience as members of the Committee on the Status of Women in India (CSWI)[12] appointed by the government in 1971, had convinced us that we had a lot to *unlearn* before we could contribute to new knowledge regarding women's situations and roles in our society. We began with the feeling that what we had learned of social science theories and research methodology in our years in the academic profession had been responsible to a very great extent for the *invisibility* of women's contributions, problems, and roles in earlier social science research in India. We attributed this failure to Eurocentric theories of social transformation and the tools and methods of research that we had borrowed from the West.

According to the Center for Women's Development Studies document, *The First Six Years and Forward* (1987),

> It was, therefore, a deliberate decision, to avoid starting with any assumptions or framework while beginning research on the situation of poor rural women in different parts of the country. We decided to expose ourselves as much as possible to the empirical reality to seek recognizable patterns within that reality, and to develop concepts that reflected the empirical reality rather than analytical approaches borrowed from any other part of the world.[13]

In repeated cases, we observed with great delight the transformation of perspectives, values, and involvement, even the sense of identity of scholars who began to take up women-focused research, especially in the poverty sectors. This process can only be described as a reversal of the normal learning process where the more educated teach and the less educated (in rural women's case, mostly illiterate) are expected to learn. In its place, women's studies or women-focused research in rural development in India (as elsewhere) has clearly emerged as a different process of generating what has been termed by a few social scientists as "organic knowledge," in which the people being researched are the real teachers and the scholars are learners.[14]

Only a fraction of educated persons, however, manage to become researchers. How are we to introduce this unlearning and rethinking perspective into the educational process? The Nairobi document *Forward Looking Strategies for the Advancement of Women to the Year 2000*[15] provides some answers. Paragraph 82 recommends inclusion of women's history and issues in the curriculum. Paragraphs 83 and 167 recommend revision of textbooks to reflect positive, dynamic, and participatory images of women, and men's involvement in family responsibilities. Paragraph 171 suggests elimination of sexual stereotypes from the educational system. Paragraphs 115 and 325 refer to the role of education in removing gender biases in development programs and projecting the centrality of women's role in development. Paragraphs 85 and 165 seek the support of education, specifically, the use of women's studies to change societal attitudes that reinforce inequalities.

None of these statements refers to the education of women but to needed reforms in educational systems—the methods and content of teaching, the value orientation, and the organization of the educational process. They also challenge some of the post-World War theories that sought to reduce the educational process and both natural and human sciences to a *value neutral* position. Such theories still dominate many educational institutions and have resulted in two parallel developments. On the one hand, critics of the value neutral position have attacked education as "a dependent function of the power and production structures" that cannot play any role in the achievement of social justice.[16] On the other side of the fence are the power bosses of the world, always suspicious of the dissent that educational institutions tend to generate and the autonomy they demand in the pursuit of knowledge and its dissemination. These bosses would like to reduce the role of educational systems to a *mere skill-generating one* in the name of either value neutrality or the manpower requirements of scientific, technological, and economic development. Yet educational institutions are expected to produce the planners, not only of tomorrow, but for the twenty-first century and beyond, assuming the power bosses leave us a world to plan for. The theory of value neutrality of educational institutions, in my opinion, is a conspiracy to reduce educators to a powerless, nonparticipatory, passive status. Academic objectivity and scientific rationality or honesty to one's data are not value neutral. They are values in themselves.[17]

All educators who reject the theory of value neutrality of education should thank the international women's movement for coming to our rescue by placing value and attitudinal transformation as a central task of educational agencies.

INSTITUTIONAL ROLES FOR CHANGE

The CSWI observed that from early childhood boys and girls were indoctrinated to accept gender inequality through a powerful socialization process. According to the CSWI report,

> The only institution which could counteract the effect of this process is the educational system. If education is to promote equality for women, it must make a deliberate, planned and sustained effort so that the new values of equality of the sexes can replace the traditional value system of inequality. The educational system today has not even attempted to undertake this responsibility. In fact, the schools reflect and strengthen the traditional prejudices of inequality through curricula, the classification of subjects on the basis of sex, and the unwritten code of conduct enforced on the public.[18]

The CSWI's challenge generated a new debate on the interrelationship between gender equality and educational development. The explosion of research-based evidence about the adverse impact of economic modernization, social change, and population dynamics on poor working women, especially in rural areas and urban slums (a majority of the latter being migrants from rural areas), encouraged a group of academics to demand the incorporation of women's studies within the educational curriculum in order to avoid the "intellectual marginalization" of women's issues in future.[19]

This increasing demand received some positive response from senior academics concerned with educational reform. In 1983 the University Grants Commission (UGC) issued a letter to all vice chancellors asking them to think seriously about incorporating problems of women's status into their teaching, research, and extension activities. At a national seminar supported by the UGC at Delhi University in 1985, several vice chancellors and senior teachers (women and men) described the role of women's studies as primarily one of changing values and attitudes as its practitioners implemented the following goals:

> ... to counter reactionary forces emanating from certain sections of the media, and economic, social and political institutions that encourage the demotion of women from productive to mere reproductive roles; to revitalize university education, bringing it closer to burning social issues, to work towards their solution, and to produce more sensitive persons able to play more committed and meaningful roles in development activities for women in all sectors; . . . to generate new and organic knowledge through intensive field work, . . . for evaluation and correction of development policies and [for] extending . . . academic analysis into hitherto neglected sectors.[20]

The debate intensified during the year-long consultations for formulating a new National Policy on Education (NPE) which was adopted by the Indian Parliament in May 1986. Part IV of the Policy Document, titled "Education for Equality," states:

> Education will be used as an agent of basic change in the status of women. In order to neutralize the accumulated distortions of the past, there will be a well-conceived edge in favor of women. The national education system will play a positive, interventionist role in the empowerment of women. It will foster the development of new values through redesigned curricula, textbooks, the training and orientation of teachers, decision makers and administrators, and the active involvement of educational institutions. This will be an act of faith and social engineering. Women's studies will be promoted as a part of various courses and educational institutions encouraged to take up active programs to further women's development.
>
> The removal of women's illiteracy and obstacles inhibiting their access to, and retention in, elementary education will receive overriding priority through provision of special support services, setting of time targets, and effective monitoring. Major emphasis will be laid on women's participation in vocational, technical, and professional education at different levels. The policy of nondiscrimination will be pursued vigorously to eliminate sex stereotyping in vocational and professional courses and to promote women's participation in nontraditional occupations, as well as in existing and emergent technologies.

Some spelling-out of the concept of empowerment was also attempted in the Programme of Action for the NPE adopted by Parliament in July 1986.

The primary emphasis was on organizing women at the grassroots level to encourage reflection, self-reliance, collective learning, and productive activity. This link between grassroots organization of women producers and their empowerment to participate more effectively in developmental and political processes by giving them "social strength" is also admitted in the Seventh Five Year Plan and in some programs adopted by different ministries.[21] There is nothing new in this idea. It has been debated and articulated in virtually all conferences on women and development, national and international. What is new is the effort to enlist the active support of educational institutions in bringing this about.

Until recently, all people concerned with planning strategies to bring about gender equality—at national and international levels—tended to depend on government action or action by nongovernmental organizations. The support of individual academics was harnessed mainly to do research—diagnostic or evaluative. The first suggestion that educational institutions also need to play a role in this field was hinted at in the United Nations Mid-Decade Conference on Women in Copenhagen, but the Programme of Action does not clearly articulate how that role should be played.

The pre-Nairobi Conference of Nonaligned and Other Developing Countries went further by stating that educational systems in these countries had actually strengthened stereotypical images of women's roles derived from the experiences of the urban middle class or the social elite.[22] Criticizing "the failure of educational systems in fulfilling their role" of promoting values conducive to women's equality, the conference members observed:

> Structurally, pedagogically, and philosophically, educational institutions need to play a far more active role in the development of a new cultural ethos that can contribute to the realization of the goals of comprehensive development of human material, and this also requires that they internalize the concern for the equality of women and the enhancement of their role—in . . . curricula, method[s], organization, and research agenda[s] . . . The promotion of new knowledge about women and new perceptions of the role of women in development should be viewed as an instrument for educational and cultural development for the younger generation.[23]

At an expert group meeting organized by UNESCO two months after the Nairobi conference, the close relationship between educational development and the incorporation of women's issues within the educational process was articulated still more explicitly:

> The exclusion of the issues of women's subordination, discrimination, and emancipation from the areas of scientific and intellectual discussion has contributed to their continuation and has facilitated the perpetuation of false rationalizations or justifications of subordination as resulting from natural or biological causes. Such facile generalizations continue to influence women's access to, and role in, all levels of education and research, including special sectors that carry

weight, prestige, and power, such as science and technology.

The process of rethinking or reevaluation of women's situation and roles has to begin from the earliest stages of education. In order to achieve that, however, efforts have also to be mounted to reorient higher stages of education. This calls for:

a. Higher level of investment in research on women's issues;

b. Inclusion of women's issues as an integral part of the teaching curriculum in various disciplines;

c. Increasing women's participation in the implementation of these activities.

Part of the task of the social and human sciences, and also of philosophy, is to articulate and bring to the surface the various paradigms and presuppositions concerning the role, status, and supposed nature of women, so as to be able to examine them in a clear and informed manner. Such paradigms continue to influence the thought and action not only of the person in the street but also of educators and researchers in their professional work. This is not to say that the social and human sciences already possess all the information and conceptualization necessary to answer the many questions that arise concerning the sources of discrimination and role determination of women; *indeed, a sustained effort continues to be needed to fill a gap that until now has been far too neglected.*

While priority in the effort to understand and change the situation of women will have to be given to the social and human sciences, the group is of the view that associating women's concerns and interests with the activities of other sciences—notably the exact sciences and technological fields, including the new technologies and their applications—is of prime importance. The fundamental changes that are taking place all over the world resulting from developments in science and technology have yet to be studied for their social and ethical implications. Examining these issues from a women's perspective is critically needed, and planning for this should immediately be undertaken if women are to be prepared for the rapid transformation taking place in their professional and private lives, and to be able to effectively influence decision making in this regard.

In recent years, women's studies and research from women's perspectives have already challenged many established theories and paradigms in the social and human sciences. However, such challenges remain inadequately reflected in the teaching curricula and research planning of institutions of higher education and all other bodies responsible for research policy and investment. Where such courses have entered, they are tolerated as adjuncts, or marginal elements. *It is important that they influence* and interact, on equal terms, with the main disciplinary courses and establish parity both on the level of teaching and on the level of associated research.[24]

In the case of developing countries particularly, intervention for women's equality and development, whether prompted by government or other agencies, always has to contain a central core of educational, information-gathering, communication, and training activities. It is impractical to expect bureaucracy to play this role. Nongovernmental organizations (NGOs) concerned with women's issues in these countries are mostly based in urban areas and lack both human and financial resources to undertake all the tasks that are involved—research, communication, mobilization, training, and obtaining resource support, including in some cases legal and political support. In many developing countries, appropriate rural-based NGOs do not exist. But educational institutions, of varied quality, do exist in most parts of the developing world. They possess some of the necessary skills, infrastructural support, and above all the human resources to play this role. In a country like India, another reason for introducing this new role for educational institutions into the education policy was their public accountability. In contrast, not all NGOs are exposed to public scrutiny nor are they committed to women's equality. Lastly, the link between this "interventionist role" and the "internalization of concern" for enhancing women's role in development projects makes for a mutually supportive, participatory relationship between grassroots groups of poor women in both rural and urban areas, and educational institutions that need to transform themselves through such exposure and intervention. The long-term effects of such an interaction can be revolutionary.

NEW ISSUES, NEW APPROACH

If education is to become an active agent for ending gender inequality, it requires a new perspective, new methods and tools, and new knowledge about: 1) the centrality of women's role in correcting the present iniquitous and destructive path of development; and 2) the origin of women's subordination in society. It is the contention of this article that the key to these two critical issues lies in the past and contemporary histories of rural women to a far greater extent than in the experiences of their counterparts in urban areas. In developing countries, one finds clearer gender differentials in the assessment of problems, priorities, values, and demands in rural as compared with urban areas.

There has been an explosion of information about the destructive consequences of ignoring rural women's critical role in the production of food, the sustenance of their families and the community, and the preservation of their environment. As this information is difficult to condense here, I will concentrate on a few crucial aspects.

According to Sarthi Acharya, in *Women and Development in the Third World*,

> The socioeconomic formations in the rural sector are the primary organization of production in which women's role has a pivotal importance in most parts of the developing world. In the rural areas of these countries, women work in all capacities, in growing food, postharvest operations, marketing, animal husbandry, and related activities. In addition, they spend considerable time in gathering fuel and fetching water. In several cases they also work as wage labor on farms. The FAO has estimated that sometimes women's work could be longer

than men's work by as much as 43 percent.[25]

Many parts of Africa have a large incidence of female-headed households where women undertake the sole responsibility of growing food. It is in spite of these facts that women have generally been seen as consumers and not as producers in the bookkeeping system of development. Such attitudes have not only adversely affected the consumer status of women, but have also put development projects in jeopardy.

Since women's role is vital in sustaining rural economic systems in these countries, it is imperative that they be included as explicit target groups in rural development, land reforms, and technological infusion. This requires an a priori understanding of women's work in different geographic and cultural settings.[26]

The problems of invisibility, undercounting, and undervaluation of women's work in agriculture surfaced with a vengeance during the women's decade, not only due to the pressure of feminist scholarship, but also to the growing developmental crisis, especially in food production, environmental destruction with deforestation, the "other" energy crisis, and mass migration of the rural unemployed to cities and metropolitan countries in search of employment. This forced various international and national agencies to revise their earlier estimates of women's contribution to agriculture.[27]

According to specialists in quantitative analysis who have been examining rural women's actual work at the field level, even these revisions are not adequate because they suffer from the basic limitations imposed on national data collection agencies such as the Census Bureau by internationally standardized definitions of work. One of the sharpest condemnations of these "fuzzy" definitions and consequent underassessment of rural women's work as "supplementary" or "nonproductive" has come, not from a feminist scholar, but a highly regarded male census expert and population analyst, Asok Mitra:

> In reality there are extraordinarily few areas where women's economic contribution could be dismissed as merely supplementary, or optional, or dispensable. But this myth has been very successfully practiced increasingly over the ages in protean form to keep woman under subjugation, politically, economically, and socially.[28]

I am no believer in the male conspiracy theory of women's subordination. But as a person who has spent fifty-four years in and around educational institutions, I have to ask the question, can we as educators absolve ourselves of all responsibility for the perpetuation and strengthening of this "protean form" of subjugation of women? Who helped to develop these definitions, the methodology, and the tools for the undervaluation of women's work? At one of the early seminars (1978) on rural women's work situations in India, a senior scholar who had been involved in designing the first farm management surveys (she was trained at Harvard) stood up and confessed that she had measured the value of women's work, not in terms of the labor input, but in terms of the lower wages that they received.

Swaminathan argues that ignoring rural women's higher skills in certain agricultural operations such as seed selection, storage, pregermination tests, pollination, transplantation, all postharvest operations, as well as cattle care and other livestock rearing has, in fact, arrested the growth of agricultural productivity. Improving their access to available new knowledge, not only in these areas, but in soil fertility and fertilizer management, integrated post and weed management, and water and soil conservation, would have a major impact on rice agriculture.[29]

A great deal of evidence is now available that links the present food crisis in Africa to the neglect of the subsistence sector, where women predominate, in agricultural development.[30] Women are the "prime movers" in the food economy but have been losing ground steadily in access to quality land, better implements, and seeds.[31] As in the case of poor rural women in Asia, their labor time has increased but the rewards are less.

Despite protective legislation in many countries regarding equal pay for equal work, all over the world rural women receive lower wages for their labor. This is acknowledged in the *World Labor Report* but is inadequately documented. One major problem that has affected both planners and analysts of rural society is the myth of the homogeneity of rural women. Rural societies, like urban societies in most parts of the world, are fragmented by divisions according to socio-economic class, occupational group, and ethnic and other cultural identity. Except in occasional isolated areas where simple communities still continue to subsist on primitive agriculture or food gathering, most rural communities have experienced radical changes in their socioeconomic organization, production systems, and relations; and they have felt the changes that come with increasing penetration of a monetized economy, state and legal control over basic resources, and population pressure. Different groups of rural women are affected differently by these changes. In the South Asian context, a hierarchical pattern of social organization emerged much earlier than elsewhere. In such societies, withdrawal of women from visible economic activity was, and continues to be, a symbol of higher social status.[32]

Based on my limited experience of rural societies, mostly confined to South Asia, rural women can be classified into five major categories, which sometimes overlap:

a. Women engaged in agriculture, who would be further subdivided into three groups: i) women from affluent, landowning families, who do not engage in field agriculture but play a major role in supervision of farm labor and postharvest operations;[33] ii) women from landowning, small farmer families, who work on the family land but do not undertake wage work in agriculture; iii) women from marginal farmer or landless households, who are compelled to seek wage work for survival.

b. Women engaged in other agriculture-based occupations, for example, animal husbandry, horticulture, sericulture, fisheries, dairying, and food processing.

c. Women artisans involved in various handicraft activities such as spinning, weaving, and pottery.

d. Women involved in forest-related activities such as the collection of minor forest produce (leaves, fruits, seeds, roots, grass, and wood), not only for their own consumption, but also for the market.

e. Women involved in retail distribution and other services often connected with one of the abovementioned activities. The capitalization of markets and the emergence of middlemerchants or monopolists who control particular products, either at the raw material end or at the finished product marketing end, have affected the retailers most adversely, pushing them more into agriculture or migration. Women in traditional service occupations—such as barbers, who also acted as midwives and healers—have also lost out to more formally trained health professionals.

It is easy to see that one set of macro-changes—such as deforestation/ afforestation; a major irrigation project drowning a large tract of land; new agricultural technology; the emergence of mass-produced consumption goods like mill cloth and aluminium pots and pans; or mechanized cereal processing—would not affect all categories of women similarly. For some it could mean increased prosperity, reduction of drudgery, and the possibility of education as well as increased chances of greater subordination within the family. For others, it could mean a temporary increase in work opportunities but no increase in time available to obtain some education or better health care. For still others, the disappearance or shrinkage of employment avenues may leave only migration as the answer. This has been the case with both artisans and women in forest-based occupations, many of whom have sought work as plantation or mine labor.

CONCLUSION

To educators who are concerned with the future role of education in achieving gender equality, I have two messages from millions of rural women in my country, which I believe are echoed in many other parts of the world. The first is to recognize and support the collective struggle for human survival, including their own, against the destruction of their productive base. Their land, water, forests, and other natural resources are threatened by types of development that are planned far away from them by people and agencies of which they have no knowledge. Further, the control over knowledge and power and its misuse by educated elites increases the women's powerlessness and deprivation.

The second message is from us, the intermediaries in the academic profession, because rural women's original contribution to human civilization has been lost even to the memories of the women themselves. We must restore this lost heritage to rural women and to educated men and women around the world.

Swaminathan has pointed out that:

> Some historians of agriculture believe that it was women who first domesticated crop plants and thereby initiated the art and science of farming. While men went out hunting in search of food, women started gathering seeds from the native flora and began cultivating those of interest from the point of view of food, fodder, fibre, fuel. This view is strengthened by the fact that women have been traditionally seed selectors. Even today, this tradition has continued in many parts of the developing world.[34]

This view is supported by many anthropologists, archaeologists, and some historians.[35] The legend has been preserved in some ancient temple murals in parts of northeastern India, where agriculture is still primarily a women's occupation. On the basis of archaeological and anthropological evidence, D.D. Kosambi has argued that pottery was begun by women on the Indian subcontinent.[36] Lastly, there is mounting evidence, from documentary[37] as well as archaeological and anthropological sources, that spinning and weaving of textiles from natural fiber was entirely initiated by women.

Food, clothing, and pots to cook in are the beginnings of productive activity or civilized living. If women were the initiators of these in a subcontinent the size of India, what was the story elsewhere? Surely it was the same in most parts of Africa.

What freedoms gave women such creative energy, which has been curbed by generations of subordination and powerlessness? Why and how did this subordination take place? Who is to find the answers to these questions and use them to build new minds that think differently about women? Only educational institutions can play this role—through research and teaching. That to me is the most important message from Nairobi.

NOTES

1. Ester Boserup, *Women's Role in Economic Development* (New York: St. Martins, 1970).

2. The product is known as *Tussar* silk, a tough fabric with great longevity.

3. Green Revolution districts are Hooghly and Burdwan, where adoption of new agricultural technology since the sixties led to sharp increases in agricultural productivity, with multiple cropping of paddies. For a detailed and moving account of the chain-reaction effect of loss of land and forests on the lives of these women and their children, see D. Bandyopadhyay, "Travails of Tribal Women," *Mainstream*, 14 June 1980. See also N.K. Banerjee, *Women's Participation and Development: A Case Study from West Bengal*, CWDS Occasional Paper no. 5 1985 (Mimeo), New Delhi.

4. This refers to the second tier of government from below, that is, elected representatives. The first tier consists of the *Gram Panchayat*, an elected council that incor-

porates five or six villages. The second tier is the Block *Panchayat Samiti* or Council. A Block is the smallest administrative unit of government from above (i.e., appointed officials including career civil servants) and generally includes a group of eight to ten *Gram Panchayats*.

5. Cotton shopping bags, woven in narrow "hobby looms," were popularized among students of Santiniketan, the educational institution in rural Bengal started by the Nobel Laureate poet Rabindranath Tagore seven decades ago in his effort to incorporate a rural reconstruction program through his educational institution. Now it is a hallmark of left-oriented students and others in Bengal and elsewhere. But because both the government and many NGOs have zeroed in on making these bags as an income-generating activity for women, the price of the bags has remained static for the last ten years, even though yarn prices have gone up by nearly 300 percent.

6. Now there are fourteen organizations with more than fifteen hundred members drawn from thirty-six villages.

7. The *Tussar* industry in this region dates back at least to the time of Kautilya's *Anthasastra* which was written sometime in the fourth century B.C. *Tussar* was a popular and paying item of export to the Roman Empire and to other parts of Europe by Middle Eastern traders through the medieval period until the eighteenth century. The East India Company first exported the fabric, but during the late eighteenth and early nineteenth century, with the company's political control over the region, it converted this flourishing cottage industry into a raw yarn-producing one to feed the British textile industry. *Tussar* produced by British manufacturers was a popular suiting for colonial regimes in all tropical regions. The forest dwellers' earnings remained confined to collection of cocoons from the forest and hand spinning of yarn by their women until the early years of the twentieth century, after which the rapid disappearance of the forests eradicated this livelihood.

8. Most of this account is based on ongoing research initiated by the CWDS; see Abhijit Dasgupta et al., *The Peasant Girl and the Goblins: Role of Women in the Silk Industry of Bengal* (forthcoming CWDS); and Narayan Benerjee, *Women's Work, Family Strategies and the Role of State: Case Study of a Forest Region in Bankura District, West Bengal* (forthcoming CWDS).

9. *The Seeds of Change: Role of Grassroots Rural Women's Organizations in Development,* Report of a training workshop for government functionaries (elected and bureaucrats) implementing the program Development of Women and Children in Rural Areas conducted by CWDS and the Ministry of Rural Development, Government of India, Mukutmanipur, Bankura, West Bengal, November 1986. CWDS, 1987.

10. M. S. Swaminathan, *Role of Education and Research in Enhancing Rural Women's Income and Household Happiness* (first J. P. Naik Memorial Lecture, 1982), CWDS, 1985; p. 38. At the time of this lecture, Swaminathan was Director General, International Rice Research Institute, Manila, and Chairman, Governing Council of the Food and Agriculture Organization. A Borlaug Award winner and Fellow of the Royal Society, his interests cover agriculture, forestry, conservation of natural resources, science, technology, and human resource development. In this document, he lists many areas of training and education for rural women to improve productivity in rice agriculture.

11. After sixteen years of university teaching, during which much of my criticism of Indian university education was formulated, I joined the Secretariat of the Uni-

versity Grants Commission to try my hand at higher education reform and development. I learned a great deal about the problems of development of a national university system, their linkages with international trends in educational transformation, and the role of colonialism and neocolonialism in widening the gap between the educational and social processes. Some of these ideas, in their initial form, were articulated in a short monograph written for the Indian Institute of Advanced Study, Simla. See Vina Mazumdar, *Education and Social Change: Three Studies on Nineteenth Century Bengal*, I.A.A.S., 1972. For a more developed, excellently written presentation in a global perspective, see R. P. Dore, *The Diploma Disease: Education, Qualification, and Development* (Berkeley: University of California Press, 1976).

12. The Committee on the Status of Women in India submitted its report, titled *Towards Equality*, on 1 January 1975. This document provided the basis for a new parliamentary mandate to the government to mount comprehensive legislative and developmental efforts "to remove disparities and disabilities that the majority of women continue to suffer from." It provided considerable fuel for the revival of the women's movement, the beginning of research focused on "invisible" women by the Indian Council of Social Science Research (ICSSR), and the beginnings of policy debates that continue to rage within and outside the government. But for the handful of persons directly involved in the committee's investigations, particularly the three academics (all of whom are now at CWDS), the effect was a transformation of perspectives, ideas, and life styles. A similar effect has been noted by many others—men and women—involved in women and development research.

13. An expert group meeting sponsored by UNESCO in Delhi, October 1982, defined women's studies as a "critical instrument for social science development to bring it closer to Asian Realities." See *Women's Studies and Social Science in Asia*, UNESCO, Office of the Regional Adviser for Social Sciences, Bangkok, 1983.

14. *The Seeds of Change: Role of Grassroots Rural Women's Organizations in Development*, op. cit.

15. *Forward Looking Strategies for the Advancement of Women to the Year 2000*, Report of the UN World Conference, Nairobi, 1985. An excellent summary has been published by the Hubert H. Humphrey Institute of Public Affairs, University of Minnesota, which also lists in an appendix the 129 paragraphs concerning education.

16. There is a whole school of these critics—Ivan Illyich, Pablo Latapi, Paulo Freire, and others.

17. For an objective statement of this position, see *Education and National Development*, Report of the Indian Education Commission (1964–66), Government of India, Ministry of Education, 1966. According to the Commission, the primary task before the Indian education system was not only to meet the manpower requirements of scientific, technological, and economic development, but to prepare the future generations for a new social order, based on the principles of secularism, socialism, and democracy. For a still more blunt and forthright statement, see J. P. Naik, *Equality, Quality and Quantity: The Elusive Triangle of Indian Education*, ICSSR, 1977.

18. *Towards Equality*, Report of the Committee on the Status of Women in India, Government of India, Ministry of Education and Social Welfare, 1975.

19. *Report of the First National Conference on Women's Studies*, SNDT Women's University, Bombay, 1981; *Report of the Second National Conference on Women's Studies*, Trivandrum, Indian Association for Women's Studies, Delhi, 1984; *Women's Studies and Social Sciences in Asia*, UNESCO, op. cit.; *Report of the Seminar on Perspec-*

tives and Organization of Women's Studies Units in Indian Universities, Department of Political Science, Delhi University, 1985; *Report of Women NGOs National Consultation on the Achievements and Failures of the Women's Decade,* 1985 (mimeo).

20. *Report of the Seminar on Perspectives and Organization of Women's Studies Units in Indian Universities,* Department of Political Science, Delhi University, 1985.

21. Such programs include the Department of Rural Development's Programme of Development of Women and Children in Rural Areas; the Department of Women and Child Development's, Programme of Support to Employment Programmes for Women (all in the rural sector); and the Ministry of Labor and Employment's Assistance to Organize Women Workers (rural and urban).

22. Ongoing research in several Asian countries by both Asian and foreign scholars is beginning to reexamine the familial role of urban elite women in countries that had experienced colonial rule. They claim that the urban elite absorbed this model of women's role in the family from their rulers, often through the system of colonial education and because of the compulsions of urbanization that called for substantial changes in the structure and life styles of the elite families.

The whole issue of women's education—its content, the values that it promoted, and the pressures that it generated on the minds of such elite women—is a fascinating example of global export of a role model that often bore little resemblance to what was demanded by the cultural traditions of the indigenous society. What was initiated by colonial education is being continued by the consumerist culture.

CWDS and the Asian Development Studies Center of Boston University are currently coordinating a United Nations University-sponsored cross-cultural study on rapidly industrializing societies, which tend to project the housewife as a consumer to promote markets, titled *Women's Work and Family Strategies in South and Southeast Asia.* The twenty-two studies under this project are nearing completion. Studies by Malavika Karlekar (CWDS, New Delhi) and Wazir-jahan Karim (University Sains Malaysia, Penang) focus especially on this issue in two different cultural contexts.

23. *New Delhi Document on Women and Development,* Report of the Ministerial Level Conference of Nonaligned and Other Developing Countries on Role of Women in Development, New Delhi, 1985, paragraphs 229 and 232.

24. *Reflections on Women's Problems in Research and Higher Education,* Report of the International Meeting of Experts, Lisbon, September 1985, UNESCO SHS/CONF/85/612/16.

25. FAO 1983, *Follow-up to WCARRD: The Role of Women in Agricultural Production,* Expert Consultation on Women and Food Production ESH, WIFP/83/11, Rome.

26. Sarthi Acharya, *Women and Rural Development in the Third World,* Tata Institute of Social Sciences (TISS), Bombay, 1987, pp. 2–3. For further information see Acharya's sources, including: UNDP 1980, *Rural Women's Participation in Development,* Evaluation Study no. 3, New York; Jennie Dey, "Gambian Women: Unequal Partners in Rice Development Projects," in Nici Nelson (ed.), *African Women in Development Process* (Totowa, N.J.: Biblio Distribution, F. Cass, 1981); J. Hanger and J. Morris, "Women and the Household Economy," in R. Chambers and J. Morris (eds.) *Mwea, An Irrigated Rice Settlement in Kenya,* Munich, 1973; I. Palmer, *The Nemow Case: Case Studies of the Impact of Large Scale Development Projects on Women,* Population Council, New York, 1979.

27. See, for example, the FAO report cited in note 25 for statistics from eighty-two

countries and the International Labor Office (ILO) Statistics cited in *Women and Rural Development in the Third World*.

28. Asok Mitra et al., *The Status of Women: Shifts in Occupation Participation Patterns*, 1961–71 (Delhi, Abhinav India, 1979), p. 49.

29. Swaminathan, op. cit.

30. See Acharya for the results of a study of participation by women and men in the labor force of 279 African agricultural communities.

31. ILO, *Resources, Power and Women*, Report of the Asian-African International Workshop on Strategies for Improving Employment Conditions of Rural Women, Geneva, 1985. International Centre for Public Enterprises in Developing Countries, *Role of Women in Developing Countries*, Ljubljana, 1985; *New Delhi Document on Women and Development*, op. cit. See also Sarthi Acharya, op. cit.

32. The sociological classic based on Indian experience that identified this process long before the Women's Decade is M. N. Srinivas, *Social Change in Modern India* (New Delhi: Orient Longman, 1972); also his *Changing Position of Indian Women* (Delhi: Oxford University Press, 1978); and *Towards Equality*, op. cit. See also Scarlett Epstein, *South India—Yesterday, Today, Tomorrow: Mysore Villages Revisited* (London, Macmillan, 1973).

33. K. Saradomoni, "Declining Employment for Labour Increasing Involvement by Land-owning Women," in *Women in Rice Farming*, International Rice Research Institute, Gower, 1985. For an excellent pen portrait of one of these women farm managers, see Mina Swaminathan, "Chellamma" in D. Jain (ed.) *Indian Women*, Government of India, Publications Division, 1975.

34. Swaminathan, op. cit., p. 9.

35. Gordon Childe, *What Happened in History* (New York: Penguin, 1985); D.D. Kosambi, *Culture and Civilization of Ancient India in Historical Outline*, p. 35.

36. Kosambi, op. cit., p. 37.

37. *Rgveda* (1500–1200 B.C.) cited in Kosambi, p. 80; *Arthasastra*, cited in Dasgupta et al., *The Peasant Girl and the Goblins: The Role of Women in the Silk Industry of Bengal*, op. cit.

A HOME DIVIDED: NEW MODELS FOR RESEARCH AND POLICY ON WOMEN AND INCOME IN THE THIRD WORLD

Judith Bruce

INTRODUCTION

Women's earned income and their ability to stretch this and other resources is vital to the survival of many households. Women pursue personal goals, as well as simple survival, in the context of stronger forces: segmented and discriminatory labor markets for which they are ill prepared; powerful family systems that use them as instruments for patriarchal or kinship ends; discriminatory customs and laws surrounding divorce and widowhood; inheritance systems that deprive them of assets or undermine their legal rights; and norms that confine women's roles to production and the nurturing of dependents.

Men and women in the same cultural setting and class group—and family—have very different prospects in life. They differ, often dramatically, in their participation in labor markets, the content of their work, the returns to their labor, the pattern of economic participation over the life cycle, daily time use, and parenting responsibilities. Their possibilities for finding adequate livelihoods, retaining assets, and maintaining their social status when marriages dissolve, whether through separation, abandonment, migration, or death, are often markedly poorer than men's.

This essay was summarized and adapted from the Introduction to *A Home Divided: Women and Income in the Third World,* edited by Daisy Dwyer and Judith Bruce (California: Stanford University Press, 1988).

SEEKING APPROPRIATE HOUSEHOLD MODELS

Bearing these contrasts in male and female experience in mind, we must reappraise various theories that treat the household as a unit. The unified household has for some time been an attractive formulation for a number of reasons. The first reason is the simplicity of making assumptions about the economic behavior of a fewer number of households in contrast to a larger number of individuals (within households). Unified households are convenient policy tools. Located within wider social and economic institutions, they become manipulable economic entities. Thus, one school of economic theory (the New Household Economics) acknowledges one central decision maker per household and views household behavior much as it would the behavior of commercial firms (for more discussion see Folbre, 1988).

A second point of resistance to conducting a search into the internal decision-making processes of households is skepticism that such potentially demanding research will bring with it explanatory powers far beyond those of the current model. What difference does the discovery of multiple decision makers with different agendas make if the outcome is still predicted by the unified household model? However, it appears that this is not always the case. Some authors (Dey, 1983; Rogers, 1983; Blumberg, 1988) have documented unexpected and unproductive outcomes of development efforts, which are probably best understood by taking into account the intrahousehold allocation process. For example, what explains the agricultural production project that simultaneously raises household incomes, leads women to withdraw labor on their key cash crops, and results in declines in nutrition and other welfare indicators? Differences between households cannot explain these effects fully, yet differences in the way men and women handle income may.

Finally, the assumption that households behave as economically rational units not only is analytically simpler to handle, but suits practical tastes as well. Policy makers, in both industrialized and developing countries, often prefer to stand clear of the issue of the internal distribution of resources in households, possibly assuming it will prove difficult to develop mechanisms to deliver benefits to specific individuals. And the household can be complicated and difficult to understand; descriptions of household dynamics differ according to the person reporting them. Yet, standard survey methodologies do not assist us in accurately viewing the household and locating economic authority in it when adult males are mechanically identified as heads of household. These adult males, when present, are often exclusively interviewed about sources and overall levels of household income. Their welfare is too often taken as a proxy for the welfare of all household members.

Supporting the analytic and practical impetus to consolidate individuals into households is a strong cultural bias. The family, especially the marital relationship, is viewed as a sanctum protected from the conflicts that characterize virtually all other social institutions. This bias, however comforting, is also incorrect. Since men's and women's access to and control of resources differ systematically in the wider world—the external world of income relations—why would their personal economies be served by a common ground plan in the internal world of income relations? Perhaps what comes closest to reality are models of household behavior in which individuals bargain, as defined by Nash (1953) and Manser and Brown (1979). Amatya Sen has developed a related idea of "cooperative conflict." Sen believes that individuals within the household contend but in many cases cannot bargain in the precise sense of this word because individual benefits from the bargaining may overlap in some areas, because perceptions of self-interest and self-worth are indistinctly defined (by self and others—an issue of extreme importance to women), and finally—in poor economies—because the ends to be attained are often fundamental elements of survival, not simply "utilities" such as satisfaction or pleasure (Sen, 1985, paragraphs 21–27).

ALLOCATION OF INCOME

A central impetus to women's earning—attaining a better life for their children, which many may view as an extension of "good mothering" (Engle, 1986)—may explain the allocational priorities they apply to their own income and other income that they control. Though difficult to research, a considerable body of information has been built up on this subject in the last decade (Blumberg, 1988). Kumar's study (1977) in Kerala, India, indicated that a child's nutritional level correlated positively with the size of the mother's income, food inputs from subsistence farming, and the quality of available family-based child care. Significantly, children's nutritional level did not increase in direct proportion to increases in paternal income. An expanding number of studies and project evaluations in Jamaica (Horton and Miller, n.d.), St. Lucia (Knudsen and Yates, 1981), Ghana (Tripp, 1981), Kenya (Carloni, 1987), Botswana (Carloni, 1987), Sri Lanka (Benson and Emmert, 1977), and a multivillage study in Guatemala (Blumberg, 1986) strongly indicate a greater devotion of women's than men's income to everyday subsistence and nutrition.

A study of landless families in Tamil Nadu and Kerala (Mencher, 1988) explores men's and women's income contributions to the family. Mencher documents that in a variety of poor classes in fourteen different villages, women consistently devote a higher proportion of their income (nearly 100 percent) to family needs than do men. Men withhold some portion of their wages for personal use even when overall income is clearly inadequate. Mencher's data challenge the hypothesis that men's and women's income contributions are fungible and cooperatively worked out. And while it is sometimes alleged that men contribute more of their earnings when women are earning less, Mencher's data show that fluctuations in men's contributions to the household go in unexpected directions. Men tend to make higher contributions to the household budget in both relative and absolute terms when women are earning the most. Curiously, they do not usually increase their contributions in times of stress (when women are finding less work or have just given birth to a child). Men's income contribution to the household varies, in most cases, not with need in the family but with their own income. From this, most men subtract a constant amount of income for personal use. The consequences of this pattern are potentially serious in communities where infant mortality is high, where all families live very close to the edge of poverty, and where malnutrition is common. Mencher also notes that planned new production techniques will bypass the poorest women and men and concentrate new technologies in the hands of a minority of wealthier men. Under present circumstances, any reduction in the income that women earn and devote to the family is liable to affect their survival.

Gender-based responsibilities are most explicit in Africa, and it is perhaps in approaching Africa that development scholars and practitioners see most distinctly the shortcomings of Western theories of household dynamics. In some societies, husbands are responsible for the provision of lodgings, children's tuition, and other educational costs. Providing income for food and clothing for children may vary as a male or female/male joint obligation. However, almost universally, women in Africa are viewed as ultimately responsible for fulfilling children's food needs (Nelson, 1981). A fuller understanding of women's roles, including women's authority over income and their production incentives, is essential if Africa's primary problems—lack of food security and the highest fertility and child mortality rates in the world—are to be resolved. Analyzing data from the Cameroons, Guyer (1988) finds both class-related aspects in household spending and distinctive male and female economies within households. At issue is not simply the ways in which women's income is used, but the degree to which men and women differ in taking personal spending money from their earnings. Though the specifics of women's consumption responsibilities vary in Africa and across the world, it is quite commonly found that gender ideologies support the notion that men have a right to personal spending money (Hoodfar, 1988; Guyer, 1988; Roldan, 1988; Mencher, 1988), which they are perceived to need or deserve, and that women's income is for collective purposes (Young, 1987). This building knowledge of the specific destinations of women's income was initially obscured by a larger debate about the possible losses to children's welfare of mothers working outside the home (Leslie, 1987). This debate initially arose in the setting of industrialized countries, but has been translated into the question succinctly posed by Engle (1986), "Can children's needs be met when their mothers work for cash income in Third World countries?" It should first be observed that many women have no choice about earning income. And research has begun to spell out in remarkable detail positive developmental impacts. Wilson (1981) noted that the children of "working" mothers have more adequate home diets at eighteen and thirty months than same aged children of non-working mothers in a set of Guatemalan villages that were studied. Recent research by Engle (1987), also in Guatemala, confirmed the positive contribution of maternal earnings (of non-domestic workers) to the welfare of one- to two-year-olds, and noted that, "two-year-old children of working mothers were significantly heavier than non-workers' children" (Engle, n.d., p. 2). Senauer (1988) evaluates the impact of the value of women's time on the next generation's food and nutritional status in three case studies, two in the Philippines and one in Sri Lanka. These analyses coincide in the conclusion that the value of women's time can be utilized as a means to indirectly change behavior and resource flows within households, and thus improve the well-being in particular of women and children" (Senauer, 1988, p. 20). This conclusion is warranted by findings that indicate that the mother and children receive a higher relative share of the household's available food when the mother's estimated wages increase. This is in contrast to a more limited or even null effect of the father's wage. In one of the two Philippine case studies, the father's wage had a negative impact on children's long-run nutritional status.

THE LINK TO POLICY

Understanding individual income streams within the household is analytically important for deciphering the determinants of economic change at both the upper and lower ends of the economic spectrum. When monitoring the health and welfare of low-income groups, it becomes crucial for the policy maker to see the link between the earning and spending priorities of women and their roles as daily financial managers of the household and primary guardians of the physical and social status of their children. Household authority patterns and norms may act to reduce the potential benefits to women of these economic opportunities by, for example, insisting that women take differential responsibility for children (and sometimes older dependents). There tends not to be a reciprocal pressure on men to contribute more to the family as their income increases; on the contrary, men may keep their bargaining edge by deciding what externally derived benefits are to be passed on to the household and to what degree. Men serve as unacknowledged gatekeepers between the family and purportedly gender-blind new economic opportunities.

The forging of an appropriate theoretical link between macro-level policy and micro-level impacts (at the household and subhousehold level) could enlighten debates about development policy, such as the current controversy about the impact of economic readjustment (e.g., changes in debt structure and internal pricing policies) on the poor. The debate—in its most simplified form—engages the economists (generally working within a neo-classical framework with its presumptive unified household) and other social scientists who tend to be more sensitive to the interclass and in-trahousehold distributional effects of economic policy. A third set of actors, also part of this debate, are the welfare planners who act principally through health and nutrition interventions.

These three groups diagnose and treat differently, but their models of the household are often similar in assuming cooperation between the adult males and adult females. Economists seek to help their households princi-pally by increasing the earnings of the main breadwinner. It is assumed that the income the male breadwinner earns from newly created employment opportunities will be distributed to his family. The degree to which this income will leak out of the household for other purposes is not formally considered, nor is the degree of actual attachment of the economically benefited males to the needy females and children. The second group, the social theorists, more attuned to the distributional effects of macroeconomic policies, are alert to decreases in real wealth; they look for polarization within societies and the creation of new class disparities. Their sensitivity to increasing class differentiation and divisions within communities has often not been extended to a concern with what happens inside households in times of stress. The third group, the health and welfare theorists and activists, have fewer resources and a good deal less in the way of policy instruments at their command; in effect, they take on "the women" as their agents. The invisible women of the economic theorists become the all-powerful mothers (within families and household units) of the health advocates. It is believed that these women, with more knowledge (but little more time or money), can heal, reconstitute, and fortify their children, while the underlying cause of much of the illness—inadequate nutrition owing to low incomes—cannot be dealt with at the level of health interventions.

One final point is worth noting when considering policy approaches: households are not permanent. By virtue of marrying men many years their senior, women in many settings face the near-certainty of widowhood, and in most cases, ensuing poverty. Women in many other societies face abandonment, extended separation, or divorce as a likely occurrence at some point in their lives. An already high—and in some settings, a rapidly increasing—proportion of women begin their families as pregnant adoles-cents without committed partners. Women's lifetime risks of being on their own are masked by survey classifications of family types that may greatly underenumerate households primarily or solely supported by women (Buvinic, Youssef, and Von Elm, 1978). Even according to the existing household headship classification techniques and cross-sectional informa-tion, as many as one third of households in the world may be woman-headed and, in some communities, the recorded figure is as high as 50 percent.[1] An important missing piece of knowledge is the manner in which many women pass through a phase in their lives when they are the primary or sole economic support of young children.

The policy message of this essay begins with the proposition that individuals rather than households should be the recipients of economic assistance, whether in the form of cash outlays, valued goods, or wage-earning opportunities, with women being the more appropriate recipients when certain ends are desired. Cultural designation of some obligation as male or as female points especially to the appropriateness of directing allocations to specific individuals. In cases in which it is determined that resources that come into the household may be used unproductively vis-à-vis the well-being of target groups, allocations of aid might be directed to women outside the household. Women's cooperatives and women's informal saving unions can be regarded as possible mechanisms to protect income and other resources for use in meeting critical needs.

Policies that earmark individual recipients for aid rather than the household as a unit are not necessarily discordant with the goals of family maintenance or strengthening. In fact, insofar as male heads of household have been de facto "individual" recipients of development allocations, our proposal is not a radical departure. Moreover, the precise delineation of recipients may reinforce, in a positive sense, differentiation regarding areas of responsibility that indigenous households already make.

To summarize, we suggest that women and men are distinctive in their economic access and similarly have distinct self-interest within the family. Male and female goals within nuclear and inter-generational households are typically pursued not through playing out cooperative plans, but rather through institutionalized inequalities. We argue for attention to these facts in pursuit of equality and economic progress. Certainly, the information gathered in this essay suggests that to the many fault lines[2] along which social changes are monitored, the economic condition of female and male within the same household should be added.

REFERENCES

Becker, Gary S. "A Treatise on the Family." Harvard University Press. Cambridge and London: 1981.

Ben-Porath, Yoram. "The F Connection: Families, Friends, and Firms and the Organizational Exchange," *Population and Development Review*, 6 (1): 1–30, March 1980.

Benson, Janet E., and Emmet, Jan Paul. "The Accelerated Mahaweli Program, Sri Lanka: A Women in Development Assessment." March 1987. A field study cited in Carloni, "Women in Development: AID's Experience, 1973–1985," Synthesis paper, Vol. 1 (1987).

Blumberg, Rae Lesser. "A Women in Development Natural Environment in Guatemala: The Alcosa Agribusiness Project in 1980 and 1985." Mimeo, August 1986.

Buvinic, Mayra, and Youssef, Nadia H., with Von Elm, Barbara. "Women-Headed Households: The Ignored Factor in Development Planning." Report submitted to the Office of Women in Development, U.S. Agency for International Development. Washington, D.C., International Center for Research on Women, 1978.

Carloni, Alice. "Women in Development: AID's Experience, 1973–1985." Synthesis paper, Vol. 1 (1987).

Dey, Jennie. "Gambian Women: Unequal Partners in Rice Development Projects?" *Journal of Development Studies*, 17 (1): 109–22, May 1983.

Dwyer, Daisy, and Bruce, Judith. *A Home Divided: Women and Income in the Third World*. California: Stanford University Press, 1988.

Engle, Patricia. "The Interesting Needs of Working Women and Their Young Children: 1980 to 1985." Report to Carnegie Corporation. Mimeo, January 24, 1986.

Engle, Patricia, and Pederson, Mary. "Maternal Work for Earnings and Children's Nutritional Status within Urban Guatemala." Mimeo, 1987.

Folbre, Nancy. "The Black Four of Hearts: Toward a New Paradigm of Household Economics." In Daisy Dwyer and Judith Bruce, op. cit.

Guyer, Jane. "Dynamic Approaches to Domestic Budgeting: Cases and Methods from Africa." In Daisy Dwyer and Judith Bruce, op. cit.

Horton, Susan, and Miller, Barbara Diane. *The Effect of Gender Household Head and Expenditure: Evidence from Low-Income Households in Jamaica*. (no date)

Knudsen, Barbara, and Yates, Barbara A. *The Economic Role of Women in Small Scale Agriculture in the Eastern Caribbean—St. Lucia*. Barbados: University of the West Indies Women in Development Unit, 1981.

Kumar, Shubh. "Composition of Economic Constraints in Child Nutrition: Impact from Maternal Incomes and Employment in Low Income Households." Ph.D. Dissertation, Cornell University, 1977.

Leslie, Joanne. "Women's Work and Child Nutrition in the Third World." International Center for Research on Women. Mimeo, 1987.

Manser, Marilyn, and Brown, Murray. "Bargaining Analyses of Intra-Household Decisions." In Lloyd, Cynthia; Andrews, Emily S.; and Gilroy, Curtis, L., eds., *Women in the Labor Market*. New York: Columbia University Press, 1979.

Nash, John. "Two Person Cooperative Games." *Econometrica*, 21: 128–35, 1953.

Nelson, Nici, ed. *African Women in the Development Process*. London: Frank Cass, 1981.

Rogers, Beatrice Lorge. "The Internal Dynamics of Households: A Critical Factor in Development Policy." Tufts University School of Nutrition, Medford, Massachusetts. Paper developed in fulfillment of an AID contract for AID/PPC/PDPR/HR. October 1983.

Sen, Amartya. "Women, Technology, and Sexual Divisions." UNCTAD/TT/79. 1985.

Senauer, Benjamin. "The Impact of the Value of Women's Time on Food and Nutrition," University of Minnesota, Department of Agriculture and Applied Economics. August 1988, mimeo.

Tripp, Robert B. "Farmers and Traders: Some Economic Determinants of Nutritional Status in Northern Ghana." *Journal of Tropical Pediatrics*, 27: 15–22, 1981.

Wilson, A. B. "Longitudinal Analyses of Diet, Physical Growth, Verbal Development, and Performance." In Balderston, J. B.; Wilson, A. B.; Freire, M.; and Simonen, M. *Malnourished Children of the Rural Poor*. Boston: Auburn, 1981.

Young, Kate. "Enhancing Gender Awareness: Household Resource Management. A Training Module for Trainers—Pilot Project." The Institute of Development Studies, Sussex, England. Mimeo, May 1987.

NOTES

1. Kossoudji and Mueller (1983); Massiah (1980); and Chaney, Simmons, and Staudt (1979) provide their own estimate of the incidence of female-headedness and see the pattern as basic to roughly one-third to two-fifths of the world's rural households.

2. We gratefully acknowledge this phrasing as Hanna Papanek's and Laurel Schwede's in "Women Are Good with Money: Earning and Managing in an Indonesian City," in Daisy Dwyer and Judith Bruce, eds., *A Home Divided: Women and Income in the Third World.* Stanford, Calif.: Stanford University Press, 1988.

II
TEACHING AND STRATEGIES FOR CHANGE

Women's Studies as a Strategy for Educational Change: The Latin American Experience

Carmen Barroso

In this essay I will examine the kinds of educational change we have achieved in Latin America through women's studies. I will try to define the "women's studies community" and the changes we are seeking. Then, I will sketch two points I think should be on the agenda for developing a strategy for the women's studies community, with special reference to our experience in Latin America. Those points are: first, the need to keep close ties with the women's movement, and second, the desirability of keeping an open and flexible approach in all realms in institution building, in substantive analysis, in methodological choices, and in style of expression.

I refer to the women's studies community, I mean the fast-growing number of researchers and university professors whose main work has been on women as a response to the challenges posed by the feminist movement. My definition seems simple enough, but it has three terms that leave room for ambiguity. First, who are the researchers? Some of us have jobs as researchers, but others do research outside any institution; some of us adhere strictly to orthodox methodologies, while others write essays, choosing their sources and methods with greater freedom. Although there is no formal certification, there seems to be some consensus that a researcher is someone who has—at some point in his or her life—adhered to and shown ability to use "bona fide" scholarly methods of inquiry. A second source of ambiguity is the reference to "main work." More than a few feminist scholars have occasionally written a piece or two on women, sometimes of very high quality, but have built their careers with work that has little to do with women. I don't see why they should be denied a women's studies ID card, but sometimes they are not interested in getting one. The third and most problematic area of ambiguity arises from the clause that stipulates that the work be a response to the feminist movement. What kind of changes are we looking for? I know, of course, of the diversity of theoretical outlooks existing within the women's studies community, but I believe that, at the most basic level, we have a common objective: we are especially engaged in abolishing hierarchical gender relations in all their manifestations, and see as our special province both the production of knowledge that is useful for this transformation and the facilitation of access to this knowledge for everybody.

HAVE WE COME A LONG WAY?

It is hard to avoid either triumph or skepticism when we evaluate the changes that have occurred in the last decades. When I recall that, as a middle-class girl, I thought I had to give up the idea of getting married and having children if I wanted a career, or the shame I felt at the dinner table when I realized that my question about the meaning of the word "midwife" was not considered proper in that setting, or my surprise in high school when a teacher told the class she actually knew a couple who shared domestic work—when I compare all this with the attitudes of my nine-year-old daughter, who takes flexible roles and her own sexuality for granted, or when I see the poor women of the outskirts of Sao Paulo now using "male chauvinism" as a household term, then I tend to agree that we have come a long way. Feminist ideas—in one version or another, and we may argue endlessly about the appropriateness of the most pervasive versions—have touched a responsive chord in the hearts of women throughout Latin America. And women's studies has been an important vehicle both for the very formulation of those ideas and for giving them legitimacy. In highly elitist societies such as those in Latin America, even feminist scholars share a small portion of the power and prestige accorded to the learned strata, and they have put these resources to subversive use by disseminating egalitarian ideas.

In Latin America, for historical reasons, research on women is much more widespread than teaching. The latter is restricted to graduate and undergraduate levels and is almost absent from secondary and primary levels. As Costa et al. have shown in the case of Brazil, women's studies practitioners have no common background, no institutional space, no specialized publication, and no formal association. However, we have been very active. In Brazil, our bibliography from 1976 to 1984 registered more than twelve hundred items, including books, articles, and papers presented at professional meetings. Informal networks have been developed primarily at the local level and sometimes at the national level. At the regional level, contacts between countries still remain a privilege of the few who can attend the occasional seminars and workshops.

Scholarship on women in Latin America started to flourish only in the late seventies. We have discovered our own past and gained a better under-standing of our plight in the present.I will give you some glimpses of this. From the unspeakable suffering and extraordinary resistance of African women who were taken to Brazil as slaves, we have learned how strong and resourceful we are. From the struggles of nineteenth-century feminists, from women's active participation in the labor movement in the early twentieth century, from Bertha Lutz's campaign for the vote won in the thirties, and her battle to insert women's rights in the UN Charter, we derived pride in our achievements and a realistic assessment of the ob-stacles we face. From sociological studies of work and the family we achieved a better appraisal of our important contribution to the economy and an understanding of the mechanisms of our exploitation from which we can derive an agenda for social reform or revolution against partriarchy. From studies on health and sexuality we have perceived how women's wonderful reproductive power has been controlled for ends that have nothing to do with our needs for pleasure and love, and how we can begin to change all this. I could go on and on, but women of many countries have had similar experiences of rediscovering their own selves and of creating a new sense of identity through women's studies.

On the other hand, when I look at the hard realities of very little change in the sexual division of labor inside and outside the home; when I note the appallingly small percentage of women in decision-making positions, even within the most progressive political parties; when I see how undemocratic those decision-making processes remain; when Brazilian politicians dare to joke that the small budget accorded to the National Council for Women's Rights is more than enough for their make-up; when I visit a Latin American office of the International Labor Organization and find no trace of intention to change traditional attitudes with regard to women's labor, even at the level of data collection; when I see that the enormous amount of knowledge amassed by research on women has remained circumscribed in the closed circle of "womanists," and regular teaching goes on as usual with no hint of recognition of women's experience; when I see that formal schooling itself remains a privilege of urban sectors in most Third World countries, I get discouraged that the effects of all the effort expended these last years have been so slight. Have we followed the wrong paths? Were our expectations too high? What would be the best strategies for the years ahead?

STRATEGIES FOR THE FUTURE

I am not prepared to lay before you detailed plans for the takeover of the citadels of male power or the agenda for a much more ambitious aim of cultural revolution—the "feminization of the world" coupled with a thor-ough democratization of access to knowledge and power. My objective is much more modest: I would like to take one step back and discuss a strategy to develop a strategy; that is, some principles I think the women's studies community should adopt in order to create the conditions for pooling our talents and experiences, so that together we devise the most effective paths to those changes for which we are all looking. My two candidates for a strategy are, first, openness and flexibility, and second, the maintenance of close ties with the women's movement.

OPENNESS AND FLEXIBILITY

We should develop an appreciation for the variety of approaches that have flourished among us in all realms: objectives, methodologies, styles, substantive analysis, and institution building. Even within a single country, our institutions are so diverse that it is impossible to prescribe a recipe for changing all of them. No single model will be effective in all situations. In Brazil, for instance, women's studies has come, as have many other educational innovations, from the top: from graduate studies and research. Individual researchers with established professional reputations had the autonomy to offer courses and to seek funds for small projects on women.

The expansion of graduate institutions, particularly in the social sciences, and the greater curriculum flexibility at this level of teaching (undergraduate, secondary, and primary schools are subject to tighter federal control) allowed for these innovations. However, there was never an institutional initiative to effect these changes; there was only the loosening of institutional control that left space for individuals to take these initiatives at their own risk. We are now at a point where several nuclei of women's studies have been created within public and Catholic universities. It seems that most of them have very little institutional backing, but at least they function as a support group that lightens the burden resting on the shoulders of individual professionals.

In the Chagas Foundation, the oldest and best-known center for research on women in Brazil, we have a history that could hardly be duplicated anywhere else. From an initial group of a few interested members of the Educational Research Department at Chagas who started doing research on women in 1984, we have created a collective that has been very succesful in a number of ways. For example, we have produced top-quality studies in a variety of areas, such as labor-force participation, public policies, the family, sex-role socialization, and sex education; we administer a large program of grants for research on women; we promote the use of innovative methodologies such as participatory research, and a variety of media such as video and newspapers. We have maintained a cohesive and supportive group throughout these years but have not been granted any kind of formal status so far. This is partly due to the unwillingness of the institution to be identified with our more radical positions, and partly to our interest in retaining an informal status in order to enhance our ability to resist. The lack of a formal status does not preclude us from hiring new reseachers, since we act as a lobby within the department in which we are researchers. It also does not preclude us from getting research funds from sources outside the institution, because these are sought by individual researchers. On the other hand, we are at a disadvantage every time an institutional policy is at stake.

Although most of our efforts are directed toward research on women—the basis of a very clear public image—each of us, in varying degrees, cultivates some of her former expertise so that we do not become isolated and vulnerable. Aside from being a survival strategy, this double allegiance has advantages and disadvantages; though it takes time away from a deepened analysis of our subject, it keeps us open to other sources of ideas and intellectual enrichment. With regard to professional associations in Brazil, the women's studies community has not created any formal association, but it has been present in every social science association as a regular committee or by organizing panels and symposia in every major congress. In spite of this integrated approach, however, it is very unusual to see a man at our meetings.

Publications have multiplied in regular issues of journals, special issues on women, and books. But again, they are seldom quoted outside the women's studies circle, and vice versa. When we consider the advantages and disadvantages of "mainstreaming" we should keep in mind that formal integration is not a guarantee of real integration, especially in the face of increasing fragmentation in the social sciences, due to the partriarchal milieu in which we are trying to develop an identity of our own.

In spite of the problems I have mentioned, the institutional approaches adopted so far have been responsible for whatever successes we have achieved. We need new approaches to go beyond these. We particularly need more systematic teaching in high schools (this has been started by a series of lectures sponsored by the Sao Paulo State Council on Women's Condition) and greater interchange among Latin American countries (perhaps through a bilingual journal, the creation of national associations of women's studies, and so on). Parallel to this need for new approaches is the importance of cherishing those which have brought us this far.

This same openness and flexibility should be applied to substantive analysis. We have wasted too much of our energy trying to determine the right theory, the true feminism. I am all in favour of the pursuit of rigor, and I would be the last one to discard the theoretical efforts that have fostered the understanding of our condition. In fact, I think we should pay much more attention to theory construction. However, we lose when one of these contributions is not thought of as one among others and instead, narrow sectarianism operates. We gain when we encourage each to follow her own theoretical path; it may cross another's sometime in the future as we tackle problems for which a single theory is not enough. In many countries in Latin America, women's participation in the labor market was once a very popular subject of study, and as Navarro has pointed out, the studies were seen by their authors—who did not see themselves as feminists at all—mostly as a strategy to understand the macro processes of capitalist societies. It was some time later that research questions were phrased from the point of view of women. Domestic labor as a research issue gained prominence, and these same researchers turned their attention to the investigation of reproduction and production, sometimes incorporating concepts such as patriarchy into their theories, giving these theories a character quite distinct from the orthodox Marxism with which they started.

The principle of openness and flexibility should also be applied to the area of style. We had hard discussions about this when the Chagas Foundation collective decided to publish a newspaper *Mulherio*. Journalists and some of the researchers among us were very critical of the academic tone of our writings. I think we should strive for communication with the noninitiated and get rid of needless jargon and excessive tables and figures. This is just common sense for those of us who aim to reach larger audiences. We should not get caught in any straightjacket, either a "free-flowing intuitive" one or an "objective rational" one. The larger the number of languages in which we are able to express ourselves, the better off we are, and this includes the language of power, through which we gain authority in certain circles.

The objective of our studies is another arena where openness and flexibility can help us grow. As changes in the political environment in some of our countries brought more democratic governments, new challenges were presented to feminists who had to redefine our relations to the state. Many of us are trying to maintain the autonomy of the movement and its pursuit of radical quests, and at the same time we are attempting to influence the state to bring about changes that might be possible in the short term. This is reflected in the academic community where, in recent years, studies aimed at supplementing public policies are being conducted. Such studies are crucial if we are to take advantage of the opportunities for intervention and change. At the same time, however, we should not lose sight of the scholarly work aimed at understanding the roots of women's oppression and creating a new identity for women.

The last area I would like to mention with regard to keeping ourselves open and flexible is in the choice of methodology. In both research and teaching, participatory methodology is consonant with women's studies. If the broad aim of women's studies is to contribute to the breakdown of gender hierarchies, nothing is more attractive than a methodology that promises a way to shake loose the monopoly of knowledge production held in the hands (or the heads) of professors, researchers, and so on. And in fact, we gained a lot when participatory methodology opened space for the subjects of research themselves to define what the research questions should be and to participate actively in a process of collective construction of knowledge. Participatory methodology enabled us to enter the niches of daily life, where cap-and-gown methods do not dare to go. In Latin America, one area of study that has particularly benefited from participatory methodology is that of sexuality, which has flourished in the last few years. In university teaching, also, participatory methods have a great potential in increasing students' motivation and creativity.

However, we should not allow ourselves to forget the merits of more orthodox methods, for there remain many areas where they are essential. We should be aware that participatory methodology so far has allowed for only a low level of generalization, which fits only too well the international division of intellectual labor, according to which the Third World remains the importer and consumer of theories produced in the countries of the north. Of course, I am not attributing our difficulty in theory development wholly or mostly to participatory methodology—for there are many other elements involved, as Costa et al. have shown—but it certainly is part of a trend that is overemphasizing the description of the concrete, as a reaction to our former fascination with Grand Theories that were so broad they hardly explained anything.

LINKAGES WITH THE WOMEN'S MOVEMENT

Some analysts whose eyes were used to observing the women's movement in industrialized countries did not recognize its existence in Latin America in the seventies. In fact, there were many women's organizations fighting for changes in access to resources and in power relations between both the sexes and different sectors of society. But their agendas and tactics were different from those of social movements of the industrialized world. In Europe and the United States, these movements had a strong cultural connotation, as they called into question the values of industrialized society and the notion of the welfare state itself, and as they tried to reinvent the social and the political. The social movements in Latin America, although they were a new phenomenon in the experience of popular classes, directed their main thrust toward the state, demanding a better distribution of social services. Therefore, they held the belief in the state as an agency for the promotion of social welfare.

To those in democratic and affluent societies, where a minimum level of civil rights and comfort is taken for granted by the majority of the population, the demands of the social movements in Latin America may sound strange: amnesty, water, electricity, schools, and so on. At the same time, however, a whole process of social change was transforming the status of women inside and outside the family and setting the scene for new ideas: urbanization, migration, increased participation in the modern sectors of the economy, higher levels of school attendance, wider dissemination of feminist ideas coming from the North, the legitimacy afforded by the UN international women's year, and disenchantment with the position of women in leftist parties. Many factors have helped to break the ground where feminist groups started to grow, initially amongst the educated middle classes in the large cities.

Although feminist groups had a distinctive place within the social movements, they sought on several occasions a common strategy built on general principles. This led feminists to downplay specifically feminist issues such as abortion, in order to avoid open conflict with the traditional Left and the Catholic church, whose progressive wings were offering support that was crucial under repressive regimes. Yet, simultaneously, in the mutual search for allies, women's studies practitioners and feminist groups sought each other's support from the very beginning. This has resulted in a constant interaction that, although not devoid of conflicts arising from different outlooks and different positions in society, has nevertheless been a source of mutual enrichment and strength.

Other linkages have put women's studies practitioners under cross-fire on some occasions. From one side, we are attacked by our colleagues in the academy, for whom we have to prove again and again that our work is scientific, not "mere ideology." From the other side, feminists demand that we show clearly that we are committed to a collective cause and not appropriating a fashionable theme for the sake of our own personal careers. Feminists for the academic community and academics for the feminists, researchers have lived dangerously in a frontier zone of tension and ambiguity.

Even so, the feminist movement has been the very source of life for the scholarship on women, suggesting themes and methodologies and helping to create a network of solidarity that is crucial for scholars confronting academic orthodoxies. What we now need is a clear definition of our role within the women's movement, so that we are allowed the distance necessary for scholarly work, which may not respond to the immediate needs of political practice but may prove of greater relevance for the women's movement in the long run. I am not arguing for a rigid division of labor that could reinforce hierarchies within the movement. But as our numbers grow, I feel we can share many of our responsibilities so that each one of us does not have to be on permanent duty for every protest, for every campaign. Thus, we simultaneously accord legitimacy to the systematic study that is so much needed and that is our special contribution both to the movement and to the social sciences.

REFERENCES

Costa, A.O., Barroso, C., and Sarti, C. *Pesquisa sobre mulher no Brasil: 1976–1984.* Sao Paulo: Fundacao Carlos Chagas, 1985.
Navarro, Marysa. Research on Latin American Women. *Signs,* 5 (1), 1979.

TRAINING AND ORGANIZING FOR CHANGE IN INDIA: VIDEO AS A TOOL OF THE SELF EMPLOYED WOMEN'S ASSOCIATION

Sara Stuart

INTRODUCTION

Training is at the heart of development work, particularly in villages and slums. Its goal is to strengthen local human resources by providing information, developing skills, and building a base of confidence and experience. Training empowers trainees to improve their lives and the lives of their families. Thereby, they become the agents of solutions to their own problems and concerns, rather than the objects of "development inputs." The experiences of Video SEWA, the video cooperative of the Self Employed Women's Association, illustrate the power and import of video as a tool in training and organizing for development.

SEWA is a trade union of some twenty-four thousand poor, self-employed women in Ahmedabad, India. The organization provides its members with skills training, cooperative mechanisms to aid in production and marketing, child care, and health benefits. SEWA also advocates for women's rights vis-à-vis municipal authorities and operates a cooperative bank. By combining struggle and development, SEWA enables its members to protect their interests and to gain their rightful place in the economy.

Leelaben Datania is a member of Video SEWA. Leelaben and her family

Sara Stuart is coordinator of the Village Video Network Secretariat. The address of the Network Secretariat is: c/o Martha Stuart Communications, 147 West 22 Street, New York, NY 10011, USA. Telephone: 212-255-2718. Telex: 508937 (STUART). This paper draws substantively on an unpublished article, "Getting an Opportunity," by Jyoti Jumani. The author gratefully acknowledges her contribution, and thanks her for all she has taught the author during the last years.

75

have sold vegetables in the Manekchowk Market of Ahmedabad for several generations. In the seventies she joined SEWA and became an organizer in order to fight the police harassment of small-scale vendors and to gain licenses and recognition from the municipal authority. As a part of this struggle, Leelaben testified in India's Supreme Court on behalf of the vendors. She is a respected leader among the market women.

FORMATION OF VIDEO SEWA

In 1982 Ela Bhatt, the founder of SEWA, met members of a Malian video team and saw their work. This experience convinced her that the members of SEWA could handle such technology and that it would be valuable in their work. Together, SEWA and Martha Stuart Communications, with financial assistance from USAID, worked to equip and train a SEWA video team. In 1984 Leelaben and nineteen other SEWA members took part in a three-week video training workshop. One-third of the participants, like Leelaben, were illiterate, and another third had less than a high school education. They included women of all ages, who were Hindus and Moslems, craftswomen, vendors, and carpenters, as well as several senior SEWA leaders.

During the workshop each participant produced her own program. "Water, Water," Leelaben's first program, focuses on the inequities of water distribution in her neighborhood. The program shows, with a brief narration, the struggle of five hundred families to fetch all their daily water from one faucet during the one hour when water flows. It is a simply made, in-camera edited program (a program recorded exactly in sequence and edited as it is recorded) that educates and raises awareness concerning this serious problem. After the workshop, the participants formed a cooperative called Video SEWA. They had regular meetings and refresher courses. Yet, a three-week workshop is not enough to fully learn production techniques. As the participants returned to their regular jobs and used the equipment less frequently, they became unsure of their video skills. Thus, regular video training, hands-on practicing, and practice recordings were planned as part of the follow-up process. As a result, a feeling of team spirit, discipline, and confidence grew among the members of Video SEWA.

EARLY IMPACT OF VIDEO IN LOCAL STRUGGLES

Several months after the initial video workshop the Municipality of Ahmedabad began, under court order, to negotiate with the vendors of Manekchowk Market. The negotiations centered on the rights of small-scale street vendors to claim space in the marketplace where they had been earning their livelihoods for generations. All along, the municipal authorities viewed the street vendors as obstructors of traffic who had to be cleared off the streets.

The municipality offered to make available to the vendors a marketplace on a terrace. After years of organizing and struggle, this was the municipality's first constructive response and it caused a great deal of excitement at SEWA. A meeting to inform the representatives of the vendors was called and three members of Video SEWA decided to tape it. Leelaben recorded sound. The vendors were comfortable with her and the rest of the video crew. Thus, the taping did not inhibit or interfere with the meeting.

The women's reactions to the municipality's offer were varied: some were skeptical; some expressed concern about the political pressures brought to bear on SEWA; some felt no price was too heavy to pay to escape police harassment; some were very enthusiastic. Eventually they formulated a list of conditions under which they would accept the offer and concerns that they still had. The camera captured the essence of this highly charged discussion and the words and faces of women making decisions about their lives.

After the taping, Ela Bhatt, general secretary of SEWA, asked herself, "Would the municipal authorities be so indifferent to the problems of these women if they had been present at the meeting?" She invited the municipal commissioner to view the tape informally. As he watched the agitated faces of the women, he was moved by their fear of the police, their distrust of the municipality, and their sense of solidarity. Listening to them on tape meant that he could be open without betraying his emotions; he could be himself and not the municipal commissioner. The women would never have spoken to him directly as they did on the tape, and he would not have been able to hear them in the same way.

This tape proved invaluable to the negotiations between the vendors and the municipality; it also shaped the way Leelaben and the members of Video SEWA understood the potential of video. In 1985, Leelaben joined Jyoti Jumani, coordinator of Video SEWA, to work full time on video. She is responsible now for screening and care of the equipment; she is a sound recordist, producer, and representative and leader of Video SEWA.

Illiteracy has been a hindrance for Leelaben and other members of SEWA. For example, in one instance, Video SEWA bought a new tape deck that was made by a different manufacturer than the rest of their equipment. The function of this new playback unit was identical to SEWA's other equipment but the layout, shapes, and colors of the buttons were different. This created considerable difficulties for the illiterate members of Video SEWA. Fortunately, a solution was found. All the Video SEWA members who could not read the English words and numbers on the video equipment received literacy training in video vocabulary. They learned words such as "eject," "rewind," and "on." To be functionally literate they had to understand fewer than twenty words and Arabic numerals. This has contributed substantially to the confidence of Video SEWA's members. Later, when Leelaben represented Video SEWA in Madras, she hired and operated unfamiliar equipment without fear or uncertainty.

"SEWA held an exhibition in Madras of products by all the SEWA cooperatives," Leelaben recalled. (SEWA has organized cooperatives of blockprinters, weavers, guilders, potters, and others, as well as their video cooperative.) "I went to present Video SEWA's tapes. Many people came to watch our programs and learn about our work. Even some television people came and didn't believe that I had made the tapes. 'How can a vegetable vendor produce videotapes?' they asked. Even after I told them about our training workshop and the tapes we have made, they were doubtful. So, I explained to them how I connect the 14-to-14 pin cable and the BNC cable, and when you need to set the white balance and audio levels, until they were convinced!"

Leelaben has combined her skills as an organizer and as a producer. She decided to produce a tape about women from Oudh who have been forced to migrate because of the drought. They earn their living by digging sand from the river bed and transporting it on donkeyback to construction sites. These women have fallen prey to police harassment. Their donkeys are frequently impounded and bribes must be paid to secure their release. To make the tape Leelaben had to gain the women's trust and learn about their problems. Her production served as a contact point between SEWA and the Oudh women. Once the taping was over they came to SEWA to screen their tape; they met with SEWA leaders and became members of SEWA. The process of participating in the taping and viewing their concerns framed by a television gave them a new perspective and was instrumental in their decision to organize. Leelaben is justly proud of this achievement.

Since the first training workshop in 1984, video has only gradually become an integral part of SEWA's activities. At first, video was new to everyone at SEWA. Effective use of the medium evolved and developed through experience. SEWA now uses tapes to motivate, mobilize, and strengthen the existing membership, to organize new trade groups, and to recruit new members for existing trade groups. Its programs are used for teaching, informing, and orienting SEWA staff members. In addition, the tapes create visibility for the issues of importance to self-employed women and are used to influence policy makers. Video SEWA members act as group leaders and facilitators when their programs are shown. Video SEWA is not an elitist, hierarchical unit. Unlike "mainstream media" producers, there is no distinction between producer and viewer; they are sisters. SEWA has discovered the potential of the medium by showing its tapes to many, many different groups of women and *listening* to their responses.

APPLICATIONS IN TRAINING, EDUCATION, AND ORGANIZING

Understanding the strength and power of collective action comes slowly to grassroots women. Thus, SEWA's organizing efforts in other parts of India and with other trade groups in Gujarat often begin with workers' education classes. These generally involve one week of training and discussion in which the goal is to raise awareness among members of a particular trade group of self-employed women workers about their common difficulties and to encourage the women to organize. For many it is a completely new idea. Video SEWA has taped several of their demonstrations, one by vegetable vendors and another by garment workers. The recordings show hundreds of poor women marching through the streets of Ahmedabad and chanting their demands. These tapes are perhaps the most powerful and most frequently used. They raise spirits, inspire confidence and solidarity, and illustrate the power of collective action.

"For example," Renana Jhabvala, secretary of SEWA, said, "we took the tape of the garment workers procession to Lucknow where we are organizing the women who do *chikan* embroidery. They are the worst paid that I have seen anywhere and they are Moslem, so very conservative. We did some training with them and talked about organizing and coming out of their homes and not wearing purdah. On the last day we showed this tape and they were so excited and jumped up to plan out the route for their own procession. In reality, they were nowhere near the stage where they could take out a procession but this enthusiasm is helping them to get organized. When women actually see that someone like them has succeeded through organizing it makes a really big difference."

Video screenings have become an important part of workers' education classes. They give new members an opportunity to see and understand issues pertaining to their own and other trade groups. The concerns of piece-rate workers are similar throughout the region, and SEWA tapes convey this similarity effectively. They help new members to feel a connection with a larger movement. New members identify with the women on the SEWA tapes. For example, some village women who viewed an interview with Chandaben, a used-clothes dealer and senior SEWA organizer, were delighted to see that even Chandaben takes snuff and speaks very quickly like they do. When SEWA organizes in slums and villages, playing videotapes acts as a magnet for people to come together for meetings and to start discussions.

Videotapes are also used for other sorts of informal training. The self-employed have no formal employer-employee relationship; therefore, they must often turn to the courts to settle their disputes with contractors or to establish their rights to a minimum wage. SEWA members attend the hearings and give evidence. "The atmosphere is very intimidating for me," explained Renana Jhabvala. "So you can imagine what it is like for the

SEWA members. The lawyers try to cut their evidence into pieces and call them liars. This is very difficult for the women to deal with and they usually change their statements." It can take years to mount a court battle and a great deal depends on the women's testimony. When a group of *bidi* workers (women who roll the native cigarettes) were preparing to testify, SEWA set up a mock court with a judge, witnesses, plaintiff's and defendant's lawyers, a bailiff, and a court audience. Video SEWA recorded the proceedings. These tapes were repeatedly shown to the women who had to testify. The SEWA lawyer had a discussion with the women after the replays. This helped the women greatly; the tape was very effective at building their confidence and preparing them to stand up for themselves in court.

Some Video SEWA tapes are made to fulfill more formal training needs. They provide specific educational information to groups of women and their children. SEWA's health programs regularly use a tape that explains the causes of diarrhea and shows how to prepare an oral rehydration solution. The tape is shown in training sessions for SEWA members as one of several teaching tools. SEWA members have learned from the group's video tapes how to build a smokeless stove, how to use SEWA's savings and credit services for illiterate women, the reasons for and timing of immunizations, and other important skills.

INTERNATIONAL CONNECTIONS

Video SEWA's experiences reach beyond the borders of India. Their tapes are used to train groups in other countries that work at the grassroots level and are interested in video as a tool for local development. Jyoti Jumani has helped to train women in Thailand and Guyana to use video. She is especially appreciated as a teacher because of her experience at SEWA and because she learned from scratch. Also, Video SEWA has received a study visit from women members of a West African video team. The exchanges among these teams were remarkable, although the cultural differences are great. Both groups work with rural women on issues related to drought. Some of their exchanges concerned practical information such as soap-making and fabric-dyeing techniques, and some were broader and more attitudinal. For the African women it was a new experience to see an all-female video team; men handle the majority of the responsibilities for operating equipment in their team.

Not all of Leelaben and Video SEWA's particular experiences with video as a tool for training are universal. Video SEWA has creatively adapted this medium to its philosophy and approach to grassroots struggle and development. Elsewhere, for example, in Brazil, where video is used very effectively in the *favelas* (urban slums), it has been adapted for use in quite different ways. Organizing there often begins with an emphasis on culture and identity, not on economic issues. Community video has developed in a very intense, competitive, and overloaded media environment. What is universal about this technology is its adaptability and its particular advantages in the hands of local organizers and extensionists.

Initial steps have been taken to explore the possibilities unlocked by video for horizontal exchange and cross-fertilization through the activities of the Village Video Network (VVN). Founded in 1982, the VVN is an informal association of video teams in twelve countries. Its members include literacy teachers in Mali, scientists and farmers in China, family planning workers in the Caribbean, and others. With start-up funding from the United Nations University and other multilateral donors, the VVN promotes and encourages video as a tool for development, provides technical assistance, facilitates exchange, and works in partnership with local governmental and nongovernmental organizations to plan, fund, equip, and train local development video teams. In the last few years, faced with shrinking finances, VNN has concentrated its efforts on training and co-production opportunities.

The flexibility and adaptability of video may be its most significant characteristic, particularly with regard to training at the local level. Video puts illiterate viewers as well as illiterate producers on a par with their literate counterparts. This leveling or equalizing action can transform relationships, encourage a high degree of participation, and consequently have great impact. As we have seen, Leelaben's work as an organizer, leader, and teacher has become more effective through the use of video. She is also more powerful. "At first," she said, "we were afraid of these machines. Now, we almost love them."

III
POLICY

Linking Research with Policy and Action

Katharine McKee

Our shelves are laden with policy-relevant research that did not have its intended effect. Why is it that so few of these studies have been read, let alone acted upon, by those in positions of power who make decisions that shape women's lives? We must admit that the failures cannot be explained wholly by the nonreceptivity and resistance from policy bodies and decision makers. This is one very important piece of learning from the United Nations Decade for Women and one on which we should reflect carefully, so that in the future we can be more strategic in using research models and methodologies with a higher likelihood of achieving success.

Rather than analyzing the many disappointments in the policy research field, I'd like to describe one such success and suggest some of the factors that may have contributed to its use for policy purposes. The case that I have selected is the Status of Women study in Nepal. The Nepal investigation was a very basic, exploratory piece of research. It focused on women's roles and time allocation in household production, especially agriculture, and on male and female decision making and management responsibilities. These variables were assessed for different ethnic groups and in different agro-environmental zones, through studies carried out in eight sites across Nepal. The study took four and a half years to complete, although it wasn't originally planned to take so long.

The research team was composed of four Nepalese researchers, including one man, and four foreigners (the project leader, Lynn Bennett, and three Ph.D. students who were in the field doing dissertation work). I am

This paper was presented at the Women's Studies International Panel on "Research, Action and Public Policy," NGO Forum, July 16, 1985.

indebted to Dr. Bennett and her counterpart, Dr. Meena Acharya, for sharing with me their insights on this project.

The research proceeded through the following stages: 1) preparation of a series of background sectoral papers and compilation of a national bibliography on women; 2) preparation and field testing of the methodology; 3) carrying out of the eight village studies over a period of six to twelve months each; and 4) the analysis. The analysis itself was carried out on two levels. Each researcher did an individual analysis, drawing, however, from the common core issues identified for focus in the overall study. Each had also collected additional qualitative data on topics of particular interest to the researcher, and this analysis was included in the overall report. The eight monographs included very specific policy and project recommendations. In addition, an aggregate analysis was carried out, based on the comparative data from each site. This was presented in the form of a report with specific policy and project recommendations, supplemented by a separate paper on institutional options for incorporating attention to women within the national planning and project implementation processes in Nepal.

What were the key audiences for this study? In the beginning, the study was aimed primarily at influencing policies within the Nepalese Ministry of Agriculture and the international donor community, including the Agency for International Development (which sponsored the study). Over time, however, the World Bank and other UN agencies were much influenced by the study's results, as were other Nepalese government bodies.

The most effective findings were those on agricultural labor input, and especially on women's management and decision-making roles. This data was crop- and operation-specific for women and men. Among the key findings were the facts that women provided half of the labor input for rice, three-quarters for wheat, and 96 percent for maize, the staple crop for the poor in Nepal. What really made members of the male agricultural establishment sit up in their seats, however, was not only this labor input data—information that any observant person might see if willing to go out to the field. The critical additional finding was that women were responsible for key farm management decisions, including those decisions that were required for the success of the major projects and other interventions in the agricultural sector being promoted by these policy makers.

The findings were disseminated in a number of ways. In addition to the series of reports, the research team organized seminars and briefings for different types of audiences.

The outcomes of this study were several. While one could debate whether they illustrate the best strategies for promoting women's advancement in Nepal, they do reflect an important change in the awareness and willingness to experiment on the part of key national and international policy makers. A first outcome was the creation of a special section on women within the Planning Commission (although the project's institutional report recommended integrating a concern with women within key ministries rather than creating a separate section). A second result was that the World Bank asked the Nepalese co-director of the study to serve on a design mission for a pilot project both to recruit women agricultural extension officers and to see that they received appropriate training. Prior to the study, women represented only seventeen of the two thousand agricultural extension staff in Nepal, and all had been trained in home economics and handicrafts rather than agriculture. The Ministry of Agriculture also responded to the key points raised in the study—particularly when the Bank made this a precondition for its loan! The study also had a big impact on the Agency for International Development (AID), especially in terms of the staffing, goals, and interventions of its Integrated Cereals Project. Finally, the UN Fund for Population Activities and the Food and Agriculture Organization have implemented pilot projects to train women agricultural extension officers. The effects were felt in other national agencies as well, such as the Ministry of Education.

What lessons can one draw from these results? I would like to highlight a number of points that can be generalized but are particularly well illustrated by this particular case of policy research:

1. The study succeeded in its basic intentions because it focused on a *strategic topic*—agriculture—that was of high priority to the target audiences.

2. Perhaps an obvious point in the utility of this study was that it *compared men and women*. What was perceived as important, for example, was that women provided almost all the labor and management input for maize, not just the hours of work they put in without reference to what the men in the family were contributing. This may seem an obvious point, but the practice is not universally followed by any means.

3. The research team was able to tailor the *project design and dissemination of results to this policy audience* because of the choices it made in terms of: a) content, including how much and what kind of data would be collected, the line of argumentation (who does the work and who makes the decisions), and the judicious use of "galvanizing statistics," which the policy audiences found striking; b) the format and style, including the language of the report and presentation; and c) the application of findings to achieve a large impact, by supplementing the reports with seminars, workshops, and information to the media.

The Nepalese researchers' knowledge of what was needed to achieve this policy impact was invaluable. Some of them had been in key development policy or program positions, and as a result they were well connected, credible, and willing to use their contacts to see that the study had a wide hearing. From their prior work, they also had an understanding of the government's perspectives on the problems and of the financial, political, and bureaucratic constraints it would face in implementing the policy recommendations that were proposed. Thus, these members of the research team had both the commitment and the ability to make workable, practical, realistic policy recommendations, which unfortunately is not typically the case with researchers from a strictly academic background. A generalizable finding from the study is the desirability of having researchers on the team who understand and have first-hand knowledge of the policy environment. If this is not possible, another useful mechanism might be an advisory committee that includes individuals who can offer that policy perspective to the study.

4. The study used a *flexible research design*. For example, individual researchers were permitted to pursue some of their own interests through the qualitative research they undertook in the village studies. Another sign of flexibility was the design of complementary in-depth studies on important agricultural questions that arose in the course of basic research.

5. The study *combined quantitative and qualitative data*. The explanatory power of the survey-type data was much greater as a result of the qualitative data with which it could be interpreted.

6. Another factor that increased the utility of the study for policy purposes is that the data was actually analyzed! This is an important achievement, given the mountains of time-use data the world over which have never been analyzed. What made the analysis possible in this case? The analysis plan was designed beforehand with clear hypotheses to be tested, so that the research team wasn't confronted at the end of the study with piles of questionnaires, a computer, and the dilemma of figuring out at that point how to combine them.

7. Another element of success was the use of case studies to draw out generalizable conclusions. The village data was comparative because of the common core questionnaire, and the analytic framework had significant payoffs in this case. Thus, a common pitfall was avoided, i.e., the isolated village study from which it is very difficult to draw generalizable conclusions, even for the local area, because there is no basis of comparison.

8. The recommendations were put into government language and expressed with a recognition of the ministries' and donors' constraints and processes.

9. And finally, there was an all too rare continuity and accountability in terms of the follow-up of the policy recommendations, because of the ongoing presence of Nepalese researchers pushing on the system to respond to the study's findings.

Finally, I would like to highlight two of the most important byproducts of this study. First, the baseline data itself is an invaluable resource for the future. Although it was expensive and time-consuming to compile, it provides an enormous resource for future policy research and for monitoring and evaluating development interventions implemented in the coming years. And secondly, the point that is perhaps the most important for all of us today, is the fact that the Nepalese members of the research team have become the core for ongoing policy and program work on feminism and on women and development issues in the country. Many have gone on to senior research and management positions. The project served an enormously important training function, as well as consolidating the expertise of the individual researchers by offering them the opportunity to work together rather than in isolation in designing the research strategy, in the analysis, and in the follow-up. This is a point well worth remembering as we assess the broader impacts of policy research undertaken during the Decade.

Integrating Gender in Research and Policy for Development in Thailand

Suteera Thomson

INTRODUCTION

Thai women play an integral role in the country's social, cultural, and economic development despite the many constraints they continue to face. At present, women in Thailand compose nearly half the population as well as nearly half the economically active population (eleven years of age and older).[1] Although the majority of women are employed in agriculture, they are also actively engaged in manufacturing, commerce, and the service industries—but at the lowest income levels.[2] As the Thai economy expands and diversifies, the questions of how to integrate the contribution of Thai women into the national development process and ensure their access to productive resources and to the benefits of their work remain pressing issues.

Recognizing the importance of women's contributions to national development, the Thailand Development Research Institute (TDRI) officially launched its Women in Development (WID) Project in January 1988 with myself as project advisor. This paper describes the TDRI-WID project's objectives and design, and analyzes some key activities that have been implemented in the first year of the project (1988–89). I begin with a brief description of TDRI and its mandate, and conclude with outcomes and lessons learned.

THE INSTITUTE

The Thailand Development Research Institute was established to conduct policy research and disseminate research results to the public and private

90

sectors. TDRI is Thailand's first policy research institute; it was conceived, created, and registered as a nonprofit, nongovernmental foundation, and is recognized as such by the Thai government. The institute provides technical and policy analysis that supports the formulation of policies with long-term implications for sustaining social and economic development in Thailand.[3] The institute's four main objectives describe the scope of TDRI's activities: (1) conducting and promoting policy research; (2) establishing an information center containing updated information on relevant policy issues; (3) creating a research network linking institutions and individuals engaged in policy research issues; and (4) disseminating the results of policy research to maximize their impact on decision making and public opinion.

To meet its objectives, the institute established seven research programs. Each program is headed by a director and is staffed with highly qualified scientists and policy analysts. The seven areas of research at TDRI are: agriculture and rural development; industry, trade, and international economic relations; macroeconomic policy; natural resources and environment; human resources and social development; science and technology development; and energy, infrastructure, and urban development. There are also currently three special projects: the Management of Economic and Social Development Project, the Rural Industries and Employment Project, and the Women in Development Project.

THE PROJECT

The TDRI-WID Project is, in part, a response to the recognition that development planning often overlooks women's needs and concerns. Indeed, one of the most significant problems in planning sound policies and effective development programs has been the dearth of information on the changing status and role of women and men: the ways in which women and men interact, divide responsibilities, allocate risks and resources, organize their labor, and plan for the future. Not much consideration has been given to women's actual and potential roles in nondomestic production and in other important aspects of national development. Policy makers and planners are not aware that certain development policies and programs affect women and men in fundamentally different and unequal ways. Women are concentrated in the lower ranks of various target groups; often policy and program benefits just do not reach women.

The TDRI-WID project team was appointed to identify critical research areas for women in development. The criteria used to select areas included:

- Importance to the establishment of national policy
- Relevance to the goals of National Development Plans and the Long Term Women's Development Plan
- Lack of policy research on particular issues
- Possible integration into the present TDRI research framework

The TDRI-WID project team decided to engage top policy makers and planners (who were mandated to strengthen women's role in national development) as well as project implementors/executors and beneficiaries (the women themselves) in a dialogue. We believe strongly that this process is fundamental to considering the actual and potential roles of women in development—to effectively meet women's needs, enhance their productivity, and ensure their access to development resources and benefits.

THE TASKS

As an advisor to the TDRI-WID Project, I work closely with four TDRI-WID team members (the project director and three researchers) and collaborate with the president, vice-president, and the seven TDRI program directors. More than half my colleagues are economists. My own background is in natural science and policy formulation with some ten years of experience. This included working at both international and national levels and with governmental and nongovernmental development agencies on issues concerning the disadvantaged populations—ranging from refugees to poor rural women. How could such diverse groups of people work together effectively? What strategies should the TDRI-WID team use to convince our colleagues of the benefits of integrating gender into their research work? How could we create a broad consensus among key players in the development arena outside the institute? How could we involve other national policy makers/planners in the process to broaden our base of support and commitment to strengthen the role of women in national development? How could we develop and use effective networks and networkers to reach key change-agents in the media, the political arena, and advocacy groups to maximize the impact on decision making and public opinion? How should we design our activities to reduce gender imbalances, to effect changes in societal attitudes and stereotypes, to raise the awareness of all concerned on specific issues, to test some hypotheses, and to network among people?

THE APPROACH

I started my work getting to know key members of the institute and identifying allies sympathetic to women's issues. Within the WID team itself were represented a diversity of viewpoints and approaches to development. To fully utilize the potential of our group, we adopted a team approach. Though this in itself took much effort, we greatly benefited from dealing with our differences, strengths, skills, biases, and the diversity of our views on any given issue. As a rule, we began at a point we could agree on and worked from there—finding ways to convince others on our team—

until we made a decision about what to do or how to approach an issue. Although the process was time-consuming, the results, some of which were unexpected, have been positive.

We adopted a participatory process to carry out our work at three levels: (1) within the TDRI-WID team; (2) with the TDRI program directors; and (3) with women who were grassroots leaders, policy makers, program planners, and project executors from the government, nongovernmental organization (NGO), and business sectors. We tried to involve as many people as possible in designing, implementing, and assessing our activities.

We have been able to achieve some success in changing the views of TDRI program directors regarding women's issues. At the beginning, some program directors conveyed to us that the policy research under their area of responsibility did not involve women's issues. Their assumption was that sex discrimination did not exist in Thailand as it did in other countries, and they had not seriously considered women's actual and potential roles in national development. Indeed, most of the aggregate data they used were not differentiated by sex. However, after we went through a number of discussions on specific research topics with each program director, it was agreed that the inclusion of sex as a variable of analysis could improve the interpretation of their data and sharpen their analysis. As a result, program directors helped us identify development issues particularly relevant to women in areas under their responsibility.

How could we build on our experience with the TDRI program directors to approach other policy makers/planners and key actors concerning the actual and potential role of women in the national development process? Could data documenting the actual contribution of women to national development and demonstrating women's economic productivity convince other policy makers/planners of women's role in the same manner as it had the TDRI program directors? For other groups of people at different levels, we needed some tools with which to work. And we asked ourselves: what tools can we use to drive home the message to all of them?

THE ACTIVITIES

1. THE CONCEPT PAPER

Consolidating Ideas with Colleagues

As mentioned earlier, through a participatory process, the TDRI-WID team and TDRI program directors identified policy research areas critical to women in development. When the TDRI-WID team first began to discuss WID issues with TDRI program directors, there seemed to be no end to the talks. We worried about how we could put together the ideas from the discussion. Some program directors, as well as some of our TDRI-WID team members, felt that our plan to consolidate these ideas was too ambitious. However, others in our team were challenged by their colleagues' reservations. Within a few months, the team put together a concept paper, "The Role of Thai Women in Development," highlighting women's contributions in four major sectors (accounting for 95 percent of the total labor force), their actual status, and their potential role. The paper also reviewed National Development Plans and other programs relevant to women, and assessed the contribution of government machinery to promote women in development issues. It also challenged assumptions concerning development planning and introduced gender analysis as a concept and tool for analyzing emerging development issues.

The concept paper was first discussed at an in-house workshop with TDRI program directors. There was no difficulty in gaining acceptance for the ideas presented. This probably resulted from a number of factors including our strategy of using the economist in our group, the project director, to present the rationale for the project and to provide background information on the status and contribution of Thai women. The paper, incorporating ideas of program directors, was revised to cover eight important research issues: socioeconomic development: determinants and impact of Thai women's status; decision making in rural development; technological development for Thai agricultural and rural development; rural income; environmental conservation; entrepreneurs; manufacturing industries: work conditions and occupational safety and health; and human resource management in the public sector.[4]

Establishing Commitment

From July 14 to 16, 1988, the eight issues highlighted in the concept paper were discussed in Pattaya, Thailand, at a seminar on "The Role of Thai Women in Development," in which seventy policy makers, program planners, project executors, and academicians participated. For this seminar, the TDRI program directors were asked to chair panel discussions on the topics of their choice, and to provide the lists of panelists. We did this in order to test the directors' commitment to the issues discussed in the concept paper. We invited Malichien Pengwong, Thailand's first elected female Kamnan (subdistrict chief), who has a fourth-grade education, to give the keynote address, "The Role of Local Leaders in Rural Development." This was a radical departure from accepted practice. Usually only very prominent, high status and senior officials or academics are called on to give a keynote address. Much to the surprise of most of the senior officials present (as they later admitted), the message of this forty-eight-year-old female Kamnan became one highpoint of the seminar and was accepted enthusiastically. She showed them that poor rural women, given the opportunity, were clearly capable of assuming public responsibility for community and rural development goals and sometimes finding unique solutions to seemingly intractable problems. She challenged the participants' stereotypic perception of the skills and concerns of relatively uneducated, middle-aged rural women, who have spent most of their adult lives raising and supporting their large families.

Participants' evaluations indicated that the seminar was highly success-ful.[5] They noted in particular Kamnan Malichien Pengwong's keynote speech; the wide spectrum of interesting and important issues discussed; the assemblage of key persons; the balanced representation in terms of sex and occupation among panelists and participants; and the relevance and utility of the data compiled in the "Thailand Women's Information Kit." (See below.) For the TDRI-WID team, one of the highpoints of the seminar was the active involvement of the TDRI program directors. All eight panel discussions were chaired by the program directors and vice-president.

2. THE THAILAND WOMEN'S INFORMATION KIT

When we worked on the concept paper, we compiled and processed a great deal of information and raw data. How useful would it be, we asked ourselves, if we selected some key statistics to prepare charts and tables for policy makers and planners? Although all of the TDRI-WID team agreed to the usefulness of such a package, we did not know how best to put it together. What key areas should we focus on? How much information should we provide in each area? How should we put the information from different sources together so that it could be easily used, as well as com-pared and contrasted with other areas? After a great deal of discussion, we decided on the format and produced a package called the "Thailand Women's Information Kit," which includes statistics (displayed as graphs, tables, and concise text) on population, migration, fertility, health, educa-tion, labor, and politics/administration.[6]

The information kit was first distributed at the Pattaya seminar and was another of the seminar's highlights. Seminar participants kept referring to it during panel discussions; some suggested that we should organize a workshop on the information kit to sensitize policy makers and planners on the actual status and role of women. Postseminar requests for the informa-tion kit have also been overwhelming, coming from people from all walks of life, and from Bangkok as well as from provinces throughout the country. The TDRI-WID team sent a copy of the information kit to each of the seventy-two provincial governors and provincial development officers. More copies were requested by the provinces for their staff in the provincial and district offices. One Thai NGO bought one hundred copies, and one government agency bought forty copies to distribute to participants in one of its own seminars. To date, we have distributed more than five thousand copies (one thousand in English and four thousand in Thai).

Exhibition on the Role and Status of Thai Women

Upon the request of the Parliamentary Committee on Women and Youth

Affairs, the TDRI-WID project team held an exhibition at Parliament based on the information kit. The exhibition (September 14–26, 1989) was held in conjunction with a seminar organized at Parliament to raise the awareness of the public and of parliamentarians on the role and status of Thai women. We received a number of requests for the information kit from members of Parliament. Later, six sets of the exhibition packages were produced and displayed at six locations in different parts of the country on International Women's Day (March 8, 1989).

A Mini-Information Kit on the Role and Status of Thai Women

A number of people from governmental and nongovernmental agencies, as well as media representatives approached the TDRI-WID project team for our WID materials for dissemination at International Women's Day activities. To reduce the cost of the information kit for the general public, we selected a few key statistics presented in graphs and charts from the kit and combined them in a pamphlet with information on the TDRI-WID Project ("Mini-Information Kit").[7] Several thousand pamphlets were distributed at the six locations where exhibitions were held in and outside Bangkok.

3. THE PARLIAMENT SEMINAR

At the time that the TDRI-WID team was considering options for strengthening national mechanisms to promote the role of women in development (one of the major concerns raised at the Pattaya seminar), we were approached by the newly appointed Minister of the Prime Minister's Office, Supatra Masdit, whose responsibilities include women's affairs. Minister Masdit had heard about the discussions at the Pattaya seminar and wanted input from the TDRI-WID team in designing a national body to coordinate governmental and nongovernmental agencies to strengthen the role of women in development.

In response to the minister's request and the concerns of the Pattaya seminar participants, the TDRI-WID team launched a study entitled "National Mechanisms for Strengthening the Role of Women in Development." On September 19, 1988, the TDRI-WID team co-sponsored with the Parliamentary Committee on Women and Youth Affairs and two newspapers (Siam Rath and The Nation), a seminar at Parliament, "New Dimensions for Strengthening the Role of Women in National Development." The seminar was opened by Minister Masdit and concluded by Ms. Yenjit Rabhibhat Na Ayudaya, the chairperson of the Parliamentary Committee on Women and Youth Affairs. Some twenty top executives from government, NGO, and media agencies with either a direct mandate for strengthening the role of women, or with clear potential for doing so, spoke at the three organized sessions. At each of the sessions, six to eight speakers were asked to respond specifically to the government's position on women's development. This had been announced to Parliament by the prime minister on August 25, 1988. At that time he stated that "the government wishes to accelerate coordination among governmental and nongovernmental agencies in women's development . . ." Speakers at the three sessions were asked to address these questions:

1. What direction(s) will the speaker/agency take in the next four years to strengthen the role of women (e.g., farmers, entrepreneurs, etc.)? What is the budget required for implementing the planned activities?
   a. In what ways are there differences between present and former directions?
   b. How will women benefit from the new directions?
2. To carry out the new dimensions/directions, what kind of support is required by the speaker/agency?
   a. policy support;
   b. legislative support;
   c. mass media support; and
   d. other support.

Seminar participants included twenty-nine senior government officials, thirteen members of parliament, twenty-six academicians and policy researchers, thirty-five executives/workers from NGOs and business institutions, and eighteen female leaders from different parts of the country. At each session presentation, a group consisting of women who are grassroots leaders, a member of Parliament, an academician, a representative from a nongovernmental agency, and a media representative, commented. Again, it was the grassroots women who stole the show. Their obvious grasp of the issues, coupled with their own practical experience, led to strong and unexpectedly articulate interventions.[8]

Where did we find such confident and effective speakers from among rural women? This was a common question of senior-level participants. In fact, the TDRI-WID project team used its network to help identify women who were successful grassroots income-earners and leaders in community development. The team believed that successful women knew how to solve difficult problems. Their insights would assist us to identify directions and effective approaches to strengthen the role of women. Each of our networkers in governmental/nongovernmental agencies, businesses, and academic institutions was asked to propose five to ten successful grassroots women. The TDRI-WID team also came up with a list. Then we selected the twenty women who were recommended by more than one networker (including the team) to participate in the seminar at Parliament.

To assist the grassroots leaders to organize their thoughts, the TDRI-WID project team invited them to come a day earlier to a workshop to share their experiences. How could we help these women communicate their insights effectively to participants at the Parliament seminar? We were able to identify an excellent team of facilitators with experience working with change-agents in rural and urban development. These facilitators helped the grassroots women share their success and their pride, articulate how they arrived where they were, as well as describe the most difficult situation they had experienced and how they overcame it. We were deeply moved by this experience. The driving force for these women was their pride in being full citizens—breadwinners and taxpayers—and in gaining family and community recognition and support for their contributions. We learned how they struggled to overcome restrictive societal attitudes and stereotypes; how government officials impeded their efforts, and contributed to the problem, *not* to the solution; how irresponsible media coverage of them and their actions exacerbated their struggle; and of their experience in labor unions.

The Parliament seminar fostered the development of new and more positive images of Thai women in development and built the ranks of allies in efforts to strengthen their role and status:

1. A much more positive image of local women leaders (which surprised the majority of the participants) was projected as a result of their outstanding contribution at the seminar;

2. A spirit of cooperation between women and men was reflected in the gender balance among moderators/speakers/discussants/participants, all focused on dealing with gender issues in development;

3. The support of the media: During the week prior to the seminar, English and Thai newspapers published a series of articles on the role of women in national development; and Radio Thailand presented documentary programs on the same subject following the morning news. Also, the media gave more than normal coverage to the seminar.

Moreover, the seminar illustrated new dimensions in efforts to strengthen the role of women in development. It provided an alternative and feasible mechanism for policy dialogue involving people from all levels of society, and portrayed the fruits of the coordinated efforts of the Minister of the Prime Minister's Office, the Parliamentary Committee on Women and Youth Affairs, the mass media, TDRI, and the grassroots leaders.

THE OUTCOMES

The most gratifying result of our work has been to witness the impact of collaborative efforts on the project design, in changing societal attitudes and stereotypes, and in raising the awareness of policy makers, development personnel, the media, and the general public on specific gender issues. Our success in presenting a locally elected woman as a keynote speaker at the Pattaya workshop, for example, had a great impact on participants' attitudes and changed some stereotypic perceptions. The outstanding performance of grassroots leaders (young and middle-aged) at the Parliament seminar also projected a positive image of this group of women. Further, media coverage on these grassroots leaders at the Pattaya workshop and the Parliament seminar helped to raise public awareness about the role of grassroots women in national development.

We have learned that to integrate "gender" in research and policy for development, it is important to involve policy makers and planners of both sexes. At both the Pattaya workshop and the Parliament seminar, we achieved a balanced representation among panelists and participants in terms of sex and occupation. Involving the media and the politicians (the Parliamentary Committee on Women and Youth Affairs) as co-sponsors of the Parliament seminar, and as active participants in the discussions, is also a new strategy toward strengthening the role of women in development. The seminar provided a mechanism for policy dialogue involving people from all levels of society. Most importantly, the Parliament seminar brought women who were rural and urban grassroots leaders together with top policy makers, for the first time, to participate in establishing national-level priorities and development directions.

The demand for our two publications—the concept paper and the information kit—went beyond our expectations. The concept paper (originally intended as an internal document) was very well received; we have exhausted our first eight hundred copies (four hundred each in English and in Thai). A second printing of the paper has just been completed. Also, we have distributed more than five thousand copies of the information kit. In addition, during International Women's Day festivities (March 3-12, 1989), we distributed more than three thousand copies of our "Mini Information Kit." At present, we are working with the Department of Nonformal Education (NFE) and the Community Development Department (CDD) to produce a set of three posters with key information on the status and role of Thai women. The posters will be designed for use by local level decision makers and development planners, and will be distributed to NFE Reading Centers and CDD Tambon (Subdistrict) Development Centers at sixty-five hundred locations throughout the country.

CONCLUSION

Integration of gender in research and policy development is a complex undertaking demanding that policy makers and planners consider women's roles and responsibilities in relation to those of men. In the past year, we found ourselves testing and preparing the ground for policy research on critical women's issues identified by TDRI's program directors and the TDRI-WID project team, and endorsed by other policy makers/planners from the governmental/nongovernmental agencies and academic institutions. Recognizing the impact of societal attitudes on the integration process, we focused our efforts to better understand how to deal effectively with these attitudes. Through action/operation research we learned how to work as a catalyst and recognized the importance of being perceived as impartial in dealing with groups of people at different levels. Further, the connection of the WID project to TDRI, a prestigious policy research institute, gave us access to other policy makers/planners and to the media.

What we have achieved so far is certainly not what we had anticipated. Our major concerns at the outset, pertaining to the diversity of viewpoints and approaches to development of our TDRI-WID team, did not prevent us from carrying out our task! Information on the status and role of Thai women in various forms, such as the information kits and the exhibition packages were our main tools used for the task of reaching out to policy makers/planners and other key actors in development. Our responsiveness to needs as they arose, and to suggestions by key policy makers and other development personnel, resulted in activities that had a significant impact on public awareness of the role of women in development. This included the decision to co-sponsor the Parliament seminar, and to develop exhibition packages and the mini-kit for the International Women's Day events across the country.

In looking back on our experience, it is clear that the key to our achievements was not the amount of money available for activities, but rather finding ways to work creatively with what was available; how to maximize the use of existing resources; how to develop, maintain, and utilize networks effectively; how to analyze and synthesize the mass of available information; and how to derive an appropriate strategy to meet the challenge before us.

NOTES

1. Government of Thailand, National Statistical Office, *Report of the Labor Force Survey*, Whole Kingdom, (Bangkok, May 1986).

2. Government of Thailand, National Statistical Office, *Report of the Labor Force Survey*, Whole Kingdom, (Bangkok, August 1985).

3. Thailand Development Research Institute, "1988 Annual Report," (Bangkok, December 1988).

4. Suteera Thomson, Orapin Sopchokchai, and Daranee Charoen- Rajapark, "A Concept Paper: The Role of Thai Women in Development," (Bangkok, Thailand Development Research Institute, April 1988).

5. Thailand Development Research Institute, "Workshop Proceedings: The Role of Thai Women in Development," (Bangkok, September 1988).

6. Thailand Development Research Institute, "Thailand Women's Information Kit," (Bangkok, July 1988).

7. Thailand Development Research Institute, "A Pamphlet: Women in Development Project," (Bangkok, March 1989).

8. Thailand Development Research Institute, "Seminar Proceedings: New Dimensions for Strengthening the Role of Women in Development," (Bangkok, December 1988).

IV

INSTITUTIONALIZATION

Women's Studies in the United States: Growth and Institutionalization

Florence Howe

INTRODUCTION

The evolution and growth of women's studies as a formal area of teaching and research is one of the major achievements of women in U.S. higher education over the last fifteen years. The idea of women's studies emerged in the late sixties under the impetus of the women's movement and its progress since then has been extraordinary. Against all odds, financial, political, and intellectual, a cadre of committed feminist scholars, joined by a few men, succeeded in gaining recognition for the legitimacy of the subject area and led the way to the establishment of courses and degree programs in colleges and universities throughout the U.S. The proportion of all institutions offering women's studies courses already exceeds 40 percent, and the number is still growing. The world of feminist scholarship as it exists today also includes research centers or institutes, and professional journals, books, working paper series, and other publications for the dissemination of the new knowledge. Here, I will briefly document the growth and institutionalization of women's studies in the United States.

OBJECTIVES OF WOMEN'S STUDIES

The early manifestos of women's studies programs were ambitious political and intellectual statements. From a study of more than fifty of these written before 1973, five goals emerge:

1. to raise the consciousness of students—and faculty alike—about the need to study women, about their absence from texts and from the concerns of scholarship, about the subordinate status of women today as in the past;

2. to begin to compensate for the absence of women, or for the unsatisfactory manner in which they were present in some disciplines, through designing new courses in which to focus on women, thus to provide for women in colleges and universities the compensatory education they needed and deserved;

3. to build a body of research about women;

4. with that body of research, to reenvision the lost culture and history of women; and

5. using all four goals, to change the education of women and men through changing what we have come to call the "mainstream" curriculum.[1]

From the outset, though the words "consciousness" and "consciousness-raising" appeared in all program manifestos, it was also clear from the course syllabi that the single most important instrument with which to raise consciousness was the new scholarship about women. Of course, in many introductory courses, then and now, students are encouraged to discuss their own experiences and comprehension of the world (often in small groups arranged expressly for the purpose), but the content of women's studies courses from the first also included an awareness that one had to gather information about many persons' experiences before one had what could be called "knowledge."

While none of the goals disappeared, by the midseventies, the strategic goal—"to change the education of all women and men"—had some focus, and there was a new goal as well. The new goal was "to open additional career options for students through development of coherent academic programs." This goal suited the process of institutionalization, for it responded to the need to justify the establishment of women's studies as an academic major through the naming of vocational areas that in our times majors need to serve. It also responded to an academic clientele increasingly focused on status, money, and vocation.

From the beginning, women's studies pioneers held that studying women was as useful a preparation for the workplace as studying history or literature or economics. If one organized this study as a dual major, moreover, one would be more richly equipped than other students for careers in many fields, as well as for graduate study. With women's studies, one would have, in addition to the traditional major, the valuable new scholarship on women. Further, for those going directly to the workplace, women's studies offered fresh perspectives on the history and contemporary condition of women to be used especially within such institutions as social work agencies, schools, or publishing houses. Less obvious even to the students themselves, and certainly to those in control of the workplace, was the fact that women were the major consumers, the major readers of books and periodicals, the major churchgoers and volunteers, and that, thus, much of the curriculum of women's studies might be seen as directly relevant to the world of work, especially within institutions that served women.

It is important to note two final objectives: first, that the women's studies curriculum ideally and idealistically aims to include not only a focus on gender, but also, and at the same time, on the intersections of gender with race, class, ethnicity, sexual preference, and other relevant characteristics of individuals and groups. Further, while the focus is unabashedly on women, there is constantly present, occasionally subtly, a comparison with men.

GENESIS AND GROWTH

Prior to 1970, there were isolated instances of courses relating to women, but the systematic study of women did not come into being until the late sixties, when the women's movement first touched the campus. Beginning in 1968, feminist scholars on several U.S. campuses began to question a simple reading of discrimination in academe and to seek the underlying causes. Certainly, fewer women than men made it to associate and full professor on any campus, including women's college campuses. Only a handful of women served as college presidents. But the more persistently difficult question was why had so many women, even in traditionally female-typed undergraduate majors, chosen not to go on to graduate school? In English, for example, while a majority of undergraduate majors were female and a minority male, the statistic at the Ph.D. level was reversed.[2]

These questions coincided with the appearance of one pioneering study of the elementary school curriculum, published in Princeton as a pamphlet called *Dick and Jane as Victims*. The authors were a group of National Organization for Women (NOW) members, some of whom were faculty wives. The study of 134 widely used elementary reading texts revealed consistent stereotypes of mothers as housewives only, and mainly unintelligent ones at that; of fathers as briefcase-carrying white-collar workers who came home to solve problems for the whole family; of a family of two children, a male older and a female younger child, and two pets, a male dog older and larger than a female cat.[3] Academics reading this study turned to their own texts to find, not surprisingly, similar stereotypes or the absence of women altogether.

In 1969, a group of feminists at Cornell University organized a conference that resulted in a faculty seminar to examine the portrayal of women in the social and behavioral sciences. The seminar led to the establishment of an interdisciplinary course on women, followed in 1970 by a coordinated female studies program of six courses from different departments of the university. At about the same time, a similar effort was underway across the continent where a women's studies program was started at San Diego State University. Included were such courses as Women in Literature, Women in Comparative Cultures, and Contemporary Issues in the Liberation of Women.

From 1970 on, women's studies courses and programs spread rapidly, fostered chiefly by two factors and two strategies, and impelled by the fact of the women's movement that continued to keep women in the media—on the front page of newspapers, on the covers of magazines, and on the television screen. The two factors were the presence among the student body of women students eager for knowledge about themselves; and the presence among the faculty, albeit at lower ranks, of a sizable percentage of women, enough at least to make a difference. Many of these women in the vulnerable positions of temporary faculty or on tenure lines risked tenure by developing and teaching new women's studies courses. A handful of senior faculty, among them Gerda Lerner, Alice Rossi, and I, risked their reputations, and did likewise.

What was needed to move women's studies forward? There was no national meeting until 1977. There were not even regional meetings until 1973. And yet, even without discussion, two strategies emerged that were critical to dissemination of the idea and details of its practice.

The first was the most obvious strategy of all academics: to use the professional association and its annual meetings for discussion and dissemination of new ideas. The Modern Language Association (MLA), for example, established a Commission on the Status and Education of Women in the spring of 1969, with a charge both to study the status of women faculty in five thousand English and modern language departments, and to review the content of the curriculum in those departments. In 1970, at the MLA's annual meeting, the commission offered to an audience of more than a thousand women and men a forum that included papers on the status of women faculty and the literary curriculum's male biases and female stereotypes and two of the first lectures in feminist literary criticism.

In 1970 also, the second and ultimately the key strategy appeared that was responsible for the rapid early spread of women's studies courses as well as for the spread of the idea of establishing women's studies *programs*. This was the strategy, first carried out under the direction of Sheila Tobias, then associate provost at Wesleyan University, of printing course syllabi for distribution at professional associations' annual meetings. *Female Studies I,* a collection of seventeen course syllabi, was distributed at the American Psychological Association's annual meeting in the fall of 1970; and *Female Studies II,* a collection of sixty-four course syllabi, at the December 1970 meetings of the Modern Language Association. More than two hundred copies were sold at each meeting, and several thousand in the next several years, when *Female Studies* numbers three to ten also appeared and were widely distributed to academics.[4]

It is important to note that part of the strategy for early dissemination of the idea of women's studies included the publication in the *Female Studies* series not only of course syllabi, bibliographies, and brief essays from such teacher-scholars as Gerda Lerner, but also the entire and often lengthy manifesto-like documents that accompanied the establishment of women's studies programs, including their rationale, their requirements, the strength of their faculty, their curricular designs, and their goals for students.

It is not surprising, therefore, to find the numbers of women's studies courses rising dramatically through the early years of the seventies. In December 1970, the MLA's Commission on the Status of Women published the first "Current Guide to Female Studies," listing more than 110 courses. The second guide, published only a year later, listed 610 courses, of which more than a dozen were graduate courses, and listed as well fifteen organized women's studies programs, five of them degree-granting, one at the M.A. level.[5]

In 1974, The Feminist Press, with a small grant from the Ford Foundation, published a comprehensive directory entitled *Who's Who and Where in Women's Studies*, which listed 4,490 courses taught by 2,225 faculty members at 995 institutions.[6] At that time, there were 112 organized women's studies programs on campus. As of 1989, there were 504 programs and the number was still growing.[7] More than two-thirds of those programs offer either a minor or an undergraduate major, in addition to more than sixty graduate programs leading either to the M.A. (fifty) or the Ph.D. (sixteen). Sixteen institutions offer the new graduate minor as part of traditional doctoral programs. Enrollments also have increased dramatically.[8]

A recent survey of women's studies programs indicates that, in the decade since 1975, there has been dramatic growth in the size and enrollments of women's studies programs and courses, dramatic increases in the size of some budgets, especially of programs located on larger doctorate-granting, university campuses. Individual course enrollments, for example, in the ubiquitous Introduction to Women's Studies have reached as high as 900 at Ohio State University, 720 at the University of Southern California, 548 at the University of Maryland, and 350 at the University of Colorado.[9]

THE PROCESS OF INSTITUTIONALIZATION

We find that thirteen primary factors have been instrumental in the process of institutionalizing women's studies. Taken roughly in order of their appearance in the process, they are: (1) the willingness of faculty to share information on teaching the new subject matter; (2) the energy and enthusiasm brought to the endeavor by students and teachers; (3) strategies for obtaining texts, which were not yet available from publishers; (4) early affiliations with established departments; (5) the establishment of women's studies programs rather than departments; (6) access to budgets and the formalization of ties to campus administrations, departments, curriculum committees, and other groups; (7) the formation of caucuses and committees within established professional associations; (8) the establishment of national fellowship programs to fund research; (9) the formation of the National Women's Studies Association and the Berkshire Conference on the History of Women; (10) the development of a network of centers for research; (11) the development of a body of literature; (12) recognition by the U.S. Department of Education; and (13) the establishment of endowed chairs in women's studies.

In the very early stages of women's studies, courses were often introduced on campus on an experimental or informal basis. Unlike such other fields as foreign area studies or urban studies, no external funding for curriculum development was available to women's studies, and the new courses were solely the result of voluntary efforts by pioneering feminist scholars on faculties. By the early seventies, it was possible to gather three hundred course syllabi from as many different faculty members, all of whom were interested in sharing them. The willingness to share new teaching information in a new field was in itself unique to academe—we know of no precedent here. We read this willingness as an indication of the strength of the feminist ideology that had spawned women's studies in the first place. While a majority of these courses were in English, sociology, and history, most other academic disciplines were also represented, along with the interdisciplinary "introduction" to women's studies, labeled in a variety of ingenious ways, depending on the departmental umbrella that had offered it the necessary academic shelter.

The excitement of teaching these new courses deserves notice. Whatever a faculty member's proper discipline, she had to read in other fields to be able to present material clearly and in appropriate context. For example, teachers of a course called "Images of Women in Literature" would need to introduce the concept "women" through the use of sociological, historical, and even economic and political ideas and contexts. While many literature faculty commonly use concepts outside of their discipline, a focus on "women" was entirely new. Perhaps as important, for the first time in her academic career, this faculty member had to focus on something directly relevant to her own life. Still more important, the students came into class with a readiness for this kind of serious study of material directly and immediately relevant to their lives. Further, the early growth of women's studies coincided with the growth in enrollments of "returning" or "older" female students, coming to college with the express purpose of changing their lives. Thus, the classroom was a living space. That there were few texts, that there were few precedents—these ultimately mattered not at all.

Faculty used what they could find, and sometimes a sexist text worked even more effectively than the unavailable ideal one. The needed texts, on occasion, appeared largely through the energies of a network of pioneers, not only in the U.S., but also in Canada. Many faculty members, for example, taught from an early version of *Our Bodies, Our Selves*, published first in Canada on newsprint in the format of a magazine. When sufficient copies were not available, faculty made photocopies. Manuscripts of essays that would not appear in print until years later also circulated through that very early network of women's studies practitioners, and were often photocopied for students.

The single most important factor in the institutionalization of women's studies was the decision, on campus after campus, by a handful of faculty feminists in each case, to attempt to organize courses in the form of a program and not a department. The model was not home economics, nor even black studies, but rather American studies. What was sought was a coordinator and office, if possible some clerical assistance, a small budget, and the right to organize a coherent curriculum through the use of faculty who would be stationed and tenured or tenurable within their respective departments. The form resembled the spokes of a wheel, or what was referred to as a center and a "network." This strategy of institutionalization served another important objective of women's studies—that of changing the traditional curriculum throughout the university. And it was common knowledge that a separate department could not be an "agent of change" for the broader curriculum.

The 1976 study *Seven Years Later* established that mature women's studies programs had passed through an initial phase dubbed "creative anarchy," and had by mid-decade entered a second phase of institutionalization. The attributes of the second phase included a paid coordinator, a formal budget or access to a dean's formal budget, a formal curriculum that passed through a women's studies committee for review by a more general campuswide curriculum committee, and a "line" relationship for all the program's activities between the coordinator and some administrator, typically a dean or vice president of arts and sciences, or on smaller campuses, the dean of faculty.

While most programs began life under the rubric of a committee, institutionalization also has included the continuation of a governing committee, often with student representation, as well as with connections to other feminist groups on campus, for example, a women's center. While only few programs in the country have department rather than program status, and can recommend their own faculty for tenure in women's studies rather than in departments, women's studies programs sometimes have been able to influence appointments informally through contributing to a review process, and in a significant number of instances, faculty hold appointments jointly in a department and in women's studies. Of necessity, therefore, women's studies must have close ties to departments. As we shall make clear, the benefits include the ability to get on with the major goal of changing the entire traditional curriculum.

Also strategic for the development of women's studies was the organization, during the late sixties and early seventies, of many caucuses and committees both within and as splinter groups outside of professional associations. Although much of the work of these committees was devoted to advancing the professional status and career opportunities of women, they also directed attention, chiefly through programming at the annual meetings, to women as a subject of teaching and research in the disciplines.

Also early in the seventies, strategic support for the recognition and institutionalization of women's studies came from the establishment of national fellowship programs for research on women by major national foundations, notably Ford to begin with, then, later, Carnegie, Rockefeller, and Mellon. Other foundations, such as Russell Sage, have been major supporters of scholars engaged in social science research relating to women. As of 1983, nationwide there were ten fellowship programs for women scholars or scholarship about women.[10] Further support for individual or project research was also forthcoming from government agencies such as the National Endowment for the Humanities, the Fund for Improvement of Postsecondary Education (FIPSE), the National Institute of Education, and the Women's Education Equity Act Program.

Important in the process of institutionalization was the founding of the National Women's Studies Association (NWSA) in 1977. The process began in 1972, when the *Women's Studies Quarterly* (then called *Women's Studies Newsletter*, published by The Feminist Press) attempted to connect a national constituency of teachers interested at least locally in the new curricular reform. NWSA's stated purpose was broad based: "to further the social, political, and professional development of women's studies throughout the country and the world, at every educational level and in every educational setting."[11] From the beginning NWSA drew a large and diverse membership consisting not only of scholars but also administrators, community activists, and other women's studies practitioners, as well as school teachers, though not as many as had been anticipated. As of 1989 its membership was about thirty-eight hundred. NWSA holds an annual meeting and publishes a quarterly newsletter and a scholarly quarterly.

Although the National Women's Studies Association has played an important role in the development of women's studies, it is more an association of generalists, and of persons committed to such reforms as "mainstreaming" or "balancing" the curriculum, rather than of faculty committed to scholarship in their own disciplines. Its sessions serve teachers and women's studies program directors as much as, or more than, the historian or the economist. No single association represents scholarship in women's studies, nor could such an association exist without subsuming all the professional associations that already exist. Rather, much of the function of representing and spreading scholarship in women's studies rests with the academic disciplines and their professional associations, and, at times, with women's caucuses, commissions, or committees within those associations. The Berkshire Conference on the History of Women, which is interdisciplinary in orientation and which takes place every three years, is the largest gathering of feminist scholars in the U.S. The Berkshire Conference is an informal organization of feminist historians that was founded in 1928 and revitalized in 1972. Its meetings have been held consistently on the campuses of women's colleges.

Probably the most strategic factor in the institutionalization of women's studies in its second decade has been the establishment of organized centers for research. As of 1989, there were sixty-two centers across the country, the majority of them campus based. Their purpose is to provide resources for research about women that strengthen the efforts of individual scholars. They offer such facilities as libraries, staff support, forums for the exchange of ideas, and assistance in project development and funding. Collectively, they have made a crucial contribution to the position of women's studies, its capacities, and its recognition in the academic community and beyond.

An essential element in the establishment of a new field is, of course, the development of a body of literature. When the earliest women's studies programs were instituted there was little by way of appropriate textbooks or other course material. The growth in volume of publications since then has been nothing short of spectacular. Such new journals as *Women's Studies and Feminist Studies* appeared in 1972, and *Signs; Journal of Women in Culture and Society* made its debut in 1975. New presses were created to serve the unmet needs of various women's studies constituencies. The largest and most successful of these, as well as the first, is The Feminist Press, which was established in 1970. Since then The Feminist Press has grown with the women's studies movement, reflected its concerns, and contributed to its development. It has published curricular material for the school and college level, has reprinted fiction, autobiography, and other books by female authors to restore the lost history, culture, and literature of women, has anticipated curricular needs by producing original texts and anthologies, and has served as a resource for reference material relating to women's studies.

Today articles relating to women regularly appear in the professional journals of most disciplines, and university presses commonly release a separate catalogue on women's studies, as do most trade presses. Female authors and reviews of feminist literature and scholarship appear in increasing numbers in the *New York Review of Books, The New York Times Book Review, Atlantic Monthly, Harper's,* and the *Times Literary Supplement.* Textbooks, previously nonexistent, are now available for women's studies courses across the disciplines, including history, law, psychology, economics, and literature, as well as for inter-disciplinary introductory courses.

A further milestone in the institutionalization of women's studies was its formal recognition as a degree specialty in 1983 by the U.S. Department of Education. The annual statistics of earned degrees conferred will henceforth provide a significant measure of the progress of women's studies, even though the Department of Education does not include subspecialties within disciplines.

There is one further step to be noted and that is the establishment during the eighties of endowed chairs in women's studies. This is another sign of the maturity and acceptance of the field. There are now upwards of a dozen chairs already in existence, including those at the University of Southern California, the University of Wisconsin, Brown University, and Rutgers University.

THE WOMEN'S STUDIES CURRICULUM

In the twenty years since its beginning, the women's studies curriculum has grown in complexity as well as in size and scope. One may describe this curriculum in terms of the disciplines it is in the process of revising, or in terms of interdisciplinary topics. The following list cuts through both types of categories, as do the titles of courses offered or coordinated by women's studies programs.

1. *Patriarchy.* While this is an overriding theme in all women's studies courses, some, including the Introduction to Women's Studies in its various guises, as well as courses in theory and methods, focus especially on this theme. The focus may take the form of the study of philosophy, theology, sociology, or psychology (Women and Philosophy, Women and Theology, etc.); however organized, a course of this kind will examine the patterns of a gender-based organization of social, economic, political, and cultural life, to describe the construction of reality that insists on male dominance and female subservience, its history, perhaps even including its origins in some prehistorical past, its contemporary construction, and the slight shifts that have begun to occur in the past twenty years both in consciousness and in action.

2. *Sex-role stereotyping.* This is a second overriding theme in women's studies courses, especially in the Introduction to Women's Studies. It often takes the form of a study of images of women and men—in literature, for example, in advertising and the media, in film, or in the Bible. The point of such study is dual: to hone the analytic abilities of students to see gender-typed stereotypes prejudicial either to women or men and to consider as well how such stereotypes might be changed, and to what visions of human potential.

3. *Sex differences.* This theme emerges in such courses as The Psychology of Sex Differences; Psychology of Sex Roles; Psychology of Gender, or, more rarely, Psycho-biology of Sex Differences. A course of this sort is a staple in all large programs, and sometimes, as at the University of Washington for example, one that is cross-listed in psychology for majors, or to fulfill a science requirement, and that attracts enrollments of more than 150 students each year. Such courses are by nature comparative, and they serve to dispel certain deeply held myths about women's alleged emotionality, men's alleged rationality.

4. *Sexuality (and health)*. Even more than the courses on sex differences, those on sexuality, especially when they are called Human Sexuality and team-taught by a woman and a man, attract very large enrollments. Such a course at the University of South Florida, offered by the Women's Studies Program and called Human Sexual Behavior, reports enrollments of more than five hundred each term. In the eighties, courses on women and health now include sexuality as a subtheme. In all cases, sexuality includes both homosexual and heterosexual behavior, as well as the sexuality connected with pregnancy and childbirth.

5. *History*. While some growing number of departments of history include at least one specialist in "women's" history who offers several courses in a particular specialization, it would be possible to replicate the entire male-centered curriculum in history with courses focused on the other half of the human race. At present, however, programs offer only selected courses in aspects of women's history in various parts of the world. By and large, most women's studies programs feel an obligation to include at least an introductory course in the history of women in the U.S., though it has become increasingly awkward to cram two hundred or more years of history—and of women of various races and classes and ethnicities—into a single course or even two. And so specialization, especially on major university campuses, has grown, and courses called American Women in the Twenties or German Women under Hitler are not unusual. At the same time, one needs to note with regard to the women's studies curriculum that the influence of history on all courses and disciplines has been ubiquitous. Women's studies faculty, whether in literature, economics, or sociology, teach with a strong sense of historical change in the status of women and the conditions of their lives.

6. *Literature and the other arts*. As in history, it would be possible to teach a women's studies curriculum parallel to all that currently exists in the male-centered curriculum. In departments of English and in foreign language departments, that process is underway, and in art history and musicology, the process has also begun. General courses called Women Writers, Women Painters, or Women Composers are commonplace, though some major universities with faculty resources offer courses as specific as Nineteenth-Century Women Novelists in the U.S. or Twentieth-Century French Women Poets, as well as courses on such individual writers as Virginia Woolf, Colette, Zora Neale Hurston, Willa Cather, and others. Women's studies courses also focus on newly recognized genres especially important to women artists: quilts, for example, is a new area of study, as is the diary literature of women, or women's autobiography.

7. *Psychology*. Critiques of Freud's view of the psychology of women, along with Erik Erikson's and those of other male theorists, provide material for courses called Women and Psychology or The Psychology of Women. By the early eighties, such courses were also focusing attention on several new perspectives about female psychology and female develop-

ment from such feminist scholars as Jean Baker Miller, Nancy Chodorow, and Carol Gilligan.

8. *The family.* Courses on women and the family may be found in departments of history, sociology, psychology, and elsewhere. Women's studies courses on the family emphasize the institution's variety of forms throughout history and into the contemporary period, and cross-culturally as well. Such courses also ask complex questions about the conservative and typically oppressive nature of the family for women and, at the same time, illuminate the quality of women's culture nurtured inside families, and both despite and because of particular family structures. Courses on the family in women's studies programs typically include a serious focus on the ideology of egalitarian families, and the social structures needed to bring such institutions about.

9. *Work.* Courses on women and work, like courses on the family, may be found in a variety of departments, including history, economics, sociology, and even literature. Such courses have redefined the work of women to include such unpaid activity as child care and housework as well as community activity outside the home. Courses on women and (or in) the labor force may be found in even some of the more conservative departments of economics. A course called History of Women and Work may focus on working-class women and their records in factories, fields, and mines, or on professional women and their inroads into law, medicine, teaching, and other areas once denied them. This aspect of the curriculum may have had a particularly profound effect on the expectations of both younger and returning women students, since, prior to women's studies, there was nothing in the curriculum to encourage the idea that women (especially middle-class women) might work as well as marry and rear children.

10. *Education.* Departments and schools of education have not been in the vanguard of women's studies scholarship. Relatively few institutions offer courses for prospective elementary and secondary school teachers on sex-role stereotyping in the schools, and still fewer offer courses on the history of women's education, an area rich in possibilities for fresh scholarship. As with the family, education is an institution that has both kept women in a subordinate position—especially through the use of a male-centered curriculum—and has also provided a vehicle for change. Women's studies courses in this area focus on the dual nature of educational institutions in a democratic society. Some courses are just beginning to include a review of the history of women's studies itself.

11. *Law and social movements.* Among the earliest women's studies courses was the unique Women and the Law, offered by a practicing Philadelphia lawyer for the Women's Studies Program at the University of Pennsylvania in the very early seventies. Such a course was unique not only because of its focus on women, but also because it was offered in an undergraduate curriculum, not a law school. It is perhaps interesting to note that male

undergraduates, interested in studying law, elected such courses for that reason. Obviously essential to an understanding of the status of women, of women's history, and women's participation in social movements to change that history, such courses may also have been instrumental in suggesting to a whole generation of female students that their future lay in legal study and practice. It is useful to note that in the mideighties the study of women and the law has become of major importance in developing countries interested in organizing women's studies curricula at the undergraduate level.

Associated with the study of law has been the study of women and social movements, in particular the nineteenth-century and twentieth century abolitionist and civil rights movements. More recently, scholars interested in peace studies and the history of women and international law and international feminist movements have been constructing courses about women and peace movements.

12. *Black women's studies, Chicana studies, working-class women's studies, Jewish women's studies, et cetera.* While women's studies teaching should ideally include the study of race and class as well as gender, the curriculum has, from the start, included at least occasional courses called The Black Woman or The Puerto Rican Woman or Jewish Women Writers, to allow for focus on the scholarship of a particular group, sometimes in a particular era as well. In large programs, especially on campuses with sizable ethnic studies programs, such courses may multiply.

13. *Women and development.* The study of women in the Third World has grown, especially since 1980, and on many campuses women's studies programs have made efforts to include such courses in their curriculum. Some of these courses focus on particular parts of the world—Women in Sub-Sahara Africa, for example, or Caribbean Women, or Women in Central America. Others focus on aspects covered topically in the curricular themes described above, as for example, Women and the Economy of Development, or Women, Kinship, and Family Structures in China. It may be useful to note here that in Third World countries now constructing varieties of women's studies curricula for use in schools and colleges, the opening theme may be this one, and all other themes reviewed here may follow from it.

Paralleling the shift in emphasis of women's studies courses has been a shift in research emphasis. During the early seventies a substantial amount of research was devoted to documenting discrimination against women and identifying sexism or patriarchy throughout society, in space and time. An early shift to survivors of that patriarchy throughout history augmented research by presenting what Gerda Lerner has called "contribution" history, including the history of prior women's movements, not only in the U.S. and the West, but in almost every country throughout the world. While these tasks continue, increasing attention is being given to the impact of the new knowledge on the fundamental assumptions of the disciplines, on public policy issues such as the impact of new technologies on the work and family roles of women, and on gender differences in general. Indeed, there is, in some quarters of the women's studies research and teaching worlds, a new shift to the study of gender that runs parallel to the study of women. While the study of gender may seem to include men more readily than women's studies per se, and while funding agencies may be more sympathetic to the study of gender rather than the study of women, feminists are alert to the fact that gender per se narrows what has been until now a very broad area of study. Gender narrows the field to discrimination and the study of differences between men and women, leaving to one side the major thrust of the women's studies movement from the beginning, the development of a body of knowledge that restores the lost history and culture. While women's studies has made inroads into the development of such a body of knowledge, the field is only at the beginning of its development. Further, only when such bodies of knowledge are extensive can scholars begin to review history or other areas of scholarship—including men as well as women in their purview.

Women's studies in the eighties has also given more attention to the international dimensions of women's issues. While feminist scholars on both sides of the Atlantic had been in touch with one another throughout the seventies and had shared ideas and controversies, the women's studies community in the United States did not at first address the concerns of women in Asia, Africa, and Latin America. There were, of course, exceptions, particularly among anthropologists who were stimulated by the women's movements to examine women's roles more closely than had been customary. Among the earliest and most influential books on women in developing countries were *Women's Role in Economic Development*, by Ester Boserup, published in 1970;[12] *Women Culture and Society*, edited by Michele Rosaldo and Louise Lamphere, published in 1974,[13] and *Toward an Anthropology of Women*, edited by Rayna Reiter.[14] There is now a substantial literature on the critical work of women in the economic systems of developing countries and of the significance of such work for development policy. The Rosaldo and Lamphere book and the Reiter book are early collections of essays by leading feminist anthropologists exploring new ways of analyzing the place of women in a wide variety of social systems. They have become classics in the field. The establishment of the UN Decade for Women from 1975 to 1985 gave further impetus to the study of women's roles worldwide.

MAINSTREAMING WOMEN'S STUDIES CURRICULUM

After a period of substantial growth since 1970, women's studies courses and programs are now firmly entrenched on college and university campuses. They have grown in sophistication as well as in size and number and they have made their influence felt abroad as well as in the United States. Yet they do not reach directly more than a small segment of the student body, most of them women. We have noted that it is one of the objectives of women's studies to integrate the new knowledge into the mainstream curriculum, thereby affecting the education of all men and women. To what extent has women's studies been successful in achieving this goal?

The first effort to measure the impact of women's studies on the liberal arts curriculum was undertaken by a group of female faculty members at Princeton in 1976. It was found that with few exceptions little or no attention was being given to women in these courses.[15] The situation in sociology was somewhat better than in the other fields largely because of the availability of an introductory text, *Sociology*, by Suzanne Keller and Donald Light, which covered a wide range of research relating to women. Based on these findings, Lois Banner concluded that methods of persuading faculty to revise their existing syllabi and to incorporate material on women were necessary. And they were not long in coming.

One was the outcome of a recommendation of the Princeton Project itself, namely the preparation of a monograph on *Teaching Women's History*, written by Gerda Lerner and widely distributed by the American Historical Association.[16] The monograph provides a guide to relevant topics and source material, including material from other disciplines, making it easier for faculty members to incorporate women's history into existing courses. This is but one of the many kinds of curriculum integration activities that have been undertaken beginning in the latter part of the seventies. A variety of approaches have been used, including workshops, summer institutes, conferences, faculty development grants, consultations and curriculum revision programs. Many of these have been funded by government agencies or private foundations.

By 1981 a directory of curriculum integration programs prepared at the Center for Research on Women at Wellesley College listed nearly fifty projects.[17] In that year, the Southwest Institute for Research on Women at the University of Arizona, one of the leaders in the mainstreaming movement, convened a conference of directors of curriculum integration projects to share information and pass on the results of their efforts to others. The conference, which was held at Princeton, resulted in the formation of an informal network and a conference report that was designed as a handbook on strategies for instituting integration projects.[18] One of the most ambitious projects in the early eighties was an institution-wide effort at Wheaton College to integrate the study of women into the liberal arts. The Wheaton project culminated in a national conference in 1983 attended by 250 women and men who were involved in curriculum integration projects or were interested in initiating them. The conference, and the ensuing report, were intended as "both a spur to the process of gender balance in the curriculum of American higher education and a means of expanding the network of those undertaking this effort."[19]

Among the recent mainstreaming efforts are several that deserve mention. One program initiated in 1985 with support from the Ford Foundation has introduced new perspectives on women into the curriculum of ten formerly all-male colleges. For example, Columbia University is in the process of redesigning its well-known Contemporary Civilization curriculum to integrate the new perspectives. At Towson State University in Maryland, a three-year project, funded by FIPSE, provided workshops, mentors, conferences, and other supportive strategies to several hundred faculty in various departments. This project has raised additional funding for outreach to faculty in a dozen nearby campuses as well as in local secondary schools, public and private.

We use the word "integrate" advisedly, rather than the word "add," since one cannot as a rule simply add new perspectives without changing traditional ways of thinking. As feminist scholar Elizabeth Minnich has pointed out, one cannot simply add the idea that the world is round to the assumption that it is flat. One must revise the whole conceptual framework. In that sense, women's studies scholars speak of new paradigms and of transforming the curriculum. In what ways and to what extent has the new scholarship influenced the disciplines? In recent years several volumes of essays on this subject have appeared. *The Prism of Sex*, edited by Julia Sherman and Evelyn Beck, shows how feminist research has challenged the premises and content of six disciplines—history, literature, psychology, sociology, philosophy, and political science.[20] A similar volume, *Men's Studies Modified*, edited by Dale Spender, looks at the impact of feminism on a number of other academic disciplines including anthropology, economics, and biology, as well as fields such as education and law.[21] A third volume, *A Feminist Perspective in the Academy*, edited by Elizabeth Langland and Walter Gove, examines feminist scholarship in the humanities and social sciences and seeks to assess the difference it has made in the mainstream curriculum. The conclusion reached is that feminist scholarship has indeed begun to alter the state of knowledge of the disciplines but that women's studies has yet to have any substantial influence on the traditional curriculum.[22]

There has been some further progress in the integration process during the six or seven years since the assessments were made. Nevertheless, it is the consensus among those engaged in integration efforts as well as others that change has been slow in coming. In a sense, this is hardly surprising. Curricular change is never rapid and it certainly cannot be expected to be rapid when basic assumptions are being challenged. In the case of feminist scholarship, the speed of acceptance also relates to the number of women in faculty positions. While all faculty women are not necessarily feminist in outlook, they are more likely than men to be sympathetic to women's studies. Until women are better represented in faculty positions, particularly tenured faculty positions, it will continue to be difficult to transfer the new insights of women's studies to the traditional curriculum.

FUTURE PROSPECTS

At the present stage of women's studies, the number of degree programs is still growing and the process of integration is underway. There is no reason to expect a reversal in these trends in the immediate future. It will be increasingly difficult for institutions that do not have women's studies courses or programs to ignore so substantial and significant a field of scholarship, particularly on campuses where the number of women in the student body exceeds that of men. With respect to graduate and professional schools, women's studies has not yet begun to reach full growth. Graduate programs are needed to produce teachers of women's studies. Among the professional schools, law is the most advanced, whereas education and social work, interestingly the traditional women's fields, are still in the early stages of developing women's studies courses and integrating women's issues into their curricula.

For these reasons, the prospect is for further expansion of women's studies beyond the eighties. There are, and will continue to be, problems, however. One has to do with the lack of departmental status of women's studies. There has been much debate about the pros and cons of this arrangement. The advantage of departmental status is that it provides control over faculty appointments and budgets. On the other hand, women's studies as a department runs the risk of being marginalized and generally ignored by the rest of the university. Underlying the debate is the issue of whether women's studies is a discipline, with its own theory and methodology, or whether it is a new area of study that is integral to the existing disciplines.[23] The preponderant structure of women's studies programs as they now exist and continue to be formed suggests that the case for women's studies as a discipline has not yet been made. At the same time, women's studies programs apart from but integrated into the disciplines are seen as essential, and that appears likely to continue for the foreseeable future. The environment for women's studies scholars in traditional departments is still likely to be one of indifference, if not disdain. But even if in the long run this was no longer the case, women's studies would still be needed to coordinate research efforts and curriculum development across the disciplines.

Problems aside, even at the conclusion of close to two tumultuous decades of development, one may still find undergraduates claiming that women's studies "changed my life" and one may still find graduate students and more established scholars making discoveries that will not only change one aspect of the curriculum or the discipline from whence it springs, but also the lives of women and men. The work of women's studies has only just begun. Generations of committed scholar/teachers will need to continue the development of both the curriculum and scholarship if academe is ever to offer a truly coeducational higher education to students. Perhaps most important for the future is the comprehension gained during the past two decades of the essential relationship between knowledge about women and the possibilities for changing the patterns of women's lives.

120

NOTES

1. Florence Howe, "The Feminist Scholarship, The Extent of the Revolution," *Change*, April 1982, pp. 14–15.

2. Florence Howe, "A Report on Women and the Profession," *College English*, May 1971. This essay was given as the opening lecture in the Forum offered by the Commission on the Status and Education of Women at the Modern Language Association's annual meeting in December 1970.

3. *Dick and Jane as Victims: Sex Stereotyping in Children's Readers* (Princeton, N.J.: Women on Words and Images, 1972). (Prepublication versions were available far earlier.)

4. *Female Studies I, II, III, IV, V* were published by KNOW, Inc. in Pittsburgh, between 1970 and 1973; *Female Studies VI, VII, IX,* and *X* were published by The Feminist Press between 1972 and 1975.

5. Florence Howe, "Women's Studies and Social Change," in Rossi, *Academic Women on the Move*, p. 393.

6. *Who's Who and Where in Women's Studies*, edited by Tamar Berkowitz, Jean Mang, and Jane Williamson (New York: The Feminist Press, 1974).

7. *Women's Studies Quarterly*, 17, nos. 1/2 (Spring/Summer 1989): 16–147.

8. In 1975, the National Advisory Council for Women's Educational Programs, a federal committee, authorized a formal study of fifteen women's studies programs, later published as *Seven Years Later: Women's Studies Programs in 1976*, by Florence Howe.

9. In 1985, I surveyed the nearly five hundred women's studies programs with a brief questionnaire. The data cited in this paper comes from that survey's return of 58 percent.

10. Catherine R. Stimpson with Nina Kressner Cobb, *Women's Studies in the United States*, (New York: Ford Foundation, 1986).

11. Ester Boserup, *Women's Role in Economic Development* (New York: St. Martin's Press, 1970).

12. Ibid.

13. Michele Rosaldo and Louise Lamphere, eds., *Women Culture and Society* (Stanford, Calif.: Stanford University Press, 1974).

14. Rayna R. Reiter, ed., *Toward an Anthropology of Women* (New York: Monthly Review Press, 1975).

15. Princeton Project on Women in the College Curriculum, Final Project, March 1, 1977.

16. Gerda Lerner, *Teaching Women's History* (Washington, D.C.: American Historical Association, 1981).

17. Martha Tolpin, *Directory of Programs: Integrating Women Into Higher Education Curricula*, (Wellesley, Mass.: Center for Research on Women, 1981).

18. Myra Dinnerstein, Sheryl R. O'Donnell, and Patricia MacCorquodale, *How to Integrate Women's Studies into the Traditional Curriculum* (Tucson, Ariz.: Southwest Institute for Research on Women, University of Arizona, Paper No. 9).

19. Bonni Spanier, Alexander Bloom, and Darlene Boroviak, eds., *Towards a Balanced Curriculum: A Sourcebook for Initiating Gender Integrating Projects,* based on the Wheaton College Conference (Cambridge, Mass.: Schenkman Publishing Company, Inc.), p. 5.

20. Julia A. Sherman, Evelyn Torton Beck, eds., *The Prism of Sex* (Madison: University of Wisconsin Press, 1981).

21. Dale Spender, ed., *Men's Studies Modified* (London: Pergamon Press, 1981).

22. Elizabeth Langland and Walter Gove, *A Feminist Perspective in the Academy* (Chicago, Ill.: University of Chicago Press, 1981).

23. For a discussion of this issue see Judith B. Walzer, "New Knowledge or a New Field Discipline?" in *Change*, April 1982, and Gloria Bowles, Renate Duelli, eds., *Theories of Women's Studies* (New York: Routledge and Kegan Paul, 1983).

INCORPORATING GENDER ISSUES IN DEVELOPMENT TRAINING

Aruna Rao

The fact that women and men have systematically different access to and control of resources has significant implications for development theory and practice. In the public domain, women have markedly lower access to productive resources. Reinforced by traditional notions of the sexual division of labor, they are frequently consigned to the less stable and poorly paid sectors of the economy. Unequal power relations in the family and restrictions on women's mobility mediate the impact of production-centered and poverty-alleviation policies and programs. Often, resources meant for women do not reach them within the confines of the household. Or, because of a failure to recognize gender differences or the lack of political will to act on this knowledge, resources that are relevant to women's productive work are often misdirected to men. In some settings, this has led to a marked deterioration of women's income-earning and educational prospects, health, and nutritional status. These detriments to women are frequently passed on to their children.

Because women's labor contributions at the household and project levels are overlooked and their need for economic incentives not always understood, large-scale projects and development policies fail to meet their goals. One strategic response to this situation has been the introduction of training programs in the First and Third Worlds to sensitize planners and program personnel to women's roles and to gender differences in development.

This paper was adapted from Aruna P. Rao, ed., *Incorporating Gender Issues in Development Training* (Bangkok: The Population Council, 1986). It draws on the presentations made at the Population Council panel at the Nairobi NGO Forum in July 1985.

122

Drawing on the momentum generated by women's movements and the United Nations Decade for Women (1975–1985), which not only focused world attention on gender inequity but also encouraged in-depth investigation of its origins and myriad manifestations, these experiments target a specific audience: policy makers who set broad directions for national development and on-line field staff whose program implementation decisions directly affect women's daily lives. While numerous efforts are underway to strengthen the capacity of women's organizations and develop projects specific to women (which often are run also by women), attempts to integrate gender into a mainstream planning framework and equip managers of major economic and social development schemes to effectively meet women's needs, enhance their productivity and ensure their access to development benefits, are few and far between.

Such programs, aimed at development personnel, share similar goals. They examine the gender implications of a range of development policies and programs and attempt to piece together a framework that incorporates gender as a key variable in the analysis of social change in societies moving from subsistence to market economies. Their differences are also instructive. As they are rooted in diverse socioeconomic, cultural, political, and institutional settings, they vary with respect to theoretical approaches and priority issues, training style and materials, as well as the levels of personnel reached.

This paper draws on the experience of five such training courses at the following institutions: the Institute of Development Studies (IDS), Sussex; the Development Planning Unit (DPU), London; the Eastern and Southern African Management Institute (ESAMI), Arusha, Tanzania; the Women and Development Unit (WAND), Barbados; and SNDT Women's University, Bombay. It examines these experiments in terms of their: (1) theoretical/ideological bases; (2) strategies for institutionalizing gender concerns in teaching/training/research; (3) mix of methodological approaches used; (4) composition of the participant group and the impact of training on participants; and (5) problem areas and future directions.

DEVELOPMENT TRAINING PROGRAMS

If one could conceptualize these training experiences as falling on a continuum from the more theoretical/formal/academic to the more practical/nonformal/action-oriented, the IDS program at Sussex, "Women, Men, and Development," would fall at the theoretical end, followed by the DPU program in London, "Planning with Women for Urban Development." At the other end of the continuum are WAND and the SNDT Women's University. The two end approaches sought to break new ground: one at a theoretical level; the other in evolving participatory development processes at the field level. The ESAMI program in Tanzania would fall in the middle, with a focus on both building analytic capacities and imparting management programs that are sensitive to women's needs.

IDS at the University of Sussex is a research, teaching, and consultancy center that offers a graduate program in development studies as well as a package of short courses in specialized fields for development personnel from the Third World and from British agencies concerned with international development work. The thirteen-week course, Women, Men, and Development, is offered once a year as part of the institute's program of short courses. Participants are drawn from the intermediary levels of government planning and programming, academicians, personnel from trade union and women's organizations, and grassroots activists. The course aims to enhance participants' abilities to evaluate policy; prepare policy briefs; conduct policy-oriented research that can promote social recognition and support for women's contribution and needs; and develop strategies and organizational mechanisms that will facilitate the adoption and implementation of policy recommendations. From its first offering in 1984, both overall enrollment and the proportion of male participants have increased.

The Development Planning Unit within the Bartlett School of Architecture and Planning of University College, London, specializes in teaching, training, and research on urban and regional development in developing countries. DPU, too, offers a series of intensive short courses, each twelve weeks in length, for senior and midcareer professionals in the field of urban development planning. The course Planning with Women for Urban Development, introduced as a DPU short course in 1984, focuses on an analysis of development and urbanization trends in the Third World in light of the needs of women and low-income households; translation of household needs into policy and program formulation in employment, housing, and basic services; and the organization of interventions that maximize and support women's active participation.

ESAMI in Tanzania is a management development institute mandated by its sixteen-member countries to strengthen national capabilities for the efficient management of economic development. The six-week course, Women, Management, and Development Planning, instituted on an annual basis at ESAMI in 1981, introduces planners, project managers, and extension personnel from both government agencies and nongovernmental organizations (NGOs), to women's critical contributions in the achievement of national development goals, and to methods of increasing women's productivity and access to development resources and benefits. The building of male and female participants' project management and evaluation skills and training of women managers in nontraditional fields such as financial management, marketing, and leadership are emphasized.

WAND was set up in 1977 with international donor assistance at the University of the West Indies, Barbados, to sensitize policy makers and staff of development projects in the Caribbean region to gender issues and to provide technical assistance, including training, directly to women and development projects. Drawing on its field experiences in facilitating participatory approaches for community development, WAND integrates both a recognition of women's work and their need for training that addresses their priorities into ongoing courses at the university for agricultural extension agents, community development personnel, and social workers. WAND's links to the Caribbean regional governmental secretariat, CARICOM, enables it to work closely with planners on policy and program design issues.

The Research Center on Women's Studies at SNDT University in Bombay has experimented with a community-based training model in which local government officials are alerted to women's needs within a specific project context. At the same time , the center intervenes to enable the training of community women in income-generating and organizational management skills. The center has also assisted the evaluation and documentation activities of nongovernmental groups that work with poor women. Its hands-on approach not only facilitates grassroots work but also adds valuable perspectives to the ongoing research, teaching, and extension program of the university.

These training programs vary in content and coverage but all have a common goal: sensitizing development agents to women's diverse roles and equipping them with the tools necessary to support women's critical contributions to their families and society. All agree on the importance of changing women's as well as men's perspectives and the difficulties of doing this. All try to enable women to think and act differently. All emphasize the use of case studies and pragmatic evaluation material to expose gender biases and/or gender invisibility in existing planning and programming techniques. Three of the programs are predominantly formal and academic in nature—those of IDS, DPU, and ESAMI. They challenge established development theories; emphasize the use of analytical techniques that are sensitive to both women's and men's roles and interests; and strengthen participants' planning and management skills. The other two, the WAND and SNDT efforts, focus on deriving lessons from field experiments to improve program planning and implementation in addressing women's needs.

IDEOLOGICAL APPROACHES

The ideological approach taken by different training programs varies. There are perceived differences between the so-called "women in development (WID)" approach and the "gender" approach in research, teaching/ training, policy, and program development. Critics of the former contend that the WID approach views women as a homogeneous group in isolation from men; emphasizes support services for women's traditional roles as housewives and mothers over their productive roles in the economy; and operates through the vehicle of women-specific rather than "integrated" projects. It is argued that this approach further marginalizes women economically, politically, and socially. Proponents of the gender approach have emphasized analysis of the experience of women in comparison to that of men within and across classes in society (including relations between the sexes). The gender approach utilizes productivity arguments to promote recognition and support for women's roles in socioeconomic development, particularly in large-scale, mainstream programs in such sectors as irrigation, integrated rural development, and forestry. In reality, the distinction between the two approaches is less clear as one approach adopts elements of the other when necessary and relevant. The language used in one institutional or country context often has connotations not seen as applicable in another. The use of the neutral term "gender" rather than "women" is also a strategic choice aimed at attracting a male readership. In a recent development, both approaches appear to converge in the priority accorded to strengthening women's organizations for collective action, advocacy, and power.

Maxine Molyneux[1] has provided yet another vocabulary for dealing with the differences between categories of women's interests that some training programs have adopted. Molyneux draws a distinction between "practical" and "strategic gender interests." The former derive from the traditional sexual division of labor and relate to women's immediate needs, such as water, income, shelter, child care, and appropriate technologies for household management. The latter, on the other hand, derive from the articulation of alternative structures and ideologies to existing ones that perpetuate the subordination of women. "Strategic gender interests" include political equality and abolition of the prevailing sexual division of labor and institutionalized forms of discrimination. Training programs have problems in approaching the "practical/strategic" dichotomy. While women drawing on their personal experience can easily articulate their "practical interests," it is much more difficult to identify long-term "strategic interests" that are not overly general. It would be incorrect to assume that all women have a clear analytical understanding of the structures that shape the parameters of their life options. Moreover, for many women differences in options delineated by class are more important than differences they face as women across classes.

An exclusive focus on short-term needs can have negative consequences for women in the long run—handicrafts promotion as an income-generating strategy is an example that attests to this. While it has provided some income to women, poor planning and management in this marginalized, low-growth but labor-intensive sector of the economy has severely constrained its long-term viability. As regards "strategic interests"—even if it were possible to identify them in relation to specific cultures—the challenge of formulating strategies including training approaches, to achieve articulated objectives remains daunting.

Training programs that have as a philosophical basis a strong commitment to meeting women's strategic interests (however defined) face a curious dilemma: should training be built into existing precepts and structures, which are disadvantageous to women in the long term, or should theory and examples of practice, which can be used to transform discriminatory structures, be integrated into training programs? Does working within a system, knowing full well that it is discriminatory toward women, constitute a strategic compromise or can it only lead to negative results?

INTEGRATION STRATEGIES

The patterns of institutionalization of training programs are varied. Some programs are independent, but isolated within existing structures; others are integrated within the existing system as one of a set of courses on a specialized field. Often sessions focusing on women are inserted into training programs in development planning and management. Rarely is attention to gender issues integrated throughout the course content in all major programs of development training institutions.

Integration relates both to structure and concepts. Training programs are faced with hard choices: whether to accept existing theoretical frameworks and find ways to introduce information on women's roles and needs; or to build a body of knowledge and strategies for change that is in isolation from the common wisdom; and/or to attempt a transformation of existing frameworks through a process of breaking down and rebuilding the base of knowledge. Do you simply add the idea that the world is round to the idea that the world is flat, or do you go back and rethink the whole matter?[2]

The experience of the few, relatively recent, institution-based efforts following the latter course of action has revealed many problems. The difficulty of restructuring social-science paradigms by introducing gender into the analysis of social change, and the opposition to "feminist" terminology (such as "the subordination of women" or "patriarchy") by both academicians and practitioners is evident. Academic establishments have been the hardest to change, yet they play a critical role through theory building and training in eliminating gender biases in policy and program development. In part, the opposition from the academic community is a reaction to the uncomfortable questions and challenges posed by feminism to long-standing ideas and entrenched values such as the definition of "work," the low value placed on women's work, and the existence of male prerogative in the public/political domain. In part, the reluctance to engage seriously with the issue of gender results from the perception that this new field of inquiry lacks rigorous academic credentials. Expectations placed on a minority field, such as the requirement of an all-embracing theoretical framework in spite of the diverse historical and cultural realities feminism seeks to address, often far exceed those which established disciplines could adequately satisfy. Nevertheless, failure to meet those expectations, irrespective of their applicability, makes it easy to dismiss the field as unworthy of serious consideration.

The challenge of feminism is fundamentally political in nature just as planning, while highly procedural, is a political act. As such, it calls for broad strategies of building alliances with progressive groups, paying attention to the language of communication and the organization of grassroots women for sustained collective action, and the expression of political will. Emphasizing links with antipoverty policies is strategically valuable because it increases the ranks of allies, enhances the possibility of transforming practical gender interests to strategic ones, and diffuses resistance.

TARGET AUDIENCES

Building alliances with a broad range of development personnel and training them to effectively intervene on behalf of women requires that training programs strategically analyze their target audiences—differentiate them and determine how to reach them. There is considerable debate over both these issues. Broadly, we can differentiate four types of audiences: (1) policy makers in governments, NGOs, and international agencies who must be sensitized on gender issues; (2) government and NGO program personnel in Third World countries who are working on issues of implementation; (3) researchers worldwide who can act as links between grassroots women, women's organizations, and government planners; and (4) Third World women's organizations who may know how to intervene in the planning process.

When talking to top-level planners, a focus on issues of national consequence such as agriculture and food production, urban basic services, or irrigation and water management is essential. Within these sectors, presenting galvanizing statistics on women's roles and comparing men and women in terms of labor allocation, management input, and resource access, and showing how variations in these affect the achievement of the stated objectives of development schemes, have proved successful strategies.

Yet, this approach of focusing at the highest levels of planning will not be effective everywhere. In India for example, where policy formulation has been achieved with relative ease, implementation through the lower echelons of bureaucracy present almost insurmountable problems. In many Latin American countries, one could argue that the impact of the debt crisis considerably weakened the credibility and outreach of the policy and planning apparatus and, therefore, change efforts should be focused on community development workers and midlevel technical personnel who continue to make decisions that directly affect women's lives. All such change efforts however, must be knowledgeable about the real resource constraints (financial, manpower, facilities) of development administrations in Third World countries. These constraints limit governments' abilities to deliver services to all disadvantaged groups, not only poor women.

SUPPORTING GRASSROOTS EFFORTS

While change efforts must continue to rely on the labor intensive, long-term and somewhat unreliable payoff work of education and training, the political sophistication of the women's movement is articulating a complementary strategy—conciousness-raising among grassroots women and their organization for collective action. This creation of an "effective demand" is an essential element for accessing development resources and monitoring local development programs. Even where women themselves have successfully organized, they still need assistance in dealing with unfamiliar institutions outside the community and in protecting their gains from backlash. The role of institutions and organizations that act as links between the government and grassroots women was highlighted in the WAND and SNDT experiences. In both cases, the status of an academic institution proved to be a powerful resource in emphasizing the need for rethinking assumptions about women's current and potential roles and in overcoming initial hostility from men in the community.

Exploiting their formal standing and mass base, women's organizations and other NGOs can take on multiple roles, including advocating for policy and program changes, involving government functionaries in a dialogue with poor women, raising women's consciousness, conducting research for the design of action programs, as well as providing direct services such as loans, service referral, and information and technical assistance for obtaining productive resources. For such mediating organizations to play effective roles in the change process, they need to retain their independence from government and to build their management capacity and political influence so that they can effectively work with and train both government personnel and grassroots women. The WAND experience suggests that working groups linking researchers, NGOs, planners and community women make for powerful combinations. Recognizing that grassroots, work-based, and women's organizations are potential areas where women and men working for gender equality can identify their needs and mobilize to meet them, the IDS, DPU, and ESAMI programs include the training of members of such organizations in needed research, management, and advocacy skills.

PRACTICAL CONSTRAINTS

There are a number of practical problems common to the five training programs. These relate to the bounded nature of the training experience, the need for appropriate training materials, financial resources, and resource constraints in relation to the recruitment of course participants. Most training courses are managed by a sole coordinator or director who is not yet in secure standing in her/his institution. To proceed with the work of transforming theoretical frameworks and developing strategies to deal with practical and strategic gender interests, they must first survive in their institutions. But survival is contingent upon conforming with rather than challenging academic and institutional norms. Trainers are placed in the difficult position of having to do both.

The course director's mission of sensitizing development planners and practitioners to issues of gender must be carried out within a limited time frame. After the training course, the participants have little contact with the trainers as they go back into environments that are often resistant to the issues raised and tools taught in the courses. Given the inclination to do so, some participants no doubt have the leeway to initiate changes in standard operating procedures. However, in many cases the hostile working environments prevent the application of new ideas about women's roles and gender. This suggests the need for follow-up activities after the training course has ended, such as network building among participants, trainers, and resource groups in their respective countries. For the same reasons, efforts to sensitize senior and junior colleagues in the participants' organization, perhaps using organizational development (OD) techniques to facilitate a team approach to problem solving and planned interventions, can also be considered.

Trainers find that existing materials on gender differences in development from both a policy and planning perspective are sparse and often inadequate. They suggest that much of the "women and development" and "women's studies" literature is not applicable to Third World planning contexts, while gender-sensitive planning techniques are still unsophisticated and limited. Consequently, the development of resource materials is a critical area for future work.

Further, recognizing the broad range of current and potential trainers, including intermediary organizations, and the variety of audiences to be reached, innovative methods of communication need to be designed. Unconscious biases about women's roles that inhibit the absorption of information also need to be revealed. Case studies are needed that document how women's groups have expanded their base. Also, in order to destroy myths about women's secondary roles and passivity, studies that examine women's organized struggles would be useful. Finally, there is a need for materials that analyze the gender-differentiated impact, both positive and negative, of particular policies and programs. Based on such analyses, alternative strategies, including those that can counter potential resistance to interventions in favor of women, must be delineated.

Probably the most difficult and universal problem that training courses experience is financial. Training at the policy level that deals with women's roles in development is not considered important by the majority of training institutions. Consequently, resources allocated to training of this sort are very limited. Also, even when training programs are available, senior male policy makers dismiss women in development as an area only of women's interest and therefore junior-level women are sent. These women, moreover, usually have little independent authority and resources with which to initiate innovation. At the same time, capable men in key positions may disdain involvement, viewing such programs as being for workers of a lower professional status. Gender biases in policy making and program design thus remain largely unchanged.

PROMISING BEGINNINGS

Battling the forces that seek to diminish their intellectual integrity and practical relevance has been a difficult, though common experience for programs that train policy makers and program personnel on gender issues. Given the odds, significant strides have been made. It is still premature to gauge their programmatic impact on the teaching, research, and consulting carried out by their home institutions, on course participants, and ultimately on the shape of development policies and projects. With the exception of the WAND program, all are fewer than ten years old. It is clear, however, that the implementation process itself has generated valuable insights on the nature and forms of resistance to gender issues and on ways to overcome them; on how to survive within mainstream institutions; and on the opportunities for and constraints on the diffusion of new perspectives. Perhaps, as with the women's movement itself, the most encouraging indicators for the future of these training endeavors are the clarity of vision, acceptance of divergence, and solidarity of action that are emerging from the intense debates and relentless questioning that lie at the core of these initiatives.

NOTES

1. Maxine Molyneux, "Mobilization without Emancipation? Women's Interests, State, and Revolution in Nicaragua," *Feminist Studies*, 1985. Quoted in Caroline Moser, "Women's needs in the Urban System: Training Strategies in Gender Aware Planning," in M. Schmink, J. Bruce, and M. Kohn, (eds.) *Learning about Women and Urban Services in Latin America and the Carribean: A Report on the Women, Low-Income Households and Urban Services Project of the Population Council* (New York: The Population Council, 1986), pp. 40–61.

2. Elizabeth Minnich quoted in Peggy McIntosh, "Women's Studies as a Strategy for Educational Change," prepared for Women's Studies International Panel A, NGO Forum, Nairobi, July 11, 1985.

V

RESEARCH ON WOMEN: NEW MODELS AND PRIORITIES

RESEARCH ON WOMEN IN LATIN AMERICA

Gloria Bonder

The emergence and early development (until the midseventies) of research on women in Latin American countries continued along similar lines across the continent. First, research began as a result of individual initiatives taken by women in various centers of social research, private and governmental. Such research concentrated on the development and composition of the labor force, and was strongly influenced by theoretical perspectives on social and economic development (particularly dependency theory) dominant in the region at the time. Moreover, these early researchers ignored and/or did not wish to be identified with feminist currents.

As Marysa Navarro[1] pointed out in 1979, "The main objective of most Latin American social scientists working on women was to analyze Latin America's social formation, to understand how the capitalist mode of production in its dependent form operates. They did not view women as a valid category of analysis but as a focus that can be used profitably in so far as it increases knowledge of the social formation. For them, women cannot be studied in isolation from socio-economic conditions ... women must be studied ... in each Latin American country, in a urban or rural environment, in their class, and especially ... their family [context]."[2]

These first research projects encouraged persistent criticism of the concepts of occupation, formal and informal labor market participation, and unemployment and underemployment on the basis of the data compiled from research on women. The majority of research projects on women

A version of this essay appeared in *Canadian Women's Studies/les cahiers de la femme* 7, nos. 1–2 (1986): 148–51.

during this period concentrated on well-established social science research areas in Latin America: labor, population, and development. Researchers tended to focus on women in poverty, and social inequalities between the sexes were viewed as a product of the sociopolitical system. During these first years, feminist theoretical approaches to gender inequalities, exercised no influence. However, from the midseventies on, another movement began to develop in research on women in Latin America, already considerably influenced by feminist ideas.

The organization of the first United Nations Conference on Women held in Mexico City in 1975, the growth and expansion of the feminist movement in Latin America, and the gradual diffusion of North American and European feminist theory into the region, contributed to sensitizing women researchers about different research fields, theoretical assumptions, the selection of research issues, and methodological approaches. Concepts such as the sexual division of labor, public and private domains, the dynamic of social production and reproduction, the reconceptualization of housework, feminist theories of gender, and the emphasis on women's everyday experiences as revealing of women's condition, spurred research in new directions. Research on women expanded both within academic institutions and among groups of women self-defined as feminists who had little or no academic background.

The most significant consequences for research can be summarized in the following manner:

1. There was a new awareness about the sexist character of the prevailing theories in each discipline; consequently, researchers increasingly felt the need to submit the theoretical assumptions that have distorted or omitted women to critical review and correction.

2. Researchers were enjoined to contribute to consciousness-raising and the transformation of women's situation.

3. The criteria of objectivity and neutrality for the evaluation of traditional theoretical and methodological approaches were questioned.

4. New forms of methodological approaches were developed—such as participatory research and action research.

5. The debate about the relationship between gender and class was deepened.

6. Researchers began to consider areas previously ignored, including "private" issues such as sexuality, motherhood, and everyday life experiences.

7. The highly "academic" characteristics of research on women began to be questioned.

One of the important consequences of the feminist movement among researchers in Latin America is a boom of new research methodologies, which began in the early eighties. The proliferation of women's centers committed to diverse programs, the participation of more women in the development of women's studies, and the criticism of traditional research paradigms and methods helped to broaden the conceptual boundaries of what is generally understood as social science research. Research on women now encompasses an extensive diversity of projects: action programs, which include a research component, participatory research, as well as essays, theses, and research projects that follow the theoretical and methodological conventions quite closely. It is mostly within the areas of action research and participatory research that the development of new methodologies can be observed, especially with regard to data gathering and analysis.

In general, participatory research methodologies are techniques that enable personal interaction between researchers and the women researched, including the active participation of the latter in different steps of the research process, as well as the use of diverse means of consciousness-raising, training, and/or organization of women participating in the project.

Commonly used techniques include:

1. Workshops or group discussions exploring and analyzing women's views and problems, with the researcher in the role of discussion facilitator.
2. Life histories, developed through close and frequent interaction, which enable researchers to capture women's past and present experiences in areas they want to explore.
3. Women's testimonials, which reflect the particularities and complexities of women's experience in different situations.
4. Games, dramatizations, and role playing, which enable the expression of women's personal experience and opinions about some aspects of their reality.
5. Audiovisual stimuli, which encourage women to articulate their true feelings.

In sum, through the use of innovative and creative methods many researchers aim to capture the most visible aspects of women's social experience and their ways of representing reality. In these new methodologies we can see the influence of popular education techniques used in Latin America and the qualitative methodologies used in anthropological studies, as well as the influence of psychological and psychoanalytical techniques and perspectives to approach women's subjectivity and reality.

But much of the exploratory research that has utilized qualitative methodologies also has its drawbacks. It is often characterized by short timeframes and in most cases has lacked followup and evaluation. Second, because most of these projects have been carried out by novice researchers who had no training and experience in other methodologies, these newcomers invented their simple research tools. Thus, not only did criticism of traditional methodologies become common, but also the idea took hold that quantitative methodologies were "difficult" and participatory ones were "easier." In fact, to yield good results, "qualitative" methodologies require highly complex procedures of data gathering and especially of data analysis.

It is well known that this complexity increases if the objectives of research include training or organizing participating women. We have the impression that many young researchers in Latin America who have gone through this "initiation rite" of using qualitative research with women may have been, in some way, negatively affected by the difficulties they have had to face during the process. Our exchange with women's studies centers carrying out this kind of research in Latin America has confirmed that this is a common concern. We believe that the development and deepening of this new methodological perspective within research on women is now facing a critical period. In our opinion, it represents a unique opportunity for theoretical development in women's studies as well as for deepening the relationship between feminist theories and practice. And in this sense, one of our current priorities is to carefully evaluate what has been done in Latin America using this new methodological perspective.

It is well known that the research agendas and program priorities related to women in the region are closely linked to the financing policies of national and international organizations that work in this field. Often, these agencies delineate their funding policies without the advice or participation of Latin American researchers, who are better acquainted with the needs and priorities of their region. To the extent that this donor-initiated agenda operates, research on women in Latin America follows an erratic development in terms of issues and perspectives rather than a systematic accumulation of knowledge and building of individual and institutional research capacities. In the long term, this inhibits our ability to formulate policies for the transformation of women's condition in society.

Participatory research with women, as it has been practiced in Latin America during the last several years, raises important questions for researchers: Are we building new methodological criteria with new concepts of validity, reliability, objectivity, and generalization? Who are the beneficiaries of research on women? What do we understand from participation? Who participates? How do they participate and for what reason(s)? How different from traditional practice are the power relations between researchers and researched? How closely linked are the proposed objectives of such research and the final achievement? In sum, what is the contribution of such research to knowledge of women's condition in Latin American society? A regional evaluation of participatory research is necessary if we are to overcome the feeling that we are always starting from zero, and especially if we want to concentrate our energies on the construction of new scientific paradigms for the comprehension of women's condition.

At the "Workshop of Research on Women," carried out at the Second

Latin American and Caribbean Feminist Meeting in Lima in 1983, two important recommendations were developed:

1. It was considered essential that the research agenda in Latin America be the result of joint action between feminist researchers and activists so that common objectives may be achieved. To this end, the need for building new channels for interchange between the feminist movement and the centers that carry out research was stressed.

2. Research on women must also lead to the reformulation of government policies and should be widely shared among scholars and activists.

But it is clear that some basic obstacles remain to be overcome. The bulk of the research on women in Latin America developed in contexts marginal to mainstream academia and governmental institutions. This limits access to economic resources, the systematic training of researchers on women's studies, and the diffusion of research results. In recent years however, we have seen a countervailing trend: the incorporation of women's studies within universities and academic centers, in particular in Argentina, Mexico, and Brazil.

It is also important that women interested in women's studies be trained in research methodologies and techniques. It is evident that small institutions and women's centers cannot mount the needed programs in research methods that might also bring more women into women's studies. For this reason, one of the priorities established at the "Seminar on Programs for Women's Studies in Latin America and the Caribbean," held at the Colegio de Mexico in June 1985, was the promotion, reenforcement, and creation of regional courses for the training of researchers and specialists in women's studies.It was felt that scholarship programs, university summer courses, and greater exchange among women's studies researchers in Latin America as well as with those in developed countries could facilitate training.

In addition, researchers face the problem of inadequate access to available documentation in the field and/or unavailability of Spanish translations of foreign works. This is an obstacle for training programs in women's studies theory and methodology. One goal is to have a Latin American journal on women's studies to spread information about research on women carried out in the region. Another goal is to establish a reliable documentation center to collect data on women from all countries.

The pursuit of these long-term goals, however, is affected by political and socioeconomic realities. Many Latin American countries went through most of the Women's Decade under dictatorships. If the repressive condition in these countries affected the development of social research in general, it is easy to imagine to what extent it has discouraged research on women's situation. That even under those conditions women researchers have sharpened their wits and have concentrated their efforts to understand women's situation in their own countries is a very encouraging sign.

Also, the critical economic situation that affects all Latin American countries will undoubtedly be reflected in the already poor state budgets relegated to research. Shrinking research budgets will affect most those less-recognized research issues. Thus, we now face a new challenge, and we believe the best response is to strengthen the cooperative bonds among researchers and institutions in each country and in the region as a whole.

In the current context, it is difficult to suggest priorities for research on women in Latin America. However, there are some important points to consider:

1. Research that provides basic, updated information about women's situation in each country is necessary. Research agendas must be informed by basic statistical data on women's situation in areas such as education, health, the labor market, and legislation. Likewise, such information will enable the elaboration of policies sensitive to the situation of the majority of women.

2. It is necessary to carry out research on the effects of the economic crisis upon women's living conditions while considering different social sectors and diverse areas: participation in the labor market, family structure, sexual roles, access to the educational system, health, women's organizations, and so on.

3. It is necessary to explore the effect of military dictatorships on women's lives, as well as to investigate changes brought about through democratization processes.

4. It is essential that research on different issues incorporate simultaneous attention to gender, class, and race.

5. Studies carried out on the everyday experience of women from different social levels in different historical periods are also important.

6. It is necessary to encourage multidisciplinary and interdisciplinary research, tolerating the cost in time, money, and effort that this kind of research demands so as to come up with useful results.

7. It is necessary to review completed action-research and participatory-research projects. Even though many of these projects have not developed formal research methods, they contain important and valuable data.

8. It is important to develop research projects focused on gender relations in the context of socioeconomic change.

Several years after the end of the Women's Decade, we find research on women in Latin America still in a period of legitimization. We have corroborating evidence on discrimination against women in all areas of social life. Starting from these certainties, we must advance towards the formulation of new questions to enrich our comprehension of women's situation in Latin America and find ways to improve it.

NOTES

1. Marysa Novarro, "Research on Latin American Women," *Signs* 5, no. 1 (Autumn 1979).
   2. Op. cit.

Research on Women in Southeast Asia: Current and Future Directions

Wazir-jahan Karim

In the recent past, institutions of higher learning in Southeast Asia have been developing women's studies programs for research while government and nongovernment agencies have begun to realize the importance of interweaving research on women with processes of development, policy formulation, and action. These developments are the result of a continuing effort to increase awareness and knowledge of women's valuable contributions to the political and socioeconomic development of Southeast Asian societies. This essay surveys past and present research on women in five countries in Southeast Asia and identifies key development issues for future research and policy.

SURVEY OF RESEARCH ON WOMEN

INDONESIA

In Indonesia, research on women and the family is carried out by various government and nongovernment organizations and institutes within and outside universities. One government organization, the Badan Penghubung Organisasi Wanita Jakarta Raya, established in 1954 in Jakarta, houses the Bureau of Consultation for Family Affairs and the Commission on the Status of Women (established 1986) and organizes educational, literacy, and welfare activities and services. It also coordinates the proposals and recommendations of its member organizations on women's issues and submits policy recommendations to the government.

Another government body, the National Institute of Economic and Social Research (LEKNAS), based in Jakarta, undertakes activities relating to research, training, documentation, conference organization, and publication. Its four member research units, the Economic Research Unit, the Social Research Unit, the Population Studies Centre, and the Political Development Unit, sponsor interdisciplinary research in the social sciences. Research relating to women covers rural development, population mobility, fertility, and family planning. The Population Studies Centre (1973) based in Gadjah Mada University in Yogjakarta, probably the most well established body in the country, conducts local and international research on women, migration, and fertility. This research complements that undertaken by another government body, the Lembaga Demografi (1973) at the Fakultas Ekonomi Universitas Syiah Kuala Darussalam, at Acheh, and a nongovernment organization, the Research and Evaluation Bureau (1957), for the Indonesian Planned Parenthood Association at Jakarta.

Research on women in the labor force is conducted by the Research and Development Centre for Manpower (1976) at the Ministry of Manpower in Jakarta. Other organizations concerned with women's labor in both the rural and urban sectors are the Yayasan Sri Kandi at Jakarta and the Rural Women Development Project (1983) at Berastagi, Sumatra Utara. The Yayasan Ilmu-Ilmu Sosial (YIIS), established in 1976, promotes scholarly research on women at the Pusat Latihan Penelitihan Ilmu-Ilmu Sosial (PLPIIS) and sponsors seminars, expert meetings, and publications on women's studies.

Despite the concerted efforts of the government to promote research on women in relevant areas of social and economic policy and to integrate social research with the developmental processes of the country, it appears that women's studies is still not fully established as an independent, interdisciplinary field in universities and other institutions of higher learning. Policies and plans of action are not generated from scholarly research interest in women's studies but rather the other way around: research is utilized to advance certain social and economic policies already formulated by the government. In this context, it might be difficult to envisage a situation when teaching/learning and research processes are able to develop critical or analytical thinking on women's issues or processes of consciousness-raising which could form the base to a women's movement or field of social action that is constructive and productive to policy and change.

THAILAND

Following Thailand's participation in the World Conference that launched the United Nations Decade for Women in 1975, the Royal Thai Government approved the establishment of a state women's organization to undertake the tasks of policy and planning for the promotion of Thai women's roles and status. After a series of events that brought about gradual development of the organization, the National Commission on Women's Affairs was set up as a permanent body in 1989 with its secretariat attached to the Office of the Prime Minister. The commission is chaired by the prime minister; the vice-chair is Minister Suptra Masdit, Thailand's first minister for women's affairs. Commission members include the heads of specialized government agencies, representatives of nongovernmental women's organizations, and individual experts.

The Commission appointed the following eight national committees to carry out specific tasks of research, formulating policy and program recommendations, and monitoring and evaluation: the Perspective Plan and Policy for Women's Development; Laws and Regulations; Education, Employment, and Culture; Health and the Environment; Social and Political Participation; Elimination of Involuntary Prostitution; International Cooperation; and the Development of a Women's Information System. Included in the commission's mandate are: (1) monitoring progress of women-related programs and activities during the Sixth National Economic and Social Development Plan period; (2) revising the Long-Term Women's Development Plan (1982–2001); and (3) formulating a master plan for women's development to be included in the Seventh Plan.

In 1981, Chulalongkorn University established the Women's Studies Program within the University's Social Research Institute. Initially, the program was meant to serve as an informal "focal point where activities concerning women are initiated and promoted" (Pongsapich, 1982:6). It has developed into an academic program that carries out research on women in Thailand, particularly on the impact of socioeconomic changes on women's status and on their responses. Research projects underway or completed include work on the urban informal sector (specifically on street vending), mobile day care centers at construction sites in Bangkok, rural women and agricultural change, rural industry, women with small rubber holdings in Southeast Asia, women in slums, and the sex trade in Thailand.

Under the leadership of Rector Nongyao, and despite the lack of full approval for a women's studies institute from the University Bureau, Thammasat University set up with its own funds a women's studies project in 1986. In its early phase, the project organized meetings and seminars on various topics and from 1989 onward has been engaged in planning broad program directions and concrete program activities such as curriculum development. In addition, beginning in August 1986, Thammasat took on the joint coordination, along with York University in Toronto, Canada, of an institutional linkage program in women's studies—the Women in Development Consortium in Thailand (WIDCIT). The program, which will continue until March 1991, links York University with a consortium of Thai universities—Thammasat and Chulalongkorn in Bangkok, and Khon Kaen University in northeastern Thailand. WIDCIT aims to support and encourage women's studies and women in development (WID) efforts in Thailand through sharing and cooperation among academic institutions, government institutions, and nongovernmental organizations committed to understanding and improving conditions for women in Thailand. WIDCIT activities include awarding scholarships (one for each university) for graduate work at York University in the student's discipline combined with women's studies; short-term faculty exchanges between York University and the Thai universities; the development of curricula in women's studies; the publication of working papers on gender issues; conferences to be held in Thailand and Canada to sum up experience gained in the program; and the launching of experimental, participatory training programs for small groups of urban and rural women in Thailand. (For more detailed information on WIDCIT, see the "Programs" section of this volume.)

Further, institutes such as the National Institute of Development Administration at Bangkok (1966) and the Institute for Population and Social Research at Mahidol University in Nakornpathom (1966) conduct interdisciplinary research, and a significant portion of their research projects—on work conditions, workers' welfare, migration and resettlement, fertility, labor force participation, policy formulation, and other topics—pertain to women.

Nongovernment organizations such as the Planned Parenthood Association of Thailand (1970), the Thai Association of University Women (1927), and the Women Lawyers Association of Thailand (1974) promote both research on and training for women, particularly in the fields of education and legal literacy. Friends of Women, a nongovernment organization set up at the end of 1980, initially brought interested academics together for joint research projects such as a bibliography of research on women, and other studies of demographic issues, labor, health, abortion, and social problems that surface in slums and among squatters. Now the organization concentrates on broadening the public's awareness of sexual crimes and harassment of women, and coordinates efforts to improve the treatment of women. Toward this end, the organization's research and information dissemination efforts focus on such activities as the publication of handbooks on laws regarding women, and publication of articles on issues concerning women in local newspapers and magazines. Similarly, the Foundation for Women focuses on helping women in distress, providing disadvantaged women with nonformal education, promoting the rights of women, and promoting as well as conducting studies related to women. The foundation's research projects concentrate on highlighting problems for women's advancement in a variety of sectors.

Women's studies as a subdiscipline and field of inquiry appears to be at an early stage of development in Thailand, but the past few years have seen many changes and rapid progress. Closer linkages among government institutions, academic institutes, and nongovernment organizations could foster more cooperation and commitment to the formalization of women's studies in universities. For this to emerge, academics who are committed, directly and indirectly, to teaching and research about women will have to play a stronger leadership role.

In the Philippines, social science research on women appears to have developed further than in other Southeast Asian countries, judging from the number of books, monographs, articles, and bibliographies on the subject published there (Feliciano, 1982:1; and Anganglo et al., 1980). Research began as early as 1910–1920, when studies dealt with sociological, political-legal, and historical accounts of women, particularly their voting rights, contributions in scientific professions, and cultural differences. In the twenties, research focused on sociological issues, such as changes in family structures and sociopsychological aspects of gender relations. The controversy of the suffrage movement, in relation to women's socioeconomic, political, and educational status, was a popular item of debate in the thirties (Feliciano, 1982:2). According to Feliciano, the number of articles on Philippine women in the fifties "increased by leaps and bounds, to 214." Women's rights, including suffrage, and women's role in industrial work and other occupations were major areas of concern.

In the sixties, both academics and journalists ventured into every conceivable subject of interest, including women's multiple roles, rights in marriage, attitudes towards sociopolitical and economic changes, and responses to modernization. Multiple social science research methods were used, including historical analysis and historiography, case studies, sample surveys, and secondary documentation. This trend of research continued in the seventies, augmented by a number of studies of media behavior, on topics such as the use and misuse of women by the media, and dissemination of information by gender. Thus by the eighties the study of women was widely known to academics, particularly social scientists, social psychologists, journalists, and communication experts. However, Feliciano (1982:3) points out a number of academic-related problems pertaining to social science research on women:

1. lack of social scientists adequately trained in methodology, particularly quantitative research;
2. lack of appreciation, concern, and commitment to problem-oriented research and action or policy research;
3. low utilization of research findings by government and nongovernment personnel, probably because of inaccessibility, poor understanding of academic concepts and jargon, and lack of clarity on the relevance of findings to policy development and social change;
4. imbalance in focus on studies undertaken, e.g., overemphasis on socioeconomic studies and insufficient psychological research on women; and
5. lack of cooperation, coordination, and communication among public

and private universities, resulting in duplication of effort and wasting of resources.

The problems elucidated here pertaining to research on women in the early eighties in the Philippines were not reflected in other Southeast Asian countries mainly because social science research on women had not yet reached the same stage of advancement. Hence, in the Philippines, the spirit of constructive criticism and evaluation of development, policy, and change could not emerge successfully. Social science research on women was still conducted in a fragmented manner and lacked the comparative perspective necessary to develop it further in both conceptual and theoretical items.

With the profusion of research, a coordinating institution was needed to integrate research activities and direct research policy. The Philippine Social Science Council (PSSC), was established in December 1968 to encourage interdisciplinary, applied research in the social sciences, including women's studies, and to orient social scientists toward development processes and problems. At least a third of the fifteen member executive board is female and a large number of the beneficiaries of the council's varied programs are women.

There was also a need to publicize the credibility and importance of social science research on women. In January 1975, the National Commission on the Role of Filipino Women, a group of twenty-six social scientists, nineteen of whom were women, was formed. This commission is an advisory body that recommends to the government ways to achieve full equality in all fields and ensures that suitable programs for women's development are monitored effectively by various institutions and agencies.

The efforts of government agencies, the PSSC, and the Commission on Women to integrate women's programs with research and training activities prompted several research institutes and centers to expand their research on women. The Asian Labor Education Center (1954) at the University of Philippines in Quezon City undertakes research studies on industrial relations that include, for example, research on workers in manufacturing establishments in Metro Manila (in which the employees are predominantly women) and on the education and information needs of Davao workers and their families. The De La Salle University Research Center (1979) has conducted women-related research projects such as "The Role of Upland Women," while the Department of Psychology at Ateneo de Manila University maintains an extensive collection of research materials on women's rights, social roles, occupational choices, and other topics. The Institute of Philippine Culture at Ateneo de Manila University has also contributed significant studies on women in rice cultivation and other areas of economic activity. Research on women is also conducted at the Institute of Social Work and Community Development (1967) at the University of the Philippines.

The Kalayaan (Katipunan ng Kababaihan Para sa Kalayaan) is a nongovernmental institute that attempts to advance research on women as well as develop women's studies programs. Its primary research areas include feminist theory, women's liberation movements in the Third World, Philippine women and culture, health, and the economy. Most of its research findings are published in its periodical, *BAI*. The Philippine Women's University (1919) maintains community education and family life education programs with a multidisciplinary approach to research on women. Other universities, such as Notre Dame University at Catalroto City, conduct health and fertility surveys through the Socio-Economic Research Centre (1972) and the Research Institute for Mindana Culture (1957) at Xavier University, Cagayan de Oro City. Finally, the Institute of Philippines Culture at the Ateneo de Manila University has expanded its research programs on women; its focus is on local problems of education and development.

These concerted efforts to improve women's participation in education and development are reflected in the significant advances of women in the social sciences: in 1982–83 the University of the Philippines registered a phenomenal female enrollment of 62 percent. Women are mainly registered in economics and communication; men form the majority in the sciences and applied sciences. In the Philippines, the advancement of women in academia is more significant than in any other Southeast Asian country. Yet, women's studies programs (at the undergraduate and graduate levels) employing an interdisciplinary perspective have yet to emerge in a significant way. Considering the popularity of professionally oriented academic programs, women's studies in the Philippines must be similarly oriented and possibly built into the content of courses in mass communication, business, economics, and human resource development and management.

Torres (1989), however, argues that women scholars have become "feminized" and are beginning to form an "intellectual collective" in gender research. Women's groups have also started to use research as an instrument of education and consciousness-raising. Hence, women's studies in the Philippines should more accurately be referred to as "impact of development on women (IDW) studies," since the concern is not study alone but change in the direction of greater parity in the sharing of economic and social resources.

SINGAPORE

At the National University of Singapore, research on women is being conducted in the departments of sociology and anthropology, social work, economics, social medicine, and public health. The Institute of Southeast Asian Studies (1968), which promotes contemporary Southeast Asian studies in the fields of economics, political science, and international relations, encourages research and publications on women. The Singapore Association of Women Lawyers (1974) focuses its research activities and legal literacy programs on women in industry, business, education, and the professions.

It appears that women's studies in Singapore can only be developed effectively if it can be seen as contributing to policies of industrialization and development. For this perception to emerge, women's studies must be directly concerned with evaluative and policy research relating to the advancement of women in educational sciences, natural sciences, business and industry, reflecting the emphasis of the government in promoting a highly skilled and innovative labor force.

Nirmala Purushotam (1989), researching on women and gender studies in Singapore, argues that the nation's politics invariably finds its way into primary areas of social research. For example, government promotion of female employment in export-oriented, labor-intensive electronic industries and the demand for university-educated women to fill lower managerial and supervisory positions in factories are reflected in research priorities such as female productivity, women in management, and the impact of industrialization and education on the Singaporean family. Similarly, the government's need to promote population growth to counter declining birth rates and maintain a youthful, dynamic work force influences research on demography and fertility.

In this sense, the themes of research are predominantly responsive to government policies and needs. Hence, social scientists have failed to develop critical questions and models for social science inquiry. To overcome this, Puroshotam suggests that gender research should be concerned with systems of social control and politicization using a Foucaultian perspective to clarify the paradigms of power in an increasingly technocratic society like Singapore. The present emphasis of research on industrialization, productivity, fertility, and the family also could be developed within the more active Foucaultian paradigm of gender politicization.

MALAYSIA

Awareness of and interest in research on women are recent phenomena in Malaysia, not only within government agencies but also in academic institutions. While the government implemented programs for women as early as 1957 (immediately after independence), these trained women in tradition-oriented activities such as sewing and embroidery, cooking, domestic and family management, home science, religious education, and family planning. The programs, implemented by agencies such as KEMAS (the community program within the Ministry of National and Rural Development) and Karyaneka in KEMAS, RISDA (Rubber Smallholders Development Authority), FELDA (Federal Land Development Authority), and MADA (Malaysian Agricultural Development Authority), reflected the immediate needs and concerns of each agency within its own sphere of economic development.

The constraints of agency goals, staffing, and funding resulted in agriculturalists and economists imposing poorly formulated programs upon the female population. More seriously, each agency continued to maintain its own philosophy and interpretation of community and family development. These had the common effect of sharpening women's traditional skills that could be commercially utilized.

In the sixties and seventies, policy or evaluative research on women was almost completely neglected. Rural development and industrialization was not in any way concerned with developing women's skills and enterprises in ways that could make them capable of management and self-representation. Only over the last several years have these agencies incorporated social scientists in policy or evaluative research on women. Previously, some of the research activities were undertaken by independent consultants, and although the programs looked viable and attractive on paper, the implementation procedures were always poor, and problems were aggravated by improperly trained community extension workers, government red tape, insufficient funding, and minimal participation in planning and decision making by the women themselves.

Recently, the Malaysian University of Agriculture (Universiti Pertanian Malaysia) at the Centre for Extension and Continuing Education (Pusat Pengembangan dan Pendidikan Lanjutan) has attempted to coordinate extension work and research on women in agriculture by including villagers in the research process, the ultimate aim of which is to increase women's involvement in decision making in primary farming activities. In 1987, these efforts crystallized in the formation of the Women Studies Unit, which held its first workshop, "Women and Technological Innovation." Student training schemes here also attempt to include innovative methods of research such as participatory action research. The regular interaction between members of the academic staff and relevant agricultural development agencies has changed the image of Malaysian academics as arm-chair theoreticians or government functionaries.

In Universiti Sains Malaysia, Penang, a research program that specifically focuses on the problems of women in development is the KANITA Project (1979). Its initial emphasis was on evaluative and participatory action research. More recently, KANITA has attempted to coordinate its research efforts with social policy and planning for women by focusing on basic structural issues that concern rural and urban women in Malaysia. (More information about KANITA can be found in the resource list in section seven of this volume.)

Through the Social Development and Administration Section in the School of Social Sciences and later the Secretariat of the International Geographical Union (IGU), then based at the university, other research programs were also initiated in the Universiti Sains Malaysia. The most productive of these was the Young Workers Project. Like KANITA, the other programs were both academic and action oriented. Social scientists and researchers attempted to grapple with actual problems encountered by young women and workers in the formal and informal sectors of the Malaysian urban and industrial sectors. Counseling services were also provided in which academics and workers jointly attempted to understand and overcome the tensions and anxieties of the younger generation arising from rapid industrialization and urban growth. The Secretariat of IGU moved out of Universiti Sains Malaysia in 1986, leaving KANITA as the only source of collaborative interdisciplinary research on women and the family. Its success in generating research and academic interest in women's studies is realized in its new status as a research unit within the School of Social Sciences. In July 1989, KANITA was made a formal research unit under the general name of Women and Human Resource Studies Unit.

Interest in integrating women's issues into academic courses was fostered by the research on women undertaken by KANITA and the Young Workers Group. KANITA has coordinated several students' projects on women, and the supervision of graduate research on women involving local and foreign scholars has become one of the more important functions of the project in recent years. Linkages have been established with several western European universities conducting research on Malaysian women, including the University of Utretch and the Katholieke Universitect in Holland, the University of Alborg in Denmark, the University of Oslo, and the London School of Economics and Political Sciences.

In general, the response from both male and female students and members of the academic staff to women's studies has been encouraging. The scope and focus of the courses are cross-cultural, utilizing case studies and experiences from other cultures, and countries. Courses employ a historical perspective to enable students to analyze the changes in position and status of different groups of women over time and across cultures. These courses include numerous guest lecturers and professionals from other disciplines within the university, as well as from the public and private sectors to give students broad exposure to issues concerning women in general and Malaysian women in particular.

The trend toward including women's studies as a subdiscipline in the social sciences reflects a growing national consciousness of the important contributions of women to Malaysian society. The National Population and Family Development Board (Lembaga Penduduk dan Pembangunan Keluarga Negara), for example, has increased its research efforts on women, fertility, and demography. Similarly, the Federation of Family Planning Association (1958) appears to be expanding its research and information dissemination focused on women and family life education. The research committee of the National Advisory Council on the Integration of Women in Development (NACIWID) sponsors policy and evaluative research on women and women's programs. It plays an advisory role to the Women's Secretariat (1983) in the Prime Minister's Department (HAWA, Hal Enwal Wanita) and submits to HAWA policy recommendations for the implementation of development programs on women.

FUTURE RESEARCH DIRECTIONS

DEVELOPING APPROPRIATE PARADIGMS

In Southeast Asia, practical application of a number of Western theoretical perspectives and concepts developed within the framework of Western women's experience is problematic. The social structures of Western and Southeast Asian societies differ significantly, requiring the reconstruction of concepts such as "power," "value," and "status." Generalizations about women's "devaluation" and "powerlessness" in the wake of modernization and urbanization processes cannot be applied without understanding systems of gender relations as they evolved in specific historical contexts.

Among many ethnic groups in the region, family and kinship structures (bilateral, and in some cases, matrilineal) have enabled women to maintain a fair share of control of family and community resources, to work independently of men, to manage their own incomes (and sometimes their spouses' as well), and to participate in agriculture, business, and trade (Illo, 1987; Sukanti, 1986; Karim, 1991). Hierarchies of age, descent, and class are as important as gender, and sometimes more so (Winzeler, 1982; Milar, 1983; Kammerer, 1988; Hutheesing, 1989). This situation is significantly different from that of South and West Asia. It also differs significantly from the West where equality has emerged through the suffrage, trade union, and women's liberation movements. In parts of Southeast Asia, gender relations is not so much concerned with achieving equality as in maintaining it. With widespread industrialization and ill-conceived development policies, negative impacts on rural women have often ensued. For example, women are recruited in factory work at the lowest rung of the industrial employment ladder at low wages and poor working conditions (Heyzer, 1986; Jamilah Ariffin, 1986). Moreover the positions of Southeast Asian women are increasingly threatened by reactionary ideologies, notably fundamentalism (Islamic, Christian, Hindu, and cult movements) (Karim, 1990).

Social scientists will need to analyze trends of change in socio-economic structures and their modes of operation in a historical perspective and compare some of these transformations with those taking place elsewhere in Asia and the West. Regional and cultural variations within Southeast Asia also need to be examined, particularly differences between rural and urban women and between minority and majority populations. It is important to review whether the existing paradigm of women's marginality created by mechanization and privatization in agriculture (Boserup, 1970) indeed applies to all societies in Southeast Asia. Heyzer (1986) and Ng (1987) have indicated that it does. However, examples from Malaysia would suggest otherwise. For example, with the current instabilities within the household economy in certain farming areas in the north, particularly Kedah, Terengganu, and Kelantan, displacement is not demonstrated so much in terms of gender variables, but rather in terms of class and ethnicity. It is the farm household that is displaced, rather than female farmers alone. Here, to maintain bilateral kinship structures as a mode of inheritance and control of land, labor, and capital in the Malay household, rural workers must be able to participate in the processes of mechanization, capital transfer, and other forms of monetization of the rural economy on the same level as non-Malays and the elite. Similar problems can be found elsewhere in Southeast Asia where those with capital accrue more wealth and power than those with land and labor.

It is also important to examine existing paradigms of power relations between men and women that uphold oppositions such as public/private, culture/nature, and real/symbolic. Overing (1980) argues with the views of writers who present women as both devalued and subordinated in real and symbolic terms. Scholarly research, Overing argues, should more deeply examine indigenous constructs of power relations between men and women and how these have changed and are changing over time.

RESEARCH METHODOLOGIES

Stereotypes embedded in methodologies utilized by statisticians have been responsible for improper accounting of women's productivity and labor force participation. For this reason, many researchers studying women have opted for time allocation measures. Unfortunately, these do not measure adequately women's contributions within and outside the household. Women's overlapping labor inputs in home production processes and participation in village activities, for example, are difficult to measure and value accurately. Researchers need to analyze current research findings on women's economic productivity that are relevant to Southeast Asia and develop more refined tools of quantifying labor and production (Acharya and Shah, 1987).

A conceptual obstacle to the development of useful methodologies in relation to work and productivity is the notion of "head of household," which generally refers to a male head unless a woman is widowed or divorced or has a husband who is disabled or working overseas. This stereotyping reflects the patriarchal biases in the computation of productivity. In farm families, an end result of this is the computation of a woman's nonpaid labor through the male head and the counting of her monetary earnings, if any, as supplementary to his. A husband who collects cash receipts from joint family production is counted as though he were the only productive earner. The problem of bias in national accounting is acute in Southeast Asia, where women put in tremendous time and energy in agricultural work and household production. Indeed, their own social and cultural values recognize the important contributions women make to the economic sector. In the future, scholars of women's work in Southeast Asia need to classify work and compute labor productivity through joint headships rather than male headships.

Regarding the definition of "housewife," researchers need to evaluate and assess the activities of women categorized as such in the context of capital investment. A woman may be unemployed in the formal sense but she may have taken a loan to purchase cattle and livestock or she may have opened her own business in the house or elsewhere. As long as she is actively involved in the acquisition of capital for investment and production, researchers should use empirically based (and/or indigenous) definitions of "work" and enter her in the census as a worker or producer or entrepreneur, even if she also defines herself as a "housewife." This is usually a convenient term of self-reference to indicate extensive contribution to home-based activities and domestic work. The category of the "unpaid family worker" in national censuses in countries such as Malaysia indicates a woman who is actively engaged in production but does not obtain a salary. National statistics should take into account the fact that such women contribute to the family earnings, and enter half of the earnings of her husband as her own in computing national income and gross national product.

The sociologist, anthropologist, historian, or educator researching women in Southeast Asia might also need to highlight certain methodological and theoretical issues concerning the use of history in cultural analysis. While a positivist, rational discourse has proved to be crucial to the development of research on women, it is important to highlight some of the more useful purposes to which postmodernist perspectives can be put in demonstrating women's contributions to history and culture in Southeast Asia.

REFERENCES

Acharya, S. and Shah, I. 1987. "Structure of Labor Force and Female Labor Force Participation in Rural Asia," paper prepared for the program, "Family Strategies and Female Labor," United Nations University, Tokyo.

Angangco, Samson, and Albino. 1980. *Status of Women in the Philippines.* (Bibliography with selected annotations.) Quezon City: Alemar-Pheonix.

Boserup, E. 1970. *Women's Role in Economic Development.* New York: St. Martin's Press.

Economic and Social Commission for Asia and the Pacific (ESCAP). 1986. Proceedings of Workshop on "Participatory Action Research Concerning Women Workers in the Non-Formal Sector," Pattaya, December.

Feliciano, G. D. 1982. "Philippines Country Report: The Social Sciences and the Filipino Woman," *Women Studies and Social Sciences in Asia,* Expert Group Meeting, New Delhi.

Goodale, G. 1986. "Diversification of Women's Training and Employment: Experience from Selected Industrialized Countries," paper presented at the seminar on "Diversification of Training and Employment of Women," Tokyo, December.

Heyzer, N. 1986. *Working Women in Southeast Asia: Development, Subordination, and Emancipation.* Stratford, England: Open University Press.

Hutheesing, O. 1989. "Emerging Sexual Inequality among the Lisu of Northern Thailand: The Waning of Dog and Elephant Repute." Leiden: Brill.

Illo, I. J. F. 1987. *Impact of Irrigation Development on Women and Their Households: The Case of the Aslong Project*. Manila: Institute of Philippine Culture, Ateneo de Manila University.

Jamilah Ariffin. 1986. "Women Workers in the Manufacturing Industries," in Evelyne Hong, ed., *Malaysian Women*. Penang: Consumer Association of Penang.

Jose, A. V. 1986. "Employment Diversification of Women in Asian Countries: An Assessment," paper presented at the seminar on "Diversification of Training and Employment of Women," Tokyo, December.

Kammerer, G. A. 1988. "Shifting Gender Asymmetries among Akha of Northern Thailand," in N. Eberhard, ed., *Gender, Power and the Construction of Moral Order: Studies from the Thai Periphery*. Madison: University of Wisconsin Center for Southeast Asian Studies Monograph no. 4 (33–52).

Karim, W. J. 1986/87. *Report on Women's Work and Family Status Production Process in Malaysia*, UNU/KANITA Workshop, Penang.

Karim, W. J. Forthcoming 1991. *Gender in Adat and Islam*. Berkeley: Center for South and Southeast Asian Studies.

Milar, S. B. 1983. "On Interpreting Gender in Bugis Society." *American Ethnologist* 10 (477–93).

Ng, C. 1987. "Agricultural Modernization and Gender Differentiation in A Rural Malay Community, 1983-1987," *In Technology and Gender*, Women Studies Unit, Universiti Pertanian Malaysia.

Overing, J. 1986. "Men Control Women? The Catch-22 in the Analysis of Gender," *International Journal of Moral and Social Studies* (Summer): 2.

Purushotam, N. 1989. "Reflections of Women Studies in Singapore," paper presented at the IGSSR International Workshop on Women Studies, Trivandrum, India, April.

Pongsapich, A. 1982. "Thailand Country Report: Status of Women Studies in Thailand," *Women Studies and Social Sciences in Asia*, Expert Group Meeting, New Delhi.

Sukanti, S. 1986. "Domestic Servants in Seven Cities on the Island of Java," paper presented at UNU/KANITA Workshop, Penang, Malaysia.

Torres, A. T. 1989. "The Filipino Looks at Herself: A Review of Women's Studies in the Philippines," in *The Filipino Woman in Focus*. Bangkok: UNESCO.

Winzeler, R. 1982. "Sexual Status in Southeast Asia: Comparative Perspectives on Women, Agriculture and Political Organization," in Van Esterik, P., ed., *Women of Southeast Asia*, Center for Southeast Asian Studies, Northern Illinois Occasional Paper no. 9 (176–213).

New Developments in Research on Women: The Commonwealth Caribbean Experience

Rhoda Reddock

In many ways one can say that the women's movement in the Common-wealth Caribbean[1] has come of age. Feminist-oriented women's organizations throughout the region, some of which have emerged recently, such as the Committee for the Development of Women of St. Vincent and the Grenadines (CDW) and the Belize Rural Women's Association (BRWA), and some long-standing ones such as the SISTERN Women's Theatre Collective of Jamaica, are using a range of new methodologies and focusing on issues relevant to their local situations. Significantly, many of the "traditional" women's organizations in this region also have to some extent been radicalized and shifted their emphasis to include issues other than social work. They now also engage in advocacy on issues related to violence against women, representation of women in political office, the legal status of women, as well as issues related to world peace, international conflict, and economic development. These shifts result from two forces: (a) the new women's movement; and (b) directives received from head organizations such as YWCA International, Soroptomists International, and the International Association of Business and Professional Women's Clubs, which work in consultation with the United Nations.

As is common with the development of the women's movement, a number of periodicals, magazines, and newsletters have emerged aimed at various audiences. These include *Sistren Newsletter*, *The Belize Women* (BRWA), and *Workingwoman* (Workingwomen, Trinidad and Tobago). In addition, the Women and Development Unit (WAND) of the Extra-Mural Department of the University of the West Indies produces a magazine, *Woman Speak!*; an occasional feature service, *Concerning Women and Devel-*

opment; and a news service, *Woman Struggle International.* Films, video, slide-tape shows, and exhibitions are also continuously produced.

Moreover, great strides have been made in both formal and nonformal education. For example, some organizations conduct educational activities for the public and staff using popular methodologies such as drama, games, and audiovisuals in addition to lectures. At the extramural (nondegree) level, WAND has worked since 1978 primarily in the smaller OECS[2] territories that do not host campuses of the University of the West Indies (UWI). In addition to working with community organizations, WAND has developed the Trainers of Trainers Programme aimed at strengthening organizational skills among community and women's organizations, and a women's studies program focused more specifically on work with the women's movement. Between 1982 and 1985, WAND administered the Caribbean subproject of the international project, Women's Movements, Organizations, and Strategies in Historical Perspective: Colonial and Contemporary, coordinated by the Institute of Social Studies at The Hague. The three Caribbean case studies were (1) "Women, Labor, and Struggle in 20th Century Trinidad and Tobago"; (2) "Women, Work, and Organization in Jamaica, 1900–1944"; and (3) "Rosehall through the Years" (including a special overview on the history of women's organizations in St. Vincent). This work made a significant contribution in this field and has been the starting point for a regional project on women's history and creative expression presently being carried out in collaboration with the Caribbean Association for Feminist Research and Action (CAFRA) as part of WAND's program on women's studies.

In March 1982, on the initiative of WAND, a meeting was held in Barbados to consider the introduction of teaching and research on women's studies within the UWI. At that meeting a regional steering committee was formed to coordinate the activities of three women and development studies groups formed on each campus—Mona, Jamaica, St. Augustine, Trinidad and Tobago, and Cave Hill, Barbados. Five research objectives were identified:

1. to pursue applied research based on needs specified by relevant groups of people;
2. to generate teaching materials;
3. to develop research that can be used to influence policy and planning;
4. to encourage people's participation in their situation, which will ultimately help them to change their situation; and
5. to encourage experimentation with innovative research methodologies and dissemination methods (Massiah, 1986:180).

In seven years this program has established undergraduate and graduate courses within the Faculty of Arts and General Studies and the Faculty of Education, as well as modules or components in a wide range of others. For material, this program drew primarily from the information generated from the Women in the Caribbean Research Project coordinated by the Institute of Social and Economic Research-Eastern Caribbean office (ISER-EC). This project, based primarily on contemporary empirical research, examined three themes—sources of livelihood, emotional support, and power and authority.

In April 1985, the Caribbean Association for Feminist Research and Action was launched. Unlike that of the UWI women and development studies program, CAFRA's sphere of operations extends beyond the Anglophone Caribbean to the wider Caribbean regardless of language or political status. CAFRA is a regional network of feminists, feminist organizations, and activist women. In its three years of existence it has succeeded in becoming a focal point for action and research of the Caribbean women's movement.

For CAFRA, research is an integral part of political action and vice versa. Thus, the research issues are those that arise during the day-to-day development of the movement. In 1985 at the inaugural meeting of CAFRA, a number of priority research/action areas were identified : (i) the Caribbean Basin Initiative; (ii) population control policies in the Caribbean; (iii) peace in the Caribbean; (iv) history of women's labor and struggle in the region; (v) women's cultural expression as an instrument of building power; (vi) sexual violence; (vii) women and trade; (viii) women in Caribbean agriculture; and (ix) women in Caribbean literature.

Thus far, CAFRA's commitment to integrate research and action and to demystify research and theorizing is evident in various forms. Data collected from 1986 to 1988 for the Women in Caribbean Agriculture (WICA) project is being disseminated through community workshops using drama and popular educational methods as well as comic booklets and video in St. Vincent and the Grenadines, and the Commonwealth of Dominica. The WICA project also facilitated the training of nongraduate activists in research and writing and contributed greatly to increasing the conscientiousness of some graduate researchers who felt they already had these skills. This type of training will continue. As part of the Women's History Project, women of the Red Thread, a Guyanase embroidery group, participated in a workshop of the BRWA in Belize on the use of embroidery in the transmission of women's history. In 1990 CAFRA, in conjunction with Sister Vision Press in Toronto, also published an anthology of Caribbean women's poetry selected primarily from unpublished poets who responded to newspaper advertisements and word of mouth. It is aptly titled *Creation Fire*.

While this grab bag description of activities and agencies is by no means an adequate reflection of the ongoing research work on women in this region, it does present a glimpse of a dynamism and growth of the women's movement here. New directions in research on women must necessarily take into account the range of organizations involved in this process, and build upon the forms of information dissemination and the variety of research utilization strategies already tested.

NEW DIRECTIONS

Clearly, priorities for future research differ from country to country and among individuals, organizations, and institutions. But in spite of the steady increase in published and unpublished material, we are continuously astounded by how much is still unknown, unexplored, and unresearched. This section will outline both ongoing programs and subjects for future consideration.

1. Ongoing Programs

(i) Caribbean Women in Transition is the provisional title of a research program being collectively developed by the WDS groups of the UWI. This ambitious program seeks to incorporate the wide-ranging research interests of group members; provide research training; and support publication of research results. While aimed primarily at providing teaching materials, this research will also be a base for advocacy at the public policy level by women's organizations. The main themes identified by the groups include: women, economy, and employment; women, power, and organizations; gender ideology; curriculum and classroom perspectives; women's history; women's health; women in Caribbean literature; culture and other art forms; legislation; religion and women (with special emphasis on fundamentalist religion); and the impact of the women's movement on men.

(ii) The Future of the Caribbean—Subtheme: Race, Class and Gender. This comprehensive research program is being coordinated by the ISERs of the UWI at a regional level. This subtheme is one of eight, but the only one specifically concerned with gender. This research theme examines the complex interrelationship between race/ethnicity, class, and gender in postcolonial societies such as Guyana, Suriname, and Trinidad and Tobago, where two or more non-European groups have sometimes had antagonistic relations within a context of overall Euro-American imperialist domination. This is quite different from the reality of race/ethnicity, class, and gender in metropolitan, industrialized societies such as the U.S.A., the United Kingdom, Canada, Australia, and even South Africa (Reddock, 1988:6).

(iii) DAWN (Development Alternatives with Women for a New Era)—Women's Visions and Movements, and Food, Energy, and Crisis. The Caribbean is also involved in the two research themes identified by DAWN for international consideration. These studies encompass a documentation of the past fifteen years of the women's movement in this region and an analysis of the political-economic context within which to analyze the development process.

2. Topics for Future Research

(i) Sexuality, Sex Tourism, and the Traffic in Women. The issue of commoditization of sexuality through various forms of international prostitution and the traffic in women must be examined. Although this has reached its most developed levels in Southeast Asia, the Caribbean is not without precedent in this area with regard to both women and men. Although prostitution has existed long before capitalism, the commoditization of female rather than male sexuality has unique characteristics under the present international division of labor. It is known that women from one country in the region are transported to another (for example, from the Dominican Republic to St. Martin, Antigua, Curacao, and Puerto Rico) or to Europe (for instance, from the Dominican Republic and Guyana to The Netherlands). Can this be perceived as part of a global informal economy? What are the conditions—social, legal, and economic—under which this traffic takes place? Do some governments turn a blind eye because of direct or indirect economic or political benefits that might accrue? And what of the women themselves? How much of their participation is the result of coercion and/or misinformation? Or is it simply a logical choice given dismal economic alternatives?

Apart from the economic aspect, this subject raises broader social-psychological questions of how women and men perceive their bodies, their sexuality, and their relationship with each other. This issue is also linked to that of race and ethnicity, where "exotic" women and men, that is, women and men of a different ethnic group, become demand items. The international marriage market between Southeast Asia and Western Europe for example, is based on the resistance of some Western European men to the new, emancipated European women and their preference for the supposedly more docile and obedient Oriental women. Although Caribbean women may never be characterized that way, the pornography characteristic of the region's tourism propaganda suggests that this subject needs to be examined further.

(ii) Science and Technology. As the Caribbean moves toward the twenty-first century, the development of science and technology is being advanced as the solution to many of the region's problems. However, the specific concerns of women are not yet reflected in these discussions.

Already within the English-speaking Caribbean, the need for a critical approach to this issue was recognized by the Caribbean Technology Policy Studies Project (CTSP). In its publication, *Technology Policies for Small Developing Countries*, the authors questioned the implicit assumption of most science and technology policy in this region that technology is "an intrinsic component of the process of cumulative causation that characterizes development and self-sustaining growth" (Girvan, 1983:11). This critique can be linked to those of feminists, environmentalists, and others who question the applicability of eurocentric and androcentric science to problems in the Third World. They challenge the Western concept of progress, which has been traditionally perceived as the increasing domination of man over nature, with science as the mechanism to achieve this. Within this schema, women have been defined as part of nature (with nature defined as female) and have become subjects of man's domination and control (Mies, 1987; Reddock, 1987:9). With progress so defined, man has set up an antagonistic relationship to nature. This has had negative repercussions not only for the physical environment but also for relations among human beings.

A recent examination of the impact of changing agricultural policies in the female agricultural labor force in Trinidad and Tobago strongly implicates an antilabor/antifemale technology. Indra Harry, in her thesis "Women in Agriculture in Trinidad and Tobago," found that mechanization was greatest in those aspects of production carried out by women, such as fertilizing and landclearing, while virtually everyone who was taught to operate the new machinery was male (1980:111). Further, it was found that women were averse to some of the available technology such as mechanical sprayers because of physical discomfort resulting from its use, a condition not felt by men (Harry, 1980:130).

An area of technological development that is presently perceived as female-oriented is the apparel and electronics industry. Most research on this subject suggests that the large-scale use of female labor is due more to considerations of labor cost and control, and management flexibility, rather than the supposed suitability of gender to certain tasks/technologies (the so-called "nimble fingers" argument). Moreover, considerable data has been generated on the health hazards affecting women workers in export-oriented apparel and electronics industries, such as chest disorders from inhaling fine particles and rapidly deteriorating eyesight, which has been recorded among women working in the Free Trade Zones (Export Processing Zones) of Jamaica.

Computer technology must also be examined in this context. While the overall effects of computerization on, for example, job displacement and health are known (although not documented for this region), the implication of computerization's potential for breaking up many secretarial/administrative functions and transferring them to the home warrants examination. Will this further isolate women and reduce the potential for labor organization?

New reproductive technologies must also be examined. Developments such as amniocentesis and the ultrasound scanner can be used to discern a child's sex prior to birth. In India, the availability of such technology has resulted in the abortion of approximately 78,000 female fetuses between 1978 and 1983 (Patel, 1984:170). In addition, technology making it possible to choose a child's sex is already in existence. Other developments include surrogate motherhood and in vitro fertilization. What has been the impact so far of these new reproductive technologies within the Caribbean context?

What trends can we see developing?

(iii) Women and Religious Experience. The reemergence of religion as a powerful political and social force during these times cannot be ignored. African-based religions in the region (such as Shango, Pocomania, Shouters, Shakers, Spiritual Baptists, and Revival Zion) have been characterized by a much greater matricenterdness than the dominant Euro-Christian, Hindu, and Muslim religions, Recent documentation suggests, however, that this might be changing and that increasing contact with Western religions has increased the power of males vis-à-vis that of females in the practice of these religions (Reddock, 1986). This is something which needs serious examination as Western values and practices may have become incorporated into the religions in a passive manner and may now be perceived as traditional.

The effects of the renewed penetration of Christian fundamentalism within the region also needs to be explored, including rates of conversion from the constituents of the African-based, as well as the Hindu and Muslim, religions. This would be important because female subordination and the primacy of the legal Western conjugal family in the fundamentalist approaches might be effecting serious changes in gender relations as well as in women's perception of their power and potential within society. At the same time studies of power relations, self-definition, and other related topics in the context of other religions practiced in the region should be explored. The impact of Hindu and Muslim fundamentalism on women and the gender relations of these religious groupings should also be examined.

(iv) Women's Interests. Theorizing on specific women's interests has been developed best in the work of Maxine Molyneux. By identifying specific gender interests, she changed the question from "why did women not organize?" to "around what issues are women willing to organize?" This concept is particularly important for Marxist theorists who have conceived of women's interests as the same as those of their associated males (specifically, the class of their husband/partner or father) and attributed women's apparent lack of consciousness to an underdeveloped or backward state. The issue of specific gender interests also raises the issue of competing interests. For example, for a black housewife married to a working-class man, what is the primary contradiction, the contradiction on which her consciousness is based?

Historical studies of women's consciousness, organization, and struggle are few in this region. But the examination of women's participation in, for example, the disturbances of the thirties in St. Vincent (1935), Trinidad and Tobago (1937), and Jamaica (1938), suggests that in all cases women's responsibility for the social and economic welfare of themselves and their children and relatives was the primary motivation for their struggles and direct action. This responsibility placed on all women (in spite of the ideology of the male provider) for the day-to-day welfare of the family, especially children, has been identified by Maxine Molyneux as an important determinant of women's "practical" gender interests as opposed to their strategic gender interests. The latter relate to their challenge to their subordination or the institutionalized discrimination that they face as women.

The identification of specific women's interests (Clarke, 1986) as well as major distinguishing characteristics of these interests go a long way toward a better understanding of women and organization. It may provide new insights into questions of why, why not, and under what conditions women participate in organizations and political movements. These questions need to be explored historically in relation to organization and struggle in the Caribbean since the postemancipation period. This could provide one mechanism for isolating trends and tendencies which could lead to the development of theory.

CONCLUSION

It is impossible in any one document to prescribe a complete agenda for research on women. The wider project of reevaluating and reconstructing knowledge itself is the task in which we are involved at present. The above represents one individual's selection from what is a vast and long-term task. In pursuance of this task, two factors should be kept in mind: first, the need to disseminate findings to all levels of society and demystify both the research process and the data it produces; and second, to link research and action, and likewise the movement with academia. This is the only means of maintaining the dynamism and essentialness of women's studies, research, and action within our region and internationally.

NOTES

1. Commonwealth Caribbean, otherwise referred to as Anglophone or English-speaking Caribbean includes Antigua, the Bahamas, Barbados, Belize, Dominica, Grenada, Guyana, Jamaica, Montserrat, St. Lucia, St. Kitts/Nevis, St. Vincent and the Grenadines, and Trinidad and Tobago.
2. OECS (Organization of Eastern Caribbean States) includes Grenada, St. Vincent and the Grenadines, St. Lucia, Dominica, Antigua, Montserrat, and St. Kitts/Nevis.

REFERENCES

Clarke, Roberta. "Women's Organizations, Women's Interests," *Social and Economic Studies* 35, no. 3 (1986).
Craig, Christine. Women and Development Studies, Three-Year Research Programme (Discussion Draft), 1988 (mimeo).

Girvan, Norman et al. *Technology Policies for Small Developing Countries: A Study of the Caribbbean*. CTSP, ISER, Mona, 1983.

Harry, Indra. "Women in Agriculture in Trinidad." Masters thesis, University of Calgary, Alberta, 1980.

Massiah, Joycelin. "Establishing a Programme of Women and Development Studies in the University of the West Indies." *Social and Economic Studies* 35, no. 1 (1986).

———. "Women in the Caribbean Research Project: An Overview." *Social and Economic Studies* 35, no. 2 (1986).

Mies, Maria. *Patriarchy and Accumulation on a World Scale*. London: Zed Press, 1987.

Molyneux, Maxine. "Female Collective Action in Socialist Revolutions: The PDRY and Nicaragua." Paper presented to Wenner-Gren Foundation Conference, Mijas, 1985.

Patel, V. "Amniocentesis and Female Infanticide—Misuse of Medical Technology." *Socialist Health Review* 1, no. 2 (1984).

Reddock, Rhoda. "Overview of Caribbean Subproject-Research Project—Women's Movements, Organizations, and Strategies in a Historical Perspective, with Special Reference to Colonial and Contemporary Societies," 1986 (mimeo).

———. "What is Feminist Knowledge?" Paper presented at the 2nd Interdisciplinary Seminar, Women and Development Studies, St. Augustine, 1987.

———. "Race, Class, and Gender: Gender Issues in the Future of the Caribbean." Working paper, Future of the Caribbean Project, ISER, 1988.

VI

PROGRAM
DESCRIPTIONS

ARGENTINA:
CENTER FOR WOMEN'S STUDIES,
BUENOS AIRES

Centro de Estudios de la Mujer
Olleros 2554 P.B.
Buenos Aires 1426
Argentina
Phone: 553-9204
Contact person: Lic. Gloria Bonder, Director

I. BACKGROUND

The Center for Women's Studies (CEM) was founded in 1979 as a nongovernmental, nonprofit organization. It was the first institution in Argentina to be dedicated to women's studies. The center grew out of the first multidisciplinary workshop on the role of women in contemporary Latin American society organized in June 1979. Its purpose was to ensure a regular exchange and in-depth discussion between all people who at the time were beginning to work on the position of women in Argentina. In this endeavor, the center offered an alternative to existing institutions such as universities, where neither criticism of the existing political and social order nor the pursuit of research on women was encouraged.

The center disseminates theoretical and methodological developments in the field of women's studies by intervening in university undergraduate and postgraduate studies. Because of the political situation in Argentina at the time, only some of the early seminars were publicly held. The seminars covered subjects such as the psychology of women, women and the family, and crises in the life of a woman. One of the first research projects, begun in 1983, was Sexual Stereotypes in Argentine Primary Education.

The center has forty members from various disciplines such as psychology, sociology, anthropology, social welfare, medicine, and law. In addition to the main center in Buenos Aires, there is a branch in the city of La Plata, founded in 1983, with fifteen members.

Currently, the objectives of the center are:

- to carry out studies on priority problems for women in Argentina;
- to disseminate results of research carried out at CEM through publications, round tables, conferences, et cetera;
- to train community agents in the field of health, law, education, and labor for the implementation of projects designed to improve the living conditions of women;
- to train and advise groups of women with a view to promoting their organization and participation in community life;
- to produce educational material designed for dissemination and training;
- to provide for regular exchanges between women's institutions and research centers within and outside the country;
- to help shape public opinion and decision making on problems that affect women in Argentina; and
- to advise governmental agencies that define policies and programs for women.

II. TEACHING ACTIVITIES

The center offers a diploma in women's studies at the University of Buenos Aires. In addition, it offers courses such as: Introduction to Women's Studies; Women and Mental Health; Female Sexuality; and Disease Prevention and Promotion of Health in Women.

Also, the center offers various training courses, including training specifically designed for community agents and basic groups. It collaborates with government agencies and NGOs in meetings and workshops for health workers, educators, and government officials. Topics covered have included the participation of women in contemporary society; the role of women in the municipality; Argentine legislation; the United Nations convention on the elimination of all types of discrimination against women; and general problems of women.

III. RESEARCH

A. *Programs*

Research programs have covered various topics and generally also include the publication of posters, booklets, guides, show cards, and audio-visual materials. Programs have been conducted on the following topics:

- Sexual stereotypes in primary school education in Argentina
- Women and the law: a critical approach
- Paid domestic service and problems in creating unions
- The UN Convention against all types of discrimination against women and related Argentine legislation
- Training women to organize a community nursery

Ongoing programs include research on:

- Gender and social class in the professional guidance program at public primary schools in the Province of Buenos Aires
- Conditions of work, health, and union participation for primary school teachers
- Women and the law: a critical approach (Part II)
- Sexual education with adolescents of both sexes from the poorer parts of Buenos Aires
- Child-mothers: a program for the prevention of adolescent pregnancy
- Sexual education with women from poor parts of the city of Campana
- Socialization of gender in "modern" families: a comparative study of families in Buenos Aires and Madrid
- Motivation, expectations, and professional projection in students at the Faculty of Engineering in La Plata, Mar del Plata, and El Comahue
- A pilot project for technical support and training in the Cooperative for Labor and Domestic Service, "Maria Pueblo," in Lomas de Zamora

The center regularly holds a workshop to evaluate its programs; monthly discussion groups; and workshops for institutional evaluation and programming. It also organizes working groups and conferences. Annual multidisciplinary meetings have covered a number of topics, including:

- The place of women in contemporary society
- Women, culture, and society
- Women and maternity
- The theoretical status of women's studies and the current debate
- A theoretical and clinical updating on psychological guidance for women

- The development of syllabi and the preparation of teaching materials for women's studies at an advanced level in Latin America and the Caribbean (sponsored by UNESCO and the University of Buenos Aires)
- The situation of women in Argentina: developments in the fields of health, education, labor, and the law

B. Library and documentation

The center has a specialized library with books, brochures, mimeographed material, periodicals, booklets, guides, and audiovisual material on subjects related to women.

C. Cooperation with other institutions

The center participates in national, regional, and international networks on subjects such as education, health, the rights of women, and the dissemination of proceedings from the UN Convention on the elimination of all forms of discrimination against women. It is also a member of the Information Network for the Social Sciences (REDISCA).

IV. ACTION PROGRAMS

The center is active in combining research with action programs of various kinds. Members of the center are active as advisors to the Committee for Sexual Education and Human Reproduction, an agency within the Ministry for Health and Social Action. They also act as advisors to the Advisory Committee on Research in Social Sciences and Health, in the National Secretariat for Science and Technology. Further, the center is represented on the Inter-American Council for Women.

As far as community services are concerned, the center assists in mental health-related programs; legal and psychological assistance for women of modest means; and in organizing groups for nonprofessional women.

CANADA:
WOMEN'S STUDIES AT THE ONTARIO INSTITUTE FOR STUDIES IN EDUCATION, TORONTO

Contact: Centre for Women's Studies in Education
Ontario Institute for Studies in Education
252 Bloor Street West, Room 5630
Toronto
Ontario M5S 1V6
Canada
Current Director: Ruth Pierson

I. WOMEN'S STUDIES AT OISE: THE STATE OF THE ART[1]

Established in 1965 as both a graduate school of education (in affiliation with the University of Toronto) and a research and field development institute, the Ontario Institute for Studies in Education (OISE) today offers unique opportunities for those who are concerned about women. According to its annual Bulletin, OISE offers students interested in women's studies either an Interdisciplinary Focus on Women's Studies in Education, which is a series of courses cutting across disciplines and departments, or a Focus on Feminist Studies and Gender Relations in Education, which is unique to the Sociology Department. In addition, OISE has established a women's center for the purpose of coordinating, promoting, and disseminating research in women's studies. But women's studies at OISE is more than a collection of courses taught by a collection of professors from

---

This project description was compiled and written by Margaret Malone and Rosonna Tite.

a variety of different disciplines. It is more than a women's center.

Approximately 10 percent of the 130 faculty members are feminist and 70 percent of OISE's student population are women.[2] Most students and professors who pursue women's studies (at OISE, or anywhere else) have their own stories about personal, intellectual, and emotional processes of developing their own feminist thinking. They can talk at length about the events that have shaped their lives in this direction. At OISE, this individual growth process is embedded in a larger challenge. Partly because of OISE's tripartite function of providing graduate studies, research, and field development, and partly because OISE draws its professors, students, and community input from a wide range of disciplinary, and social, political, and occupational backgrounds, the challenge for women's studies practitioners here is to create an environment that nurtures supportive communication, flexible boundaries between disciplines, and community outreach. In practical terms, this means blending feminist theory and practice.

The conditions that set the stage for OISE's initial response to the collective demands for women's studies were facilitated by the political climate of the social revolution and the women's liberation movement of the sixties, combined with attempts to create a more open, responsive, and experimental education system. Within this climate, the faculty of the Sociology in Education Department developed and institutionalized a democratic participatory constitution, based on egalitarian principles. All the department constituencies—faculty, support staff, and students—were represented on all standing committees and participated in the monthly departmental assembly. In fact, the support staff and students (and more recently research officers) were and continue to be represented on a parity basis with faculty in all the department's major decisions including faculty hiring. The constitution also included representatives for two special interest groups— the liaison to part-time students and the women's advocate.

The presence of women and the concerns of women in the new department had already been recognized, but there were no women's studies courses until women students began to ask for courses that addressed their concerns. The faculty recognized the need, but initially the necessary institute support was not forthcoming. By 1973, the students put together their own course and found instructors from among the women's student body to teach it. It was a collective and energetic effort strengthened by the support of the Women's Caucus in the sociology department. The Women's Caucus[3] continued to push for additional courses and eventually a feminist faculty position was established. The institutionalized democratic structure created the environment that allowed the various constituencies' needs to be voiced, heard, and eventually acted upon. However, students, faculty, and support staff all agree that none of these changes occurred without struggle.

As is the custom today in the sociology department, candidates for new positions were invited to apply, submit their curriculum vitae for review by all members of the department, and give a talk, followed by an open and often quite vigorous debate. The sociology department appointed Margrit Eichler to be the first feminist scholar at OISE in 1975. Other women were teaching at OISE, notably Alison Prentice (Department of History and Philosophy of Education) and Jeri Wine (Department of Applied Psychology), but they were not specifically appointed as feminists. The Group for Research on Women (GROW) was established to provide, among other purposes, an interdepartmental link for these isolated feminists. Two years later, two additional feminist scholars, Mary O'Brien and Dorothy Smith, joined the faculty of the sociology department.[4]

The hiring of feminist scholars played a crucial role in the development of women's studies at OISE since they brought with them many works in progress. *Resources for Feminist Research/Documentation sur la Recherche Feministe (RFR/DRF)* is a good example. Founded as the *Canadian Newsletter of Research on Women* by Margrit Eichler and Marylee Stephenson,[5] it had the double focus of research and teaching with a Canadian perspective. Originally used as a means of communication between isolated feminist scholars across Canada, *RFR/DRF* is now recognized as an officially refereed publication and OISE journal. While *RFR/DRF* has become known for the annual book review and interdisciplinary issues, some theme issues have been particularly significant. Some examples include Immigrant Women in Canada, Women and the Criminal Justice System, Women as Elders, and the Lesbian Issue, which at the time was the only Canadian feminist publication and resource on lesbians and the politics of lesbian identity. *RFR/DRF* has, among its goals, the objectives of stimulating research into gender relations and the conditions of women's lives, and the dissemination of research findings and critical analyses relevant to feminist theory and activism.

At the same time, the institute, in meeting its tripartite functions, began to produce many innovative educational tools. Among them was the Women's Kit, a learning resource for teachers. This project, originally developed by feminist photographer Pamela Harris, involved extensive outreach to the wider community, which set in motion a still continuing interchange between the institute and the community. The "Kit"—initiated in 1972—and the space required to produce it, eventually led to the development of the Women's Educational Resources Centre (WERC) in 1976. While Frieda Forman has been the creative force behind WERC's scholarly work and networking interaction between and within the staff and user groups, the combination of hiring another feminist faculty member, Mary O'Brien, who took this project on, and the sociology department's democratic constitution, made it possible to give WERC a secure home in the sociology department. Also during this period women were struggling to implement a day-care center, which was eventually housed in OISE. Clearly, women's studies at OISE was not limited to academic studies, but like so many of women's activities, there were direct connections between the everyday lives of women and their work.

As the other departments within OISE began to develop an interest in women's studies—a result of the concerns articulated by the students, community, and faculty—the need for an all-encompassing women's center was evident. Women's concerns regarding their educational needs were often marginalized and isolated within OISE departments other than sociology. The eventual establishment of the Women's Centre[6] in 1983 created the necessary environment, focus, and administrative support for the various women's projects, research, workshops, special lecture series, and liaison work both within OISE and the community. Policy matters pertaining to the center are decided on at a biweekly meeting of its coordinating committee in which every constituency (students, research officers, support staff, and faculty) is represented.

A current example of community outreach is a series of public forums organized by the Older Women's Network, which emerged from the community and was subsequently given support and co-sponsorship by the center. As an attempt to bring a feminist perspective to the problems plaguing older women, the forum provides opportunities for the audience (five hundred at the first forum) to speak out about their personal experiences, and to make recommendations for task force activities.

Other activities sponsored by the Women's Centre, which fall within their mandate for scholarly and professional development of faculty, staff, and students include: the Popular Feminism Series,[7] drawing on the work of feminist scholars from many different fields;[8] the Brown Bag Feminist Lecture Series, providing an informal, supportive setting for students and visiting scholars to share their work; the General Lecture Series, pulling together many feminist scholars from around the world; and a number of additional workshops and conferences. In 1984, for example, the Women's Centre organized an International Conference on Women and Peace.[9] Other events co-sponsored by the center have focused on issues such as women's organizations, day care, problems encountered by immigrant women, technology, and media violence.

In addition to responding to the needs of the community in ways that draw people and issues into a feminist focus, OISE feminists participate in a wide range of service activities directed at bringing the feminist focus out to a broader public and to the various groups involved in formulating public policy. At the federal level, OISE feminists have been called on to consult with and appear before royal commissions and Parliamentary hearings. Examples include, the Royal Commission of Inquiry on Equality in Employment (1985), and the recent Parliamentary Hearings on Free Trade (1987), at which Marjorie Cohen presented a brief. Members have also sought to create a Royal Commission of Inquiry when an issue of extreme importance to women needs to be addressed. For example, Margrit Eichler, among others, formed the Coalition for a Royal Commission on the New Reproductive Technologies. Similar actions are taken at the provincial level vis-à-vis the Ontario Women's Directorate, and the Ministry of Education, and the municipality for the Metro Toronto School Boards, and the Metro Toronto Police Force. For journalists, OISE feminists provide a regular source of information about women's issues. The Women's Centre enhances the function of each of these efforts and its establishment has brought a permanence to the women's studies focus within OISE. Along with the Women's Educational Resource Centre, the Women's Centre provides an integrated focus and service to the community both within and outside the institute.

The Women's Educational Resource Centre (WERC) offers a unique Canadian, contemporary, and archival collection of books, periodicals, and multimedia resources. WERC members provide consultation, advisory services, and resources for professors, students, and a wide range of users in education, government, service organizations, women's groups, and the media. In addition, WERC members generate, organize, co-sponsor and provide material resources for conferences, workshops, and public events. WERC's periodical collection, second to no other in Canada, provided the early foundation for an important indexing project.

The Canadian Women's Indexing Group includes academics and librarians from another Canadian university, library schools, the Canadian Congress for Learning Opportunities for Women, and other feminist organizations. *The Canadian Women's Periodical Index,* designed to provide an index and accompanying thesaurus of women's studies terminology, will soon take its place on library shelves alongside other indexes such as *Sociological Abstracts* and the *Canadian Periodical Index*. These volumes are expected to provide a major new research tool supporting all scholars' attempts to focus on women's issues.

Multidisciplinary and interdepartmental research and development is reflected in the ongoing collaborative work on many other projects and activities. For example, Ruth Pierson, a social historian from the Department of History and Philosophy of Education as well as Sociology in Education, and Marjorie Cohen, an economist from the Department of Sociology, are collaborating on a study of women and unemployment insurance. Joint research is also undertaken between center members and feminist researchers from other universities. Alison Prentice, a historian from the Department of History and Philosophy, and Paula Bourne and Beth Light, two researchers with the Canadian Women's History Project, recently completed writing a textbook, *Canadian Women: A History,* with historian Gail Cuthbert Brandt and political scientist Naomi Black from York University and historian Wendy Mitchinson from the University of Waterloo.

The Sex Equity and OSIS (Ontario Schools, Intermediate and Secondary) Project represents a similar type of activity. Principle investigators Paula Bourne, Beth Light, and Pat Staton are currently preparing nineteen new teacher resource guides in consultation with practicing teachers, which promise a unique contribution to school program development. Dorothy Smith's Latch Key Family: Coordinating the Family School Relation Project investigates mothers' work in the school starting from the position of the subjects.

Finally, encompassing all of the women's studies efforts across Canada is the Canadian Women's Studies Project 22,[10] which investigates the development of women's studies as an academic discipline in Canadian universities. Project members are currently analyzing survey data collected from nine hundred professors who are presently teaching or who have taught women's studies in the past. In addition, they are transcribing interviews conducted with a follow-up sample of close to two hundred professors. Also underway is an analysis of women's studies courses and programs as they appear in university calendars, and preparations for interviewing the most popular feminist thinkers, as identified by the professors.

Students' input into the process of building women's studies at OISE has been crucial. Not only were students involved in initiating the first courses leading to the establishment of the first feminist faculty position, but they also continue to contribute in very significant ways. Many women who come to OISE for graduate studies bring with them experiences from a wide range of volunteer activities and occupational roles, such as work in women's hostels, sports, teaching, nursing, religious life, business, race relations, the arts, and community development. The students' community work and occupational backgrounds most often shape their academic studies, and frequently, as many faculty members have indicated, the theoretical stance and focus of the courses offered.

Graduate courses reflect faculty responsiveness to the diversity of students' academic and community interests. Currently, the Interdisciplinary Focus on Women's Studies falls within four departments: Adult Education, Applied Psychology, History and Philosophy, and Sociology. Among the selection of available courses that might form a core for such a focus are: Feminist Issues in Counselling Psychology and Psychotherapy; The Psychology of Motherhood and Its Relatedness to Education; Women's Learning in the Development of Critical Consciousness; Adult Learning and Social Change: Global Feminist Perspectives; The History of Women and Education; Women, Literature, and Education; Women and the Educational System; Women in Relation to War, Peace, Revolution, and Violence in Ideology and Experience; Advanced Research Seminar on Feminist Theory, Methodology, and Education; Education and the Sociology of Women and Gender Relations; Women, Work, and Education: Production and Reproduction; Nonsexist Approaches to Stratification; and The Social Organization of Knowledge.

OISE's responsiveness to the needs of the community of people interested in women's issues is reflective of the continually developing democratic processes that encourage the participation of students, faculty, and staff in the administration of the institute. The recent hiring of an Employment

Equity Officer, for example, emerged from an institute subcommittee on employment equity, affirmative action, race relations, and ethnocultural- ism. However, what ultimately distinguishes the creative, intellectually stimulating, and endlessly challenging Women's Studies Focus at OISE, are the forward-thinking women (within and outside OISE) who are on the cutting edge of new theory, methodology, and healthy social change. They are the housewives, the factory workers, the cleaners, the feminist scholars, the nurses, the support staff, the economists, the teachers, the filmmakers, the lawyers, the union workers, the artists, the women in every aspect of life. The process of intellectual debate, graduate studies, research, field develop- ment, and community outreach and input touch all women's everyday lives. The unique blend of feminist theory and practice is its strength, its source of creative energy, and its inspiration to continue to labor to make our world more equal, more humane, and more peaceful for everyone.

II. EDUCATIONAL ACTIVITIES: SOME EXAMPLES

A. Courses

Currently, OISE women's studies courses are offered in the Departments of Adult Education, Applied Psychology, History and Philosophy of Edu- cation, and Sociology in Education.

The following are examples of selected excerpts of some of the many women's studies courses offered at OISE. Courses and course content vary year to year depending on the course instructor and the needs of the community of people interested in women's issues.

1. Women, Literature, and Education

Instructor: Deanne Bogdan
The purpose of this course is to give an overview of the major trends in women's writing and feminist literature. It tries to bring together a number of aims and subject matters by focusing on the "creative" and "constructed" nature of women's "self" as reader and writer. The course content concen- trates primarily, though not exclusively, on Anglo-American writers. The aim is to integrate the classes of literary theory with reading and responding to works of literature; to give students the opportunity to share responses; to encourage literary research; and to encourage academic writing that incorporates and integrates scholarship, personal experience, and theoreti- cal analysis. It seeks to develop an authorial voice that breaks down barriers between the creative and critical, the academic and the experiential.

The course is structured along the following topics:

- Images of Women and the Reader's Self
- Feminism, the Literary Self, and the Romantic Imagination

- Patriarchy and Woman's Romantic Self
- Patriarchy and Writing the Self
- Virginia Woolf: The Literary/Political Self
- Utopian Vision and Romantic Self-Creation
- Dystopia as Annihilation of Women's Self
- Marginalized Selves I: Towards a Theory of Self-Representation
- Marginalized Selves II: Minority Literature

Examples of readings include:

Atwood, Margaret. *The Handmaid's Tale.* Toronto: McClelland and Stewart, 1985.

Belsey, Catherine. *Critical Practice.* London: Methuen, 1980.

Chopin, Kate. *The Awakening: An Authoritative Text, Contexts, Criticism.* Edited by Margaret Culley. New York: Norton, 1976.

Mellor, Anne K., ed. *Romanticism and Feminism.* Bloomington: Indiana University Press, 1988.

Moi, Toril. *Sexual/Textual Politics: Feminist Literary Theory.* London: Methuen, 1985.

Radway, Janice. *Reading the Romance: Women, Patriarchy, and Popular Literature and Theory.* New York: Pantheon, 1985.

Showalter, Elaine, ed., *The New Feminist Criticism: Essays on Women, Literature and Theory.* New York: Pantheon, 1985.

Woolf, Virginia. *Three Guineas.* London: Hogarth, 1938. Reprint. New York: Harcourt, Brace, Jovanovich, 1966.

2. The History of Women and Education in Canada

Instructor: Alison Prentice

This course undertakes a survey of the history of women's education and of women's work in educational settings in Canada. On the one hand, the course examines the various institutions—both formal and informal—that, over time, have been involved in the education of girls and young women. Secondly, it deals with the evolution of teaching, paying particular attention to the sexual division of labor within the occupation.

The scholarly literature on the history of women and education in Canada has grown rapidly over the past fifteen years. One of the main objectives of this course is to become familiar with, and to critically assess, this body of literature. It will also explore the different sources that can be drawn upon in this field, as well as the methodologies that can be used. A further goal is to explore questions in the history of Canadian women and education from a feminist perspective. How can a feminist historical analysis help to illuminate educational structures and patterns of work in our schools, colleges, and universities?

A final goal is the development of students' skills and insights into their

own particular situation. As active participants in the field, students have the opportunity to develop their skills in historical research and writing.
The course is structured along the following topics:

- Methodology
- Convents and Early Private Schools
- From "Private" to "Public" Schooling
- The Teachers: Nineteenth-Century Transitions
- Women's Work in Schools
- Women, the Family, and Education
- The Professional Training of Women: Improved Status or Ghettoization
- "Higher" Education: Access to Equality?

Examples of readings include:

Axelrod, Paul, and John G. Reid, eds. *Youth, University and Canadian Society: Essays in the Social History of Higher Education.* Montreal: McGill-Queen's University Press, 1989.
Danylewycz, Marta, and Alison Prentice. "Teachers' Work: Changing Patterns and Perceptions in the Emerging School Systems of Nineteenth- and Early Twentieth-Century Central Canada." *Labour/le travail* 17 (Spring 1986).
Fahmy-Eid, Nadia, and Micheline Dumont. *Maîtresses de maison, maîtresses d'école: Femmes, famille et éducation dans l'histoire du Québec.* Montreal: Boréal Express, 1983.
Prentice, Alison et al. *Canadian Women: A History.* Toronto: Harcourt, Brace, Jovanovich, 1988.

3. Adult Learning and Social Change: Global Feminist Perspectives

Instructor: Angela Miles
This course is organized into two parts: Part I: General Feminist Principles, and Part II: Feminist Principles and Educational Practice Globally.
Part I is organized into the following topics:

- Early Feminist Classics
- Anthologies of Early Writing
- About the Early Movement (the sixties and early seventies)
- Consciousness-Raising and Feminist Process
- Later Theoretical Developments

Examples of readings include:

Cooke, Joanne, Charlotte Bunch-Weeks, and Robin Morgan, eds. *The New Woman: An Anthology Library.* Greenwich, Conn.: Fawcett, 1970.

Cade, Toni, ed. *The Black Woman: An Anthology*. New York: Mentor,
New American Library, 1970.
Koedt, Anne, ed. *Radical Feminism*. New York: Vintage, Random House,
1970.
Miles, Angela. *Feminist Radicalism in the 1980s*. Montreal: Culture Texts,
1985.

Part II examines feminist educational practice in a variety of contexts and
countries. Examples of readings include:

Bhasin, Kamla. *Towards Empowerment*. Rome: Freedom from Hunger
Campaign/Action for Development, Food and Agriculture Organization
of the United Nations, 1983.
Bunch, Charlotte, and Sandra Pollack, eds. *Learning Our Way: Essays in
Feminist Education*. Trumansburg, N.Y.: Crossing Press, 1983.
hooks, bell. *Feminist Theory: From Margin to Center*. Boston: South End Press,
1984.
Kiswar, Madhu, and Ruth Vanita, eds. *In Search of Answers: Indian Women's
Voices from Manushi*. London: Zed Books, 1984.
Mies, Marie. *Patriarchy and Accumulation on a World Scale: Women and the
Division of Labour*. London: Zed Books, 1986.
Sen, Gita, and Caren Grown. *Development, Crisis, and Alternative Visions:
Third World Women's Perspectives*. New Delhi: The Dawn Secretariat, Insti-
tute of Social Studies Trust (ISST), 1985; New York: Monthly Review
Press, 1987.
Sistren. *Lionheart Gal: Life Stories of Jamaican Women*. Toronto: Sister Vision,
Black Women and Women of Color Press, 1987.
Smith, Barbara. "Introduction." In *Home Girls: A Black Feminist Anthology*.
New York: Kitchen Table/Women of Color Press, 1983.

4. Feminist Organizing and Community Psychology

Instructor: Jeri Wine

This course is an attempt to bridge the gap that frequently appears
between theory and practice—a product of masculinist dualist thought that
is often concretely manifested among feminists as a division between
academic and activist women. The reading list includes readings focused on
practice, ones that integrate theory and practice, and some strictly theoretical readings that are considered essential. Students are required to form
small collectives and carry out feminist organizing projects. In the context
of the project, students are required to give evidence of familiarity with
activism in the area of their project both through reading and contact with
feminist activists, as well as to provide ongoing analysis of the theoretical
grounding for their work.

Much activist work "reinvents the wheel," that is, it is carried out as though it is the first time such work were undertaken and the same mistakes are repeated, similar issues arise, and so on. There is now a considerable literature, much of it unpublished, that provides information from feminists on the work of other activists. It is also possible, of course, to learn from feminist organizers by word of mouth. The class is expected to serve as a forum for this kind of learning, and class members are expected to seek out knowledgeable informants in the area of their project. It is also frequently the case that feminist organizing is carried out without a clear understanding of the theoretical bases and implications of the work. The class is expected to make creative connections among overarching theory, writings on particular issues, and specific projects, strategies, and goals.

The course is organized along the following topics:

- Feminist Directions: Locating Ourselves
- More Feminist Theory and Directions
- Collectives: Process, Promise, Problems, Critique, and Comparison with Other Organizational Forms
- The Canadian Feminist Movement: History and Contemporary Activism
- Organizing Strategies
- Race and Class
- Women's Bodies—Site of Struggle
- Noncollective Structures and Strategies
- Women's Health
- Women and Peace

Examples of readings include:

Adamson, Nancy, Linda Birskin, and Margaret McPhail. *Feminist Organizing for Change: The Contemporary Women's Movement in Canada.* Toronto: Oxford University Press, 1988.
Bunch, Charlotte. "The Reform Tool Kit." In *Building Feminist Theory: Essays from* Quest, a Feminist Quarterly. New York: Longman, 1981.
Lyons, Gracie. *Constructive Criticism: A Handbook.* Berkeley, Calif.: Issues in Radical Therapy Collective, 1976.
Ward, Sue. *Organizing Things: A Guide to Successful Political Action.* London: Pluto Press, 1984.
Women's Self-Help Network. *Working Collectively.* Campbell River, B.C.: Ptarmigan Press, 1984.

5. The Social Organization of Knowledge

Instructor: Dorothy Smith
This course is primarily concerned with exploring the forms of knowledge that are essential constituents of the textually mediated forms of

governing, organizing, regulating, planning, and exercising initiative for contemporary capitalist societies. The course deals with aspects of everyday life as they are socially organized and form part of consciousness. The critical interest is in developing, through investigation, an awareness of processes through which the relations of the ruling apparatus are produced and reproduced.

The course is organized along the following main topics:

- The Rise of the Ruling Apparatus
- Charting the Shift In Consciousness
- The Problematic
- The Question of Method
- The Social Organization of Textual Reality
- Facts as Social Relations
- Ideology as an Inscriptive and Interpretive Practice
- Inscription
- The Social Organization of Reading
- Textually Mediated Discourse
- The Textually Mediated Relations and Apparatuses of Ruling

Examples of readings include:

Atkinson, J. Maxwell. *Discovering Suicide: Studies in the Social Organization of Sudden Death.* London: Macmillan, 1978.

Eisenstein, Elizabeth L. *The Printing Press as an Agent of Change: Communication and Cultural Transformations in Early Modern Europe.* Cambridge: Cambridge University Press, 1979.

Foucault, Michel. *The Archaeology of Knowledge.* London: Tavistock Publications, 1974.

Garfinkel, Harold. "Suicide for All Practical Purposes." In *Studies in Ethnomethodology,* ed. Harold Garfinkel. New York: Prentice-Hall, 1967.

Marx, Karl, and Friedrich Engels. *The German Ideology.* Moscow: Progress, 1976. (Section on Feuerbach)

Noble, David. *America by Design: Science, Technology, and the Rise of Corporate Capitalism.* Oxford: Oxford University Press, 1979.

Smith, Dorothy E. *The Conceptual Practices of Power: A Feminist Sociology of Knowledge.* Toronto: University of Toronto Press, 1990.

————. *Texts, Facts and Femininity: Exploring the Relations of Ruling.* London: Routledge, 1990.

Weber, Max. *Economy and Society.* Edited by Günther Roth and Claus Wittich. Translated by E. Fischoff et al. 1968. Reprint. Berkeley: University of California Press, 1978.

6. Women, Work and Education: Production and Reproduction

Instructor: Marjorie Cohen

The kind of work women perform and how it is valued by society is shaped by the complex interaction of sexual relations, cultural perceptions, economic conditions, and social action. In this course the nature of women's work and the relationship between the division of labor by gender and women's subordination are examined. The course examines the relationship between domestic labor and other forms of labor; the nature of women's labor force participation and the theories that attempt to explain discrimination; and the effect of public policy and political movements on the conditions of female labor.

The course is organized along the following main topics:

- Public Policy and Women's Work: Election Issues
- Economic Change and Women's Labor—Historical Differences and Perspectives
- Theoretical Explanations for the Economics of Women's Paid and Unpaid Work
- Household Labor
- The Future of Women's Work

Examples of readings include:

Amsden, Alice, ed. *The Economics of Women and Work.* New York: Penguin, 1980.

Armstrong, Pat, and Hugh Armstrong. *The Double Ghetto.* Toronto: McClelland and Stewart, 1984.

Cohen, Marjorie. *Free Trade and the Future of Women's Work.* Toronto: Garamond, 1987.

————. *Women's Work, Markets and Economic Development in Nineteenth-Century Ontario.* Toronto: University of Toronto Press, 1988.

Connelly, Patricia. *Last Hired, First Fired: Women and the Canadian Workforce.* Toronto: Women's Press, 1978.

De Bresson, Chris, Margaret Lowe Benston, and Jessie Worst. *Work and New Technologies: Other Perspectives.* Calgary: Socialist Studies, 1987.

Folbre, Nancy. "Hearts and Spades: Paradigms of Household Economics." *World Development* 14 (1986): 245–55.

MacDonald, Martha. "Economics and Feminism: The Dismal Science." *Studies in Political Economy* 15 (Fall 1984).

Mackintosh, Maureen. "Gender and Economics: The Sexual Division of Labor and the Subordination of Women." In *Of Marriage and the Market,* edited by Kate Young et al. London: Methuen, 1984.

Sanday, Peggy Reeves. *Female Power and Male Dominance: On the Origins of Sexuality, Inequality.* Cambridge: Cambridge University Press, 1981.

7. Nonsexist Approaches to Stratification

Instructor: Margrit Eichler

This course takes the form of a research seminar in which participants will be jointly engaged in trying to develop and apply a nonsexist approach to social stratification. The course has four aims:

1. to provide an overview of critiques of sexism in stratification studies that have been made in the past;

2. to familiarize students with a means of identifying sexism in research;

3. to apply these analytic tools to selected recent publications in the area of social stratification;

4. to work with an alternative framework that tries to avoid sexism, as well as other problems to be identified in the contemporary social stratification literature.

Examples of readings include:

Acker, Joan. "Women and Social Stratification: A Case of Intellectual Sexism." *American Journal of Sociology* 78, no. 4 (1973).

————. "Women and Stratification: A Review of Recent Literature." *Contemporary Sociology* 9 (1980).

Armstrong, Pat, and Hugh Armstrong. "Beyond Sexless Class and Classless Sex: Towards a Feminist Marxism." *Studies in Political Economy* 10 (1983).

Benston, Margaret. "The Political Economy of Women's Liberation." In *Roles Women Play: Readings Towards Women's Liberation,* ed. Michele Hoffnung Garskof. Belmont, Calif.: Brooks/Cole, 1971.

Boyd, Monica, and Hugh A. McRoberts. "Women, Men, and Socioeconomic Indices: An Assessment." In *Measures of Socioeconomic Status: Current Issues,* ed. Mary G. Powers. Boulder, Colo.: Westview, 1983.

Dale, Angela, G. Nigel Gilbert, and Sara Arber. "Integrating Women into Class Theory." *Sociology* 19, no. 3 (1985).

Delphy, Christine. "Women in Stratification Studies." In *Close to Home: A Materialist Analysis of Women's Oppression.* London: Hutchinson, 1984.

Eichler, Margrit. *Nonsexist Research Methods: A Practical Guide.* Boston: Allen and Unwin, 1988.

————. "Women as Personal Dependents: A Critique of Theories of the Stratification of the Sexes and an Alternative Approach." In *Women in Canada,* ed. Marylee Stephenson. Don Mills, 1977.

Erikson, Robert. "Social Class of Men, Women, and Families." *Sociology* 18, no. 4 (1984).

Goldthorpe, John H. "Women and Class Analysis: A Reply to the Replies." *Sociology* 18, no.4 (1984).

Heath, Anthony, and Nicky Britten. "Women's Jobs Do Make a Difference: A Reply to Goldthorpe." *Sociology* 18, no. 4 (1984).

Seccombe, Wally. "The Housewife and Her Labour under Capitalism." *New Left Review* 83 (1974).

Smith, Dorothy. "Women, the Family and Corporate Capitalism." In *Women in Canada*, ed. Marylee Stephenson. Don Mills, 1977.

Stanworth, Michelle. "Women and Class Analysis: A Reply to Goldthorpe." *Sociology* 18, no. 2 (1984).

B. Popular Lecture Series

Since 1985, the Centre for Women's Studies in Education has sponsored the Popular Feminism Lecture Series and the Brown Bag Lunch Series. Lecture topics have included:

- Approaches to Anti-Racist Education
- Black Feminist Issues
- Women and Religion
- Violence Against Women
- Infertility and Sterility: The Alibi of Reproductive Technologies
- Sexuality and Empowerment

III. PUBLICATIONS

In response to the perceived need for inexpensive women's studies material, the Center for Women's Studies in Education has published three separate papers series as well as book publication projects.

A. Occasional Papers

Brodribb, Somer. Reproductive Technologies, Masculine Dominance and the Canadian State.

Carter, Betty. A Feminist Perspective on "The Badgley Report": Sexual Offenses Against Children.

Haddad, Jane. Sexism and Social Welfare Policy: The Case of Family Benefits in Ontario.

Pimento, Barbara. Native Families in Jeopardy—the Child Welfare System in Canada.

Van Kirk, Sylvia. Toward A Feminist Perspective in Native History.

B. Critical Perspectives Papers

Gates, Eugene. Creative Women in Music: A Critical Review of Seven Psychological Studies.

Harris, Carol E. Women in Roles of School Leadership: Theoretical Reflections upon Selected Administrative Studies, 1968–1987.

Lynett, Elizabeth. A Critical Review of the Social Role Theory as an Explanation for the Sex Differences in Depression.

C. Popular Feminism Papers

Armitage, Kay. Reverse Angles: Feminist Filmmaking.
Caplan, Paula. Psyching Women Out.
Gerrard, Nikki. Undoing Crazymaking: Feminist Therapy—A Stitch in Time Saves Nine.
Rockhill, Kathy. The Chaos of Subjectivity in the Ordered Halls of Academe.

D. Books (published by the Centre for Women's Studies in Education)

O'Brien, Mary et al., eds. *Feminism and Education: A Canadian Perspective*, 1990.
Staton, Pat, Joyce Scane, and Dormer Ellis, eds. *Toward the Future: Proceedings of a Workshop on Women in Non-Traditional Occupations*, 1987.

Numerous books and scholarly papers written by the OISE feminist faculty and associated feminist scholars have been published through a variety of other publishers and/or journals. For further information, please contact the Center for Women's Studies in Education.

E. Bibliography (published by the Center for Women's Studies in Education)

Gelman, Susan, and Alison Prentice. *The History of Gender and Teaching*, 1990.

F. Visiting Scholars

Over the years, OISE has had visiting scholars from a variety of countries. Some of their research topics include:

- Girls and Schooling in Australia 1950-1970
- Care and Its Role in Moral Education
- History of the Education of Working-Class Women and Girls
- The Implementation of Equal Opportunities Policies within Schools in England

NOTES

1. The authors would like to express their appreciation to Margrit Eichler and Ruth Pierson, who encouraged us to write this paper and assisted with editorial comments. We would also like to acknowledge the assistance of Paula Bourne, Frieda Forman, Pamela Harris, Edward Harvey, Gloria Geller, Helen Lenskyj, David Livingstone, Paul Olson, and Lucy Tantalo. Special thanks to the Women's Centre, who allowed us liberal access to their resources for the preparation of this paper.
2. When the first feminist faculty member was appointed, the proportion of female

students to male students was estimated to have been the reverse.

3. The Women's Caucus is now OISE-wide and is supported by the Centre for Women's Studies in Education.

4. Mary O'Brien, recently retired from OISE, is internationally known for her contributions to feminist theory. Her book, *The Politics of Reproduction* (New York: Routledge and Kegan Paul, 1981) was written in English, has been translated into French and Greek, and is soon to be translated into German. A second book, *Reproducing the World: Essays in Feminist Theory* (San Francisco: Westview, 1990) has just been released.

5. A consultant, Vancouver, British Columbia.

6. The Women's Centre, established in 1983, brings together an existing core of feminist faculty, research officers, and graduate students involved in the study of women and education. All are considered "members" of the Women's Centre, but many may in fact develop and conduct their research and other activities quite separately from the center, though the center can play a supporting role.

7. All the Popular Feminist Series lectures are available in cassette from WERC, OISE. Some of these lectures are also available in print from the Centre for Women's Studies in Education.

8. The Toronto Area Women's Research Colloquim, established approximately ten years ago by feminists from York University, University of Toronto, and OISE, also coordinate a series of multidisciplinary lectures in which many OISE feminist scholars participate.

9. The Women and Peace Conference gave rise to *Women and Peace: Theoretical, Historical and Practical Perspectives*, Ruth Roach Pierson, ed. New York: Croom Helm, 1987.

10. Major researchers include Margrit Eichler, Rhonda Lenton, Rosonna Tite, and Louise Vandelac.

ENGLAND: WOMEN, MEN, AND DEVELOPMENT, INSTITUTE OF DEVELOPMENT STUDIES, SUSSEX

Women, Men, and Development
The Institute of Development Studies
at the University of Sussex
Brighton BN1 9RE
England
Phone: 0273- 606261
Telex: 877997 IDSBTN G
Contact person: Naila Kabeer

I. BACKGROUND

The course, Women, Men, and Development at the Institute of Development Studies (IDS), is open to approximately twenty-four participants per year, who are recruited from government ministries and offices, nongovernmental organizations (NGOs), particularly those undertaking their own development projects, grassroots and trade union organizations, women's groups, universities, and institutions and agencies responsible for providing and interpreting data for government policies. Most of the participants come from the Third World, and the course aims to have equal numbers of men and women participants.

The course provides participants with an understanding of gender's key

---

While the course retains a core set of issues and lectures, it changes from year to year in response to the interests and expertise of the person running it. The course description and reading lists reprinted here provide an illustration of the course based on the one offered in 1988.

role in determining how men and women participate in economic, social, and political activities. A basic premise of the course is that men's and women's lives are structured in fundamentally different ways and therefore that development policies and programs affect them differently and provoke different responses. Seemingly well-thought-out projects that ignore gender differences or make incorrect assumptions about the sexual division of labor have often encountered costly difficulties or led to a marked deterioration in the educational prospects, health, and nutritional status of women and children. To achieve development aims, it is essential to examine carefully the gender implications of a wide range of policies and programs. Such an examination requires an adequate understanding of the structure of gender relations, available in terms of both personnel trained in gender issues and data generated by gender-focused research.

The course identifies a number of major issues concerning women's participation in economic and social processes in societies undergoing rapid transformation. It emphasizes a number of critical interventions that can help ensure social recognition of, and support for, women's distinct contributions and needs: policy-useful research; formulation of policy alternatives; and development of organizational strategies to influence policy-making decisions. Grassroots, work-based, and women's organizations are seen as potential areas where women and men working for gender equality can identify their needs and mobilize around meeting those needs. The course enables participants to evaluate policy and prepare policy briefs, to organize more effectively around meeting women's needs, and to prepare for policy-focused research. It also aims to give participants a keener sense of the strategical planning and organization necessary to ensure that changes in policy or implementation of existing policies are given serious consideration.

II. TEACHING ACTIVITIES

A. Structure

Teaching methods include lectures, exercises, and practical work, together with discussion with people working in local government, NGOs, and women's organizations on issues of gender equity and social change. Speakers come from the IDS as well as from other agencies involved in development work. Particular importance is attached to small group discussion of conceptual and policy issues and participants' own experiences. All participants are requested to bring material with them to make an oral presentation early in the course on their work and present concerns.

A one-week field trip enables participants to get a comparative and firsthand impression of some economic and social problems in Britain today. During the trip, participants meet groups organizing around gender-specific problems. At a conference in the final week, participants present a paper based on their work during the course. Specially invited outsiders comment on the papers and help course participants plan further work.

B. Contents

The first half of the course covers: 1) the direction and aims of development; 2) gender relations; 3) identification of the critical issues in rural and industrial development as regards women's access to paid work including: a) agricultural modernization and changes in land use and ownership, in crop patterns and production methods, in the end use of production, and in women's access to land, labor, markets, income, credit and training; b) import substitution or export promotion strategies: the logic behind them and their implications for economic growth and social equity; employment generation and the sexual division of labor; inequality and impoverishment in the urban and rural sector; provision of welfare services; and the state, market, and NGOs; c) technological innovation; and 4) economic crisis, structural adjustment policies, and their implications for gender divisions in labor and well-being.

C. Course lists

Below is a list of the topics covered in the course, with some of the required and recommended reading under each heading.

1. What Is Development? Group Exercise

Briefing paper No. 2A. "The Development Debate."
Seers, Dudley. "The Meaning of Development." In *Development Theory: Four Critical Studies*, ed. D. Lehmann. Frank Cass, 1979.

2. Women and Development: Group Exercise

Briefing paper No. 2B. "The Development Debate and Women."
Oakley, A. *Sex, Gender, and Society.* London: Temple Smith, 1972.
Rubin, G. "The Traffic in Women: Notes on the Political Economy of Sex." In *Toward an Anthropology of Women*, ed. Rayna R. Reiter. New York: Monthly Review Press, 1975.

3. Women and Development: A Historical View

Beneria, L., ed. *Women and Development.* New York: Praeger Publishers, 1982.
Boserup, E. *Women's Role in Economic Development.* New York: St. Martin's Press, 1970.

Briefing papers, mimeos, and lectures listed for the course are unpublished and may be available from IDS.

Briefing Paper No. 2B. "The Development Debate and Women."
Maithreyi, Krishna Raj. "Women and Development." *Lokayan Bulletin* 4, no.
6 (1986).

4. Women and Development: The Theoretical Underpinnings

Banderage, Asoka. "Women in Development: Liberalism, Marxism, and
Marxist Feminism." *Development and Change* 15, no. 4 (1984).
Beneria, L., and G. Sen. "Class and Gender Inequalities and Women's Role
in Economic Development." *Feminist Studies* 8, no. 1 (1982).

5. Women and Development: Socialist Approaches

Engels, Friedrich. "The Origin of the Family, Private Property, and the
State." In *Marx and Engels: Selected Works*. London: Lawrence and Wishart,
1970.
Kollontai, A. *Autobiography of a Sexually Emancipated Woman*. London:
Orback and Chambers, 1972.
Molyneux, M. "Family Reform in Socialist States: The Hidden Agenda."
Feminist Review 21 (1985).

6. Alternative Approaches to Women and Development: Discussion

Allison, H., G. Ashworth, and N. Reclift, comps. "Hard Cash: Man-Made
Development and Its Consequences." In *Change, War on Want*, 1985.
Sen, Gita, and Caren Grown. *Development, Crises, and Alternative Visions:
Third World Women's Perspectives*. New Dehli: DAWN (Development Al-
ternatives with Women for a New Era), 1985; New York: Monthly Review
Press, 1987.

7. Antecedents to Gender and Development

Anand, R. "Rethinking Women and Development: The Case for Feminism."
CUSO Journal, 1984.
Young, Kate. "The Four Feminisms." Lecture, 1988.

8. Gender and Development

Oakley, A. *Sex, Gender, and Society*. London: Temple Smith, 1972.
Whitehead, A. "Some Preliminary Notes on the Subordination of Women."
IDS Bulletin 10, no. 3 (1979).
Young, K. "Gender and Development: A Relational Approach." Lecture,
1988.

9. Condition: Position: Welfare: Equity

CIDA (Canadian International Development Agency). "Managing the
Process of Change in Women in Development." Parts 2 and 3 of presen-

tation to President's Committee Policy Branch, 1984.

Sen, A. *Women, Technology, and Sexual Divisions.* UNCTAD (United Nations Conference on Trade and Development), 1984. (Shorter Version).

Young, Kate. "Some Reflections on Women's Needs." Mimeo, 1988.

10. Class, Race and Ethnic Differences

Kaze, H. "The Beginning of a Debate Long Due: Some Observations on Ethnocentrism and Socialist-Feminist Theory." *Feminist Review* 22 (1986).

Lees, S. "Sex, Race and Culture: Feminism and the Limits of Cultural Pluralism." *Feminist Review* 22 (1986).

Mirza, H. S. "The Dilemma of Socialist Feminism: The Case of Black Feminism." *Feminist Review* 22 (1986).

Ramzanoglu, C. "Ethnocentrism and Socialist-Feminist Theory: A Response to Barrett and McIntosh." *Feminist Review* 22 (1986).

11. Gender and Development: State Socialist Experience—Cuba

Greer, Germaine. "Cuba." In *Women: A World Report.* London: Methuen, 1985.

Holt-Seeland, Inger. *Women of Cuba.* London: Zed Press, 1982.

Larguia, I., and J. Dumoulin. "Towards a Science of Women's Liberation: A View From Cuba." *Red Rap Pamphlet* 1 (1975).

"On the Full Exercise of Women's Equality: Thesis to the First Congress of the Communist Party of Cuba." In *Women and the Cuban Revolution,* ed. Elizabeth Stone. New York: Pathfinder Press, 1981.

12. Gender and Development: State Socialist Experience—Tanzania

Andersson, C.H. *Domestic Water Supply Improvements in Tanzania: Impact on Rural Women.* Report to Institute of Resource Assessment, University of Dar Es Salaam, 1985.

Government of the United Republic of Tanzania and United Nations Children's Fund (UNICEF). *Analysis of the Situation of Children and Women,* 465-83. Dar Es Salaam: UNICEF, 1985.

13. The State: Can the State Be Used as a Neutral Agency for the Redistribution of Resources in Capitalist Societies?

Anglade, C., and C. Fortin. *The State and Capital Accumulation in Latin America.* Vol. 1, chap. 1. Pittsburgh: University of Pittsburgh Press, 1985.

Friedman, M. *Capitalism and Freedom.* Introduction and chaps. 1 and 2. Chicago: University of Chicago Press, 1962.

Miliband, R. *The State in Capitalist Society.* Chaps 1 and 3. London: Quartet Books Limited, 1969.

14. Development: The Debates in the Sixties and Seventies

Singer, H.W. "Poverty, Income Distribution, and Levels of Living: Thirty Years of Changing Thought on Development Problems." *Reflections on Economic Development and Social Change,* ed. Hanumantha Rao et al. Columbia, Mo.: South Asia Books, 1979.

Toye, John. "Development Policy in the Shadow of Keynes." Chap. 2 in *Dilemmas of Development: Reflections on the Counter-Revolution in Development Theory and Policy.* Oxford and New York: Blackwell, 1987.

15. Industrial Development Debates

Briefing Papers 6, 6B, 7.

Prebisch, R. "The System and Social Structure of Latin America." In *Latin American Radicalism,* ed. Irving L. Horowitz. 1969.

Sutcliffe, R. *Industry and Underdevelopment.* Chap. 1. London: Addison Wesley, 1971.

16. Industrialization Case Study—Brazil

Evans, P. *Dependent Development: The Alliance of Multinational, State, and Local Capital in Brazil.* Princeton: Princeton University Press, 1979.

Humphrey, J., and D. Wield. *Industrialization and Energy in Brazil.* Case Study 6. Milton Keynes, U.K.: Open University Press, Third World Studies, 1983.

17. The Informal Sector

McEwen Scott, A. "Who are the Self-Employed?" In *Casual Work and Poverty in the Third World Cities,* ed. R. Bromley and C. Gerry. New York: Wiley, 1989.

Moser, C. "Informal Sector or Petty Commodity Production? Dualism or Dependence in Urban Development?" *World Development* 6, no. 9/10 (1978).

18. Technological Change and Informal Sector Employment

Murray, F. "The Decentralization of Production: The Decline of the Mass-collective Worker?" *Capital and Class* 19 (Spring 1983).

Schmitz, H. *Microelectronics: Implications for Employment, Outwork, Skills and Wages.* IDS (Institute of Development Studies) Discussion Paper no. 205, Sussex, June 1985.

19. Technological Change and Formal Sector Employment

Humphrey, J. "Gender, Pay and Skill: Manual Workers in Brazilian Industry." In *Women, Work and Ideology in the Third World,* ed. Haleh Afshar. London and New York: Tavistock, 1985.

20. Socialist Development in the Third World

Coraggio, José L. "Economics and Politics in the Transition to Socialism: Reflections on the Nicaraguan Experience." In *Transition and Development Problems of Third World Socialism,* ed. Richard R. Fagen et al., 143–170. New York: Monthly Review Press, 1986.

White, Gordon. "Developmental States and Socialist Industrialization in the Third World." *Journal of Development Studies* 21, no. 1 (October 1984): 97–120.

———. "Revolutionary Socialist Development in the Third World: An Overview." In *Revolutionary Socialist Development in the Third World,* ed. Gordon White et al., 1–34. Lexington, Ky.: University Press of Kentucky, 1983.

21. Introduction to Agricultural Development Debates and Links with Development Strategies

Goodman, D., and M. Redclift. *From Peasant to Proletarian: Capitalist Development and Agrarian Transition.* Oxford and New York: Basil Blackwell, 1983.

Mellor, J. "Rural Growth Linkages." Chap. 7 in *The New Economics of Growth.* Ithaca, N.Y.: Cornell University Press, 1976.

Myint, H. "Agriculture and Economic Development in the Open Economy." In *Agriculture in Development Theory,* ed. Lloyd G. Reynolds, 327–55. New Haven, Conn.: Yale University Press, 1975.

22. Cash Crop/First Food Debate, National Food Self-Sufficiency/Security Arguments

Cheater, A. "Women in Commercial Agricultural Production: Medium Scale Freehold in Zimbabwe." *Development and Change* 12, no. 3 (1981).

Henn, J. K. "Feeding the Cities and Feeding the Peasants: What Role for Africa's Women Farmers?" *World Development* 11, no. 12 (1983).

Maxwell, S., and A. Fernando. "Cash Crops in Developing Countries: The Issues, the Fact, the Policies," parts 3, 4, and 5. Mimeo, 1987.

23. The Gender Implications of Technological Change in Agriculture

Agarwal, B. "Rural Women and the High Yielding Variety Rice Technology." *Economic and Political Weekly, Review of Agriculture* 19, no. 13 (March 1984).

Whitehead, A. "A Conceptions Framework for the Analysis of the Effects of Technological Change on Rural Women." In *Rural Women and Technological Change,* ed. I. Ahmed. London: Allen and Unwin, 1985.

24. Rural Development, Poverty, and the Livelihood Strategies of the Poorest

Chambers, Robert. *Rural Development: Putting the Last First.* New York: Longman, 1983.

Gulati, Leela. *Profiles in Female Poverty: A Study of Five Poor Working Women in Kerala,* 63–98. Oxford and Elmsford, N.Y.: Pergamon, 1982.

Hartmann, Betsy, and James K. Boice. *A Quiet Violence: View From a Bangladesh Village.* San Francisco: Institute for Food and Development Policy, 1988.

Rahmato, Dessalegn. *Peasant Survival Strategies.* Geneva: International Institute for Relief and Development, Food for the Hungry International, 1988.

25. Socialist Strategy and Agrarian Transformation

Deere, C. D. "Agrarian Reform Peasants and Rural Population and the Organization of Production in the Transition to Socialism." In *Transition and Development: Problems of Third World Socialism,* ed. Richard R. Fagen et al., 143-70. New York: Monthly Review Press, 1986.

Fitzgerald, E. V. K. "Agrarian Reform as a Model of Accumulation: The Case of Nicaragua since 1979." *Journal of Development Studies* 22, no. 1 (1985).

———. "The Problem of Balance in the Peripheral Socialist Economy: A Conceptual Note." *World Development* 13, no. 1 (1985).

Mackintosh, M. *Agricultural Marketing and Socialist Accumulation: A Case Study of Maize Marketing in Mozambique.* Milton Keynes, U.K.: Open University DPP Working Paper no. 1, 1985.

Selden, Mark. "The Crisis of Collectivisation: Socialist Development and the Peasantry." *IDS Bulletin* 13, no. 4, (1982).

26. The Global Economy in the Eighties

Lipietz, Alain. "From the Configuration of Success to Crises in Peripheral Fordism." In *Mirages and Miracles,* by A. Lipietz, 131–87. London: Verso, 1987.

Raj, K. N. "Structural Changes in the World Economy." In *Economic and Political Weekly,* December 26, 1987.

27. Debt

Brett, E. A. *The World Economy since the War.* Chap. 9. London: Macmillan; New York: Praeger, 1985.

Delvin, R. "Economic Restructuring in Latin America in the Face of the Foreign and External Transfer Problem." *CEPAL Review* 32, Economic Commission for Latin America, 1987.

Griffiths-Jones, S., and R. Green. *African External Debt and Development: A Review and Analysis.* Prepared for the African Center for Monetary Studies and the United Nations Conference on Trade and Development (UNCTAD), 1984.

Payer, Cheryl. *The Debt Trap: The IMF and the Third World.* New York: Monthly Review Press, 1975.

28. Structural Adjustment

Brett, E. A. *The World Economy since the War.* Chaps. 7 and 8. London: Macmillan; New York: Praeger, 1985.

Cornia, A. et al. *Adjustment with a Human Face: Protecting the Vulnerable and Promoting Growth.* Oxford: Clarendon Press, 1987.

Elson, D. *The Impact of Structural Adjustment on Women: Concepts and Issues.* Manchester: DSA Annual Conference, 1987.

Williamson, J. "The Lending Policies of the IMF." In *IMF Conditionality,* by J. Williamson. Washington: Institute for International Economics, 1985.

29. Structural Adjustment: a Discussion

Cornia, A. et al. *Adjustment with a Human Face: Protecting the Vulnerable and Promoting Growth.* Oxford: Clarendon Press, 1987.

Elson, D. *The Impact of Structural Adjustment on Women: Concepts and Issues.* Manchester: DSA Annual Conference, 1987.

30. State or Market

Deepak, L. *The Poverty of Development Economics.* London: Hobart Paperback, 1983.

Green, R. H. "The Role of the State as an Agent of Economic and Social Development in the Least Developed Countries." *Journal of Development Planning* 6 (1974): 1–40.

Toye, John. "Dirigisme and Development Economics." *Cambridge Journal of Economics* 9 (1985): 1–14.

White, Gordon, and Robert Wade. "Introduction." In *Developmental States in East Asia,* ed. G. White. London: Macmillan, 1988.

31. State and Civil Society

Nayar, B. R. "Political Mobilization in a Market Polity." In *Aspects of Political Mobilization in South Asia,* ed. R. Crane, 135–59. Syracuse, N.Y.: Maxwell School of Citizenship and Public Affairs, Syracuse University, 1976.

32. Civil Society and the Political Process

Bailey, F. G. *Stratagems and Spoils.* London and New York: Basil Blackwell, 1960.

Bayart, J. F. "Civil Society in Africa." In *Political Domination in Africa,* ed. P. Chabal. Cambridge: Cambridge University Press, 1986.

Geertz, Clifford. "The Integrative Revolution." *Old Societies and New States,* ed. C. Geertz, 105–57. New York, 1971.

Stream: In addition to the lecture series, the course is divided into three streams—research, policy and organization—each of which emphasizes different topics.

D. Research Stream

1. Theory and Method in Social Sciences

Giddens, Anthony. "The Prospects of Social Theory Today." In *Central Problems in Social Theory*, ed. A. Giddens. London: Macmillan, 1979.

Morgan, Gareth, ed. *Beyond Method: Strategies for Social Research.* Newbury Park, Calif.: Sage, 1983.

2. Qualitative Research Methods Reconsidered

Bhavnani, Kum Kum. "Empowerment and Social Research: Some Comments." *Text* 8, no. 1/2 (1988): 41–50.

Grimshaw, R., D. Hobson, and P. Willis. "Introduction to Ethnography at the Center." In *Culture, Media, Language.* London: Hutchinson, 1980.

3. Quantitative Research Methods Reconsidered

Bowles, G., and R. Duelli-Klein. "The Value of Quantitative Methodology for Feminist Research." In *Theories of Women's Studies*, ed. G. Bowles and R. Duelli-Klein. London: Routledge and Kegan Paul, 1983.

Glendinning, C. "Women and Poverty in the Twentieth Century." In *Women and Poverty in Britain*, ed. C. Glendinning and Jane Millar. Brighton, U.K.: Wheatsheaf, 1987.

White, Benjamin. "Measuring Time Allocation, Decision-Making and Agrarian Changes Affecting Rural Women: Examples from Recent Research in Indonesia." *IDS Bulletin* 15, no. 1 (1984): 41–50.

4. Alternative Approaches

Karim, Wazir-jahan. *Evaluation of Participatory Research as a Method in Developing Community Skills in Leadership and Decision-Making.* Penang: University of Science, Malaysia, School of Social Sciences, Kanita (Women and Children) Project.

Rahman, M.A. "The Theory and Practice of a Participatory Action Research." Draft Working Paper for the Tenth World Congress of Sociology. Geneva: ILO (International Labor Organization), 1982.

Zachariah, M. et al. *Analysis and Evaluation of a Participatory Research Project in Wang Tepus, Kedah.* Penang: University of Science, Malaysia, School of Social Sciences, Kanita (Women and Children) Project.

E. Policy Stream

1. Joint Streams: Needs, Interests, and Transformation Potential

Asia and Pacific Center for Women and Development (APCWD). *Report, Part II: The Critical Needs of Women.* Tehran: Report of Expert Group Meeting, 1977.

Young, Kate. Revised Introduction to UNESCO, *Women's Concerns and Planning*. Mimeo, 1988.

2. Limitations of Planning

Allan, B., and K. Hinchliffe. *Planning, Policy Analysis, and Public Spending: Theory and the Papua New Guinea Practice*. Hampshire, England: Gower, 1982.
Caiden, N., and A. Wildavsky. *Planning and Budgeting in Poor Countries*. New York: Wiley, 1974.

3. Policy as Process

Boneparth, Ellen. "A Framework for Policy Analysis." In *Women, Power and Policy*, ed. E. Boneparth and E. Stoper, 1–19. 2nd ed. New York: Pergamon Press, 1987.
Cleaves, P. "Implementation Amidst Scarcity and Apathy: Political Power and Policy Design." In *Politics and Policy Implementation in the Third World*, ed. M. S. Grindle, 281–303. Princeton, N.J.: Princeton University Press, 1980.
Grindle, M. S. "Policy Context and Content in Implementation." In *Politics and Policy Implementation in the Third World*, ed. M. S. Grindle, 3–34. Princeton, N.J.: Princeton University Press, 1980.
Staudt, K., and J. Jaquette. "Women's Programs: Bureaucratic Resistance and Feminist Organizations." In *Women, Power and Policy*, ed. E. Boneparth and E. Stoper, 263–81. 2nd ed. New York: Pergamon Press, 1987.

4. Gender-Aware Approaches to Economic Policy

Elson, D. "The Impact of Structural Adjustment on Women, Concepts and Issues." Harare, Zimbabwe: Commonwealth Secretariat Memorandum for Second Meeting of Commonwealth Ministers Responsible for Women's Affairs. Mimeo, 1987.
UNICEF. *Adjustment with a Human Face: Protecting the Vulnerable and Promoting Growth*. Oxford, U.K.: Clarendon Press, 1987.

5. Statistics and Indicators: Concepts and Methods

Blacker, G. "A Critique of the International Definitions of Economic Activity and Employment Status and Their Applicability in Population Censuses in Africa and the Middle East." Mimeo.
Evans, A. *Enhancing Gender-Awareness: Socio-Economic Statistics*. Training for Trainers. Draft, 1987.
Graham, H. "Do Her Answers Fit His Questions?" In *The Public and the Private*, ed. E. Gamarnikow et al. London: Heinemann, 1983.
Leon, M. "Measuring Women's Work." *IDS Bulletin* 15, no. 1 (1984).

6. Basic Concepts and Their Implications for Policy

Commonwealth Secretariat. "The Policy Process: Integrating Women and Development Initiatives." Paper presented to the Second Meeting of Commonwealth Ministers Responsible for Women's Affairs, Havare, Zimbabwe, 1985.

Edwards, M. "Individual Equity and Social Policy." In *Women, Social Sciences, and Public Policy*, ed. J. Goodnow and C. Pateman. Australia: The Academy of Social Sciences, 1985.

Evans, Alison. "Household Economics in Agrarian Societies." Paper presented to the International Development Issues Seminar, 1987.

Folbre, Nancy. "Hearts and Spades: Paradigms of Household Economics." *World Development* 14, no. 2 (1986): 245–55.

7. Ideas about Equality: The Example of Protective Legislation

McAllister, Elizabeth. *Managing the Process of Change: Women in Development*, 1-8. CIDA (Canadian International Development Agency), 1984.

O'Donovan, Katherine. "Reforming the Public: Why Can't a Woman Be More Like a Man?" In *Sexual Divisions in the Law*, 160–76. London: Weidenfeld and Nicholson, 1985.

Rhode, Deborah L. "Feminist Perspectives on Legal Ideology." In *What Is Feminism?* ed. Juliet Mitchell and Ann Oakley, 150–60. Oxford: Basil Blackwell, 1986.

8. Case Study: Strategies for Rural Women, Colombia

Lopez, C. "Rural Women's Work: An Economic Issue." Mimeo.

9. Case Study: Conceptual Framework for Gender Planning: The Housing Sector

Moser, C. "Women, Human Settlements, and Housing: A Conceptual Framework for Analysis and Policy-Making." In *Women, Human Settlements, and Housing*, ed. C. Moser and L. Peake, 12–32. London: Tavistock, 1987.

Nimpuno-Parente, P. "The Struggle for Shelter: Women in a Site and Service Project in Nairobi, Kenya." In *Women, Human Settlements, and Housing*, ed. C. Moser and L. Peake, 70–87. London: Tavistock, 1987.

10. Case Study: Project Planning

Dixon, Ruth B. *Assessing the Impact of Development Projects on Women.* USAID Program Evaluation Discussion Paper no. 8, 1980.

Weekes-Vagliani, Winifred. *The Integration of Women in Development Projects.* OECD Development Center, 1985.

11. Case Study: Institutional Change: Making Women Visible

Mackintosh, Maureen and Hilary Wainwright. *A Taste of Power: The Politics of Local Economics*. London: Verso, 1987.

Stone, Isabella. *Equal Opportunities Initiatives in Local Authorities*. London: HMSO, 1988.

12. What Kind of Project?

Buvinic, Mayra. "Projects for Women in the Third World: Explaining Their Misbehavior." *World Development* 14, no. 5 (1986): 653–64.

Sen, Gita, and Caren Grown. *Development, Crises, and Alternative Perspectives*, 41–46. New Dehli: DAWN (Development Alternatives with Women for a New Era), 1985; New York: Monthly Review Press, 1987.

13. Case Study: Policies and Policy Change to Address Violence against Women

Commonwealth Secretariat. *Confronting Violence: A Manual for Commonwealth Action*. 1987.

14. Institutionalizing Gender Issues: Approaches/Differences

Commonwealth Secretariat. *Ladies in Limbo: The Fate of Women's Bureaux*, 1–30, 101–24. 1984.

McAllister, Elizabeth. *Managing the Process of Change: Women in Development*, 1–18. CIDA (Canadian International Development Agency), 1984.

Summers, Anne. "Mandarins or Missionaries: Women in the Federal Bureaucracy." In *Australian Women: New Feminist Perspectives*, ed. Norma Grieve and Aisa Burns, 59–67. Melbourne: Oxford University Press, 1986.

Weber, Paul. "Bureaucratic Resistance to Women in Development Policy at CIDA (Canadian International Development Agency)." Mimeo, 1986.

15. Is Violence against Women a Development Issue?

Kamuguisha, Stephanie. "Violence against Women." In *Women of the Caribbean*, ed. Pat Ellis. London: Zed Books, 1986.

16. Goals and Strategies

Asia and Pacific Center for Women and Development (APCWD). *Report, Part II: The Critical Needs of Women*. Tehran: Report of Expert Group Meeting, December 1977,

Chambers, Robert. "Seeing What to Do." In *Rural Development: Putting the Last First*, ed. R. Chambers, 140–67. New York: Longman, 1983.

UNESCO. *Women's Concerns and Planning: A Methodological Approach for Their Integration into Local, Regional and National Planning*. Chap. on Ecuador, 53–85. 1986

Young, Kate. Revised Introduction to *Women's Concerns and Planning*. Mimeo, 1988.

F. Organization Stream

This stream uses the following literature as essential readings:

Aridoo, Ama Ata. *Ghana: To Be a Woman.*

Draft Summary of Conclusions of the Third Meeting of Ministers with Responsibility for the Integration of Women in Development, 4–8.

Elshtain, J.B. *Women and War,* 92–120. Hertfordshire, England: Harvester Press, 1987.

Katz, Daniel, and Robert Kahn. "The Concept of Organizational Effectiveness." In *Social Psychology of Organizations.* London: Wiley Eastern Publishers, 1970.

Kumarswamy, Jacintha. "Systems of Linkages: Organising Rural Women in Collective Action." Paper presented at the Training Conference of SAARC (South Asian Association for Regional Cooperation), 1987.

Kumunhini, R. "Organising Women in Free Trade Zones: Sri Lanka." *ISIS Women's Journal.*

Minuchin, Salvador. "A Family Model." Chap. 3 in *Families and Family Therapy.* Cambridge, Mass.: Harvard University Press, 1974.

———. "Restructuring the Family." Chap. 8 in *Families and Family Therapy.* Cambridge, Mass.: Harvard University Press, 1974.

Ngiabo, Lauretta. *The African Woman Writer.*

———. *The Caribbean Woman as a Writer.*

Sashkin, Marshall. "An Overview of Ten Management and Organizational Theorists." In *The 1981 Annual Handbook for Group Facilitators.* San Diego, Calif.: University Associates, 1981.

Weiss, R. *The Women of Zimbabwe.* Harare, Zimbabwe: Nehanda, 1985.

Williams, Kathy. *My Life and My Writing.*

G. Gender Workshops

1. Relations between Men and Women

Goode, W. "Why Men Resist." In *Rethinking the Family,* eds. Barrie Thorne and Marilyn Yalom. New York: Longman, 1982.

Hastuti, L., and B. White. "Different and Unequal: Male and Female Influence in Household and Community Affairs in Two Javanese Villages." Mimeo, 1980.

Sen, A. *Women, Technology and Sexual Divisions,* short version. United Nations Commission on Trade and Development (UNCTAD), 1985.

Whitehead, A. "Some Preliminary Notes on the Subordination of Women." *IDS Bulletin* 10, no. 3 (1979).

2. Power and Powerlessness

Bell, C., and H. Newby. "Husbands and Wives: The Dynamics of a Deferential Dialectic." In *Dependence and Exploitation in Work and Marriage,* eds. D. Leonard Backer and S. Allen. 1976.

Dumas, Rhetaugh. *Dilemmas of Black Females in Leadership*. London: Tavistock, 1985.

Handy, Charles B. "On Power and Influence." In *Understanding Organizations*. London: Penguin, 1976.

Lukes, Steven. *Power: A Radical View*. London: Penguin, 1984.

Rogers, S. "Female Forms of Power and the Myth of Male Dominance." *American Ethnologist* 2, no. 4 (1975).

3. Difference and Ideology

Archer, J., and B. Lloyd, eds. "Aggression, Violence and Power." In *Sex and Gender*. Harmondsworth, U.K.: Penguin, 1985.

Birke, L. *Women, Feminism and Biology*. Chaps. 2 and 3. Hertfordshire, England: Harvester Press, 1986.

Connell, R. W. *Which Way Is Up? Essays on Class, Sex and Culture*. London: Allen and Unwin, 1983.

Harris, Olivia. "Households as Natural Units." In *Of Marriage and the Market*. London: Methuen, 1981.

Mead, M. *Male and Female*. Chaps. 5 and 9. London: Penguin, 1950.

Ortner, S. "Is Female to Male as Nature Is to Culture?" In *Women, Culture and Society*, eds. M. Rosaldo and L. Lamphere. Stanford, Calif.: Stanford University Press, 1974.

4. Divisions, Affinities, and Equality

Mitchell, Juliet. "Women and Equality." In *The Rights and Wrongs of Women*, ed. J. Mitchell and A. Oakley. London: Penguin, 1976.

Whitehead, A. "Women's Solidarity and Divisions Among Women." *IDS Bulletin* 15, no. 1 (1985).

India: Research Center for Women's Studies, SNDT Women's University, Bombay

Research Center for Women's Studies
SNDT Women's University
Sir Vithaldas Vidyavihar
Santa Cruz (West)
Juhu Road
Bombay 400 049
India
Phone: 612-8462 Ext. 18
Contact person: Dr. Maithreyi Krishna Raj, Director

I. BACKGROUND

The center was founded in 1974 to undertake studies pertaining to women's status and role in society. In 1981, it received support from the University Grants Commission and the Ford Foundation, and in 1982 it was designated a Center for Advanced Studies at the university.

The original objectives of the center were:

- to identify issues and problems of women and undertake studies pertaining to women's role and status in society;
- to collect information and build documentation and reference material on women;
- to assist in the preparation and teaching of women's studies;
- to liaise with individuals and institutions in India and abroad on women's studies; and

- to encourage and support action programs for the improvement of women.

In its community outreach activities, the center involves government planners and practitioners in the review of on-the-ground programs, and sensitizes government officials to women's practical needs in specific communities. Thus, the center plays an intermediary role between government agents and the women of the community concerned. Funding has come from various sources, including the Indian Council of Social Science Research, and such multilateral and bilateral donor agencies as UNICEF, UNDP, and NORAD.

II. TEACHING ACTIVITIES

The center has played a leading role in planning and conducting a women's studies program in India's university system. It has hosted institutes for orientation and training of university teachers, both at local and national levels. The faculty also provides guest lectures at women's studies courses in four other departments, and at constituent and affiliated colleges of the university. The aim of the teaching and research activities is primarily to enrich university teaching, research, and advocacy functions by providing a more accurate picture of women's lives and possibly a clearer sense of the type of development interventions needed to sustain them.

In the training workshops on women's studies and women in development, participants include both teachers and government functionaries. Also, teachers have been trained in women's studies perspectives separately at the center's winter institutes. This experience has been documented in a book, *Women's Studies in India—Some Perspectives* and resulted in a manual called *Getting Started—A Teacher's Manual*. The research methodology developed by the center has been used by the UNDP, and its audiovisual kit, "Women and Development," is being used by the Indian Department of Women and Children, and by UNICEF. The center has also participated in the United Nations University's regional study, Women's Work and Family Strategies.

The center also runs a research methodology workshop for center staff where various research methodologies are discussed. Qualitative methods include anthropological fieldwork, folk material, and oral history. Various tools for quantitative research methods are discussed as well, including the use of computers. These workshops are held to train people in traditional methods of research and to include gender perspectives in the studies.

The center assists other institutions in curriculum building to include gender perspectives. Cooperation with other institutions is strengthened through participation of foreign visitors at the center and by the fact that the center offers three junior research fellowships for Ph.D. candidates in social sciences. Every year two or three scholars from abroad affiliate with the center for their research.

III. RESEARCH

A. Focus

Research at the center aims at analyzing women's problems and improving conceptual tools to better inform program design and policies for women. Central issues studied are the subordination and ideological oppression of women, as well as the impact of development processes on women, including the evaluation of government programs. Significant work has been done on how to understand women and development; on the concept of "work"; and on androgyny and motherhood. Specific projects have included research on women's movements, prostitution, health issues, myths pertaining to women, the future employment and career prospects of technically qualified women, and the portrayal of women in the media.

B. Specific Programs

Current research projects include:

- Designing women's components for development projects in land reclamation areas (Raigad)
- An all-India study to generate a data base and make policy recommendations on women in handicraft industries
- Women workers in the diamond trade
- Preparation of a sourcebook for development schemes for women
- Estimating job opportunities and training requirements for women in the information industry
- Women cane-bamboo workers
- Evaluation of the Development of Women and Children in Rural Areas (DWCRA) program
- Theoretical exploration of gender in economics
- Female labor migration
- A guide to research methodologies in women's studies

C. Library and Documentation Center

The library was started in 1982 and houses the largest collection of gender-related texts in the region. It offers a clipping service and has an archive with material on women in regional languages. Holdings include Gujarati and

Marathi journals dating from 1850 to 1920, and newspapers in Maharashtra from 1978 to 1982.

In addition, the library contains abstracts, bibliographies, and data sheets. The bibliographies cover subjects such as dowry, the women's movements in India and the Third World, violence, family planning and migration, and women's organizations. Available indexes cover India's periodical literature and facts about Indian women. The Documentation Center also contains audiovisual material—slides, video cassettes, posters, and photographs—which are used mainly as teaching aids.

D. Publications

The center regularly publishes books, research reports, occasional papers, seminar abstracts, and a newsletter. Recent titles include books on the Widow Remarriage Movement, 1800-1900; the political status of women in India; self-reliance for women; progress made in India toward the achievement of the objectives of the United Nations Decade for Women; women and health; women's studies in India; women and society in India; women, law, and the media; women's lives; and political participation of women in the Indian Parliament.

Research reports have covered topics such as unorganized women workers in the slum areas of Bombay; the plan for the study of sexism among primary school teachers; women and mass media; women, urbanization, and modernization; bank credit to women in the informal sector; impact on women's roles of the changes in the food-processing industry; women workers in the garment industry; gender discrimination in computer technology; women stage actors; the experience of menstruation; women and the church; and women and sports.

Occasional papers have focused on the emergence and development of women's organizations in India; middle-class women's entry into the work force; teaching and research on women in India; voluntary development organizations; Marxism and feminism; and the relevance of Western feminist perspectives to India. Other publications include a series on facts about Indian women, and various bibliographies.

The center also publishes seminar abstracts. These seminars have covered a wide range of topics, with lecturers coming from institutions all over the world. For example, seminars have been held about the situation of women in the U.S., Mexico, and the Soviet Union, and about specific research topics such as the use of photography and oral history.

E. Cooperation with Other Institutions

The center cooperates with other institutions in course construction and material preparation. It has provided assistance to other academic institutions in Kerala, Pune, and New Delhi, and has collaborated with UNESCO in putting together a textbook for undergraduates titled Women and Society.

There is also cooperation and pooling of resources with institutions in other countries, such as Sri Lanka, Nepal, and Bangladesh. Also, in collaboration with the center for Women's Development Studies in New Delhi, the center has formed the Women's Information Network to pool resources from various countries in the compilation of a resource guide.

IV. ACTION PROGRAMS

The center gives priority to programs that combine research and action, and has had good results with this. As a result of its action programs, a Rural Development Cell and an Evaluation Cell have been set up at the center. The Rural Development Cell undertakes women's development activities in villages, including production activities, upgrading traditional skills, providing inputs in science and technology, and legal aid and awareness training. The Evaluation Cell studies the impact of training programs on the rural women.

A. Rural Development Program at Udwada

This program covers nine villages within a 150-kilometer radius of Bombay. It was set up by the Government of India in light of a center study on the problems of rural women in the areas of health, education, and income generation. A local cadre comprising seven women and two men with working experience in community development were trained to take on leadership roles in the project. In turn, the cadre trained village women to manage their activities and deal with government officials.

The Udwada program has evolved into a learning laboratory for all three groups involved—the university staff, government officials, and the community women. In particular, this experience taught women that publicly supported resources were available and how they could be accessed. Furthermore, the contact with male government officials as peers gave all the women a greater sense of confidence.

The university's presence played an important role in shielding the village women from some of the opposition in the rest of the community to their participation in the cross-caste/cross-class activities of the project. Since the university is not perceived as having political ambitions, the project was acceptable among the local people.

B. Other Programs

The center has also undertaken other action programs such as the Awareness Training Program for Women Employees, which aims at making women aware of their role in production and of their strengths and the opportunities available to them. In the Kharland (Saline) Reclamation Project, the center is encouraging development agencies to include community women in the program's planning and execution.

V. FUTURE DIRECTIONS

The center plans to conduct more research to promote opportunities for women in technology development, as well as research in areas such as women and family and the mental health of women, on which very little information is currently available.

LEBANON: INSTITUTE FOR WOMEN'S STUDIES IN THE ARAB WORLD, BEIRUT

Institute for Women's Studies in the Arab World (IWSAW)
Beirut University College
P.O. Box 13
5053 Beirut
Lebanon
Phone: 811968
Telex: 23389 LE
Contact person: Dr. Julinda Abu Nasr, Director

I. BACKGROUND

The institute was founded in 1973 with a grant from the Ford Foundation. Its formal mandate is to conduct, encourage, evaluate, and disseminate original research on the role, status, and condition of women and children in Arab society. It also aims to investigate how traditions in the Arab world impinge on women's opportunity for advancement. The director, who has been with the center from the start, is Dr. Julinda Abu Nasr. At present, there are two full-time and two part-time members, in addition to staff contracted for special projects.

Over time the institute's objectives have expanded to include:

- to serve as a data bank and a resource center to provide knowledge on subjects pertaining to Arab women and children;
- to assess the impact of change on the role of women;

- to develop awareness among women of their own potential and help them to develop it;
- to improve the quality of life for women and children in the Arab countries;
- to serve as a catalyst for policy makers;
- to promote better understanding of Arab women and children;
- to promote and facilitate communication among individuals, groups, and institutions concerned with women and children in the Arab world;
- to integrate information on the role of women in the Arab world into the Beirut University College curriculum; and
- to provide functional education in the hope of meeting the needs of illiterate and semiliterate Arab women.

II. TEACHING ACTIVITIES

A. University Courses

Since 1978, the institute has offered courses on women in the Arab world. The courses aim to create an awareness of the role and status of Arab women in contemporary Middle Eastern culture; to enable the students to discover the true dimensions of their cultural background and its effect on the status of women; to raise questions on the role of women in society within the context of a scientific and academic approach; and to initiate interest in research topics relevant to women and social transformation in the Arab Middle East. Lecturers for these courses have come from various institutions, such as the American University of Beirut, the Lebanese University, and United Nations organizations.

Topics discussed in the courses include: feminism and feminist consciousness; sex roles and gender; the ideology of the family; women's roles and status in the Arab world; concepts of women in modern Arabic novels; Islam and women; Christianity and women; women and law in the Arab world; women and politics in the Arab world; and the economic contributions of women.

B. Conferences and Workshops

Various international workshops have been held by the Institute, mostly outside Lebanon, due to the difficult political situation in the country. The first workshop was the Wellesley Workshop, held in the U.S. in 1976. This was co-sponsored with the Ford Foundation, and its purpose was to develop criteria for organizing, evaluating, teaching, and coordinating existing theories and research on Arab women. Other conferences were: Women in Industry (1984), Women and Development (1985), Planning for Integration of Arab Women in Economic Development (1985), Basic Living

Skills (1986), and Children's Literature Workshops for Writers and Illustrators of Children's Quality Books in Arabic (1988).

III. RESEARCH

A. Focus

As studies on Arab women are scarce, the institute has focused on this topic. Being a pioneer in this field in the Arab world, the institute has developed its own instruments and tools. In doing so, it has stressed the importance of creating links with other researchers with similar interests in other parts of the world, and has created a network through which a number of projects in Lebanon and other Arab countries have been carried out. The institute continues to seek contacts with other researchers.

Although the present political situation makes research difficult in Lebanon, research projects have included: contemporary Arab women poets and novelists; sex role images in Lebanese textbooks; women workers in Lebanese industry; women, employment, and development in the Arab world; educational and employment problems facing Arab women; Arab women and education; and the compilation of a bibliography on Arab women. In addition, researchers are engaged in studying women and the war and the effects of war on children's social, emotional, and moral development.

B. Library

The institute has a unique collection of more than twenty-five hundred books and two thousand periodicals, individual articles, bibliographies, and unpublished papers in Arabic, English, and French relating to various aspects of women in the Arab countries and in other parts of the world. This collection is housed at the Beirut University College Library. A related effort, the Portable Library Project in Lebanon, is an innovative way to get books to women and children wherever they are.

C. Communications

In addition to workshops and seminars, the institute uses radio and television programs in Arab and Western countries, articles in local and international newspapers and magazines, as well as teaching and action programs to serve as vehicles of communication. It publishes a quarterly journal, *Al-Raida*, in English. The journal deals with the Arab woman today and contains news on conferences, publications, reports, and articles on current issues related to women in the Arab world.

IV. ACTION PROGRAMS

A. *The Basic Living Skills Project*

The Basic Living Skills Project is a nonformal, integrated educational program designed for illiterate and semiliterate Arab women. Its objectives are to improve the quality of life for Arab women, their families, and society at large, and to increase the active participation of Arab women in the process of development by alerting them to their responsibilities, potentials, and opportunities. The program uses simple learning materials to maximize learning among women who do not have reading skills. It is divided into eight units:

- Environment
- Home management
- Health
- Child care
- Civic education
- Sex education and family planning
- Legal rights
- Nutrition

The program uses audiovisual materials, colored illustrations, slides, and games to accompany the written text. It has developed a complete manual of instructions for the teacher on how to use the material and how to evaluate the teaching process. The institute also provides training for the implementation and evaluation of this program.

B. *Nanet*

This is an income-generating program for displaced women in Lebanon. More than 700,000 Lebanese have been forced to move from their homes due to the ongoing conflict in the country. The program organizes women to produce and sell handicrafts such as hand-knitted woolen baby clothes, embroidery, and tatting, and explores other means of improving women's socioeconomic situation. It stresses the importance of collective action for consciousness-raising and for promoting self-reliance.

C. *Other Programs*

Other action-oriented programs include in-service training for social workers; a preschool in-service training program; a workshop for Arab writers and illustrators of children's books; children's library workshops; radio programs for women on health and nutrition; radio programs for children and youth in Lebanon on health and nutrition; and career counseling for high school and college students.

MEXICO: INTERDISCIPLINARY PROGRAM ON WOMEN'S STUDIES, MEXICO CITY

Interdisciplinary Program on Women's Studies
El Colegio de México
Camino al Ajusco No. 20
C. P. 01000
Mexico, D.F.
Mexico
Phone: 568-60-33
Telex: 1777585 COLME
FAX: 652-6233
Contact person: Elena Urrutia, Coordinator

I. BACKGROUND

The Interdisciplinary Program on Women's Studies (PIEM) was founded in 1983. It responded to the growing awareness among scholars of the need to formalize the impetus to examine women's issues triggered in Mexico by the 1975 United Nations International Women's Year Conference and several others subsequently held.

The PIEM is housed at El Colegio de México, one of the country's most prestigious higher education institutions within the social sciences and the humanities. The program is run by a coordinator and has an advisory board. Its staff consists of five researchers, one librarian, five research assistants, and four secretaries. Several faculty members from El Colegio participate in decision making on the PIEM's program directions and management, and conduct seminars.

II. CURRENT ACTIVITIES

At present, the PIEM is involved in four main academic endeavors:

1. Supporting research: For the fifth consecutive year, PIEM has launched a program calling for research projects, including master's and doctoral theses, which are then selected for financial and academic support. Twenty-five to thirty projects are supported annually.

2. Teaching: Since 1983, the PIEM has organized seminars, courses, and workshops on such topics as: the family; women and domestic organization; work and feminine identity; peasant women and agrarian development; Mexican women writers; women's speech; women in Asia and Africa; women in Mexican history; and work, power, and sexuality. The PIEM attracts nearly one hundred students each year. Also, the program has already organized two summer courses for women scholars from the rest of the country, and will soon offer a specialization course in women's studies.

3. Documentation unit: The PIEM offers a collection of materials mainly on women in Mexico and Latin America. It has more than five thousand documents and a daily news-clipping service. The collection is regularly visited by students and researchers from the major universities of the country.

4. Publications and meetings: Publications include research reports and anthologies, such as Massolo and Schteingart, eds., *Participación social, reconstrucción y mujer: El Sismo de 1985*, 1987; Ramos et al., *Presencia y transparencia: La mujer en la historia de México*, 1987; Salles and McPhail, eds., *La investigación sobre la mujer*, 1988; López-González et al., *Mujer y literatura mexicana y chicana: Culturas en contacto*, El Colef, 1988; de Oliveira, ed., *Trabajo, poder y sexualidad*, 1989.

Colloquia have been organized with different groups working for women, NGOs, and universities with related interest in women's studies. These groups include UNESCO, UNICEF, El Colegio de la Frontera Norte, and the University of California. Publications resulting from these meeting include *Organizaciónes No-Gubernamentales que trabajan en benficio de la mujer, 1988;* and *Directorio de investigatidoras sociales y programas de estudio e investigación sobre la mujer en América Latina y El Caribe*, 1989.

NETHERLANDS: WOMEN AND DEVELOPMENT PROGRAM, INSTITUTE OF SOCIAL STUDIES, THE HAGUE

Women and Development Program
Institute of Social Studies
P.O. Box 90733
2509 LS The Hague
Netherlands
Phone: (073)-510100
Telex: 31491 ISS NL
Fax: (073) 549851
Contact person: The Convener of the program

I. BACKGROUND[1]

"They are isolating themselves" was a comment often heard in the corridors of the Institute of Social Studies (ISS) in The Hague, when people discussed the Women and Development Program of that institute. Such a remark reminds me of Sandra Coyner's discussion of ghettoization, where she points out that we very well misinterpret the reasons why, for example, black studies and home economics are seen as weak and not influential: "The problem is not just separation but continuing racism and sexism. These scholars do not fail to communicate with their colleagues, but the rest of academia often refuses to listen."[2]

The Institute of Social Studies, founded in 1952 by the universities of the Netherlands, is a center for development studies with worldwide institutional linkages. The composition of its staff and student body is international. The main goal of the ISS is to contribute to national and international efforts to understand and solve problems related to the development process. It also aims at helping to evolve the policy skills and techniques that are needed for finding solutions to such problems.

To date, more than six thousand participants from some 120 countries have taken part in the institute's programs. Participants come from a great variety of academic and career backgrounds, usually having worked for a number of years prior to turning to the ISS for further study. The main teaching activities of the ISS are a fifteen-month M.A. in Development Studies with seven specializations—of which Women and Development is one—and a number of six-month, postgraduate diploma programs. In addition to these, the ISS also offers a M.Phil. and a Ph.D. program. Policy workshops, seminars, and various other activities are held in The Hague and elsewhere.

As in most institutions of higher education, the sex ratio among the academic staff is unbalanced: sixty-four men and fifteen women, of which seven are part of the Women and Development Program. In recent years the sex ratio among students has improved substantially: of the approximately 160 students in the master's degree program, 40 percent are women. This figure, however, drops to 22 percent when the Women and Development students are excluded. Offering a course that is of direct interest to women has no doubt contributed to an increase in the number of female students. In addition, a conscious admission policy of the ISS, combined with a policy to increase the numbers of fellowships for qualified female applicants by the Ministry for Foreign Affairs/Development Cooperation, has contributed to this result.

The origins of the Women and Development program—as of so many institutions that work on women's issues—go back to the International Women's Year and the United Nations World Conference on Women that took place in 1975 in Mexico City. To mark the International Women's Year, the ISS decided to initiate a project on the role of women in development. One of the then very few female staff members of the ISS participated in the Tribuna, the meeting of nongovernmental groups and organizations held in conjunction with the UN conference in Mexico. In the many discussions with Third World women on the impact of development processes and change on women, the idea emerged of organizing a workshop at the ISS to further discuss and analyze the issues involved in these processes. This idea was realized in the organization of a workshop in the summer of 1977. For four months, the workshop participants, the majority of whom came from Africa, Asia, and Latin America and the Caribbean, analyzed the problems women face in their countries, and in particular the problems of poor rural women. The importance of action, research, analysis, theorizing, policy making, and the development of strategies was emphasized. A need was expressed for more such opportunities—a permanent space for women to do such work. Therefore, a specific recommendation was made that the ISS, as an institute of social studies focusing on development problems and their solutions, should develop a master's degree course on women and development.[3] This workshop was followed by a two-month workshop on similar issues in Peru in 1978. Since that time a few women, supported by a few male colleagues at the ISS, have put a lot of energy in establishing such a course: finding the financial resources and staff, developing a curriculum, and overcoming the resistance inside as well as outside the ISS against the development of such a course.

In 1978/79, two courses in women and development were offered within Comparative Development Studies, an existing specialization in the master's degree program in Development Studies, and in 1979/80 the first ten-unit option on women and development was offered. In the academic year 1983/84, Women and Development was made a full fifteen-month master's degree specialization in the ISS teaching program. It attracts participants from all over the world.

Why a Separate Program?

At the two workshops mentioned earlier, Third World women had expressed a clear demand for space in an international development institute like the ISS to work on women's issues in relation to the development process, a demand which had its base in the growing feminist movement of the late sixties and early seventies. It was felt that women needed to research, analyze, and theorize on their own terms. Much more was needed than just adding women as the forgotten category to the existing teaching programs. Over the years it has become increasingly clear that a feminist perspective represents a serious challenge to the existing paradigm of development theory, and a challenge as well to the social sciences such as anthropology, economics and sociology, which contribute heavily to development thinking. It rejects among others the generally accepted methodological approach in these sciences. As Mies states: "The methodological principle of value-free, neutral, uninvolved research, of a hierarchical, nonreciprocal relationship between research subject and research object, is still the cornerstone of the prevalent methodological and theoretical paradigm in the social sciences."[4]

Taking a feminist perspective not only leads to the demand for fundamental changes in theory and methodological approach, but it also requires rethinking of research methods and, in the ISS case, rethinking of the policy skills and techniques that are advocated to solve development problems. It also has great consequences for the student-teacher relationship: teaching should become a process of mutual enrichment through sharing of experiences and insights, instead of a one-way delivery of knowledge.

Such fundamental changes need space and resources to be worked out and practiced. Therefore, the emphasis of feminist women at the ISS has been on establishing a relatively autonomous women and development program, which has the following objectives:

- to increase, in cooperation with women from Third World countries, the understanding of women's recognized and unrecognized contribution to society in all countries and within a historical perspective;
- to develop a theoretical framework for the analysis of the root causes, forms, and dimensions of their oppression and exploitation, and various ways in which this is manifested internationally;
- to stimulate critical evaluation of present-day development strategies from the perspective of their effects on women;
- to search for alternative methods, policies, and strategies that will strengthen women's autonomy, and support and strengthen women's movements, women's groups, and women's organizations in their struggles;
- to assist in building up international communication networks related to issues on women and development; and
- to render advisory services to a wide variety of groups, organizations, and people concerned with women and development issues.

Special emphasis is placed on the documentation and analysis of women's organizations and on their struggles to change the situation of women, particularly in Third World countries.[5]

Over the years some basic principles underlying the teaching part of the program have emerged, as formulated by Reddock:

- that women's studies emerged from the women's movement and thereafter that link should always be actively maintained if women's studies is to maintain its relevance and dynamism within the society;
- that the aim of women's studies is to understand the mechanisms through which asymmetrical and hierarchical power relations of sex, race and class developed within human society, . . . [to understand] they have been reproduced, and to work out strategies for their transformation;
- that the women's problem is an international problem, common to all countries but it has to be understood within the historical and socioeconomic context of each society or group of societies within the international setting;
- that women's studies by definition is interdisciplinary, although specific aspects can be more closely related to specific disciplines; it can therefore be seen to be both interdisciplinary and multidisciplinary.[6]

In our view, the process of implementing the stated objectives and putting such principles into practice can best be realized by a group of women working from an established base. Close cooperation and the exchange of insights and views make it possible to engage in the development of a research base and a theoretical framework, to build a library, and to function as an advisory and resource center.

However, it has never been the intention to build an isolated, separatist program. On the contrary, it was felt that women's issues should be integrated in all courses at the ISS. Such a process of integration, however, would leave unimpeded the need for an autonomous women's program. Therefore, combined courses were established with other master's degree specializations, for example: Agricultural and Rural Development, Labor and Development, and Politics and Alternative Development Strategies. In addition, Women and Development staff teach in other courses. This brings staff members with different perspectives on women's issues in development together for discussion and for working out the details of such a course. It also provides a wider range of students who hold different views with the opportunity to challenge each other and thus enrich their learning process.

Based on the experience so far, a first preliminary conclusion is that such a combined course is more effective in increasing the students' insight into and openness toward women and development issues when the students from other specializations have been exposed already to women's issues in their own course by their own staff. Courses such as Labor Theory or Colonial Agrarian Structures and Social Formations can be used to introduce some relevant issues before the students participate in a combined course. Over the years, questions raised by students have also had an impact on staff sensitization.

For the future, the integration of a feminist perspective in the overall ISS teaching and research program deserves high priority. However, in our view this process of integration can only take place when it is nourished by a strong autonomous women's studies base.

Struggles, Strategies, and Contradictions

The whole process of establishing an autonomous women's studies base has not been easy. It involves struggles at different fronts and the development of appropriate strategies. At the same time, it gives rise to many contradictions.

First of all, the struggle involved acquiring permission to set up courses with a special focus on women and getting the curricula approved. The next hurdle was to secure the appointment of feminist staff members in a situation of limited resources and thus in competition with the other programs.

Next, fellowships needed to be obtained from the fellowship program of the Dutch government (again, in competition with the other programs). Also, we struggled to secure admission for women older than the age limit set for applicants, which is 40 years.

In the process of pursuing these objectives various strategies were developed. Looking back, one can identify two major efforts: (1) using the available ISS instruments for innovation and (2) at the same time showing other relevant people the quality of the work being done. In addition, networks and support groups were built within the ISS, but also in the Netherlands and internationally.

An important instrument for innovation that was used is the "policy workshop." In it the ISS brings together, for a period from six weeks to a few months, knowledgeable people from all over the world who can explore and contribute to what is known about a certain issue. From such a workshop suggestions emerge on what needs to be done in the areas of teaching, research, and policy making, and also what role the ISS should play. The policy workshop instrument was used to organize the 1977 workshop mentioned earlier, the Peru workshop in 1978, and another workshop held in 1980, called Women's Struggles and Research.[7] In addition, in 1984 the International Seminar on Women's Studies Curricula and Programmes in Higher Education was organized in cooperation with UNESCO.

Other instruments employed to sensitize a wider audience to the work being conducted are:

- Seminars that are open to all staff and students;
- Public lectures aimed at attracting a wider audience outside the institute, including Women and the State, Beyond the Decade, Women and Environment, and others;
- The organization of an Open Day, which usually involves the presentation of audiovisuals, photo exhibitions, songs, poetry, discussion groups, theater, book displays, and so on. In recent years, the Open Day has become part of the celebration of an International Women's Week around March 8, organized by participants.

It is also very important to disseminate high quality but low-cost publications such as research papers, public lectures, and books. The outside demand for publications is an excellent means by which to increase colleagues' awareness of the growing importance of women's studies. For example, public relations staff in charge of selling ISS publications were impressed when, at a book fair in India, the publications of the Women and Development Program immediately sold out.

The other major strategy has been the building of support groups and networks. Women's studies has emerged from the women's movement and in our view needs strong links with the women's movement. Our methodology of work not only leads to a relatively greater involvement of students in the classroom, whereby exchange of experience is emphasized, but also encourages their involvement with women's groups and organizations in the Netherlands through the mechanism of field visits. In addition, links have been established with women's studies groups at other universities. Most important, however, are the international links, established in particular through our alumnae. If they did not think that a program such as the Women and Development Program was important and if they did not encourage others to participate, the program would not be able to survive. Contacts are maintained through a newsletter.[8] In it alumnae write about their experiences once they are back home in their own work situation, and through it they are kept informed about the developments in the program. The collaborative research project, Women's Movements and Organizations in a Historical Perspective, in five countries and one region[9] is another way of strengthening international networks and support groups.

Since the program also depends on the political will in the Netherlands to support our work, it is important to strengthen its political base. For that reason, regular contacts exist between the staff, the students, and the wider Dutch public. In particular, contacts are maintained with women and men working in the relevant ministries (Foreign Affairs/Development Cooperation and Education and Sciences), particularly with those who are feminists or at least are interested in working for women's issues. Staff play an active role in a national lobby network called *Vrouwenberaad*. This network aims at influencing Dutch development cooperation policies, of both the government and NGOs, in such a way that these organizations will respond to women's needs and interests. All of this is not one-way traffic, but involves advisory services related to feminist activities provided by the staff and increasingly by alumnae of the program, on behalf of both the Netherlands government and nongovernmental organizations.

For the same political reason, the staff regularly informs journalists and other media people about the activities of the program and invites them to attend events such as public lectures, seminars, and the Open Day. Contacts are also cultivated with members of Parliament, in particular those who sit on parliamentary committees that deal with issues that are relevant to the program. These activities are very labor-intensive; they require a selective approach, accuracy, and consistency. For this, living in a small country has some advantages—it is possible over time to build solid support groups through personal trust in addition to gaining respect for the quality of one's work.

Last but not least, our overall strategy involves identifying colleagues in our own institute, in particular those participating in governing and administrative bodies, who are willing to support women's studies. Their support is important, for example, when decisions have to be made about the selection of staff, about criteria for admission of students, and about the content of teaching and research in the Women and Development Program.

Feminist teaching and research in a regular institution of higher education also implies a number of contradictions.[10]

First, there is the contradiction of focusing on feminist issues in processes of development and change, with an 80 to 90 percent participation of Third World students, in a program that has more resources than most other women's studies programs at Dutch universities.

Another major contradiction is found in teaching. Here processes of interactive learning between staff and students are encouraged, while at the same time staff is required to assess the students' work and grade their papers in a traditional educational setting with a hierarchical relationship between teacher and student. To overcome such contradictions, small intensive workshops are organized partly within and partly outside the established curriculum and innovative nonhierarchical teaching methods are tried. Some of these are quite successful and other ISS programs show a keen interest in the teaching methods that are being developed in the Women and Development Studies Program.

Instead of being accused of striving for isolation, as was the case in the early days of the program, Women and Development Studies is now recognized as an important part of the ISS teaching and research profile.

Have Our Strategies Worked?

Without hesitation the answer is yes. Through the efforts of many committed women and a few men, a strong women's studies program has been established. This is underscored by the fact that at present the Women and Development Program is the largest of the seven master's degree specializations in Development Studies at the ISS. It is a program that has made and is making a valuable contribution to a growing global feminist movement.

Increasingly our strategies are also effective in channeling the overall educational process in the ISS in a feminist direction. This process is further strengthened by the appointment of feminist staff in other teaching programs. In spite of this latter phenomenon, however, our experience has taught us that a relatively autonomous women's studies program with its own resources is needed. It is only from such a base that linkages with other programs can be built and efforts toward transformation of those programs sustained.

II. TEACHING ACTIVITIES

The Women and Development Specialization

Objective. Within the overall framework of strategies for human emancipation and development, the Women and Development specialization has as its objective to increase, in cooperation with other groups and individuals in different parts of the world that are concerned with similar issues, the understanding of women's recognized and unrecognized contributions to society in all countries and within a historical perspective. Within the specialization, the aim is to develop a theoretical framework for the analysis of the causes, forms, and dimensions of women's oppression and exploitation, and the various ways in which this is manifested internationally; to stimulate a critical evaluation of present-day development strategies from the perspective of their effects on women; and to search for alternative methods, policies, and strategies that will increase women's autonomy and power and strengthen their movements, groups, and organizations. This effort requires the continuing documentation and analysis of women's organizations and women's struggles to change their situation, particularly in Third World countries.

These objectives imply a critical approach toward development models and the underlying social science theories, with a view to identifying and overcoming their inherent androcentric and Eurocentric biases. This includes the collective development of a methodology within which practice and theory, teaching and research may be integrated.

Organization. Six main elements can be distinguished in the program: Basic Courses, Core Courses, Subspecialization Courses, Field Visits, Research Paper, and Synthesizing Exercise. These elements are interlinked and build on each other in such a way that the various dimensions of women and development issues can be studied in an integrated manner.

In the Basic Courses, participants are introduced to women's studies and development thinking. Fundamental to an understanding of the differential impact of development on women and men is the analysis of social science theories in light of their underlying assumptions on women's role in society and the methodology used. Basic concepts are covered and the main schools of economic development theory are reviewed.

Core Courses then follow. In Term I, these are conceptual and theoretical in nature, providing participants with a framework of analysis used to deal with practical problems. The Core Courses in Term II focus on issues of specific importance in the area of women and development: domestic labor and subsistence production; sexuality: concepts and issues; women and agrarian change; and the effects of the internationalization of capital on women.

In Term III the Women and Development Program offers one full subspecialization and one joint subspecialization with the Politics and Alternative Development Strategies specialization. The Women and Development subspecialization is based on the conceptual and theoretical insights gained in Terms I and II. A more in-depth analysis is given of the concrete and practical problems that women face in a changing world. Gains and losses in the worldwide struggle for women's liberation will be reviewed through case studies. This subspecialization is open to participants of other specializations. For those wishing to participate in this subspecialization, some extra reading may be required. In addition, attendance is expected at the Women and Development open seminars and lectures, which are an integral part of the Women and Development Program.

Throughout the core program, participants are given the opportunity to relate their new theoretical and analytical insights to aspects of the women's movement through field visits in the Netherlands. Methodological issues are central to the program, particularly in Term I, with study visits conducted in Terms II and III.

During Term IV, participants are required to write a research paper which is then discussed during research seminars in Term V. The Synthesizing Exercise, which also takes place in Term V, is policy-oriented and combines individual and group work. It provides the opportunity to reflect on the work done in earlier sections of the program and to synthesize theoretical insights and practical experience in dealing with one or more concrete policy issues.

Basic Courses. In the Basic Courses an introduction will be given to the field of women and development studies. Through sharing and analyzing the participants' experiences, basic concepts, central issues, and methodological aspects will be introduced. To encourage the process of interactive learning, a workshop will be organized at the beginning of the course.

Main currents in social science theories will be reviewed, with particular stress laid on the implications of their underlying assumptions about male/female relationships in relation to development processes. The emergence of a feminist critique of of social science theories will also be examined. For a full understanding of the implications for women of development strategies and policies, special attention will be given to basic economic concepts and various development theories and approaches to development.

1. Introduction to Women and Development Studies and Critique of Social Science Concepts and Approaches

Participants are introduced to literature that represents main currents in social science theories. Attention is focused in particular on the androcentric and Eurocentric assumptions of such theories and their methodological implications. This will facilitate the understanding of the feminist critique and the formation of feminist theories.

Readings include:

Beechey, Veronica. "Women and Production: A Critical Analysis of Some Sociological Theories of Women's Work." In *Feminism and Materialism: Women and Modes of Production*, ed. Annette Kuhn and AnnMarie Wolpe, 153–72. London and Boston: Routledge and Paul, 1978.

"The Enslavement of Women." In *Selections from the Writings of Marx, Engels, Lenin and Stalin*, 9–26. Westport, Conn.: Greenwood Press.

Harding, Sandra. "Is There a Feminist Method?" In *Feminism and Methodology*, ed. Sandra Harding, 1–14. Bloomington: Indiana University Press; Milton Keynes, U.K.: Open University Press, 1987.

Hubbart, Ruth. "Have Only Men Evolved?" In *Discovering Reality: Feminist Perspectives on Epistomology, Metaphysics, Methodology and Philosophy of Science*, ed. Sandra Harding and Merill B. Hintikka, 45–69. Dordrecht,

Boston, and London: D. Reidel Publishing Company, 1983.

Leacock, Eleanor. "Introduction: Engels and the History of Women's Oppression." In *Myths of Male Dominance: Collected Articles on Women Cross-Culturally*, 13–29. New York and London: Monthly Review Press, 1981.

Young, Kate, and Olivia Harris. "The Subordination of Women in Cross-Cultural Perspective." In *The Woman Question: Readings on the Subordination of Women*, ed. Mary Evans, 453–72. London: Fontana Paperbacks, 1982.

2. Introduction to Development Economics

This course is divided into two parts. The first part aims to provide some of the essential concepts necessary for participants who have not had a background in economics. The second part will explore the various theories and approaches to development within their historical context and in relation to the relevant debates on the economic development process.

Readings include:

Brewer, Anthony. *Marxist Theories of Imperialism: A Critical Review*. London and New York: Routledge and Kegan Paul, 1986.

Cole, Ken, John Cameron, and Chris Edwards. *Why Economists Disagree: The Political Economy of Economics*. London and New York: Longman, 1983.

Feminist Review, ed. *Waged Work: A Reader*. London: Virago, 1986.

Bottomore, Tom. *Theories of Modern Capitalism*. London: Allen and Unwin, 1985.

Heilbronner, Robert, and Lester Thurow. *The Economic Problem*. 5th ed. Englewood Cliffs, N.J.: Prentice Hall, 1978.

Core Courses

The Core Courses in Women and Development are divided into two blocks. The first, given in Term I, includes courses that are conceptual and theoretical in nature, providing a framework of analysis for practical problems. The second block extends the conceptual and theoretical insights thus gained to a set of specific issues that are of great relevance to women in different parts of the world: domestic labor and subsistence production; sexuality: concepts and issues; women and agrarian change; and the effects of the internationalization of capital on women.

1. The Social History of Women's Work

This course introduces participants to the methods of examination and analysis of women's history within the context of the changing nature of women's work. The course demonstrates the changing labor patterns for women in Western Europe as part of the emerging capitalist relations of production, and illustrates the ways and means through which the existing sexual division of labor in the colonial territories was transformed, used, and/or imposed through ideological and material means. This analysis is extended to certain Third World countries at present, thereby exploring further the bases of manipulation of women's labor and the trends and directions apparent in this control. Through illustration of the processes of change, and through increased comprehension of the methodology of historical analysis, participants gain an understanding of the possibilities for women to appropriate history, in order to make history.

Readings include:

Cockburn, Cynthia. "Technology, Production, and Power." In *Machinery of Dominance: Women, Men, and Technical Know-how*, ed. C. Cockburn, 15–34. London: Pluto Press, 1985.

Gaitskell, Deborah, and Elaine Unterhalter. "Mothers of the Nation: A Comparative Analysis of Nation, Race, and Motherhood in Afrikaner Nationalism and the African National Congress." In *Women-Nation-State*, ed. Nira Yuval-Davis and Floya Anthias, 58–78. Basingstoke and London: Macmillan, 1989.

Kelly, Joan. "The Doubled Vision of Feminist Theory." In *Sex and Class in Women's History*, ed. Judith L. Newton, M. P. Ryan, and J.R. Walkowitz, 259–70. London: Routledge and Kegan Paul, 1983.

Lovett, Margot. "Gender Relations, Class Formation, and the Colonial State in Africa." In *Women and the State in Africa*, ed. J. L. Parpart and K. Staudt, 23–46. Boulder, Colo.: Lynne Rienner, 1989.

Stoler, Ann. "Social History and Labour Control: Feminist Perspectives on 'Facts' and Fiction." In *Fighting on Two Fronts: Women's Struggles and Research*, ed. Maria Mies, 86–101. The Hague: Institute for Social Studies, 1982.

2. Feminist Theories

This course introduces participants to contemporary feminist theories and examines their applicability in different cultural contexts. The plurality of "feminisms" are explored through the conceptualization of the relation between sex, class, and race in different feminist theories. Historical and cross-cultural variations in the structures of patriarchy are illustrated through examples of the control over women's labor, fertility, sexuality, and mobility at the level of the household, the community, and the state. Recent theories of power and theories of the state in relation to women's subordination are explored with a special focus on state ideology and emerging trends of religious fundamentalism.

Readings include:

Amos, Valerie, and Pratibha Parmar. "Challenging Imperial Feminism." *Feminist Review* 17 (1984).

Chhachhi, Amrita. "The State, Religious Fundamentalism, and Women: Trends in South Asia." *Economic and Political Weekly*, March 18, 1989.

Edholm, F., O. Harris, and K. Young. "Conceptualising Women." In *Critique of Anthropology* 3, nos. 9 and 10 (1977).

Jayawardena, Kumari. Introduction to *Feminism and Nationalism in the Third World*. London: Zed Press, 1986.

Lerner, Gerda. "Origins: A Working Hypothesis." In *The Creation of Patriarchy*. London and New York: Oxford University Press, 1986.

Mouffe, Chamsal, ed. *Gramsci and Marxist Theory*. London: Routledge and Kegan Paul, 1979.

Segal, Lynne. "Beauty and the Beast II: Sex, Gender and Mothering." In *Is the Future Female?* London: Virago, 1987.

Weedon, Chris. *Feminist Practice and Post-Structuralist Theory*. Oxford and New York: Basil Blackwell, 1987.

3. Theory and Method for Change

This course concentrates on developing integrated approaches to theory and methods for women's liberation and development. The implicit politics of many traditional research methods are examined in the light of both anti-imperialist and feminist critiques. The processes by which research can reinforce or challenge dominant local and global social divisions of class, race, and gender are examined at all levels of the research process. Participants are introduced to a range of qualitative and quantitative research techniques, as they have been developed and applied by feminists, including oral history and action research. Group work is undertaken in which participants critically appraise contemporary methodologies of women's studies and feminist research, with a view to developing research and study skills that are relevant and applicable to their own contexts and concerns.
Readings:

Atiya, Nayr. *Khul Khaal: Five Egyptian Women Tell Their Stories*. London: Virago, 1988.

Lather, Patti. "Feminist Perspectives on Empowering Research Methodologies." *Women's Studies International Forum* 11, no. 6 (1988): 569–81.

Mohanty, C. "Under Western Eyes: Feminist Scholarship and Colonial Discourse." *Feminist Review* 30 (Autumn 1988): 61–88.

Morsy, Soheir. "Fieldwork in My Egyptian Homeland: Towards the Demise of Anthropology's Distinctive-Other Hegemonic Tradition." In *Arab Women in the Field*, ed. S. Altorki and C. Fawzi El-Solh. Syracuse, N.Y.: Syracuse University Press, 1988.

White, Ben. "Measuring Time Allocation, Decision-Making and Agrarian Changes Affecting Rural Women: Examples from Recent Research in Indonesia." *IDS Bulletin* 15, no. 1 (1984).

4. Methodology and Fieldwork

This course focuses on the practical aspects of the methodological insights gained in Theory and Method for Change. Participants will select themes or topics in which they have an interest because of past experience and/or planned future work. Working groups will be organized according to Synthesizing Exercise themes, and practical fieldwork will be conducted in Terms II and III. The experiences and insights gained through this field work will serve as a source of information for the Synthesizing Exercise later in the year.

Readings include:

Mahoney, Pat. "Oppressive Pedagogy: The Importance of Process in Women Studies." *Women's Studies International Forum* 11, no. 2 (1988): 103–08.

Lycklama, Geertje, and Renee Pittin. "Feminist Teaching and Research: Contradictions and Challenges." *LOVA Nieuwsbrief* 3 (1986): 66–73.

Lather, Patti. "Feminist Perspectives on Empowering Research Methodologies." *Women's Studies International Forum* 11, no. 6 (1988): 569–81.

5. Domestic Labor and Subsistence Production

The course examines the meaning, content, and effects upon women of subsistence production and domestic labor in the Third World and in Europe/North America. Problems of recognition and measurement of women's work in labor force and associated statistics are analyzed in the light of underlying expectations regarding women's roles. Theoretical analysis of domestic labor and subsistence production provides a stage from which to focus upon the existence of a global dimension to women's domestic subordination. The importance of historical and material specificity in understanding and acting upon such subordination is reflected through the use of relevant case studies.

Readings include:

Bennholdt-Thomsen, Veronika. "Why Do Housewives Continue to Be Created in the Third World Too?" In *Women: The Last Colony,* ed. Maria Mies et al., 159–67. London: Zed Press, 1988.

Gaitskell, Deborah, Judy Kimble, Moira Maconachie, and Elaine Unterhalter. "Class, Race, and Gender: Domestic Workers in South Africa." *Review of African Political Economy* 27/28 (1984): 86–108.

Mitter, Swasti. "Industrial Restructuring and Manufacturing Homework: Immigrant Women in the UK Clothing Industry." *Capital and Class* 27 (Winter 1986).

Molyneux, Maxine. "Family Reform in Socialist States: The Hidden Agenda." *Feminist Review* 21 (Winter 1985): 47–64.

Pittin, Renee. "Documentation and Analysis of the Invisible Work of

Invisible Women: A Nigerian Case Study." *International Labour Review* 123, no. 4 (July-August 1984): 473–90.

6. *Sexuality: Concepts and Issues*

This course focuses on the way in which sexuality is conceptualized in theories and practices of relations of power and oppression. Special attention will be paid to the development of theories on sexuality as a social construct. Since every culture has its own history of sexuality and its own historical conception of the female body and related practices of sexual expression and oppression, the course will start with a workshop to identify commonalities and differences in the domain of sexuality. Underlying assumptions about sexuality in religions, cultural traditions, and science, as well as the way in which these have been translated into practices of control and domination of women's sexuality, will be examined in their specific cultural, socioeconomic, political contexts. Practices of fertility control, prostitution, sexual violence, and heterosexism will be addressed.

Readings include:

Bland, L. "Purity and Motherhood: Pleasure or Threat? Definitions of Female Sexuality, 1900–1970." In *Sex and Love: New Thoughts on Old Contradictions*, ed. S. Cartledge and J. Ryan. London: The Women's Press, 1987.

Mama, A. "Developing an International Perspective on Violence against Women." In *The Hidden Struggle*. London: London Race and Housing Research Unit, 1989.

Truong, T. "Sexual Labour and Prostitution." In *Sex, Money, and Morality: Political Economy of Prostitution and Tourism in South East Asia*. University of Amsterdam, 1988.

Weeks, J. "A Never-Ceasing Duel? 'Sex' in Relation to 'Society.'" In *Sexuality and Its Discontents: Meanings, Myths and Modern Sexualities*, ed. J. Weeks. London: Routledge and Kegan Paul, 1985.

7. *Women and Agrarian Change*

The course examines the roles of women in various types of agricultural production systems, and the consequences of various accumulation strategies for the living and working conditions of rural women. Attention is given to the differential effects of agrarian transformation patterns on production and gender relations and to the neglect of gender-related issues in major rural development strategies such as land reforms and agricultural intensification programs. Particular attention will be given to analytical approaches and conceptualization problems. Beside the conventional lecture approach, simulation games will be used as a teaching instrument.

Readings include:

Cecelski, E. "Energy and Rural Women's Work: Crisis, Response and Policy

Alternatives." *International Labour Review* 126, no. 1 (January–February 1987).

Deere, C., I. Humphries, and M. Leon de Leal. "Class and Historical Analysis for the Study of Women and Economic Change." In *Women's Roles and Population Trends in the Third World*, ed. R. Anker, M. Buvinic, and N. Youssef, 87–112. London: Croom Helm, 1982.

Deere, C. D. "Rural Women and State Policy: The Latin American Agrarian Reform Experience." *World Development* 13, no. 3 (1985).

Palmer, J. *The Impact of Male Out-Migration on Women in Farming*, 1–14, 65–75. West Hartford, Conn.: Kumarian Press, 1985.

Sen, G. "Women Workers and the Green Revolution." In *Women and Development*, ed. L. Beneria. New York: Praeger, 1982.

8. The Internationalization of Capital and Women

This course examines the different phases of capital accumulation and the process by which the work of rural and urban women is integrated into a global market system. The aim is to elucidate contemporary developments in the world economy through the operations of international business and financial institutions, national economic policies, and the developments in new technology. The effects of these on women in both developed and developing countries are discussed with the aim of developing a global feminist perspective on changes in the world economy.

Readings include:

Arizpe, L., and J. Aranda. "The Comparative Advantage of Women's Disadvantages: Women Workers in the Strawberry Export Agribusiness in Mexico." *Signs* 7, no. 2 (1981).

Elson, D., and R. Pearson. "The Subordination of Women and the Internationalisation of Factory Production." In *Of Marriage and the Market*, ed. K. Young et al. London: Routledge and Kegan Paul, 1984.

Mather, Celia. "'Rather Than Make Trouble, It's Better Just to Leave': Behind the Lack of Industrial Strife in Tagerang Region of West Java." In *Women, Work, and Ideology in the Third World*, ed. Haleh Afshar. London: Tavistock, 1985.

Mitter, Swasti. "The Capital Comes Home." In *Common Fate, Common Bond: Women in the Global Economy*. London: Pluto Press, 1986.

Roldan, Martha. "Industrial Outworking, Struggles for the Reproduction of Working Class Families and Gender Subordination." In *Beyond Employment*, ed. Nannecke Redclift. New York: Basil Blackwell, 1985.

Sen, Gita, and C. Grown. "Systematic Crisis, Reproductive Failures and Women's Potential." In *Development, Crises and Alternative Visions*, by Gita Sen and Caren Grown. New Dehli: Development Alternatives with Women for a New Era (DAWN), 1985; New York: Monthly Review Press, 1987.

9. Synthesizing Exercise

The general objective of the Synthesizing Exercise is to provide participants with the opportunity to relate conceptual and policy issues to a concrete and relevant problem in the field of women and development. The Synthesizing Exercise combines the experience and knowledge that participants gained in their work in their home countries and during the period of study at the ISS (including the introduction workshop, coursework, field work, subspecialization, research paper writing, and living in a multicultural setting). The process of synthesizing, through workshops and group work, entails reflection, conceptualization of strategic issues, focusing on one specific problem or challenge, blending the theoretical and practical insights into a policy/action-oriented paper, and addressing conclusions and recommendations to a clearly defined audience, such as (inter)national policy making bodies, NGOs, and action groups.

The selection of themes and organization of working groups are usually discussed and decided upon during Term II or III.

Subspecializations

Subspecialization: Women Organizing for Change: Strategies and Struggle. This subspecialization is open to any master's participant who has an interest in and/or experience with issues related to women's struggles. This may be in the context of women's organizations and movements, or in the area of policy making.

In this subspecialization, parameters involved in analysing change processes are discussed in relation to women's issues based on past experiences of women's movements and organizations, and on present-day attempts by women to transform the relations of gender subordination. In this context, the focus is on the dynamics between the alternative strategies and policies envisaged by women's groups and organizations, and government policies related to women and development. These dynamics will be analyzed in terms of the specificities of class, ethnicity, and geographical area. The latter part of the course will center on case studies of both capitalist and socialist formations.

1. Theoretical and Historical Aspects of Women's Movements and Organizations in Relation to the State

In this first part of the subspecialization, the most important theoretical issues related to women's movements and organizations as well as issues central to the formation of modern states are dealt with. In a workshop session, participants' experience will be taken as the starting point of this course. Direct and indirect ways in which women have resisted repressive and exploitative structures are discussed in comparative perspective. Various basic concepts related to women's struggles and strategies will be examined in historical context.

Readings include:

Anthias, Floya, and Nira Yuval-Davis. Introduction to *Woman-Nation-State*, ed. Nira Yuval-Davis and Floya Anthias, 1–15. London: Macmillan, 1989.

Coward, Rosalind. "The Woman Question and the Early Marxist Left." In *Patriarchal Precedents: Sexuality and Social Relations*, by Rosalind Coward. London: Routledge and Kegan Paul, 1983.

Lalita, K. "Women in Revolt: An Historical Analysis of the Progressive Organization of Women in Andhra Pradesh." In *Women's Struggles and Strategies*, ed. S. Wieringa. Aldershot, U.K.: Gower, 1988.

Topley, Marjorie. "Marriage Resistance in Rural Kwangtung." In *Women in Chinese Society*, ed. M. Wold and R. Witke. Stanford, Calif.: Stanford University Press, 1975.

Wieringa, Saskia, ed. *Women's Struggles and Strategies*. Aldershot, U.K.: Gower, 1988.

2. Analysis of the Emergence of Strategies and Policies of Women and Development

In this section of the subspecialization, the impact of development strategies, policies, and policy instruments on women of different classes in society is examined, and the underlying assumptions about women are analyzed both at the international and national levels and from different political perspectives. The role of the state in policy-making for women and development receives special attention as do women's action and resistance vis-à-vis such policies. Subsequently the strategies, policies, and instruments involved are reviewed from the perspective of the women's movement and in terms of their potential for the empowerment of women.

Readings include:

Ford-Smith, Honor. *Ring Ding in a Tight Corner: A Case Study of Funding and Organizational Democracy in SISTREN, 1977–1988*. Toronto: Women's Program ICAE, 1989.

Lycklama, G. "The Fallacy of Integration." *Netherlands Review of Development Studies* 1 (1987).

Maguire, Patricia. *Women in Development: An Alternative Analysis*. Amherst: Center for International Education, University of Massachusetts, 1985.

Sen, Gita, and Caren Grown. *Development, Crises and Alternative Visions: Third World Women's Perspectives*. New York: Monthly Review Press, 1987.

Yudelman, Sally W. "The Integration of Women into Development Projects: Observations on the NGO Experience in General and in Latin American in Particular." *World Development* 15 (1987, supplement).

3. Empowerment of Women: Capitalist versus Socialist Experiences

The last section of this subspecialization will be devoted to analysis of the actual experience women have had with various strategies, both in capitalist and in socialist settings. The main issues discussed are: the relationship of women's groups or movements with the state and/or political parties and the relevance of feminism as a mass movement versus smaller, more radical groups. Also, socialist theories on the woman question will be critically assessed, from the perspective of their organization and strategies and their theoretical implications in relation to elements which may lead to the construction of alternative strategies.

Readings include:

Kabeer, Naila. "Subordination and Struggle: Women in Bangladesh." *New Left Review* 168 (1988): 95–121.

Molyneux, Maxine. "Mobilization without Emancipation? Women's Interests, the State and Revolution in Nicaragua." In *New Social Movements and the State in Latin America*, ed. David Slater. Amsterdam: CEDLA, 1987.

Obbo, Christine. "Sexuality and Economic Domination in Uganda." In *Woman-Nation-State*, ed. Nira Yuval-Davis and Floya Anthias, 79–91. London: MacMillan, 1987.

Ong, Bie Nie. "Women and the Transition to Socialism in Sub-Saharan Africa." In *Africa: Problems in the Transition to Socialism*, ed. Barry Munslow. London: Zed Press, 1986.

Sen, Gita and Caren Grown. *Development, Crises and Alternative Visions: Third World Women's Perspectives.* New York: Monthly Review Press, 1987.

Subspecialization: Communications and Development: Problems and Challenges. This subspecialization is offered jointly by the Women and Development and the Politics and Alternative Development Strategies specializations. After a general introduction to the understanding of the role of mass communications in social systems, participants can select one from the two different streams. One option concentrates on the status and image of women in the mass media; the other option focuses on alternative communication. The tutorials will be organized separately in the two streams.

The subspecialization is open to interested participants from any of the master's programs.

Readings include:

Callagher, Margaret. "The Image Reflected by Mass Media: Stereotypes." In *Images of Women in the Mass Media*. Document prepared for the International Commission for the Study of Communication Problems, General Conference of UNESCO, 19th Session.

———. "Redefining the Communication Revolution." In *Boxed In: Women and Television*, ed. H. Baehr and G. Dyer, 19–37. London: Pandora Press, 1987.

Mattelart, M. "Modernity 1: The Feminine Ideal." In *Women, Media, Crisis: Femininity and Disorder*, 24–56. London: Comedia, 1986.

Steeves. H. Leslie. "Feminist Theories and Media Studies." *CSMC (Critical Studies in Mass Communication)* 4, no. 2 (June 1987).

Williamson, Judith. "Woman Is an Island: Femininity and Colonization." In *Studies in Entertainment: Critical Approaches to Mass Culture*, ed. Tania Modleski. Bloomington: Indiana University Press, 1986.

Other Training Programs. For two years, a special training program for a group of women from SWAPO, the Namibian liberation movement, was organized by the program in cooperation with the SWAPO Women's Council, UNESCO, the Commission of the European Communities, and the Netherlands Ministry of Development Cooperation. Its aim was to provide the participants with practical and theoretical training in issues of women and development, including the organization and implementation of field research, and the formulation and implementation of project proposals aimed at improving women's conditions. As women are playing a vital role both in the struggle for Namibian national liberation and in the construction of a new society, the SWAPO Women's Council took a particular interest in this program. Main elements of the program were national liberation and women's liberation, social and economic issues within the southern African region, women's participation in the process of social and domestic production, women and agrarian change, family planning and birth control, a methodology of women's studies, contemporary debates in the women's movement, development economics, and field research.

III. RESEARCH

Research activities in the Women and Development Program are based on the perspectives outlined under the teaching activities, and are therefore action-oriented and focused on concrete issues confronting women. Areas of theoretical focus based on staff research include: women's movements and organizations, state and government, industrialization, labor migration, and women as workers in the tourist industry.

One research project, Women's Movements and Organizations in a Historical Perspective, with Special Reference to Colonial and Contemporary Societies, has been an important part of the research effort. This project was initiated largely as a result of a felt and expressed need among women in such societies. Its aim was to promote a better understanding of the current experience of these women through a historical analysis of their organization, in order to strengthen existing women's organizations and movements.

Women from organizations or movements in the Caribbean, India, Indonesia, Peru, Somalia, and Sudan participated in this research project. The project staff at the ISS had mainly a monitoring and support function in the research process; the women from the six countries or regions mentioned were the main researchers.

Research studies included issues such as women's participation in labor struggles, anti-price-rise movements and other social movements, and the organization of women in their communities and in the household. In some cases, where little prior documentation on women's organizations existed, an entire national women's movement was the object of study. The research methodology used involved the collection of primary and secondary data, using both oral and written sources. This meant that archival research, participant observation, recording of oral history, and group discussion were combined, with the emphasis varying according to the different needs of each project. The results of this research are available in the form of monographs, popular educational booklets, and audiovisual material.

In addition, members of staff are involved in a research project concerning the female industrial labor force in Pakistan in cooperation with the Pakistan Institute of Labour Education and Research (PILER). The objectives include the compilation of an elaborate profile of the female industrial labor force and identification of the sexual division of labor, gender hierarchy, and gender typing in job allocation. Also included in the analysis are the factors enhancing or impeding women's participation, job satisfaction, and discrimination or protection rooted in social, economic, or legislative spheres. On the basis of the above, members recommend appropriate ameliorating measures and facilitate women workers' participation in the process of collective bargaining through training, consciousness-raising, and dissemination of information.

In cooperation with the Women's Programme of the Asian and Pacific Development Centre (APDC), research is organized in a number of Asian countries concerning the international migration of female domestic workers. The countries involved are Bangladesh, the Gulf States, Indonesia, Malaysia, Pakistan, the Philippines, Singapore, and Sri Lanka. The research aims at identifying the causes, mechanisms, and consequences of this type of migration and providing the data on which policies and programs can be developed that minimize the negative and maximize the positive impact and effects.

At present, the staff is preparing a new research project focusing on women organizing in industry. This project is concerned with patterns of industrialization and their effects on women in employment, the household, and the community. The interaction between state policies, patterns of accumulation, and the sexual division of labor, both within and outside the household, raises issues concerning the inevitable process of polarization other than traditional class cleavages; the project also involves the identification of multiple survival strategies and a questioning of the assumption of either a single evolutionary pattern of industrialization or a qualitative difference between the First and the Third World. The project intends not only to establish a sound empirical base for understanding the wider relationship but also to attempt new theory-building by reconceptualizing and transcending the dichotomies of production and reproduction.

The perspective of the project will be on how women can and do organize themselves around issues that affect their livelihood, their homes, their communities, and themselves. In the context of the ISS Working Papers, the Women and Development Program produces a subseries called Women, History, and Development: Themes and Issues. Through this series, research findings of staff and participants are communicated in an early stage.

IV. SUPPORT OF REGIONAL EFFORTS

The Women and Development Program has been able to reach a considerable number of women from a wide range of Third world countries. It is felt, however, that the scope of this outreach is still too limited and that it is important to reach larger numbers of women at different levels of society. Over the last few years, efforts have been made in a number of countries to assist in developing women's studies at a local level. An example is the cooperation with the University of the West Indies (UWI). Through a program of staff exchange and staff development, Women and Development Studies is strengthened at the three campuses of UWI. The program involves curriculum development, expansion of the libraries, training of documentarists, and staff development through a series of disciplinary and interdisciplinary seminars.

Several other, more incidental forms of cooperation between the ISS Women and Development Program, or its individual staff members, and other universities have been realized. Apart from supporting institutions, ISS staff have also been involved in ongoing regional workshops which involved grassroots organizers and activists from nongovernmental organizations. A month-long South Asian workshop was held in 1986 in Bangladesh. Similar workshops are planned for Southeast Asia as well.

At present, due to lack of time and other resources, the Women and Development staff is limited in its possibilities to respond positively to a number of requests for institutional cooperation over a longer period of time. Nevertheless, through its dynamic and highly motivated alumnae, the program is able to make a significant contribution to the growth and enrichment of women's studies in many places in the world.

NOTES

1. This section is excerpted from Geertje Lycklama, Women's Studies as a Strategy for Change: The ISS Experience. Paper prepared for Women's Studies International, Nairobi, 1985.

2. Sandra Coyner, "Women's Studies as an Academic Discipline," in *Theories of Women's Studies*, Gloria Bowles and Renate Duelli Klein, eds. (London: Routledge and Kegan Paul, 1983)

3. ISS, Women and Development Workshop, 1977, Recommendations.

4. Maria Mies, "Women's Studies: A New Paradigm in the Social Sciences." Address at the Institute of Social Studies, The Hague, 26 October 1979, 14.

5. ISS, "Women and Development Program, Four-Year Plan, A Draft," November 1983, 3–4.

6. Rhoda Reddock, "The Institute of Social Studies Women and Development Teaching Program and Its Relevance to the Caribbean: A Discussion Paper," St. Augustine, February 1985, 3–4.

7. Maria Mies and Rhoda Reddock, eds., *National Liberation and Women's Liberation*. The Hague: ISS, 1982.

8. *The Women and Development Programme Alumnae Newsletter*, published once a year.

9. The five countries are India, Indonesia, Peru, Somalia, and Sudan; the region involved is the Caribbean.

10. For a more elaborate discussion of contradictions, see G. Lycklama and R. Pittin, "Feminist Teaching and Research: Contradictions and Challenges," *LOVA Nieusbrief* 3 (1986): 66–73.

Linking Institutions: The Women in Development Constorium in Thailand and Canada

Women in Development Consortium in Thailand (WIDCIT)
Office of the Rector
Thammasat University, Bangkok, Thailand,
Contact person: Malee Pruekpongsawalee

WIDCIT
Thai Studies Project
Department of Anthropology
Ross Building
York University, North York, Ontario
Contact Person: Penny Van Esterik

BACKGROUND

The last decade has witnessed a number of different approaches to implementing development projects. One such initiative is the Institutional Linkage Program (ILP) between Thai and Canadian universities begun in 1985. Funded by the Canadian International Development Agency (CIDA), the program encourages joint projects between universities in Canada and Thailand to further development goals in Thailand. Specifically, the ILP program goals are to strengthen the capability of Thai universities to

This essay was written by Penny Van Esterik, Professor of Anthropology and Co-Director of the Thai Studies Project at York University, in Toronto, Canada.

contribute to the development of Thailand through institutional cooperation among themselves and with Canadian institutions, and to improve the knowledge and understanding in Canada concerning Thailand, its development priorities, and possible opportunities for future cooperation. The Women in Development Consortium in Thailand (WIDCIT) was the first project funded under the ILP program. It began in August 1986 and will continue until March 1992. This project links York University (Toronto) with a consortium of Thai universities—Thammasat and Chulalongkorn in Bangkok, and Khon Kaen University in northeastern Thailand. WIDCIT aims to support and encourage women's studies and women in development (WID) efforts in Thailand through sharing and cooperation among academic institutions, government institutions, and nongovernmental organizations (NGOs) committed to understanding and improving conditions for women in Thailand.

Project Components

WIDCIT activities include awarding scholarships (one for each university) for graduate work at York University in the student's discipline combined with women's studies; short-term faculty exchanges between York University and the Thai universities; the development of curricula in women's studies; the publication of working papers on gender issues; conferences to be held in Thailand and Canada to sum up experience gained in the program; and launching of experimental, participatory training programs for small groups of urban and rural women in Thailand. These training programs are being developed by each Thai university on the basis of stated needs of the groups of women with which they have chosen to work. The WIDCIT team at Khon Kaen University has begun a project to assist rural women in northeastern regions in developing leadership skills. After conducting a thorough needs assessment and village surveys, the group at Khon Kaen identified "natural" women leaders in the poorest districts in the Khon Kaen region. These women participate in a training program that focuses on group management techniques, public speaking, and the identification of information sources relevant to their concerns. The training program hopes to encourage women to take a more active leadership role in the development of their villages.

The WIDCIT team at Chulalongkorn University has set up linkages with government programs on agricultural extension. They aim to improve the delivery of extension services to rural women in Suphanburi Province in central Thailand by making extension workers more sensitive to gender issues and to agricultural women's needs. Workshops with rural women will be used to develop a gender-sensitive manual that will be used by extension workers in central Thailand. The manual will indicate how agricultural training programs can meet the needs of female farmers more effectively. A second manual designed for development workers will focus on how to organize effective workshops for rural women. If the government finds these manuals helpful, it may use them in other parts of the country.

Thammasat University is working with female factory workers in Bangkok. Many of these factory workers have migrated from the countryside and are remitting salaries back home to alleviate poverty in rural districts. Eventually, many of these women will return to their home villages. The project aims to inform these women about their legal rights and discuss with them improvements in working conditions including occupational health issues. In this project, WIDCIT is working with the Labor Department.

Thammasat University has been designated as the WIDCIT secretariat. At Thammasat, women's studies has benefited from the dedication and commitment to women's issues of its former rector, Khunying Nongyao Chaiseri, whose vision of an institute for women and youth studies inspired the development of WIDCIT. Without the support of such a highly respected academic woman, the administration might not have been so willing to invest in women's issues at the university.

The Model

The consortium model is one arrangement for linking institutions and individuals with common interests. It is a loose, flexible association that allows institutions to maintain maximum independence while cooperating to achieve related objectives. While the specific interests of each participating institution differ, they all deal with the development of women's studies and women's projects. Though the consortium model appears unwieldy and awkward—and sometimes it is—it allows individual faculty members to draw on a broader range of resources and expertise than would be available at any one institution. This is particularly important for the study of women and gender issues because the subject is both complex and sensitive. Moreover, the consortium model links service providers, activists, and academics in the planning, preparation, and delivery of courses and projects related to women. Thus, people working in NGOs that implement programs for women, but who seldom have time to analyze and write up their experiences, are brought together with academics who may have a mandate to publish on women's issues but may have little experience with grassroots organizations working on women's projects. Government departments responsible for labor, agricultural extension, and community development have all been involved, along with such nongovernmental organizations as Friends of Women and the Women's Information Centre. In addition, the consortium plans to expand to include Chiangmai University and Prince of Songkla University. Including these institutions would make it a unique nationwide network of individuals and groups concerned with women and development issues in Thailand.

Management Issues and Conceptual Problems

The original proposal for WIDCIT was crafted to meet the development priorities expressed in the Fifth Thai National Development Plan (1982–1986), the Thai government's long-term development plan for women, and CIDA's guidelines related to women and development. During the first two years of WIDCIT, however, a number of management and conceptual problems developed. Grappling with these problems has resulted in some common understanding about women's issues among the WIDCIT working groups in both countries. These concerns may be common to other institutional linkage programs. I mention them here, so that future linkage programs can be better prepared at an early stage in the planning process to overcome them.

1. Management Issues

Communication difficulties are particularly complex in linkage projects. While project coordinators have yearly visits between Canada and Thailand, most communication is through letters and telexes, both of which can be easily misunderstood. To date, most queries concern reports and money. Rapid, regular communication through computer networks is not yet available in Thailand. Communicating by FAX has been expensive and awkward, since the FAX office at Thammasat used only to accept messages between 9 AM and 4 PM local time (9 PM to 4 AM in Canada). The distance and the time gap between questions and responses breeds misunderstandings and provides excuses for delaying work and avoiding difficult issues on both sides of the world. Also, translation problems are both literal and conceptual. Reports to Canada in Thai can be translated to English, but with a three-to-four-week time gap that engenders a feeling of complacency and a lack of urgency. Currently, more regular document exchanges are occurring, and since September 1989, WIDCIT working papers have been produced in English.

Thammasat, as the secretariat for WIDCIT, has a particularly difficult position among the consortium of Thai universities. It handles all administrative and budgeting tasks and therefore has access to more funding than the other universities. At the same time, the consortium model hopes to encourage cooperation among Thai universities and discourage competition, particularly in women's studies, where resources are so scarce. The secretariat, therefore, must struggle to balance the position of being first among equals.

Academics in developed and developing countries are often treated by government and development agencies as if their time commitments are flexible and light. Many projects such as the ILP program assume that project directors do not need any time off from teaching and administrative responsibilities, and that project work will actually be performed by more junior assistants. This has been a serious problem, particularly in Thailand where academics committed to gender issues are few in number and overcommitted. Each project person in WIDCIT wears many hats: academic, consultant, administrator, and activist. Also, WIDCIT meetings in Thailand take place only three times a year; because of the Thai team's need for consensus, it may take six to eight months to resolve difficult issues.

WIDCIT's cross-cultural characteristics also pose challenges to management. In Thailand, a successful interaction is one that is pleasant and where there are no significant disagreements or open confrontations. However, with subjects as sensitive and complex as gender issues, arguments are crucial to establishing the shared and unshared assumptions about women and gender in Thailand. Often arguments in Thai settings lead to a reluctance to act. When confrontations occur, a common solution is for the individuals or groups involved to simply disappear, leaving the group devoid of both valuable experience and diversity of opinion. These abdications may result in the setting up of a new faction or new group, which may or may not cooperate with the parent group. One can argue that fissioning groups are well adapted to the Thai NGO community, since each can seek separate funding and focus on separate issues. Certainly, there are enough women's issues to go around. But this pattern does not encourage cooperative joint action or the development of a common frame of reference. Lack of both makes it easier for national policy makers to deal with gender issues on a piecemeal basis. Fortunately, this factionism has not ocurred in WIDCIT, thanks to the skill and patience of the Thai administrator, Malee Pruekpongsawalee.

2. Conceptual Issues

The following conceptual issues reflect the fact that work with the different Thai universities and their training projects is just beginning. It is too soon to consider any problems emerging from the training projects themselves. And many problems and questions will continue to be raised many years after the ILP has ended.

As WIDCIT begins the task of examining gender issues from the perspective of both teaching women's studies and producing manuals for training programs geared to specific groups of Thai women, the need for conceptual guidelines is abundantly clear. What is less clear is from what source these are to be drawn. In Thailand, women's studies as an academic discipline is in its infancy, and its role in the university curriculum is far from clear. How exactly will women's studies fit into Thai university curricula? It is difficult to determine the women's studies content for undergraduate courses when only a few professors see the need for it. And, in the absence of student demand and a supportive administration, changes in the curriculum will be accomplished only very slowly.

In North America, women's studies emerged out of the women's movement as feminism's "academic arm." In Thailand, there is no strong tradition of women's protests or nationwide struggles for independence. As Pongsapich points out, the early effort to form women's groups and raise women's issues (1855–1935) resulted primarily in welfare activities (1980:1). The current wave of interest in women's problems emerged as part of the democratic movement of the midseventies. In this climate of political reform, women's studies and gender issues became more prominent. These efforts were encouraged by the United Nations Decade for Women (1975–1985).

Although a number of Thai universities undertook some initiatives in the area of women's studies during this period, these efforts were not always successful. There is, as yet, no consensus on the meaning of feminism in the Thai context beyond a shared awareness of women's oppression and exploitation. As Pongsapich indicates, "Concepts and theories related to women have been presented as translations and interpretations of Western theories" (1986:34). These theories "reflect the pattern of male-female relations in Western countries where there are different sociopolitical contexts" (Tingsabadh and Tanchainan, 1986:77). According to some activist Thai women, many supporters of the women's movement in Thailand are not feminists, and/or reject the label because of its perceived inappropriateness to the Thai context. Yet, these authors accept women's studies as a "tool for analyzing women's subordination for the purpose of understanding how to change the power relations between sexes in society" (1986:75). Thus, a key task for WIDCIT, Thai academics, and activists is to clarify the meaning of feminism in this context, primarily through an analysis of the historical and cultural conditions that shape Thai women's lives. This task should precede the development of women's studies curricula for Thai universities.

Projects funded by CIDA, such as WIDCIT, do not contain research components. But it is impossible to develop women's studies curricula or workshops on gender issues without considering the adequacy of available information on Thai women. The United Nations Decade for Women encouraged the publication of directories on women's groups and bibliographies of existing publications on women. A number of international organizations are funding projects that require the collection of indicators regarding the status of women in different sectors of Thai society, including statistics on the percentage of women in the labor force, male and female literacy rates, and wages for skilled and unskilled labor. Even if gender disaggregated statistics were available and accurate, they would not provide insight into the mechanisms of gender subordination in Thailand nor suggest the most suitable entry point for encouraging change within the existing gender system (Van Esterik, 1987). Moreover much of the available research on Thai women is concerned with family planning and health (Sirisambhand, 1988), and tends to describe and count rather than analyze and synthesize. WIDCIT hopes to encourage more analytic work, which is necessary if research is to influence policy formulation and the planning of development programs that have a long-term, beneficial impact on Thai women.

WIDCIT pressures both Thai and Canadian team members to rethink the relation between advocacy and project tasks, such as teaching, training, and writing. Often technical problems related to WID programs are far removed from both feminist rhetoric and action. For example, WID planners caution against getting sidetracked by narrow advocacy issues such as sex tourism, prostitution, or Buddhist ordination for women. But these narrow, unpopular issues may be fundamental to analyzing gender issues in Thailand. WIDCIT participants will have to find their own balance between academic legitimacy and advocacy/action during the course of the project. Their Canadian counterparts face similar dilemmas.

Finally, women's studies programs also have to deal with the issue of institutionalization, so that programs dependent on external funding last beyond the funding period. Programs that fit into existing structures such as faculties of social science may fare better than programs lodged within single departments. Although women's studies in Thailand is interdisciplinary, it is crucial to have an institutional base with separate faculty lines. When this is impossible, women's studies committee members may settle for introducing single courses on women or gender issues into different departments, or encouraging the development of modules or units on women to insert into existing courses.

Creating Common Understandings

In order to move forward on WIDCIT's objectives, an extraordinary number of common understandings must be developed among individuals and groups in Canada and Thailand. Some of these that are emerging include:

1. Awareness of gender issues: WIDCIT often encounters the argument that Thai women are already equal to men, or that Thai women dominate men. Awareness of gender inequalities is not widespread, and one cannot assume that a commitment to deal with manifestations of women's subordination will follow from the addition of women's programs or research on women in development projects. This lack of commitment is not always apparent, given that the language of project proposals and policy guidelines (which are often Thai translations of international guidelines such as those prepared for the United Nations Women's Decade) suggest otherwise.

2. Interdisciplinary approaches: Gender issues are best approached from an interdisciplinary perspective, in research methods, curriculum development, and project planning. In contrast, most current research on Thai women is conducted solely from an economic or a demographic perspective.

3. Interinstitutional collaboration: Collaboration in research and program development among NGOs with practical experience working with disadvantaged women, academics who can suggest analytic frameworks for understanding experience, and key government individuals and agencies responsible for designing and implementing programs that affect women's lives, is the best way to insure that successful initiatives are begun under WIDCIT and continue after the linkage program formally comes to an end. For example, NGO workers' observations on increasing rural-to-urban female migration from some areas, or changing patterns of land ownership could become a focus of research among women's studies faculty and students. Similarly, women's studies could develop curricula, case studies, and so forth based on the experiences of NGOs and governmental agencies in designing and implementing programs for women. However, this kind of cooperation is difficult to orchestrate because, although Thai government officials are used to working with academics (who are also civil servants), they are wary of cooperating with women's NGOs. Nevertheless, efforts to work with government bureaucracies are important because, while they may not be as sensitive to gender issues as NGOs or some academics in women's studies, their decisions have in comparision a much greater impact on women. And they will, of course, outlast linkage programs.

4. Participatory approaches: Project personnel on both the Thai and Canadian sides are convinced that participatory methods are the only viable strategies for training projects. Projects using a lecture format make minimal impact on women. WIDCIT training workshops build from women defining their own situations, and then working with facilitators to develop suitable strategies for solving their own problems.

Benefits to Canadian Institutions

The ILP program between Canadian and Thai universities is meant to benefit institutions in Canada as well as in Thailand. Although CIDA is not directly concerned with university development in Canada, the agency will benefit indirectly from having Canadian academics familiar with development processes in Thailand. York University benefits directly from the association with Thai universities by having Thai graduate students experienced in gender and development problems in their social science departments, and when visiting Thai faculty give seminars and consult with York faculty.

The benefits to York University are most directly felt in the area of women's studies, international development, and Southeast Asian studies. Women's studies, although already interdisciplinary at York, strengthens its experience with Third World women's concerns by having an opportunity to associate with women actively involved in the Asian women's movement. Also through association, graduate students in international development studies can explore how gender issues fit in with existing curricula on, for example, policy or evaluation.

The Thai Studies Project at York University is the most direct result of the linkage program with Thailand. Thai studies seeks to increase Canadians' knowledge of Thailand's social, political, economic, and cultural institutions. To this end, the project organizes seminars and orientation programs, puts out working papers, and develops language and library resources on Thailand at York for use by students, faculty, and the general public. While it would be an exaggeration to say that academic interest in Thailand, and in particular in gender issues in Thailand, have blossomed due to the linkage program, a number of unanticipated developments in the areas of women and environmental issues and English-language testing for Asian students have begun, using WIDCIT and Thai studies as local resources. Also women's studies courses and development courses now cite examples from Thailand.

WIDCIT provides an opportunity to rethink the relationship between First and Third world universities. Universities, like consortiums, may appear to be unwieldy, inefficient institutions for administering development aid programs. They are essentially elite institutions devoted to teaching and research. But they are ideal locations for changing aid expert/aid recipient relations (cf. Stamp, 1988). Universities are the most appropriate place to begin to transform the inappropriate relationship between the aid expert as the giver of knowledge and money, and the aid recipient as receiver of knowledge and money. Academics in both Canadian and Thai universities are "experts." In the case of the Thai WIDCIT team, they are possessors of localized, indigenous, appropriate knowledge about Thai women; in the case of the Canadian WIDCIT team, they are possessors of external, abstract, theoretical knowledge whose appropriateness in the Thai context is untested. In both countries, universities are a potential arena for social criticism and a source of alternate visions for the future. Thus, the ILP program could be viewed as an opportunity to assist in strengthening the role of Thai universities in independent and creative thinking, and in the development of indigenous concepts and ways of organizing development in Thailand. Thai universities reflect and influence changes in Thai society, and will increasingly be called upon to practice "the art of knowing oneself by being critical and the art of stepping down from the ivory tower and seeing things heretofore neglected" (Wanthana, 1988:99).

REFERENCES CITED

Pongsapich, Amara, 1986. Status of Women's Activities in Thailand. In *Women's Issues: Book of Readings*. A. Pongsapich, ed. Bangkok: Chulalongkorn University Social Research Institute.

Sirisambhand, Napat, 1988. *Research on Women in Thailand*. Bangkok: Chulalongkorn Social Research Institute.

Stamp, Patricia, 1989. *Technology, Gender, and Power in Africa*. Ottawa: International Development Research Centre.

Tingsabadh, Chirati, and Sucheela Tanchainan, 1986. Theories in Women Studies. In *Women's Issues: Book of Readings*. A. Pongsapich, ed. Bangkok: Chulalongkorn University Social Research Institute.

Van Esterik, Penny, 1987. Ideologies and Women in Development Strategies in Thailand. *Proceedings of the International Conference on Thai Studies*. Vol. 3(2):579–604. Australian National University, Canberra (also WIDCIT working paper series, York University).

Wanthana, Somkiat, 1988. Thai Studies in Thailand in the 1980s: A Preliminary Remark on the Current State of the Arts. *Social Science Review*. Bangkok: Chulalongkorn University Social Research Institute.

USA: Center for Women's Studies, The Ohio State University, Columbus

Center For Women's Studies
The Ohio State University
207 Dulles Hall
230 West 17th Avenue
Columbus
Ohio 43210-1311
Phone: 614-292-1021
Contact person: Susan M. Hartmann, Director

The Ohio State University is a state-supported, century-old institution with forty thousand undergraduates, fifteen thousand graduate and professional students, four thousand faculty members, more than one hundred academic departments, and a billion-dollar budget. Its main campus is located in Columbus, Ohio, the state capital. The metropolitan area has a population of around one million and a relatively strong feminist community.

MISSION OF THE CENTER

The mission of the Center for Women's Studies is to promote the development and dissemination of knowledge about women and gender. The center offers its own courses and promotes feminist research among its own

This essay was written by Susan Hartmann, Mary Margaret Fonow, and Marlene Longenecker.

faculty members, and it supports and encourages scholarship and teaching about women throughout the university and beyond.

The center's teaching mission is to expose undergraduate and graduate students to a substantive body of knowledge and to develop their critical and analytical skills, their capacity for imagination, and their ability to articulate alternatives. Through subject matter and feminist pedagogy, the faculty aspires to empower students and offer them the opportunity to apply their learning to the conditions of their own lives.

The research mission of the center is to evaluate critically and restructure traditional androcentric knowledge in virtually all of the conventional disciplines of academic inquiry. In promoting feminist research, the faculty seeks to contribute to the development of public policy and to advocacy for social change necessary to overcome the historical and universal subordination of women and other marginalized groups.

The center's service mission is to apply feminist knowledge and research to analyzing and changing women's position in both the university and society. The center serves as a resource for state and local government, women's organizations in the community, and other units on campus. The faculty provide lectures, conduct research, and consult on a wide range of topics and projects relevant to women's interests. The office also acts as an informal information and referral service for female faculty, students, and staff with concerns related to gender.

HISTORY

After several years of political struggle begun in the early seventies by university and community women, women's studies achieved official status at Ohio State in 1975. The university created the Office of Women's Studies to develop new courses and coordinate existing courses about women, but the office did not have the the the authority to offer a degree in women's studies nor to hire faculty. That authority was granted when the Office of Women's Studies was upgraded to the status of a center in 1980.

The field of women's studies—as well as our particular program at Ohio State—originated and developed within a specific social, historical, and political context. This context provided opportunities and resources as well as constraints, as will be evident in the following historical overview.

It took five years of work (1970–1975) and the support of numerous constituent groups to bring the program into existence. Encouraged and supported by the local women's liberation movement, students made establishment of a women's center a part of a general list of demands proposed by the student movement at Ohio State University in 1970. During the following academic year, faculty from various departments who were already teaching courses on women became a catalyst and resource for establishing a formal women's studies program. That year seven courses about women were offered in the departments of comparative literature, health and physical education, history, psychology, and sociology, enrolling a total of 491 students. These courses were not centrally coordinated, had little publicity, and frequently were taught as temporary, experimental courses that could not be used to fulfill any university general education or "major" requirements.

Women librarians made the first attempt to coordinate and disseminate information about courses and library holdings on women. They began a newsletter that contained a list of course offerings on women each quarter as well as annotated bibliographies of books and periodicals of interest to women and available through the university library. These early efforts led to the eventual formation of the Women's Studies Library as an integral part of the program.

A feminist administrator in the Office of Student Affairs organized a special task force on women students in 1972 as part of a larger effort to address the future of student development. After conducting hearings and a survey to ascertain the needs of female students, the task force recommended the development of support services for women, including career counseling, child care, rape prevention, and curriculum reform. They recommended specifically that the university should teach about women throughout the curriculum and create a non-degree granting center for women's studies to plan interdisciplinary courses that would be taught by faculty with joint appointments between women's studies and already existing departments.

As support for women's studies grew, the Division of Comparative Literature and Languages sponsored a workshop on women's studies in the fall of 1972. Participants expressed so much interest in the establishment of a formal program in women's studies that scheduled presentations were cancelled and participants began concrete discussions about the formation of a program. Following this meeting, the Ad Hoc Committee on Women's Studies, comprised of women faculty, students, and administrators, worked over the next two years to develop a proposal.

This committee mobilized a number of resources. Among the most important were the media (particularly the student newspaper), a federal law suit, student and community pressure, and sympathetic faculty and administrators on campus who provided legitimacy and "insider" knowledge of administrative channels.

Community support was rallied through formation of the Women's Caucus, a political action group composed of women faculty, students, alumnae, and friends who were concerned about the status of women at the university. With a sizeable membership of women from local feminist organizations on and off campus, the caucus served as a pressure group. Members wrote letters supporting the establishment of women's studies to their friends and contacts among deans, department heads, and administrators, spoke to various groups on campus about the need for women's studies, collected a thousand signatures on a petition, and wrote letters to editors of the local newspapers. The university administration could only guess who and how many were a part of the caucus, and this served to the group's advantage.

During this phase of the campaign, the Ad Hoc Committee developed a formal proposal to establish a center for women's studies. Controversy existed between liberal and radical members of the committee over an academic versus an activist focus and between the committee and university administrators over the size of the budget, the need to offer a degree, and the committee's insistence on a strong feminist orientation for the center.

When negotiations with the university faltered, members of the Women's Caucus filed a suit with the federal government charging the university with sex discrimination in hiring, promotion, wages, governance, and access to athletics. The suit also noted the university's failure to act favorably toward a proposal for women's studies. On November 11, 1974 the caucus announced to the press that they had filed the suit. On the next day, the student newspaper quoted a university official to the effect that an Office of Women Studies had been allocated $60,000 for start-up costs.

During its first year of operation, the Office of Women's Studies was directed by the Interim Governing Board whose charge was to establish the administrative unit, set priorities, and hire staff. The early priorities of the office were to develop the major, establish an introduction to women's studies course that students could use to fulfill the university-wide basic education requirements, explore the feasibility of joint faculty appointments with other academic units, develop library space, establish a program to fund research on women, sponsor lectures and colloquia, and develop ties with other women's studies programs in the region and nationally.

Administratively, the new Office of Women's Studies was attached directly to the Office of Academic Affairs and administered by a director who reported to the provost, but had no faculty appointment. The first Introduction to Women's Studies course was offered in the spring of 1976, and the first permanent director was appointed July 1, 1976. The final budget authorized by the university for the first full year of operation (1976–1977) was $11,500.

Although the demand all along had been for the establishment of a center, the university would initially authorize only the Office of Women's Studies. An "office," as defined by university by-laws, could not offer a major nor hire faculty. Nonetheless, the staff proceeded to act as if "center" status was a forgone conclusion: in 1977, they hired the first women's studies faculty member (with a joint appointment in the history department), followed by two more (with joint appointments in comparative literature and in management and human resources). The Office of Women's Studies also received approval to offer a major and a minor and prepared the proposal that would grant the Office of Women's Studies the status of a center. Achievement of center status and the appointment of a tenured faculty member as director occurred in 1980 with little controversy.

In the summer of 1983, the center hosted the annual meeting of the National Women's Studies Association. This was an enormous undertaking that consumed the time and energy of faculty and staff for more than a year. It brought approximately two thousand feminist scholars to campus and did much to strengthen its own legitimacy on campus and national visibility.

CRITICAL DECISIONS IN PROGRAM STRUCTURE

Critical decisions made in the early years had consequences for later developments. For example, early activity on the part of feminist librarians created a communications network that kept the various constituent groups informed and simultaneously served as a lobby for the establishment of the present Women's Studies Library, one of the largest of its kind in the United States, with one full-time staff member and one part-time librarian, a collection of more than twelve thousand volumes, more than one hundred serials, and a large microfilm collection. It is the fastest growing unit of the university library system.

Another important decision was the separation of women's support services from the academic mission of women's studies. This was accomplished in 1973 with the establishment of the Office of Women's Services. In addition to providing information and referrals and publishing a quarterly calendar of events, Women's Services conducts programs in the area of rape education and prevention, assertiveness training, leadership development, and support groups for reentry women, lesbians, and women of color. The separation of nonacademic service from academic programming meant that each unit was free to focus expertise and programming to meet rather diverse needs, thereby avoiding duplication of activities and a drain on resources.

The decision to move women's studies from the direct jurisdiction of the provost in the Office of Academic Affairs to the College of Humanities resulted in the further legitimization and institutionalization of the program. The College of Humanities was chosen because it was the unit most hospitable to interdisciplinary work, already housing black studies and a number of area studies programs. In addition this placement gave the center the same administrative channels as other regular academic departments, including a dean to lobby for resources. While placement of the Center for Women's Studies within the College of Humanities facilitated joint faculty appointments with other departments in the humanities, it has also made joint appointments with other colleges more problematic, though several have been achieved.

Another critical choice for women's studies programs is that between full-time faculty appointments in women's studies and joint appointments between women's studies and other academic units. At Ohio State each center faculty member holds a joint appointment, 50 percent with women's studies and 50 percent with another academic unit which serves as the tenure home. Both units must agree on the initial appointment and on salary increases, and the center participates fully in tenure and promotion decisions. Thus, if the center does not recommend tenure, the joint appointment is terminated. At the same time, the center can hire a faculty member only with the cooperation of another academic unit, and it cannot retain a faculty member if her department recommends against tenure.

Over the years, the center has become aware of several advantages of 100 percent appointments over joint appointments. Full-time appointments provide greater control over hiring, salaries, tenure and promotion of faculty; eliminate the extremely heavy burdens on individuals who owe service obligations to two units; offer a curriculum based more on academic decisions and less on the vagaries of making joint appointments; and promote the development of women's studies as an interdisciplinary field. Full-time appointments also provide greater stability. With the current fifty-fifty structure at Ohio State, a women's studies professor may move full-time into her departmental home, and over the years we have lost four faculty members through such decisions. (This mobility is not entirely negative; we have been able to replace these faculty, and they have remained supporters of and contributors to the program).

Center faculty at Ohio State have discussed this question at length and have—for the present—opted for joint appointments and center status, rather than for departmental status with 100 percent appointments. The arguments for center status include the continuing disciplinary bias of many feminist scholars, a bias which could hinder recruitment and which would result in a faculty divided between those with 50 percent appointments (our current faculty, all of whom want to retain their ties with traditional departments) and those with 100 percent appointments (new and probably junior faculty); inability of faculty with 100 percent women's studies appointments to teach in their disciplines or work with Ph.D. students unless they could make special arrangements with departments; the potential weakening—at least symbolically—of our varied and extensive connections with other academic units and our situation as the focal point for feminist research that takes place throughout the university; the greater visibility and legitimacy afforded to women's studies through joint appointments; the avoidance of "ghettoization"; and opportunities to reach a broader audience.

FACULTY AND STAFF

The center employs a director, 80 percent of whose time is allotted to women's studies and 20 percent to the department with which she holds a joint appointment. The current director is a full professor with a joint appointment in history. The full-time assistant director holds a Ph.D. and is responsible for training and supervising graduate teaching associates, undergraduate advising, preparing grant proposals, and maintaining ties with community and government organizations. The center also employs an administrative assistant and a secretary at full time, a part-time student assistant, and at least two work-study students.

At present there are nine tenure-track faculty and one open line. Eight of the faculty are at the main campus in Columbus and one at a regional campus in Newark. Specific fields represented by the tenure-track faculty are: history (3); English (1); black studies (1); French (1); social work (1); nursing (1); and agricultural economics and rural sociology (1). The center is heavily oriented toward the humanities (six faculty members), with three faculty members holding joint appointments outside the Colleges of Arts and Sciences. Two fields are notably lacking in the disciplinary expertise of the faculty: political science and the natural sciences. Of the nine faculty members, five have achieved tenure. All are women.

In addition to the faculty who hold joint appointments in the center, there are more than thirty faculty members at Ohio State who define research on women or gender as their specialty and who regularly teach courses on women in their disciplines. Among the areas represented by these professors are anthropology, black studies, classics, communication, education, English, German, history, journalism, law, psychology, social work, and sociology. These professors are integrated into the governance structure of the center, the central advisory board to the director. Twenty-one of them serve on the women's studies graduate faculty.

UNDERGRADUATE PROGRAM

The center offers both a major and a minor in women's studies; at present there are seventy majors and forty minors. Because of its interdisciplinary focus, a degree in women's studies complements many other fields; in fact, many of our majors are double majors, combining women's studies with fields such as English, psychology, political science, history, social work, journalism, and nursing.

The major in women's studies requires 45 credit hours (out of 196 quarter-hours required for the bachelor's degree), of which 10 may overlap with another major. The minor requires 23 credit hours. The core requirements for the major—all interdisciplinary courses taught by center faculty—are Introduction to Feminist Analysis; History of Western Feminist Thought; and at least one course (chosen from four currently offered) on women of color. The student selects additional hours from a complement of interdisciplinary courses offered by the center and discipline-based courses offered by other academic units.

Women's studies courses provide students with subject matter and perspectives that traditional disciplines continue to omit or slight. The center's contribution to general education is growing and is likely to increase even more under a new curriculum adopted by the Colleges of Arts and Sciences. This new curriculum requires every student in Arts and Sciences to take a course that focuses on race, class, and gender in the United States. The new basic education requirements also call for integration of women and ethnic minorities throughout the curriculum.

These new requirements are due substantially to a center project, Feminist Research and the Construction of Knowledge. The center obtained a grant from the Office of Affirmative Action for a lecture series in 1987 that brought to campus eight prominent feminist scholars to speak and consult with various curriculum bodies throughout the university. These scholars—Barbara Christian, Johnnetta Cole, Bonnie Thornton Dill, Anne Fausto-Sterling, Sandra Gilbert, Sarah Hanley, Sandra Harding, and Barbara Nelson—impressed upon the body designing the new curriculum requirements the need to integrate race and gender throughout the curriculum and to require each student to take a specific course on social diversity.

During the 1989–1990 academic year, more than twenty-five hundred students enrolled in interdisciplinary women's studies courses, an increase of 15 per cent over the preceeding year. A comparable number enrolled in discipline-based courses on women taught in some twenty departments throughout the university. The most popular courses have been introductory courses, which students may use to fill a basic education requirement.

Results of a survey conducted in introductory courses in the spring of 1987 indicate that we serve a very diverse student body. Twenty-four percent of the students were male, 8.2 percent were black (twice the percentage of blacks in the total student body), and 11.6 percent were enrolled through continuing education. The curriculum pays considerable attention to social diversity, and every course must deal with issues of race, class, and sexual orientation.

After graduation around half of women's studies majors attend graduate or professional school, while others find employment in government and nonprofit agencies and organizations. Women's studies graduates have been involved in the following areas of work: counseling women, affirmative action and sex equity, rape education and prevention services, domestic violence, substance abuse and health concerns, career development and job training, and planning and implementation of public policy.

GRADUATE EDUCATION

During the past three years the center's involvement in graduate education has been increasing rapidly. In addition to offering interdisciplinary graduate-level courses, providing faculty who serve on master's and doctoral committees in a variety of departments, and employing graduate students in other disciplines to teach introductory women's studies courses, the center provides an individualized master's degree in women's studies through the university's Master's of Liberal Studies Program. By the fall of 1990, twenty students were enrolled in the MLS program with a concentration in women's studies.

In 1987, the center began to develop a proposal for a new M.A. degree in women's studies, among the first of its kind in the United States. The degree program consists of fifty quarter hours (around ten courses), and students may choose a thesis plan or nonthesis plan. Three courses form the core requirements for all M.A. students: Introduction to Feminist Scholarship; Race, Class, and Ethnicity; and a course on feminist theory. Students choose the remainder of their curriculum from interdisciplinary courses taught by center faculty and discipline-based courses taught by feminist scholars in other academic units.

The M.A. program is housed in the center and governed by the women's studies graduate faculty, composed of center faculty and feminist scholars in other units whose research focuses on women and gender. The program is designed to prepare students for Ph.D. work in traditional disciplines or for careers in agencies and organizations that serve women. Most of the MLS students currently enrolled will transfer into the M.A. program; the first full class of around fifteen new M.A. students will begin in the fall of 1991.

The center employs twenty-five graduate associates. Among these associates, the graduate research associates (GRAs) work on center publications or assist faculty with research and the graduate teaching associates (GTAs) teach most of the introductory courses. GTAs receive extensive training, ongoing evaluation, and assistance as they teach for the center. Consequently, when they go on the job market they are experienced in teaching not just in their discipline, but also in interdisciplinary women's studies courses.

The GTA training program conducted by the assistant director consists of an intensive two-week workshop during which new GTAs observe women's studies classes and meet in sessions that cover course content and design, teaching techniques, evaluation, classroom climate, theories of learning, and feminist pedagogy. At the conclusion, TAs are videotaped and critiqued.

GOVERNANCE

Five standing committees comprise the governance structure of the center. Students at both the graduate and undergraduate level serve on these committees as do faculty and administrators from outside the center. These committees are the Advisory Council, responsible for advising the director on all major policy decisions; the Curriculum Committee, which conducts the ongoing planning and development of the academic program; the Library and Publications Committee, which advises the Women's Studies Librarian on acquisitions and center staff on in-house publications; the Small Grants Committee, which is responsible for the administration of research funds; and the Graduate Studies Committee, which oversees the new M.A. program.

DIVERSITY

A major concern of the center has been to promote diversity in all areas of endeavor, and particularly to integrate in our curriculum, research, and programming the concerns and perspectives of women of color, lesbians, poor and working-class women, and women outside the United States. Each course is monitored for attention to diversity among women and for efforts to create a classroom climate hospitable to all students. To encourage attention to women of color, the Common Differences Award is presented for the best student paper written about the perspectives and contributions of women of color. The center collaborates closely with the Department of Black Studies and with the Women of Color Consortium on campus with whom programs are regularly co-sponsored. The center also recruits professors and staff from other units to ensure diversity on our hiring and governing committees.

In addition, strenuous efforts are made in hiring faculty and graduate teaching and research associates. At present, four of the nine professors specialize in the study of women of color and two of these are themselves black; one-third of current GAs are women of color. Lesbians are well represented among the faculty and GAs, and the first course in lesbian studies was offered in 1988.

RESEARCH

Areas of research expertise among center faculty include: African and African-American women, feminist theory, Latin American women, literary and visual arts, women's health, social and political movements, public policy, and women and development. The center also contributes to research on women across the university through its Small Research Grants Program, which allocates $10,000 each year for research on women by faculty and graduate students. In addition, the center coordinates an informal group of more than one hundred scholars from various university units who conduct research on women, gender relations, and sex equity. Examples of areas of research supported by these programs are: women in sports; women on welfare; homeless women; black female entrepreneurs;

women writers; artists and contemporary composers; women in classical Greece and Rome; women in rural America; and black women's political participation.

PUBLIC SERVICE

The public service expectations of women's studies are substantially greater than those of most academic disciplines. The center serves as a liaison between the university and women's organizations in the community; and the faculty provide lectures and consultation to community groups involved in various women's issues such as reproductive freedom, rape prevention, working with victims of domestic violence, social work practice with lesbians, and the like. The center is a member of Columbus Women's Roundtable, a consortium of women's organizations, and it has recently completed a needs assessment survey of Columbus women for the roundtable.

The center's location in the state capital provides important links to the public policy arena. In fact, the past director was employed as a special advisor to the governor on women's issues during a leave of absence. The assistant director serves as special advisor to the Governor's Interagency Council on Women and Policy. A number of our students have served internships in state government offices, and some have found employment there upon completing their degrees.

PUBLICATIONS

In 1987, the center promoted the establishment of the *NWSA Journal*, published by the National Women's Studies Association and featuring interdisciplinary feminist research. The center became the journal's first editorial home and secured university funding for part of its costs, which are shared by the national association. The university provided the salary for the editor, who also taught part time for the center, two graduate research associates, and one student office worker.

The center also produces *Feminisms*, which is published every two months. This collection of essays, poetry, book reviews, and articles celebrates a variety of feminist expressions and serves as a link between the center and the women's community. The editorship is held by a graduate research associate and the publication is sold on a subscription basis.

FEMINISM, LEGITIMACY, AND INSTITUTIONALIZATION

Women's studies at Ohio State was born in a climate of campus and community activism that created the political pressure essential to its establishment and acceptance by university officials. That political climate also informed its intention to be inclusive in curriculum and governance and to infuse its teaching and programming with feminist principles. Once established, women's studies gained legitimacy and respectability through the teaching and scholarship of its faculty and graduate teaching associates and through its ability to attract large numbers of students to its classes. Due in large part to the inclusion of women's studies courses as options for students fulfilling basic education requirements, enrollments have continued their upward climb, and university administrators have committed additional faculty lines and a relatively generous budget that now exceeds $500,000. (Faculty and staff salaries and GA stipends accound for most of this budget; around $35,000 is used for operating expenses, including programming.)

With growth, institutionalization, and academic legitimacy have also come challenges to feminist principles. Collective decision-making processes sometimes give way to the imperatives of a university bureaucracy, and the center faces pressures to emphasize research in ways that could compromise feminist teaching and diminish ties with the community. At the same time, the academic respectability of women's studies has enabled the center to thrive and was particularly decisive in its ability to influence the new basic education requirements and to secure support for the new M.A. program. The center's challenge in the next decade will be to steer an acceptable path between the demands of a university establishment and its initial goal of empowering all women through education and advocacy.

TEACHING ACTIVITIES

Course descriptions

1. W.S. 210: Women, Culture, and Society

Through lectures (including guest speakers), discussions, individual and group exercises, and films, this course provides an introduction to the life experiences of women in the U.S. Special attention is given to diversity among women through an examination of the ways in which gender, race, class, and sexuality intersect to define and modify women's realities. Historical and cross-cultural comparisons of the status of women are incorporated. Topics include: diversity and theories of oppression based on difference; cultural representations of women; socialization and the nature of sex differences; race and ethnicity; work, social class, and the feminization of poverty; reproduction and family; sexuality and sexual orientation; violence against women; and feminist politics and women's movements.

Selected readings:

Cole, Johnnetta, ed. *All American Women: Lines That Divide, Ties That Bind.* New York: Free Press; London: Collier Macmillan, 1985.

Freeman, Jo. *Women: A Feminist Perspective.* Mountain View, Calif.: Mayfield, 1989.

Richardson, Laurel, and Verta Taylor. *Feminist Frontiers II: Rethinking Sex, Gender, and Society.* New York: Random House, 1989.

Rothenberg, Paula. *Racism and Sexism: An Integrated Study.* New York: St. Martin's, 1988.

Sapiro, Virgina. *Women in American Society: An Introduction to Women's Studies.* Palo Alto, Calif.: Mayfield, 1985.

————. *Women: A World Report.* New York: Oxford University Press, 1985.

2. W.S. 505: Women's Worlds

This course introduces students to a comparative perspective on women in the Third World, examining differing conceptions of gender, women's roles and status, and history. The course concludes with an examination of international feminist movements. The emphasis is on women's own articulation of their situation through the inclusion of life histories, novels, international speakers, and films. Topics include: social construction of gender; psychology of gender; ideology of gender; women's religious roles; women in households as wives and nurturers; women in the household economy and agriculture; women in trade and manufacturing; cultural mediation; domestic service; prostitution; education; social class; and global feminism.

Selected readings:

Davis, Miranda, ed. *Third World, Second Sex.* London: Zed Press, 1983.

Emecheta, Buchi. *The Joys of Motherhood.* New York: G. Braziller, 1979; London: Heinemann, 1980.

Fuentes, Annette, and Barbara Ehrenreich. *Women in the Global Factory.* Boston, Mass.: South End Press, 1983.

Moore, Henrietta. *Feminism and Anthropology.* Cambridge, U.K.: Polity Press, 1988.

Sabbah, Fatna. *Women in the Muslim Unconscious.* New York: Pergamon, 1984.

Ning Lao T'ai-t'ai. *Daughter of Han: The Autobiography of a Chinese Working Woman.* Stanford, Calif.: Stanford University Press, 1945.

3. W.S. 700: Feminism and Black Political Thought

This course examines the politics and perceptions of womanhood in the black community in an effort to understand the origins, development, and consequences of a womanist consciousness. Historical, literary, visual, and aural products are analyzed within the relevant socioeconomic, political, and historical contexts for what they reveal about the particular world views of black women in the U.S. The focus is on black women's ideas about womanhood in the black community. Topics include: late eighteenth- to mid-nineteenth-century black women's history and politics; black women as visual, literary, and performing artists; black women as community activists and educators; black working-class women; contemporary black activism; and contemporary black women's studies and womanist theory.

Selected readings:

Cooper, Anna Julia. *A Voice from the South.* New York: Oxford University Press, 1988.

Garrow, David, ed. *The Montgomery Bus Boycott and the Woman Who Started it: A Memoir by Joanne Gibson Robinson.* Knoxville, Tenn.: University of Tennessee Press, 1987.

Harding, Vincent. *There Is a River: The Black Struggle for Freedom in the United States.* New York: Harcourt Brace Jovanovich, 1981.

Richardson, Gloria. *Maria Stewart: America's First Black Woman Political Writer.* Bloomington: Indiana University Press, 1987.

Shakur, Assata. *Assata: An Autobiography.* Westport, Conn.: Lenox Hill, 1987.

4. W.S. 370: Varieties of Female Experience: Lesbian Lives

This course explores a variety of lesbian experiences and perspectives in the U.S. Readings and discussion focus on social, political, and legal issues facing lesbians. Topics include: social, racial, and cultural diversity and variability in women's sexual identities; history of political activism among lesbians; influence of homophobia and heterosexism in U.S. society; work and workplace discrimination; motherhood and child custody; lesbian health issues and the experiences of lesbians as health care providers and consumers; identity formation and the coming- out process; and the social and historical construction of lesbian sexuality and relationships. Some attention is given to the role of art and culture in the creation of lesbian communities.

Selected readings:

Boston Lesbian Psychologies Collective, eds. *Lesbian Psychologies: Explorations and Challenges.* Urbana: University of Illinois Press, 1987.

Darty, Trudy, and Sandee Potter, eds. *Women-Identified Women.* Palo Alto, Calif.: Mayfield, 1984.

Freedman, Estelle et al., eds. *The Lesbian Issue: Essays from* Signs. Chicago: University of Chicago Press, 1985.

Lorde, Audre. *Sister Outsider.* Trumansburg, N.Y.: Crossing Press, 1984.

Pharr, Suzanne. *Homophobia: A Weapon of Sexism.* Inverness, Calif.: Chardon Press, 1989.

Selections of writings by Paula Gunn Allen, Beth Brant, Adrienne Rich, bell hooks, Jewelle Gomez, Gloria Anzaldúa, Joan Nestle, Melanie Kaye/ Kantrowitz, and Marilyn Frye.

VII

RESEARCH AND TEACHING ABOUT WOMEN: A RESOURCE LIST

RESEARCH AND TEACHING ABOUT WOMEN: A RESOURCE LIST

The following list of centers, institutes, groups, and organizations represents the diverse strategies responsible for the rapidly increasing knowledge about women through the establishment of institutions devoted to research and teaching. The list includes as many organizations as we have been able to identify that are involved in relevant work today. It draws on many sources, beginning with the Women's Studies International Network established in Copenhagen in 1980, maintained by The Feminist Press and by the National Council for Research on Women, and augmented in Nairobi in 1985, and through subsequent international meetings, visits, and visitors. Where included, descriptions are based on responses to a questionnaire that has been circulated beginning in 1987. Space limitations preclude descriptions of U.S.-based centers for research on women. Readers are referred to the *Women's Studies Quarterly*, The Feminist Press at CUNY, 311 East 94th Street, New York, NY 10128, U.S.A. or to the National Council for Research on Women, 49 East 65th Street, New York, NY 10021, U.S.A. for annotated lists.

The institutions included here are growing and changing and others will be founded. The Feminist Press is hopeful that this list will continue to be maintained, and will be published separately every three years. To add an institution to this list, send a three-hundred-word description, descriptive materials, and sample publications to The Feminist Press at CUNY.

ARGENTINA

The Alicia Moreau De Justo Foundation
Corrientes 1485
1st "A"
1042
Buenos Aires
Telephone: 40-5077 and 40-1805
Contact: Elana Tchalidy, Coordinator

The Alicia Moreau de Justo Foundation was founded in July 1986, in honor of Dr. Alicia Moreau de Justo, a feminist, medical doctor, politician, and pacifist, who died at the age of one hundred on August 12, 1986. The foundation's research focuses on preserving the history of women, social research on women's problems, and the life and work of Dr. Justo for inclusion in an archive. The foundation is currently sponsoring research on the lives of women to be used in its annual calendar, and on family violence in which women are victims.

Community outreach programs offer free legal and psychological assistance to poor women. The foundation holds conferences, short courses, and seminars in subjects of interest to women. Films about violence, sexuality, and education are shown with opportunities for discussion.

Publications: Publications include calendars; various brochures; and a monograph entitled *Some Critical Considerations for Feminism about Socialist Ideas about the Origin of the Oppression of Women.*

Center for the Study of Women
Olleros 2554 P.B.
Buenos Aires 1426
Contact: Gloria Bonder, Director
For a description of this program, please see pp. 167–70 in this volume.

Centro de Estudios de Estado y Sociedad
(Center for the Study of the State and Society)
Hipolito Yrigoyen 1156
Buenos Aires 1086
Contact: Elizabeth Jelin

CENEP
Corrientes 287, piso 7
Buenos Aires

GT Condicion Femenina CLACSO
(The Feminine Condition)
Consejo Latinoamericano de Ciencias Sociales
(Latin American Council of Social Science)
Avda. Pueyrredon 510-70
Buenos Aires 1032
Contact: Maria del Carme Feijo, Coordinator

Equipo de Investigacion Asistencia para la Mujer
(Research Team for Women's Assistance)
Beruti 3032 c.p.
Buenos Aires 1425
Contact: Maria Cristina Villa de Ge

Multinational Women's Center for Research and Training of the Inter-
american Commission on Women
Av Veléz Sarsfield 153
Cordoba
Telephone: 45750
Contact: Dra. Alicia Malanca de Rodrigez Rojas, Director

In 1969 the idea of creating a women's institute was proposed by the Inter-
American Commission on Women, a specialized agency within the Organization of American States (OAS). This idea resulted in the funding of the
Multinational Center for Women in November 1977, through an agreement
between the Argentinian government and the Inter-American Commission
on Women; activities officially started in 1978.

Current research projects focus on the situation of aboriginal women in
Argentina, Paraguay, and Bolivia, and on the careers of sociocultural
workers.

The Center has a permanent art gallery and a specialized library. Training
courses for women are available. Courses are also available in secondary
schools and in the interior of the Cordoba Province.

Publications: More than fifteen reports and manuals resulting from Center
projects have been published by the Inter-American Commission on Women.
Topics include women and education, research and work, and political and
economic analyses of the status of American women.

Participacion Social para Mujeres Argentinas
(Argentinian Women's Social Participation)
Dorrego 2373
Codigo 1425
Buenos Aires
Contact: Beatriz Schmukler

Women and Family, Argentinian Society of Family Therapy
Julián Alvarez 239
Buenos Aires
Telephone: 854-2147
Contact: Maria Christina Ravazzola

The program on women and family at the Argentinian Society of Family Therapy began in 1988 with the following goals: promoting the program and the Argentinian Society of Family Therapy nationally and internationally; compiling bibliographical material and organizing courses about women and health, women and stereotypes, women and family, and other topics concerning women in general, including sexuality, maternity, abortion, legislation, and work; promoting reflection on the situation of women in various fields; conducting clinical case studies to examine sexist practices in medical and psychological therapy; organizing meetings, discussions, and film debates; and organizing a consultancy for the public on the problems of everyday life.

Recent research projects include a study of the relationship between gender stereotypes and mental illness in a sample of Argentinian families, and therapy for women aimed at resolving oppression.

Publications: Articles written by program participants have been published in the *Journal of Family Systems* and the *Bulletin of the Argentinian Society of Family Work*.

AUSTRALIA

International Women's Development Agency
P.O. Box 372
Abbotsford Victoria 3067
Telephone: (03) 419 3004
Contact: Wendy Poussard, Executive Director

The International Women's Development Agency (IWDA) is an Australian-based aid agency that supports development assistance projects in partnership with women of other countries. IWDA also provides consultancy services to governments and international NGOs. Its research is action-oriented and participative, is usually communicated through reports and projects rather than research papers, and covers a wide range of topics. Some recent projects have focused on women in development in the South Pacific, women in rural Thailand, prostitution in Southeast Asia, violence against women, and the means by which institutions can take women's needs into account in the planning of aid programs. IWDA has a community outreach program that includes radio programs, workshops, and a quarterly report to associates and friends.

The staff of IWDA sometimes teach in university development studies programs and other advanced educational institutions and in training programs for overseas students. They also design training courses and teaching materials and undertake a few short-term exchange programs and internships.

Future directions include an expanded program of development assistance, especially in Asia and the Pacific, stronger links with women's networks internationally, and more publications based on project experience.

Publications: IWDA distributes a quarterly newsletter and an annual report, as well as occasional publications.

Office of the Status of Women
Department of Prime Minister and Cabinet
Canberra, A.C.T. 2600
Contact: Helen Ware

Research Centre for Women's Studies
University of Adelaide
G.P.O. Box 498
Adelaide, SA 5001
Telephone: 61 8 228 5267
Contact: Susan Magarey, Director

Following an inquiry into the position of women at the University of Adelaide, the university established the Research Centre for Women's Studies in 1983 to (1) initiate individual and group research projects by staff and students; (2) facilitate cross-disciplinary research; (3) supervise and assist students working toward honors or postgraduate degrees on topics in the field of women's studies; (4) organize seminars, conferences, and publications for the dissemination and critical discussion of research on women and of feminist theories; (5) attract outside grants and commissions from government and other agencies for research on policy and other social issues concerning women; and (6) offer collective and diverse expertise to departments that wish to incorporate recent scholarship concerning women into their courses.

Research is conducted in the areas of feminist history and political studies and feminist theory and cultural studies. Recent research projects include: a book provisionally titled *The War of the Sexes: Australia 1801–1914;* eight doctoral theses ranging from an examination of economic change in rural China and its implications for women, through a reading of the contemporary German novelist Christa Wolf, to an examination of gender and postgraduate performance in South Australia. A Research Associateship for 1988–90 was awarded to Dr. Jaclyn Gier, a graduate of Northwestern University in the U.S.

Center staff currently teach two courses for honors-level students from the departments of education, English, history, and politics. The center's future plans include a five-year study of domestic life in Australia and the design of a curriculum for an M.A. in women's studies.

The center's director is a member of the Advisory Committee on Women in Tertiary Education (which advises two ministers in the South Australian Government); the Management Committee of the Working Women's Center; the Women's Liberation Archives Collective; and several Adelaide University committees.

Publications: S.M. Magarey, *Unbridling the Tongues of Women: a Biography of Catherine Helen Spence* (1985); L. Parkes et al., *Family History in Australia: a Bibliography* (1985); *Australian Feminist Studies,* a biennial journal, begun December 1985.

Women's Policy Coordination Unit
Department of the Premier and Cabinet
1 Treasury Place
Melbourne 3002 Victoria
Telephone: (03) 651 5109
Contact: Information Officer

The Women's Policy Coordination Unit (WPCU) is a government unit that provides policy advice to the premier on all matters relevant to women in Victoria. The unit undertakes policy and development review; monitors legislation affecting women; responds to reports and submissions from other government agencies; assesses the impact of governmental budget allocations on women; incorporates women's views into the decision-making process; and maintains the *Women's Register,* a statewide directory of women with a wide range of experience and expertise who are available for nomination to government boards and committees. In addition, WPCU annually produces *The Women's Budget,* a report that aims to describe the funds, services, and programs available to women through government departments and agencies.

The WPCU maintains links with various community organizations through subscriptions to newsletters and publications published by these groups. The unit services the Victorian Women's Consultative Council (VWCC) whose main focus is to consult with community women on issues affecting women as referred by the premier, and on issues initiated by VWCC as approved by the premier.

Publications: In addition to those items mentioned above, WPCU has published a pamphlet, *New Laws on Violence in the Home, Your Rights.* Through WPCU, the VWCC has published *Women in the Home: A Report and Summary* (June 1987; translated into Italian, Greek, Polish, Vietnamese, and Arabic); *Women and Small Business Report* (March 1988); and *The VWCC Newslettter.*

Women's Research Unit
The University of Sydney
127 Darlington Road
Sydney, N.S.W. 2006
Contact: Gretchen Poiner, Senior Research Officer

AUSTRIA _____

Dokumentation Frauenforschung
(Women's Research Documents)
Institut für Wissenschaft und Kunst
1090 Wien
Berggasse 17/1
Vienna 1090
Contact: Edith Proust

BANGLADESH _____

Foundation for Research on Educational Planning and Development
(FREPD)
64/A Green Road
Dhaka-1205
Contact: Rasheda K. Chawdhury, Senior Research Associate

Institute for Development Studies
E-17 Agargaon
Sher-e-Bangla Nagar
Dhaka-7

International Women Studies Institute
71 Satmasjid Road
Dhanmandi R. A.
Dhaka

Women for Women: A Research and Study Group
15 Green Sq.
Green Rd.
Dhaka
Telephone: 50-46-97
Contact: Nazma Chawdhury, President

Women for Women: A Research and Study Group is a registered voluntary organization formed in late 1973 to research the lives of women in Bangladesh and present the findings in published form. The group also conducts a series of bimonthly seminars on women with a view to disseminating information and exchanging ideas. To promote research on women, the group offers a course on research methodology and women's issues. In addition, Women for Women conducts workshop training courses for university students on the concept of women and development. Another important project focuses on capturing the life and activities of rural Bangladeshi women through videos.

Other activities of Women for Women include conducting an annual national convention that brings particularly significant issues to the attention of the public; maintaining links with interested groups at home and abroad; and developing a research library.

Women for Women members are all engaged elsewhere in full-time work. Their research and writings for the group are part-time voluntary activities. The current membership strength is twenty-five. The six-person elected executive committee serves for two years, implementing and administering policies and programs. Six subcommittees, each with specific responsibilities, work independently, but in close communication with the executive committee, which works as a membership subcommittee.

Publications: Women for Women publishes a quarterly newsletter in Bangla.

BARBADOS

DAWN
(The Development Alternative with Women for a New Era)
c/o Women and Development Unit
School of Continuing Studies
University of the West Indies
Pinelands, St. Michael
Telephone: 809-426-9288
Contact: Peggy Antrobus, General Coordinator

The Development Alternative with Women for a New Era (DAWN) was established in 1984 in Bangalore, India by a group of Third World women— researchers, activists, and policy makers—to address the need for analysis of the impact of the global economy on the lives of poor women. Now, it is an expanding network of Third World feminists proposing development alternatives. DAWN promotes research programs, publications, communication, training, and advocacy. Research themes include: alternative economic frameworks; reproductive rights and population; and the environment.

Publications: Development, Crises, and Alternative Visions, available in English, Portuguese, and Spanish.

The Women and Development Unit
Extramural Department
University of the West Indies
Pinelands, St. Michael
Telephone: 809-436-6312
Contact: Peggy Antrobus, General Coordinator

The Women and Development Unit (WAND) was established on August 1, 1978 and is located within the Extramural Department of the University of the West Indies. Since its establishment, WAND has served as a catalyst in promoting and supporting a wide range of programs and projects for women. It has collaborated with women's agencies as well as development programs concerned about women's development.

There are two major aspects of the WAND program: 1) Strengthening the capability of national/local agencies by collaborating with them in the development of projects and programs at the community level; 2) A program of publications and audiovisual productions as well as innovative approaches for support of a community based outreach program of women's studies aimed at uncovering women's role in history, and supporting the growth of a women's movement in the Caribbean. This outreach complements the academically based Women and Development Studies program at the three campuses of the University of the West Indies. There are many collaborating and complementary linkages between these two groups. The unit's specific objectives are: to assist women in their own development and in that of their countries; to build the consciousness and sensitivity of women and men from community levels regarding issues concerning women's role in development; to foster cohesion in women-in-development programs at regional, national, and international levels.

WAND's publications provide information that can be used in training programs at national and regional levels. The unit sees this as an important advocacy role as it works to build the awareness of policy makers and decision makers at both senior and middle management levels of governmental agencies about the issues that affect women's participation in development. WAND has also sought to use radio in innovative ways to build women's awareness of wider options for their lives and for earning an income. Increasingly the unit has been seen as an important focal point and collaborator for both regional and international agencies concerned with supporting programs for women's development.

Publications: WAND publishes a newsletter, *WOMAN SPEAK!*, which informs the Caribbean community of women's programs and activities.

WAND also sponsors a series of issues papers titled *Concerning Women and Development*, and Woman Struggle, an international newsclipping service.

BELGIUM

CREW: Centre for Research on European Women
38 Rue Stevin
1040 Brussels
Contact: Michele Bo Bramsen

BOLIVIA

Centro de Informacion y Desarollo de la Mujer
(Center for Women's Information and Development)
22433 Av. Villazón, of. 3A
La Paz

BRAZIL

Carlos Chagas Foundation
Avenue Professor Francisco Morato 1565
Sao Paulo 05513
Contact: Carmen Barroso

Institute de Estudios Economia, Politica, y Sociologia
(Institute for the Study of Economics, Politics, and Sociology)
Av. Dr. Arnaldo, 1973
CEP: 01255-Sumare
Sao Paulo
Contact: Cheywa R. Spindel

Institute de Universite de Pesquisas
de Rio de Janiero
(Institute of the University of Pesquisas
of Rio de Janiero)
Rua Paulino Fernandes, 32
Rio de Janiero 22270
Contact: Neuma Aguiar, General Coordinator

Nucleo de Estudios Sobre a Mulher
(Center for the Study of Women)
The Pontifical Catholic University
Rua Marques de Sao Vicente, 225 Gavea
Rio de Janiero 22453
Telephone: 529-9288
Contact: Fanny Tabak, Director

Nucleo de Estudios Sobre a Mulher (NEM) is the first women's studies center to be established within a large university in Brazil. Created in 1981, it forms part of the Department of Sociology and Politics of the Pointificia Universidade Catolica do Rio de Janiero (PUC). NEM's objectives are: to promote courses relating to women's problems; to develop studies of subjects relevant to women and publicize the results; to bring together Brazilian and international publications as well as unpublished university work; to aid teaching and research.

NEM aims to contribute to the elimination of all forms of discrimination and the improvement of the situation of women. It acts not only at the academic level, but promotes the sharing of experiences and mutual support among women so that each one may better attain her objectives.

NEM organizes seminars, round tables, talks, meetings, film sessions, and audiovisual shows, with the aim of bringing together students and professionals in different areas to exchange information among themselves and the members of PUC (students, professors, and nonacademic staff). NEM's members, both teaching and research staff, come from various disciplines, which permits a wide diversity of activities. Women's studies courses are offered in PUC's academic program.

NEM seeks to involve women outside the university, in particular those in the low-income sector, in activities affecting community life. Recently, NEM has developed a research and action project with the Vidigal slum community in the metropolitan area of Rio de Janiero. The organization is currently developing a project of education for migrant women of the urban population sectors.

Publications: NEM publishes a monthly newsletter, *Boletim*, and books, articles, essays, and monographs on work carried out by its members.

CANADA

The Canadian Advisory Council on the Status of Women
110 O'Connor St., 9th Floor
P.O. Box 1541, Sta. "B"
Ottawa, Ontario K1P 5R5
Telephone: (613)992-4975
Contact: Sylvia Gold, President

The Canadian Advisory Council on the Status of Women (CACSW) was established in 1973 as an independent organization funded by the federal government. The council's mandate is to advise the government and inform the public on matters concerning women.

The council consists of up to thirty members appointed by the prime minister. Members are chosen so that the council collectively represents the regional, cultural, and ethnic diversity and both official languages of Canada. The council reports to Parliament through the minister responsible for the status of women. All council members meet regularly with community leaders.

Research is conducted on a wide variety of isssues affecting women, including women in agriculture, pay equity, child care, pornography, the impact of free trade on women in maufacturing, and the effects of Canadian jobs strategy on the lives of women. The current and future research directions for the CACSW are described in its three-year strategic plan, *Fine Balances: Progress Toward Equality for Women in the 1990s.*

Publications: CACSW publishes its research findings as books, pamphlets, background papers, and fact sheets. They are available free of charge in both English and French. Among CACSW publications are: the *CACSW Newsletter; Women Entrepreneurs: Building a Stronger Canadian Community; Pay Equity: Issues in Debate; Reality Gap: The Disparity Between Women's Needs and Existing Programs and Services;* and *Brief on Pornography: An Analysis of Proposed Legislation.*

Centre for Women's Studies in Education
Ontario Institute for Studies in Education
252 Bloor St. West, Room S630
Toronto, Ontario M5S 1V6
Contact: Ruth Pierson, Director
For a description of this program, see pp. 171–87 in this volume.

Canadian Research Institute for
the Advancement of Women
151 Slater Street, Suite 408
Ottawa, Ontario K1P 5H3
Telephone: (613)563-0681 or 563-0682
Contact: Linda Chippingdale, Executive Director

The Canadian Research Institute for the Advancement of Women (CRIAW), a bilingual (English and French) national nongovernmental organization, was founded in April 1976 in response to International Women's Year. There are currently more than twelve thousand members. CRIAW's purpose is to encourage, coordinate, and disseminate research, and to ensure an equal place for women and women's experience in the body of knowledge and research about Canada, its people, culture, economy, and politics. The institute encourages the participation of women in all facets of the research process. Members of CRIAW are involved in scholarly and scientific research; action research; journalistic research; and artistic research. Many members teach at universities and community colleges.

Recent research projects include preparation of a resource kit about new reproductive technologies (such as surrogacy, in vitro fertilization, reproductive and genetic manipulation, sterility, and infertility) for women's and community groups, and a number of community-based and collaborative research projects on the theme "Family Violence: Women's Solutions Across the North," which led up to a conference about northern women in November, 1989. In addition, CRIAW maintains a computerized database of feminist researchers from all disciplines and their research.

The institute's annual conference is aimed at bringing together academic and community-based researchers for the purpose of sharing research and networking. The institute runs a resource center that is open to the public.

Every year CRIAW awards approximately twelve research grants-in-aid of $2,500 each to innovative proposals promoting the advancement of women. In addition, the Marta Danylewycz Memorial Award (worth $2,000) is given annually to a research project in women's history. It is for Canadians or Canadian content only. Research Associate status is available to assist unaffiliated researchers applying to funding agencies. No salary or stipend is offered. Several prizes are awarded annually for scholarship, journalism, and contributions to the women's movement.

CRIAW's long-term goal is to be more engaged in doing its own research and to become established as a fully independent research institute. At the present time CRIAW is funded largely by the Women's Program of the Secretary of State (federal government) with additional revenue derived from membership dues, donations, the sale of publications, and the occasional research contract.

Publications: The CRIAW Papers, original research papers and review articles drawn from various disciplines, as well as interdisciplinary works; *Feminist Perspectives,* a series of topical, issue-oriented papers; a quarterly newsletter for CRIAW members; a research funding directory; an index of articles appearing in Canadian women's periodicals; proceedings from annual conferences; and reports based on CRIAW-sponsored research.

Institute for the Study of Women
Mount Saint Vincent University
166 Bedford Highway
Halifax, Nova Scotia B3M 2J6
Contact: Susan Clark

Simone de Beauvoir Institute
1455 de Maisonneuve Blvd. West
Concordia University
Montreal, Quebec H3G 1M8
Telephone: (514) 848-2370
Contact: Arpi Hamalian, Principal
Elizabeth Henrik, Acting Principal

Founded in 1978, the Simone de Beauvoir Institute is a unit of the Faculty of Arts and Science at Concordia University. The institute exists to provide an environment in which teaching and research in women's studies can flourish, to stimulate research into the historical and contemporary roles of women in society and the dissemination of that research, and to encourage women to develop their potential to the fullest. Research is conducted by collectives, such as the Center for Feminist Studies on Peace; Le Centre de Recherche et d'Enseignement sur la Francophonie des Femmes; and the Center for Research and Teaching on Women and Work, and by individual scholars on such topics as immigrant women, women and science, and women and power in organizations.

The institute sponsors conferences and other activities intended to serve women and men within the institute, the university, and the larger, international community. Recent activities have included an international conference on teaching and research related to women; an INSTRAW (International Research and Training Institute for the Advancement of Women, based in Santo Domingo) workshop on women and development; an international colloquium on the new technologies of human reproduction; an international conference on women and development; and several open seminars and workshops for the public at large. The institute provides feminist counseling and also maintains a documentation center (Documentarist, Joan Kohner, (514) 848-2375) and a reading room.

The institute offers a B.A. major, a minor, and a certificate program in women's studies. An M.A. program is at the proposal stage and special arrangement for graduate studies is possible on an individual basis.

Two entrance scholarships are offered by the institute: the Provost Scholarship for first-entry students (about $500 each) and the Mair Verthuy Scholarship for highest ranking third-year student (about $500). Opportunities exist for research assistantships and postdoctoral fellowships. Faculty and professional staff from Concordia University can be formally affiliated as resident or associate fellows.

Future directions include moving to the graduate level; strengthening research funding; strengthening outreach and dissemination functions.

Publications: The institute publishes in three series: *Reprints/Reimpressions, Communication,* and *Working Papers/Inedits.* Conference proceedings and a newsletter are available.

Women and Environments
Centre for Urban and Community Studies
455 Spadina Ave.
Room 426
Toronto, Ontario M5S 2G8
Contact: Judith Kjellberg, Editor

Women in Development Consortium
Thai Studies Project
York University
4700 Keele St.
North York, Ontario M3J 1P3
Contact: Penny Van Esterik
For a description of this program, see pp. 238–47 in this volume. See also
Women in Development Consortium, Thammasat University, Thailand,
p. 331.

Women's Bureau, Department of Labour
Ottawa, Ontario K1A 0J2
Telephone: (819) 997-1550
Contact: Linda Geller-Schwartz, Director General

The Women's Bureau of the Federal Department of Labour was established
in September 1954 with a mandate "to promote and strengthen, through
research, policy development and information on women's efforts to achieve
equality in the labor force," and to offer "leadership and services to women
in paid employment." Research is conducted in the following areas: women's
employment and related issues such as maternity and child care leave; leave
for workers with family responsibilities; equal pay for work of equal value;
technological change; part-time work; job sharing; sexual harassment in the
workplace; reproductive health hazards in the workplace; and statistical
analyses of women's employment situation.

The Women's Bureau organizes exhibits, videos and publication displays
and distribution at conferences, seminars, career days for students, and
annual meetings of unions, women's, and other community organizations.
Speakers or discussion group leaders may also be provided as appropriate.
The bureau's Reference Centre, which houses a wide collection of publications, is open to the public and handles requests for information and
materials.

Publications: The bureau's regular publication, *Women in the Labour Force,*
contains in-depth statistical information on women's employment situation. A number of publications based on research undertaken by and for
the bureau are published each year.

Women's Studies Research Unit
University of Saskatchewan
Education Bldg.
Saskatoon, Saskatchewan S7N 0W0
Contact: Dawn Currie, Co-Chair

CHILE

Centre de Estudia y Atencion del Nino y la Mujer
(Center for the Study of Women and Children)
Enrique Foster Sur 24
Dpto. 10
Santiago

Centre de Estudios de la Mujer
(Center for Women's Studies)
Bellavista 0547
Santiago

Facultad Latinoamericana de Ciencias Sociales (FLASCO)
(Latin American Faculty of Social Sciences)
Programa Santiago
Leopolodo Urrutia T950, Nunoa
Santiago
Contact: Teresita Valdes, Professor

COLUMBIA

Center of Economic Development Studies (CEDE)
University of Los Andes
Apartado Aereo 4976
Bogota
Contact: Elssy Bonilla, Director, Program on Gender Studies

COSTA RICA

ASESORA
Centro Nacional para el Desarrollo de la Mujer y la Famila
(National Center for the Development of Women and the Family)

Ministerio de Cultura, Juventud y Deporte
Apartado 10.227-1000
San Jose
Contact: Dina Jimenez Munoz

Programa de Informacion para la Mujer
(Women's Information Program,
National University)
Apartado 1009
Centro Colon
San Jose
Telephone: 376363 ext. 2458
Contact: Mafalda Sibille M., Coordinator

The Women's Information Program in Costa Rica has established an information system that consists of a documentation center specializing in women and development and a national network of information about women and development, with participation from thirty national institutions.

Publications: Bulletin of the National Network of Information; Bulletin of Bibliographic News; Evaluation of the Present Situation, and Proposals for the System of Information for Women in Costa Rica.

Programa Interdisciplinario
de Estudios del Género
(Interdisciplinary Program for the Study of Gender)
Universidad de Costa Rica
San Jose
Contact: Yolanda Ingianna, Director

DENMARK

CEKVINA
(Women's Research Center in Aarhus)
University of Aarhus
Finlandsgade 26
DK-8200
Aarhus N
Contact: Elisabeth Flensted-Jenson, Associate Professor

Center for Development Research
Kongensgade 9
DK-1472 Copenhagen K
Telephone: 14-5700
Contact: Kirsten Westergaard, Senior Researcher

The Center for Development Research (CDR) is a research institution under the Foreign Ministry, founded in 1969. Research on Third World women is one of CDR's priority areas. The focus of the theoretical and empirical work within this area is on gender relations and social change. Within the latter, stress is laid on the potentials for action and forms of resistance adopted specifically by women.

The center's research projects have included women in production and reproduction: small-holder tea production in Kenya; gender and socioeconomic differentiation in Kericho, Kenya; women's utilization rates of primary health care and family planning services in Kenya; changing male roles and gender relations in Kisii District, Kenya; and domestic outworkers and artisans: subcontracting in Mexico.

Publications: The CDR Annual Report, free upon request, lists publications.

Center for Feminist Research and Women's Studies
University of Copenhagen-Amager
Njalsgade 106
DK-2300 Copenhagen S
Contact: Bente Rosenbeck, Associate Professor

Center for Women's Studies
Odense University
Campusvej 55
DK-5230 Odense M
Contact: Nina Lykke, Associate Professor

KULU/Women in Development
Kobmagergade 67, 1
DK-1153 Copenhagen
Contact: Kirsten Jorgensen

KVINDEFORUM
(Center for Feminist Research)
University of Aalborg
Fibigerstraede 2
DK-9220 Aalborg
Contact: Anna-Birte Ravn, Associate Professor

KVINFO
(Center for Feminist Research)
Laederstraede 15,2 SAL
1201
Copenhagen K
Contact: Jytte Larson, Acting Director

Women's Research Center in the Social Sciences
Adelgade 49 st. tv.
DK-1304 Copenhagen K.
Contact: Else Cristensen

DOMINICAN REPUBLIC

Centro de Investigacion para la Action Femenina (CIPAF)
(Center for Research on Women's Action)
Benigno Filomeno Rojas no. 307
Apartado 1744
Santo Domingo
Contact: Magaly Pineda, General Coordinator

International Research and Training Institute for the Advancement of
Women (INSTRAW)
Calle César Nicolas Pensón 102 A
Apartado Postal 21747
Santo Domingo
Telephone: (809) 685-2111, 2112, 2113, 2114
Contact: Eleni Stamiris, Deputy Director

INSTRAW was established by a resolution of the United Nations Decade for
Women (1975–85) Conference in Mexico in 1975. Since 1983, it has been
operating worldwide from its headquarters in Santo Domingo.

The institute undertakes research, training, and information and communication activities to ensure that all phases of development plans and
projects include women and address their needs and demands.

Among INSTRAW's programs, the improvement of statistics and indicators about women in development occupies a vital place. This includes
redefining the concepts and methods used to measure the work and
condition of women; improvement of household surveys; evaluation and
measurement of women's work in the informal sector; and national and
regional workshops for users and producers of statistics.

Other programs deal with economic relationships, both micro and macro.
They include the position of women in the international economy; directo-

ries and checklists about women for development plans and projects; individual and collective self-sufficiency in developing countries; women and technology; access to credit; and women and cooperatives.

Sector programs include women, water, and sanitation; women and renewable energy; women as administrators and entrepreneurs in industry; food security; and elaboration of prototype methods for studies of women and development.

INSTRAW pays particular attention to training, and prepares multimedia modules for the personnel of the United Nations about women, drinking water, and environmental sanitation; women and the sources of renewable energy; and women and development.

INSTRAW News, the biannual journal of the institute, is published in English, French, and Spanish. The Unit of Public Information also produces promotional material about the institute's programs, such as a series of posters and art postcards. The book *Woman in the World Economy* has been published in Spanish by the publisher Siglo XXI, as well as in English and Japanese. A complete list of publications is available on request.

Programa de Estudios de la Mujer
(Program for the Study of Women)
EQUIS-INTEC
Santo Domingo
Contact: Ginny Taulé, Director

ECUADOR

Centro Ecuatariano par la Promocion y Accion
de la Mujer, Los Rios
(Ecuadoran Center for the Promotion and Action of Women)
2238 y Gandara
Apartado Postal 182-C
Secursal 15
Quito

EGYPT

Center for Egyptian Civilization Studies
18, Saray el Guezireh, Apt. 7
Cairo Zamalek
Contact: Nawal M. Hassan, Director

ETHIOPIA _____

African Training and Research Center for Women
United Nations Economics Commission for Africa
Box 3001
Addis Ababa
Contact: Mary Tadesse

EUROPEAN ECONOMIC COMMUNITY _____

Women's International Studies Europe (WISE)
University of Maryland
European Division
APO, New York 09102
or
Institut für England-und Amerikastudien
Johann Wolfgang Goethe-Universität
Kettenhofweg 130
6000 Frankfurt am Main 60
Germany
Contact (for both addresses): Tobe Levin

On November 10, 1990 in Driebergen, The Netherlands, Women's International Studies Europe (WISE), the first EC-initiated women's studies exchange network, was formally constituted. Following five years of efforts by an international initiative group, representatives from eleven European Community countries voted to accept a constitution whose preamble defines the aims of WISE, a feminist studies organization, as promoting knowledge to improve the quality of women's lives and supporting activities and groups seeking to establish or extend women's studies teaching and research.

During the conference participants met in subject-based workshops: "Women, Science, and Technology"; "Women's Work, Resources, and State Policies"; "Contemporary Feminism and Its Strategies"; "Cultural Practice and Communication"; "Racism and Discrimination in Refugee and Immigration Policies in Europe"; and "Research on Violence." The activities initiated by these subject divisions will form the basis of future working papers, conference presentations, and publications.

WISE will be open to the widest membership possible, including national women's studies networks, institutions, and individuals with established expertise in women's studies teaching.

FINLAND_____

Council for Equality between Men and Women
Box 267, 00171 Helsinki
Telephone: (0) 160 5701
Contact: Eeva-Liisa Tuominen, General Secretary

Founded in 1972, the Council for Equality between Men and Women is a parliamentary advisory body. The council has thirteen members and a permanent secretariat within the Ministry of Social Affairs and Health. The council promotes research, education, and information activities in various fields concerned with equality between women and men; prepares reforms in collaboration with national and municipal authorities, labor organizations, and others for the purpose of promoting equality; promotes equality in community planning; takes initiatives and makes proposals to develop legislation and administrative activities related to equality; and follows the development in other countries of issues relating to equality.

One of the main tasks of the council is to coordinate research conducted in various fields, and since 1981 it has had a research coordinator. Recent research projects focus on sexual harassment in the workplace and pay equity. The council has arranged research seminars on women and medical science and women in the natural sciences and technology. It also assists in establishing women's studies curricula in Finnish universities.

Community outreach programs include activation campaigns before municipal and parliamentary elections. The council maintains a widely used information service on women's studies and women's issues in general and a small library that specializes in equality issues and women's studies.

Publications: The council publishes the series *Tasa-Arvojulkaisuja* ("Equality Publications") in Finnish and Swedish in collaboration with the Equality Ombudsman's Office. Several publications in the series deal with women's studies. It also publishes the quarterly *Tasa-Arvo* ("Equality"; in Finnish with Swedish and English summaries); and a women's studies newsletter, *Naistutkimustiedote*, in Finnish.

Institute of Women's Studies
Abo (Turku) Akademi
Gezeliuksenkatu 2 A
SF-20500 Turku
Contact: Christina Flemming, Librarian

FRANCE

Group for the Study of Sex Roles, Family, and Human Development
National Center for Scientific Research
87 rue Carchinet
Paris 75017
Contact: Andrée Michel

Center for Historical Research
School of Advanced Studies in Social Science
University of Paris VII
54 Boulevard Raspail
Cedex 06 75270
Paris

GERMANY

University Center for the Promotion of Women's Studies and Research
on Women
Free University of Berlin
Konigin-Luise-Strasse 34
D-1000 Berlin 33
Contact: Ulla Bock, Director

Society for Social Science Research and Praxis for Women
Julicher Strasse 22
Cologne 1 5000
Contact: Illona Kickbusch

GREECE

Mediterranean Women's Studies Institute
Leof. Alexandras 192b
115 21 Athens
Telephone: (01) 64-36-604 64-36-436
Contact: Yota Papageorgiou, Documentation Head

The Mediterranean Women's Studies Institute (KEGME) was founded in
October 1982 following a resolution drawn up at the first Mediterranean
Women's Conference held in Athens in October 1980. Its aims are to study
the roles and position of Mediterranean women in the socioeconomic

development of the region; to mobilize women to save the Mediterranean basin from pollution; to assist Mediterranean women to preserve their heritage; and to promote peace. KEGME is an NGO with consultative status to the United Nations Economic and Social Council.

Social science research is conducted from a feminist perspective with the purpose of producing knowledge and information that will be used for changing women's lives. Recent research projects have included: 1) Young Women in Greece: Problems and Opportunities; 2) Women and Drugs in Greece: A Feminist Perspective; 3) Women and Sexuality: The Case of Greece; 4) Educational Trends and Career Opportunities of Greek Women.

The institute has a Women's Studies Program that focuses on teaching in the summer and conducting research in the winter. KEGME organizes conferences and workshops for the presentation of current research, and runs an information and documentation center.

Publications: The institute publishes a newsletter twice yearly; reports of research findings and workshops, including *Immigrant Women on the Move: The Employment, Health and Education of Migrant Women* (1987, English); *Women's Cooperatives in Greece* (1987, Greek); *Women's Cooperatives in the Mediterranean* (1987, English); *Women and Technology in Urban Greece* (1988); and *Women and Technology in the Mediterranean* (1987, English); and a book, *Readings on Women's Studies in the Mediterranean* (1987).

GUYANA _____

Women's Studies Unit
Faculty of Social Sciences
University of Guyana
P.O. Box 10 11 10, Georgetown
Telephone: 63691
Contact: Janice M. Jackson, Program Officer

The Women's Studies Unit at the University of Guyana, which grew out of the interdisciplinary women's studies group, was established on September 1, 1987 to promote research and teaching on and off campus and to influence social policy and upgrade the quality of women's lives. Research is conducted in the areas of women and work, violence against women, women and health, and women in higher education. Recent projects have focused on the incidence and problems of early pregnancies, women's participation in higher education, and the creation of a directory of female resource persons.

The unit offers a course on literature and modules in other literature and sociology courses. Members of the academic community serve as lecturers and associate researchers in the unit.

The unit plans to publish a newsletter, a journal, and a monograph series, and to establish a documentation and resource center.

HONDURAS

Association of University Women in Honduras
El Centro
Tegucigalpa, D.C.
Casa No. 1241 y 7a Ave
Telephone: 37-0294
Contact: Dra. Maria Luisa de Bertrand Anduray, Correspondent

The Association of University Women in Honduras (AMUH) was founded in 1950 and obtained legal status in 1958. Its objectives are to obtain equal opportunities in work for women, with salaries equal to those of men.

AMUH research centers on development and Honduran women in their various economic and cultural situations. It offers training courses at all levels. General education, literacy, vocational training, and preventive medicine programs are also available.

AMUH is striving for free, professional health and legal services for poor women and families. It also wishes to obtain scholarships for other Spanish speaking countries.

Publications: A monograph on Honduran women and a short history of feminism in Honduras.

HONG KONG

Gender Roles Research Programme
Centre for Hong Kong Studies
The Chinese University of Hong Kong
Shatin, New Territories
Contact: Dr. Fanny M. Cheung

INDIA

Anveshi Research Center for Women's Studies
Osmania University Campus
Hyderabad-500 007
Contact: Shanta Rameshwar Rao

Centre for Development Studies
Ulloor Trivandrum
Kerala State 695011
Contact: Leela Gulati, Professor

Centre for Informal Education and Development Studies
No. 7, Balaji Layout
Wheeler Road Extension
Bangalore 560 084
Contact: Corinne Kumar-D'Souza

Center for Women's Development Studies
B-43 Panchsheel Enclave
New Delhi 110017
Telephone: 6438428
Contact: Vina Mazumdar

The Center for Women's Development Studies (CWDS) was established in May 1980 in response to a need for major policy changes on several fronts to avert the process of marginalization of women. CWDS undertakes research of an evaluative, critical, and exploratory nature on the processes that influence women's socioeconomic and political status. CWDS also collaborates with central and state governments to translate its research findings into reality. Recent research projects have been concerned with wasteland development through women's own organizations; women's development and the need for child care; the gender dimension of migrant labor; and women's access to land and other productive resources.

The center plans new economic activities for women that would be viable and also produce the desired result of participatory development at the grassroots level. Teaching activities center on training workshops for government officials of various levels to reorient their approaches to women's role in rural develoment. CWDS aims to play the role of catalyst in promoting research, training, teaching, action, and policy debates in women's develoment issues.

Publications: CWDS publishes an annual journal on women's studies, *Samya Shakti*, and the *CWDS Bulletin* (biannually). Research findings of CWDS's academic staff appear as occasional papers, books, mimeo reports, and annotated bibliographies on varied subjects. Among these are: *The Non-aligned Movement and the International Women's Decade: A Summary of Decisions; Women in Focus*, by Kumud Sharma, Sahba Hussain and Archana Saharya; *Who Cares? A Study of Child Care Facilities for Low Income Working Women in India*, by Mina Swaminathan; and *International Women's Decade: A Balance Sheet*, by Lucille Mathurin Mair.

Centre for Women's Studies and Development
Banaras Hindu University
228 Faculty of Social Sciences
Varanasi 221005
Contact: Dr. Surinder Jetley, Director

The Centre for Women's Studies and Development was one of the first five centers set up by the University Grants Commission in 1987–88 to promote and strengthen women's studies in the higher education system. It caters to the Hindu-speaking states, the largest language region.

The center's current focus is on understanding the situation of women among the rural poor as well as evaluation of programs for their development. Besides constructing the social mapping of the region, the center is developing a resource center for wider understanding of issues of common concern internationally. Ongoing research concerns women in the coal-producing area and the political economy of dowry, with reference to women's access to their family's productive resources. The center has initiated an action-oriented research project on the improvement of the rural environment through safe drinking water and rural sanitation. It also organizes rural women in their neighborhoods and provides a forum where they can discuss issues of common relevance and decide upon solutions to shared problems.

Through workshops and seminars, the center encourages a constant review of syllabi in different disciplines. It offers research fellowships for work on women's studies for a period of four years. The researcher can come from any discipline, although preference is given to the social sciences. Currently, the center is designing a diploma course in women's studies.

The center publishes the *Newsletter of the Indian Association for Women's Studies.*

Institute of Social Studies Trust
M-1 Kanchenjunga
18 Barakhamba Road
New Dehli 110001
Telephone: 3323850 or 3312861
Contact: Devaki Jain, Director

The Institute of Social Studies Trust (ISST) is a private nonprofit research and educational organization that was founded in 1964 to provide research and information input into development studies, especially for development aimed at the elimination of poverty among women and children. ISST became a trust in 1980, with trustees drawn from the fields of social action, publishing, and medicine. On May 10, 1985 the institute was granted consultative status with the United Nations Economic and Social Council in Category 2. At present, ISST focuses on data collection, research, and analysis; influencing policy-making and planning bodies; social action and service; and maintaining its library.

Research into women's issues is an important function of the institute. The focus is on the economic roles of women with a view to identifying areas for action and assisting in the integration of women in development, including preparing block-level plans for the integration of women in development projects. Recent research projects have focused on child survival; the impact of mining on women in Kumaon; and case studies of Lakshmi Ashram and Nivali Ashram. In 1981, ISST opened its reference library, which houses literature and documents relevant to women, the poor, and action agencies. The collection includes approximately four thousand documents from conferences, research groups, government and other agencies that focus on poor women and children, and more than forty periodicals relating to social welfare and the social sciences in India and elsewhere.

ISST acts as a facilitation center for the group Mahila Haat, which is also registered independently. Mahila Haat provides low-income women with support services for marketing their products. In 1985, ISST opened a small counselling center. In the future, the institute plans to continue working on issues concerning poor women and to identify policy changes that would benefit women workers in various occupations.

ISST also has an office at Tharanga, 10th cross, Raj Mahal Vilas Extention, Bangalore, 560080.

Publications: ISST has published more than twenty books, case studies, and reports, including: *Impact of Women Workers—Manarashtra Employment Guarantee Scheme Evaluation; Women Migrant Workers from Kerela in Fish Processing in Three States; Linking Fertility and the Socio-Economic Activity of Rural Women; Small Scale Forest-Based Enterprise with Special Reference to the Role of Women.*

Martec Center for the Advancement of Women
25 Cathedral Road
Madras
Tamil Nadu 600086
Contact: Kamakshi Sundaraman, Chair

Mother Teresa Women's University
Kodaikanal 624 102
Tamil Nadu
Contact: Jaya Kothai Pillai, Vice Chancellor

Research Center for Women's Studies
SNDT Women's University
Sir Vithaldas Vidyavihar
Santa Cruz (West)
Juhu Road
Bombay 400 049
Contact: Dr. Maithreyi Krishna Raj, Director
For a description of this program, see pp. 203–08 in this volume.

Streevani
c/o Ishvani Kendra
Off Nagar Rd., Pune 411014
Telephone: 661820
Contact: Augustine Kanjamale, Director

Streevani (Voice of Women) was founded in 1982 as a feminist research project of the Women's Department of Ishvani Kendra. Streevani's objectives are to discover the images that women have of themselves; describe the problems that women encounter in the family, at work, in the community, and in religion; capture the language women use to talk about themselves; help women to take initiative in their own interests; and encourage male writers who are writing about poor women to reflect on how they portray female characters.

Streevani's first major research project was conducted with the above goals, with four groups of women in Maharashta: two groups of Dalit (most oppressed) women, a group of middle-class women who work with victims of family violence, and single Christian professional women. Using the oral history documented in this project, Streevani hosted a curriculum development workshop with Ishvani Kendra that demonstrated in an actual classroom situation how the stories can be used to teach women's studies and social work. Three lesson plans from this workshop are available for distribution. Faculty from two professional schools of social work and the Research Center for Women's Studies, SNDT Women's University participated. Also based on its research into images of Maharashta women, Streevani produced the film Baj ("Women") which won an Indian Government award for the best social/family welfare film of 1985. This film has been widely circulated to various audiences in India.

Other recent projects include case studies on outstanding women activists, a manual on how to carry out such case studies, views on feminism of Indian women activists, a film on Gandhian women activists based on one of the case studies, and a reinterpretation of Hindu and Islamic myths about women.

Publications: Pan on Fire: Eight Dalit Women Tell Their Stories (Marathi and English), Struggling To Be ... Myself (English), Images of Women in Dalit Men's

Autobiographies (Maharathi), and *A Streevani Collage* (English), teaching methods and materials used by Streevani.

Unit for Family Studies
Tata Institute of Social Sciences
Sion-Trombay Road
Deonar, Bombay 400 088
Telephone: 5510400, 5510409
Contact: Meenakshi Apte, Head
Murli Desai, Reader
Shalini Bharat, Lecturer

The Unit for Family Studies was set up in the Department of Family and Child Welfare of the Tata Institute of Social Sciences in 1984 to conduct research in the areas of marriage and the family in India. Topics covered include single-parent families, adoption, working women, female heads of households, chronically ill women in the family, separation and divorce, and particular problems of minority groups (for example, Parsees and Muslims).

Members of the unit teach courses for M.A. students of social work specializing in family and child welfare.

Looking ahead, the unit plans to continue doing research in the above areas and in addition, to analyze government policies and programs in these areas and document and evaluate relevant social work interventions, and to conduct seminars for the purpose of dissemination and discussion of research findings.

Recent research projects have included: "Family in India: An Annotated Bibliography," S. Bharat (1986); "Status of Mother and Deprivation of Family Care among Children," M. Apte, M. Desai, and K. Parwan (a series of surveys from 1986–1987); "Incidence, Nature and Causes of Single-Parent Families in Slum Area of Bombay," S. Bharat (1986); "Bibliography on Family Social Work," M. Desai and R. Dixit (1986); "Case Study of Mrs. Mehrunnisa Dalwai, an Outstanding Woman Activist Working With Muslim Women," M. Desai (1987).

Vimochana, Forum for Women's Rights
P.O. Box 4605
Bangalore 560 046

Vimochana was organized to resist increasing violence against women and to promote both the political analysis of personal life and the integration of women into programs for economic development. The group's politics and philosophy is based in feminist socialism, and it is structured as an autonomous democratic collective. Members are from diverse social strata and occupations; in addition to the group's urban membership, more than five hundred rural women subscribe to and participate in the publication of Vimochana's journal.

In its effort to end violence against women, Vimochana registers legal cases, meets with police, secures legal aid, and engages in pickets and boycotts of businesses connected with violence. It has also initiated campaigns against sexist advertising and has developed street theater programs depicting women's experience of violence and economic exploitation. Two of its additional programs, Womanart and Cinewoman, critique the role of women in the media and present Vimochana's alternative point of view.

Publications: Vimochana's publications include a bimonthly journal in the local language (Kannada) geared to reach rural women and to serve as a forum for women's expression. The group also publishes an occasional newspaper.

Women's Studies Unit
Tata Institute of Social Sciences
P.O. Box 8313 Sion-Trombay Road
Deonar, Bombay 400088
Telephone: 5510400
Contact: Dr. Suma Chitnis, Professor and Head

The Women's Studies Unit is an academic center within the Tata Institute of Social Sciences. It offers both an M.A. and a Ph.D. program in social work and is currently developing curricula and compiling material for teaching in the following subject areas: women and work, women and the law, and women and health. The unit provides both financial and intellectual support for its researchers.

Recently, four members have been researching historical writings of the reform period in Maharashtra to trace the transforming identity of women. Another member has been investigating state development policies for underprivileged groups and researching ways in which academic institutes can help grassroots activists understand the development process.

The unit conducts workshops for policy makers and seminars for teachers interested in teaching women's studies. It also provides a specialized documentation center for students, researchers, faculty, and community activists.

Publications: The unit has published a teaching guide, *Health Status of Indian Women,* and will publish research findings and more teaching material in the near future.

IRAN

Center for Women's Studies
P.O. Box 13145-654
Tehran
Contact: Parvin Derakshan, Director

IRELAND

Council for the Status of Women
54 Lower Mount Street
Dublin 2
Telephone: 607731/611791

The Council on the Status of Women was formed in 1973 by twenty women's organizations. The council now represents fifty-four groups and organizations. Its aims are to provide a liaison between government departments, the European Economic Community, and women's organizations; to press for the implementation of the Report of the Commission on the Status of Women; to provide educational and developmental programs for women and to highlight areas of discrimination; to examine cases of discrimination against women and to take appropriate action; and to consider legislative proposals of concern to women.

The council provides information and referral service for women throughout the country and highlights women's issues in the media. It organizes courses in assertiveness training and sexuality and sponsors conferences relating to women's issues. It funds and facilitates the National Women's Talent Bank to ensure the participation of women at the policy-making level and acts as consultant to the Curriculum and Examinations Board of the Department of Education.

Publications: The council publishes a quarterly newsletter.

University College Dublin Women's Studies Forum
University College, Dublin 4
Telephone: 1-693244, Ext. 8129
Contact: Ailbhe Smyth, Lecturer

University College Dublin Women's Studies Forum (WSF) was founded in 1983 by female members of the academic, administrative, and library staff along with undergraduate and postgraduate students to provide a forum in which women from different disciplines and backgrounds could share their ideas and opinions, research and resources, and collectively and creatively challenge the assumptions and processes of patriarchal knowledge-making. The Women's Studies Forum is especially concerned to ensure that research and resources in women's studies are accessible to women in the community as a whole, and to integrate creative work with the research process.

WSF is open to research on a broad range of areas within women's studies, and especially to the development of research relating to Irish women. Fortnightly, interdisciplinary research seminars involve teachers, post-graduate students, and women involved in research/action projects.

Since 1984, with funding from the Arts Council, WSF has sponsored a series of poetry readings and talks by women writers, artists, and composers. The seminar and the series are open to all women in the community. Regular one-day conferences are held off campus to encourage the participation of women from a wide variety of backgrounds. Topics addressed have included emigration and exile, reproductive technologies, women and folklore, creative writing, women and the law, and the myth of the perfect body.

Members of WSF teach undergraduate courses in women's studies. Master's degree and diploma courses are in the planning stages; validation is required for 1990–91.

The forum is currently in the process of compiling a databank of resources on Irish women's studies, including publications, research in progress, theses, reports, scholars and practitioners, programs and courses in Ireland. For the future, WSF plans to develop a women's education, resource, and research center, which will entail the appointment of researchers and awarding of research grants. WSF also plans to expand its publication list and to establish an international exchange program.

Publications: The forum launched its first series of reports and working papers in July 1987. These include the following: *In the Law of the Father: Report of Seminar on Women and the Law; Abortion Trials and Tribulations; The Politics of Abortion: Ireland in Comparative Perspective;* and *The Universal and Particular: Gender, Class, and Reproduction in Second-Level schools.* WSF also publishes three bibliographies: *Short List of Recent Work on Women in Ireland; Women's Studies—Irish Style;* and *Select List of Creative Writing by Irish Women.*

ISRAEL

International Network for Sex Equity in Education
22 Yehuda Halevi St.
Raanana 43556
Telephone: 052-445795
Contact: Judith Abrahami-Einat, Founder

The International Network for Sex Equity in Education (INSEE) was established in Dublin in July 1987 at the Third Interdisciplinary Congress on Women. The objectives of the network are to create liaisons with other groups with similar interests through the exchange of teaching materials, research projects, and reports; to notify members of relevant conferences; to plan joint publications; and to prepare for an international conference or study program of its own.

INSEE conducts workshops on sex equity in education at international conferences and maintains a mailing list of more sixty individuals from eighteen countries and several international organizations.

INSEE is planning various activities and projects for the future, including publication of members' papers on the meaning of sex equity in education, measures taken to promote it, and the value of such projects; international gatherings both as part of related conferences and as separate study groups; and the exchange of teaching aids on an international basis.

Publications: The *INSEE Newsletter* provides information on conferences, relevant study programs and future plans.

Women's Studies Program
University of Haifa
Mt. Carmel, Haifa 31999
Telephone: 240 111
Contact: Marilyn P. Safir, Director

The Women's Studies Program at the University of Haifa was established in 1983 as a multidisciplinary program encompassing a wide range of topics in the humanities, social sciences, education, social work, and religion. The program offers approximately seventy undergraduate courses. There are more than four hundred students enrolled in the B.A. minor program, and hundreds of others taking elective courses.

The women's studies faculty has conducted research on many subjects in many disciplines. The following is a sampling of topics: sex differences in intellectual functioning; single parents; psychological androgyny and sexual adequacy; sex role socialization/education on the kibbutz; feminization of education; Arab women; violence in the family; the status of women faculty and staff at the University of Haifa; sexual harassment at the university; depression in women following hysterectomies; identifying and training Jewish and Arab women in community development skills; and Arab and Jewish women's attitudes towards family, work, and society.

The KIDMA project is a community outreach program provided by the program to make women's studies accessible to nonuniversity women— women of all ages, from development towns, from varied socioeconomic, cultural, and ethnic backgrounds. In addition, female soldiers and their officers, policewomen, and women's groups such as Na'amat, WIZO, and Ha Gesher (The Bridge), an Arab/Jewish women's peace dialogue, have attended special seminars developed for them under this framework. More than 2500 women participate in the KIDMA programs every year.

The program sponsors lecture series featuring local speakers and speakers from countries such as the United States, Norway, and the Soviet Union.

The program is working towards establishing a center for research and teaching on women with a focus on Jewish and Arab women's status in Israeli society. The goals of this center will be to: sponsor and coordinate research; promote the teaching of women's studies; promote interaction among academics working in women's studies throughout Israel; initiate and develop ties with women's studies scholars and programs abroad; provide a resource center for information about the status of women; publish research findings; and organize conferences and seminars.

Publications: The women's studies faculty writes books and articles in both Hebrew and English. Recent publications include: *The Struggle for Equality: Urban Workers in Prestate Israeli Society; Women's World; Sexual Equality: The Israeli Kibbutz Tests the Theories;* and *Women in Politics.*

ITALY

GRIFF
(Group for Research on Family and Feminism)
University of Milan
Department of Political Science
via Conservatorio 7
Milan
Contact: Laura Balbo

Gruppo Onda
(Group Onda)
Via Savonarola 27
44100-Ferrara
Telephone: 40219
Contact: Gabriella Rosetti

Gruppo Onda was founded in 1983 by representatives of three women's organizations and one academic institution. Its areas of research include women and work, women in school, and women's training programs. Currently, it is conducting research on women and work in Ferrara, a project sponsored by the European Economic Community and the regional government.

Gruppo Onda members participate in the Equal Opportunities Commission of the town council. The group also conducts training programs for women based on the results of its research. Its teaching activities include discussion of research methodology and gender issues, and seminars with university students on women in development. The group plans to develop a documentation and training center for personnel in international programs dealing with women's issues.

Publications: Gruppo Onda has published *Foemina Faber: immagini e condizione del lavoro delle donne,* Milan, Angeli, 1989.

Isis International
Via San Saba 5
00153 Rome
Telephone: (06) 574-6479
Contact: Marilee Karl, Coordinator

Isis International was established in 1974 as a network for sharing information and promoting communication and solidarity among women and groups in the South and the North concerned with women's empowerment and participation in development. Isis has resource centers in Rome, Italy, and Santiago, Chile, and an international network of several thousand individuals and groups. Isis's computerized resource centers contain a unique collection of thousands of publications and materials produced by women in developing countries.

Isis International coordinates the Latin American and Caribbean Women's Health Network, linking some six hundred groups and organizations in the region and around the world working on health issues, providing an information service and a bimonthly health journal in English and Spanish, and coordinating health campaigns.

Other activities include training in audiovisual techniques, computerization of women's resource centers, and computer literacy. Isis plans to link with other groups and networks in developing countries via modem to create a more rapid mobilization of information and solidarity.

Publications: Women in Action, a quarterly magazine that focuses on women's groups in developing countries; The Isis International Book Series with recent publications such as *Rural Women in Latin America; Women and Popular Education; Women and the Economic Crisis;* and *Women's Struggles and Strategies in the Third World.* Two resource guides, *Women in Development: A Resource Guide for Organization and Action* (1983; updated Spanish edition, 1989) and *Powerful Images: A Women's Guide to Audiovisual Resources,* also have recently been published.

Research Center for Archives on Women
Orientale University
30 Piazza So Giovanni Maggiore
Naples 80134
Contact: Maria Teresa Chialant

JAPAN _____

National Women's Education Center
728 Sugaya, Ranzan-machi
Hiki-gun
Saitama-ken 355-02
Contact: Mizue Maeda, Director-General

Institute for Women's Studies
Ochanomizu University
Otsuk 2-1-1, Bunyo-ku
Tokyo 112
Contact: Hiroko Hara, Professor

Women's Studies Society of Japan
Shokadou Women's Book Store
Nishinotouinn-Nishiiru, Shimodachiuri
Kamigyouku, Kyoto-shi, Kyoto
Telephone: 075-441-6905
Contact: Toyoko Nakanishi, Manager

The Women's Studies Society of Japan (WSSJ) was established in 1978 by teachers, students, housewives, and writers concerned with the liberation of Japanese women from traditionally oppressive gender roles. It is the oldest and largest women's studies group in Japan, with a membership of two hundred, including university and high school teachers, students, homemakers, older women, and men. The society conducts studies on Japanese and foreign women in areas such as literature, history, sociology, psychology, economics, and the politics of women's liberation. Research is funded by private companies and city governments.

Seven ongoing seminar series, focusing on feminist therapy, women and employment, modern women's history, sexuality of women, women's studies, female writers, and feminist projects, are affiliated with WSSJ. Women from Kyoto and Tokyo participate in these seminars. WSSJ also sponsors a monthly seminar in Kyoto or Osaka.

Publications: WSSJ publishes *Voice of Women,* a monthly newsletter; *Annual Report on Women's Studies,* the only academic journal of feminist studies in Japan; and a history of the first ten years of the group.

LEBANON _____

Institute for Women's Studies in the Arab World (IWSAW)
Beirut University College
P.O. Box 13
5053 Beirut
Lebanon
Phone: 811968, Telex: 23389 LE
Contact: Julinda Abu Nasr, Director
For more information about this program, see pp. 209–12 in this volume.

MALAYSIA _____

Project KANITA
School of Social Sciences
University Sains Malaysia
11800 Penang, West Malaysia
Telephone: 04-883822 Ext. 436
Contact: Wazir-jahan Karim, Director

Project KANITA, a women's studies research program, was originally founded in 1978 with UNICEF funding. In January of 1982 funding for the project was taken over by the Prime Minister's Department in Kuala Lumpur. From 1982 to 1984, the project focused on the major issues affecting and inhibiting women's full participation in development. Since January 1984, the project has functioned as a research and consulting body, acting for national and internationl agencies including the Commonwealth Secretariat, Ford Foundation, and the Ministry of Social Welfare.

The objectives of Project Kanita are to identify the needs of rural and urban women; to develop research tools and strategies comprising academic, action-oriented and evaluative research; to assist in the development, implementation and coordination of policies and programs concerning women, youth, and children; to ensure that the research process, from data gathering to policy framing, will enable women, youth, and children to realize and develop their full potential in leadership, entrepreneurship, and community organization.

Areas of research include: health and medicine; child development; patterns of female employment; female leadership; entrepreneurship; culture and ideology in tradition and change; participation of women in national planning; evaluation of government programs for women. Much of this material has been presented in seminars and workshops at both the local and national level and for government and nongovernment agencies, as well as the general public.

KANITA's community outreach activities include working with other women's groups, youth groups, and workers to pursue common goals; and producing audiovisual materials, talks, and exhibitions for a wide variety of audiences about issues of concern in Malaysia and other countries. Kanita participates in international networks, attends and helps to organize national and international conferences and seminars, and contributes to local and international newsletters and publications. Its research will continue to center on the issues and problems facing women, youth, and children, particularly those related to socioeconomic planning and development.

Publications: Proceedings from seminars, workshops, forums, and research findings are published as working papers or articles.

Women in Development Program, Asian and Pacific Development Center
Pesiaran Duta, P.O. Box 12224, 50770
Kuala Lumpur
Telephone: 03-2548088
Contact: Noeleen Heyzer, Coordinator

The Women in Development Program of the Asia and Pacific Development Center (APDC) has its roots in the Asian and Pacific Center for Women and Development (APCWD), which was established in 1977 as an initiative of the Decade for Women. In 1980, the center was integrated with three other regional United Nations centers into one main development center for the region. The program provides a forum for women's concerns to be aired and helps to ensure that women are included in mainstream development policy and programs.

The program carries out research on key development issues that have policy and planning implications for women. Research on agricultural change and rural women, women and development planning, and the participation of women in the industrial process has been undertaken and the findings have been published (see the first three publications below). Other recent research projects are "International Migration and Women," the causes, consequences, and mechanisms of women migrating as domestic workers; "Women and Poverty," the documenting of interventions that have relieved poverty and reduced the total number of poor women; and "The Impact of Food, Energy, and Debt Management on Women."

Community outreach programs include two pilot projects on credit for low-income women, started in 1988 in Papua, New Guinea for some of the poorest women in the region.

Most of the program's training activities focus on improving skill development in planning and implementing effective programs for women. One current training project is "Research and Training of Women and Development Management."

Publications: Women Farmers and Rural Change in Asia: Towards Equal Access and Participation, Noleen Heyzer, ed. (1987); *Missing Women: Development Planning in Asia and the Pacific,* Noeleen Heyzer, ed. (1985); *Daughters of Industry: Work, Skills and Consciousness of Women Workers in Asia,* APDC (1988); occasional papers, conference and seminar reports, and the Women's Resource and Action Series, begun in 1988 with *Women in Law,* Radhika Coomaraswamy, ed.; *Women, Health and Environment,* Vanessa Griffin and Lena Chan, eds.; *Women, Science and Technology,* Ruth Lechte, ed.; *Women and Media,* Kamla Bhasin, ed. Further details about the program, its activities, and publications are available in the 51-page booklet, *The Women in Development Programme.*

MEXICO ──────────────────────────────────

Interdisciplinary Program on Women's Studies
El Colegio de México
Camino al Ajusco No. 20
C.P. 01000
México D.F.
Contact: Elena Urrutia, Coordinator
For a description of this program, see pp. 213–14 in this volume.

THE NETHERLANDS ──────────────────────────

Centrum voor Vrouenstudies KUN
(Center for Women's Studies KUN)
Thomas van Aquinostraat 2
Nijmegen
Contact: Maria L. Van Der Sommer

Department of Women's Studies
Agricultural University Wageningen
Hollandseweg 1, 6706 KN Wageningen
Telephone: 08370-83374
Contact: Joan Wolffensperger, Agricultural Engineer

The Department of Women's Studies was founded in 1980 as a result of student pressure on the university board. Its objectives are to conduct research and teaching in areas of interest to all women's studies students. Research topics include gender and rural development in Third World and European countries and gender and agricultural sciences. Projects recently in progress have focused on developing educational and research methods, of which theory on gender is a substantial part; the development of theory of gender and rural development; and a joint research and education project undertaken by the Agricultural University and the University of Zimbabwe.

The department offers courses on feminist methods and methodology. Members of the department are working toward integrating women's studies and research projects into the curricula and programs of other departments. The number of courses offered will be extended from three to seven in the near future, including a general course on women's studies in the agricultural sciences.

Publications: Publications are primarily in Dutch, but several congress papers are available in English, such as *Engendered Structure* by Joan Wollfenperger, a conceptualization of the alliance between gender and social system, and *The Gender of Power* by M. Leijenaar (Leiden: DSWO-Press). The department also publishes a quarterly bulletin documenting articles and books available within the university.

Dutch Women's Studies Association
Heidelberglaan 1, 3584 CS Utrecht
Telephone: 30.531881
Contact: Erna Kas

The Dutch Women's Studies Association was founded in 1979 as a national platform for women's studies aimed especially at current national politics. It earned the legal status of a foundation in 1982, with a mandate to collect and disseminate information; suppport staff members, students, and jobless women's studies activists; influence policy making; and organize conferences.

The association sponsors research programs, community group lectures, and workshops on research skills, such as where to find money for research and how to write good research proposals. Current research projects include a study of the career success of women's studies majors.

The association is working toward a full recognition of women's studies as an academic discipline.

Publications: The association publishes *Money Boxes for Women's Studies: Where and How to Find Money for Your Research,* and *Women Studies and the Labor Market.*

Interfacultaire Wergroep Vrouwenstudies
(Interdisciplinary Women's Studies Group)
Rijksuniversiteit Utrecht
Heidelberglaan 1
Centrumgebrouw Zuid
Utrecht 3584
Contact: R. Braidotti, Chair

International Information
Center and Archives for Women
Kaizergrach 10
Amsterdam 1015 CN

Promotion Committee for Emancipation Research
Lutherse Burgwal 10, 2512 CB
The Hague
Telephone: 070-614321
Contact: Riky Van Og

Since 1974 the Dutch government has conducted an emancipation policy. In the Netherlands, emancipation, generally accepted to mean the emancipation of women, refers to women's liberation, equal opportunity, and equal rights. One component of this policy is the promotion of women's studies. Because it believes that women's studies must gain a foothold in established research, the Dutch government founded the Promotion Committee for Emancipation Research (STEO) in 1985.

STEO aims to promote emancipation research and women's studies at universities and other institutions of advanced education, by government, foundations, private business, and individual researchers; encourage the inclusion of emancipation aspects in standard research; and help emancipation research and women's studies acquire financing.

STEO designates priority areas in women's studies every year. In 1989 health, justice, and law; and language and signs were explored.

STEO maintains contact with individuals and groups of similar interest such as university boards, the Ministry of Education and Science, women's studies coordinators at universities, and work groups made up of women's studies researchers. National and international foundations and organizations that fund research are also an important part of STEO's networking. STEO keeps track of the available research expertise in women's studies in the Netherlands and brings researchers together.

STEO was first established with a time limit of six years. By 1991, it is hoped that women's studies emancipation research will occupy a permanent place in traditional research.

Publications: Verslag van drie jaar STEO (Three Year Report of STEO), 1988; *Congres in Beeld* (Conference Report), 1988. A publication about theories of power is planned.

Research and Documentation Center
Women and Autonomy (VENA)
Faculty of Social Science
P.O. Box 9555
2300 RB Leiden
Contact: Mary A. Boesveld-Ornstein

The Union of Turkish Women in the Netherlands
Van Musschenbroekstraat 108
Amsterdam
Telephone: 020-941854
Contact: Maviye Karaman

The Union of Turkish Women in the Netherlands (in Turkish, Hollanda Türkiyeli Kadinlar Birliĝi: HTKB) is a Turkish migrant women's organization founded in 1975. It has five branches in Amsterdam, Rotterdam, The Hague, Hijmegen, and Eindhoven.

The primary task of HTKB is to draw attention to the triple exploitation of migrant women (as women, as migrants, and as workers) and to mobilize and organize the women themselves to struggle for their rights. At the same time, HTKB members support democratic forces fighting against the military junta in Turkey.

Because of their lack of education, many Turkish women who have come to the Netherlands to join their families are unemployed; when they do find work, conditions are severe. In order to gain for these women the same rights as citizens of the host country, HTKB cooperates with Dutch women's organizations and other migrant groups. HTKB sponsors literacy programs; informs women about their legal status as well as about issues surrounding health, child care, and birth control; teaches Dutch people about their international neighbors; and organizes activities for second and third generation Turkish girls living in the Netherlands.

Publications: HTKB publishes a periodical, *Union of Women,* five times a year.

Women and Development Program
Institute of Social Studies
P.O. Box 90733
2509 LS The Hague
Phone: (070)-510100
Telex: 31491 ISSNL
Fax: (070)-549851
Contact: Geertje Lycklama
For a description of this program, see pp. 215–37 in this volume.

NEW CALEDONIA

Pacific Women's Resource Bureau
South Pacific Commission
P.O. Box D5
Noumea Cedex
Contact: Marie-Claire Beccalosi; Hilda Lini

NEW ZEALAND

Centre for Women's Studies
University of Waikato
Private Bag, Hamilton
Telephone: (071) 62-889
Contact: Jane Ritchie, Director

The Centre for Women's Studies at the University of Waikato was established in 1986. Although women's studies courses have been taught at the university since 1974, the founding of the center contributed to formal recognition of the field. Research has been conducted on various women-related issues including women and work, women and education, women and smoking, women and trade unions, feminism and racism, and women's health. Recent research projects have focused on eating attitudes and behaviors of intermediate and secondary school girls; feminism and racism; and the professionalization of New Zealand female teachers.

The center works in collaboration with the Centre for Continuing Education's Women's Program. Teaching activities include a supporting major in women's studies for the Bachelor of Social Sciences degree, courses at the master's level, and a postgraduate Diploma in Women's Studies. The center intends to add a Maori dimension to its program by appointing Maori staff.

Publications: The center publishes *Celebration*, a collection of addresses delivered at the inauguration of the center.

Society for Research on Women
P.O. Box 13-078
Johnsonville
Wellington
Contact: Mary J. Mowbray

NIGERIA _____

Women in Nigeria
P.O. Box 253, Samaru, Zaria
Kaduna State
or P.O. Box 5600, Benin City
Bendel State
Contact: Glory Kilanko, Acting National Coordinating Secretary
or Bene Madunagu, Secretary-General

Women in Nigeria (WIN) was formed in 1982 to work for the improvement of the lives of Nigerian women. WIN is a national, independent, nonreligious organization, open to all those who subscribe to its aims and objectives. It works through research, dissemination of information, policy making, and action. Research has been conducted in the following areas: women and the family, women and education, women in rural areas, consciousness-raising and mobilization, what women want for Nigeria's political and socioeconomic system and, most recently, violence against women and children.

Community outreach programs include workshops, with more than twenty-four hundred working-class and poor rural women throughout Nigeria, both to raise women's consciousness about the political and socioeconomic system of Nigeria, and to ensure that the views of ordinary women are represented to the Political Bureau. In addition, WIN has fought individual cases of discrimination against and sexual harassment of women, such as sexual assault and harassment of students; the attempted closing of the mosque road to women; the case in which a village head tried to force a teenage girl to marry him instead of continuing school; the Federal Housing Project discrimination against single women; and the nonextension of medical facilities to some married female workers. WIN organizes numerous small seminars and workshops and produces radio and television programs and popular theater to raise public awareness about gender and class relations at local levels. WIN is in the process of building a resource and documentation center of materials relating to women's struggles and gender/class issues.

Publications: Women in Nigeria Today, proceedings of the 1982 seminar, London: Zed Press, 1985; *Women and the Family*, proceedings of the 1983 seminar, Dakar: CODESRIA, 1985; *The WIN Document: Conditions of Women in Nigeria and Policy Recommendations to 2000 AD*, Zaria: WIN, 1985.

Women's Research and Documentation Centre
Institute of African Studies
University of Ibadan
Ibadan
Telephone: 22/400550 Ext. 2345
Contact: Bolanle Awe, Director and Chairperson

The Women's Research and Documentation Centre (WORDOC) was established in 1986 to provide a focus for women's studies in Nigeria through coordination of research projects, promotion of new methodologies, and the seeking of sources for funding. It further exists to set up a women's network, to promote understanding of the concerns of women in Nigeria and West Africa through projects, publications, seminars, and other activities with a view to providing a basis for policy formation, and to provide a documentation center for scholars, policy makers, and other interested people.

Research focuses on agriculture, government and politics, culture, history, the legal system, health, family, education, literature, religion, science, and urban economy. WORDOC's 1988 research project is titled "Women in Agriculture in Nigeria."

WORDOC sponsors monthly seminars/symposia on issues related to women. Members of WORDOC teach courses on women in history and literature.

Publications: WORDOC Newsletter; a special issue of *African Notes* on "Women in Agriculture"; and a directory of scholars in women's studies in Nigeria (forthcoming).

NORWAY _____

Arbeidsforskningsinstituttet (AFI)
(Work Research Institute)
Stensberggate 25
P.b. 8171 Dep/
N 0034 Oslo 1

The Gender and Development Group
Centre for Development Studies
Stromgaten 54
N-5007 Bergen
Telephone: (05) 213305
Contact: Tone Bleie, Researcher/Social Anthropologist

The Gender and Development Group was formed in 1986 by female researchers as a response to the lack of priority given to gender-focused research. The group aimed at a multidisciplinary approach and initially included history, comparative religion, anthropology, geography, and philosophy in its program. Research is focused on the relationship between the cultural construction of gender and its social organization. In September 1988, the group arranged the symposium "Gender Relations and Identity Management: Symbolic Analysis and Interpretations."

Additionally, members of the group are involved in the popularization of gender-relevant basic research and locating current development debates within a gender-aware framework.

Publications: The Gender and Development Group plans to publish an anthology based on the Gender Development and Identity Management symposium.

Institutt for Samfunnsforskning (ISF)
(Group Research about Equality)
Munthesgate 31
N 0260 Oslo 2
Contact: Helga Hernes

Secretariat for Women and Research
Sandakerveien 99
0483 Oslo 4
Telephone: 02 15 70 12
Contact: Aina Schiotz

The secretariat was established as part of the Norwegian Research Council for Science and the Humanities (NAVF) policy for strengthening the position of women in research and higher education. It was founded in 1977 as a secretariat solely for the social sciences. Since 1982, it has expanded into the natural sciences, medicine, technology, and the humanities. Its aims are to increase the number of women in research and to initiate, coordinate, and promote research on women. Four to five persons are on staff.

From 1979 to 1984, the secretariat conducted a comprehensive research project, "Employment Procedures and Equal Opportunity at Norwegian Universities and Colleges." A second project, on Norwegian research policy, has also been completed. In the fall of 1988 a research director who focuses on feminist research in medicine was appointed. Through the end of 1990, the secretariat will concentrate on the recruitment of women to medicine, the natural sciences, and technology.

Publications: The journal *Nytt on Kvinneforskning* (News on Women's Studies) is issued five times per year. The secretariat also publishes conference reports, and the results of the two research projects mentioned above.

Senter for Humanistisk Kvinneforskning
(Center for Feminist Research in the Humanities)
University of Bergen
Herman Fossgt. 12
5007 Bergen
Telephone: 212471/212472
Contact: Gerd Vatne, Secretary

The Senter for Humanistisk Kvinneforskning (Center for Feminist Research in the Humanities) was founded in August 1985 at the University of Bergen for a trial period of five years and is currently staffed by a secretary, a scholarship holder, and two assistant professors. The center also has an advisory board that coordinates its activities. The purpose of the center is to initiate, stimulate, and coordinate feminist research in the humanities. The center's research is interdisciplinary and aims at developing theory.

Research has been conducted in various areas of interest to women: feminist theory, literary analysis, gender ideology in Christianity, religiously legitimated wife abuse, exorcism, and the social mobility of Norwegian women.

Teaching activities include seminars on theoretical issues and research projects.

Senter for Kvinneforskning
(Center for Women's Research)
University of Trondheim
Hakon Magnussonsgate 1B
N 7055 Dragvoll
Contact: Rannveig Dhale

Senter for Kvinnefoskning
(Center for Women's Research)
P.O. Box 1040
University of Oslo
0359 Oslo 3
Telephone: (02) 454370
Contact: Fride Eeg-Henriksen, Administrative Head

The Senter for Kvinnefoskning at the University of Oslo is an interdisciplinary unit that is intended to strengthen women's research and increase the recruitment of women to research. It was established in 1986 to work for the integration of women's perspectives in research and teaching in the various departments at the university.

The center conducts seminars and meetings about women's research, emphasizing interdisciplinary approaches and epistemological problems. In addition, it offers courses for researchers, for example how-to courses in writing applications for research funds and scholarships, and courses in the art of writing.

The center offers office space to researchers and students, and welcomes visitors from abroad. It is working to promote contact between female researchers and those doing research on women within and outside the University of Oslo.

Publications: The center publishes an information bulletin twice a year.

PAKISTAN

Applied Socio-Economic Research
Flat No.8, 2nd Floor Sheraz Plaza
P.O. Box 3154
Gulberg, Lahore
Telephone: 877613
Contact: Nighat Said Khan, Director

Applied Socio-Economic Research (ASR) is an intermediary nongovernmental organization that was founded in 1983. It initiates or acts as a catalyst for a wide range of activities, primarily research, publishing, training, film production, documentation, and networking.

Research has been conducted on issues relating to women and gender in the areas of agriculture, media, industry, religion, development, activism, and feminist theory, and on other issues related to the transformation of society. Recent research projects have focused on women and land, oral histories of women, women and Islam, the left and the women's question, feminist theory in South Asia, and women and the 1974 partition of South Asia.

ASR collaborates with grassroots women's organizations on participatory action research, organizing women in the informal sector, health programs, and consciousness-raising in the community.

ASR also conducts regular workshops at grassroots and national levels. Some of these are conceptual or theoretical workshops on issues such as women and development and feminism; others are skill-related—for example, training women in video production.

Future goals of ASR include steering research activities toward more theoretical issues; continuing the training program especially on feminist issues; and moving into film production.

Publications: ASR has published more than thirty books and pamphlets on topics such as feminism, research and action methodologies, women and development, and women and industry, and an annotated bibliography of works about women.

PANAMA

Instituto de Investigaciones y Capacitacion para la Promocion de la Mujer en Panama
(Institute for Research on and Promotion of Women in Panama)
Apartado Postal 6-5950 "El Dorado"
Panama City
Contact: Marcela F. de Rodriquez

PARAGUAY

Centro Paraguay de Estudios de la Mujer
(Paraguayan Center for Women's Studies)
Facultadad de Derecho
Universidad Catolica
CC 1718 Asuncion

Grupo de Estudio de la Mujer Paraguaya
(Group for the Study of Women in Paraguay)
Eligio Ayala 973 C.C. 2157
Asuncion
Telephone: 443734
Contact: Graziella Corvalan, Coordinator

The Grupo de Estudio de la Mujer (GEMPA) was founded in 1985 to promote research and discussion on women's issues in Paraguay. It is a private, autonomous group of social scientists working together to achieve the following objectives: (1) to develop a theoretical and methodological body of knowledge about women in Paraguay in order to generate an alternative perspective about the condition of women; (2) to support and collaborate with women's groups and individuals working on women's issues; (3) to build a conceptual framework for considering Paraguayan women within the economic, political, social, and cultural processes. GEMPA is affiliated with the Centro Paraguayo de Sociologia.

The group is particularly interested in conducting research on women from a sociological perspective, on such topics as women and the labor market, women's movements, women and education, women and politics, and images of women in the media. In addition, recent research projects have focused on women in the rural sector and women's participation in the informal sector of the Paraguayan economy (as street vendors and domestic workers, for example).

Publications: GEMPA publishes a journal, *Enfoques de Mujer* (Focus on Women), four times a year and *Bibliografía de la Mujer Paraguaya* (Bibliography of the Paraguayan Woman). Future publications will include an anthology, *Condicion Social de la Mujer en el Paraguay* (The Social Condition of the Woman in Paraguay).

PERU

Flora Tristan Peruvian Women's Center
Parque Hernan Velarde 42
Lima 1
Telephone: 248008, 240839
Contact: Virginia Vargas, Director

The Flora Tristan Center was founded in 1979 to demonstrate the specific forms of the subordinate and oppressed situation of women in Peru.

The center is researching the roots and formation of the women's movement in Peru, and gender studies in the university. Community outreach programs focus on family planning for women in marginal urban sectors, and are also concerned with reproductive and sexual rights of women. Legal services and labor training programs for women workers are also available.

Publications: Publications include brochures about work and health. The center also publishes a bimonthly journal called *VIVA!*

Labor Association for Development
León Velarde 890-Lince
Lima 14
Telephone: 705682, 705688, 701446
Contact: Maruja Barrig, Responsible for Research

The Labor Association for Development (ADEC-ATC) was begun in 1979 with the merging of two organizations, the Association for Defense and Legal Training and the Association of Labor and Culture. Its goal is to strengthen the labor movement, with an emphasis on research on women and employment. Research has been carried out since 1983 on various topics

including the fish canning industry, pharmaceutical laboratories, manufacturing industries, and the informal urban sector. Current research projects
focus on the tendencies to insert women into the urban labor market, and
the relationship between economic activity and the domestic unit.

The association carries out action research and commmunity outreach
projects. Training workshops are held with workers from every sector.
Brochures and videos about feminine socialization and double workdays,
for example, have been produced for these workshops. Teaching activities
include union organization and training courses for union leaders, both
men and women, in which talks are held about the situation of working
women. The association also has a daily radio program.

Publications: The association publishes two magazines of general labor
information, in which aspects of working women's situations are included.
Numerous brochures and folders with teaching materials for working
women are available. Five books concerning women and employment have
been published, as have books about women and the law.

Peru Mujer
(Peru Woman)
Avenue Espana 578
Lima 5
Contact: Jeanine Velasco

Women's Documentation Center
CENDOC-Mujer
Av. LaMar 170
Lima 18
Contact: Barbara Jochamowitz, Director

PHILIPPINES

Center for Women's Resources
43 Roces Ave., 2nd. Floor
Mar Santos Bldg.
Quezon City
Telephone: 99-27-55
Contact: Carolyn Medel Anonuevo, Executive Director

The Center for Women's Resources (CWR) is a nonprofit, private institution
established in 1982. Its activities are primarily in education, publishing, and
research. A major objective of CWR is to respond to specific needs of women
of different socioeconomic sectors, including workers, students, urban and
rural poor, and professionals.

The center conducts participatory research on the conditions of women from these different sectors. Research projects have focused on the effects of militarization, on women in fisheries, women's health concerns, and on investigating the historical roots of patriarchy in Phillipine society. In addition, the center is currently developing a women-specific data bank.

CWR's main area of focus is the development of popular education modules on the condition of women in the Phillipines. The center has developed an orientation module complete with a workbook demonstrating how education modules can be used by different women's groups.

CWR also conducts a free community clinic and provides help for different women's organizations in their programs.

Publications: The center publishes a quarterly, *Piglas-Diwa* (Liberating the Spirit); a journal, *Marso 8* (March 8), which discusses research findings; the text of an education module titled "How Do We Liberate Ourselves?"; and a booklet for organizers, *From Bonding Wires to Banding Women.*

Development Institute for Women in Asia (DWIA)
The Philippines Women's University
Taft Ave.
Manila
Contact: Amelou B. Reyes, Executive Director

Institute of Women's Studies
St. Scholastica's College
P.O. Box 3153
Manila
Telephone: 50-77-86
Contact: Sr. Mary John Mananzan, OSB

The Institute of Women's Studies at St. Scholastica's College emerged after activists developed the first introductory women's studies course in 1986. The excellent evaluation of the course by both students and faculty led to the decision to make the course a part of the General Education Component and a prerequisite to graduation. In 1988, the Women's Studies Program developed into the Institute of Women's Studies consisting of four components: the curricular program; research and publication; the outreach program; and the resource development program.

The outreach program has conducted four awakening awareness seminars for peasant women, women workers, urban poor women, and women in service industries. An international course on women and society was offered to fifteen Asian and Pacific women from September to December 1990.

Publications: The research and publication program has published three volumes in its women's studies series.

Labor Information Desk,
Ateneo Center for Social Policy and Public Affairs
Rm 230 Faura Hall, P.O. Box 154
Manila
Telephone: 99-87-21/98-25-41 location 325 or 326
Contact: Eleanor R. Dionisio and Stella D.
Pagsanghan, Program Officers

The Labor Information Desk (LID) is a unit of Ateneo Center for Social Policy and Public Affairs (ACSPPA), a university-based nongovernmental organization that aims to support the formation of public opinion in favor of advocacy for social reform. LID works to support and shape the labor movement's participation in social reform.

Research has focused on various issues, such as labor relations and the state, gender equality in development, labor's vision of development, and women in the trade union movement. A recent research project focused on the state of trade union education for women.

As part of its community-based activites, LID offers secretariat support for the Industrial Workers Committee of the group Legislative Advocates for Women; participates in the development of an education and training module series for female workers; and conducts seminars for female workers and union leaders.

Future directions include: conferences on issues that concern women workers; development of a database on labor, with a special section on women workers; and the integration of a feminist perspective in workers' political education.

Publications: LID publishes a newsletter on the labor movement and its position on various national issues, including a regular section on women workers. The Tagalog edition is titled *Bigkis-Manggagawa;* the English edition is *The Worker's Advocate.*

Mediawatch Collective
12 Pasaje Dela Paz, Proj. 4
Quezon City
Telephone: 77-53-41, 721-68-69
Contact: Pennie S. Azarcon-de la Cruz, Project Coordinator

The Mediawatch Collective was established in 1987 as the action component of a 1985/86 Mediawatch research project sponsored by Pilipina (see below) on the images and treatment of women in the local media. The project focused on the characterization of and roles given to women in radio and TV programs, magazines, tabloids and other newspapers, advertisements, and movies. The collective monitors images of women in local media and lobbies for responsive legislation to regulate media and advertising.

The main thrust of the Mediawatch Collective's research is to examine: (1) the treatment of women in local media on issues such as rape; (2) headlines on women's issues; (3) the placement of women's stories in the news; (4) the working conditions of women in media; and (5) the different perspective that women in the media bring to the field. Recently research has focused in particular on the response of grassroots women to such media images; advertisers' response to women's actions; and legislative response to the issue.

The Mediawatch Collective sponsors seminars based on a fifteen-minute slide show, "How to Catch and Keep a Man," and organizes letter writing campaigns and petitions against offensive ads and radio and TV programs.

In the future, the collective plans to continue the above activities and to organize women on a grassroots level to forge a boycott force (if needed) and convene women writers to write and produce alternative and women-oriented scripts for radio and television.

Publications: The collective publishes the monthly, *Mediawatch Newsletter*, and *From Virgin to Vamp: Images of Women in Philippine Media*.

Pilipina, Inc.
12 Pasaje de la Paz Street, Project 4
1109 Quezon City
Telephone: 77-53-41 and 721-68-69
Contact: Delores de Quiros-Castillo, Executive Coordinator

Pilipina was founded in 1981 by Teresita Quintos-Deles, Remedios Ignacio-Rikken, Irene Santiago, and Mary John Mananzan. The organization currently has 350 members with chapters at Metro Manila, Davao, Cebu, Cagayan de Oro, and Naga. Pilipina works for the acceptance by Philippine society of the central significance of the women's struggle for social transformation. It promotes economic justice and equity for women; women's right to be free from sexual harassment, abuse, and rape; and shared parenting toward nonsexist child-rearing.

Research is conducted in areas such as child care, the portrayal of women in the media, and policies and laws affecting women. A recent project, "Work Support Systems: Focus on Child Care Support Structures," studied the child care support needed by mothers from various grassroots socioeconomic groups, as well as existing child care support facilities of the Department of Social Welfare and Development and of nongovernment organizations, and sought to formulate policies integrating the viable existing strategies and the needs of mothers.

The "Women's Media Watch Monitoring Project" was undertaken in 1985 to monitor the roles of women in print and broadcast media. As a result of this research project, Pilipina and other concerned women's organizations formed the Mediawatch Collective mentioned above. The collective continues to monitor the images and treatment of women in the local media.

As conveyor organization and secretariat base for Legislative Advocates for Women, a broad coalition of women's organizations that seeks to advance a legislative agenda for women, Pilipina is very active in monitoring government policies and laws relating to family relationships, child care, divorce, overseas women workers, industrial women workers, health and population, sexual violence, mail-order brides, AIDS, prostitution, women in arts and culture, women in media, and peasant women and agriculture.

Community outreach programs include social credit for poor self-employed women in public markets and slum communities; legal resources for women such as paralegal training, legal literacy, advocacy, litigation, research, documentation, and publication; and community health with emphasis on women's health. Pilipina also conducts consciousness-raising sessions on feminist issues with grassroots women, students, social workers, and professional women; women's livelihood projects, for example, soap making and crafts making; media awareness seminars; health and child care training for urban poor women and rural women; and seminars and lectures on legislative advocacy and lobbying.

Publications: Pilipina publishes a pamphlet series by the Philippine Women's Research Collective, which includes the following titles: *Towards Our Own Image, Towards Our Own Image II, Women of the Soil, Life on the Assembly Line, Economic Refugees, Filipinas for Sale,* and *Too Little, Too Late,* which will cover health, the law, religion, and women's movements in future releases. Also available are *Kamalayan,* an anthology of feminist writings, edited by Pennie Azarcon-de la Cruz and *From Virgin to Vamp: Images of Women in Philippine Media.*

Women's Resource and Research Center
Katipunan Parkway
Loyola Heights
Quezon City
Telephone: 97-28-60, 98-24-21
Contact: Lucia Ticzon, Executive Director

Established in October 1987, the Women's Resource and Research Center is a service-oriented institution for women and men who are committed to educating and empowering Philippine women. The center's objectives are to serve as an advocate for the full participation of Philippine women, particularly grassroots women, in national development and social transformation; to support national and global women's movements, particularly in the Third World; to encourage nonsexist scholarship and relevant research on women within the educational system; and to promote a national and international communications network for groups and individuals addressing women's issues.

The Women's Resource and Research Center operates through five programs: the Institutional Development Program; the Network Development Program; the Research Development Program; the Women's Studies Program; and the Information Resource Management and Development Program. Current directions in scholarship include feminist education and training for poor women; feminist participatory health care; women and international migration; women's information needs; nonsexist learning in the educational system; women and spirituality; theoretical studies in Third World feminism; and feminist analysis and critique of macro development policies and programs.

Publications: FLIGHTS News Bulletin and monographs, proceedings, and occasional papers series.

Women's Studies Resource Center
2nd Floor Santos Building
Malvar Extension
Davao City
Contact: Mae Fe Ancheta-Templo

REPUBLIC OF CHINA ─────────────────────────────

Research Program on Gender and Society
National Tsing Hua University
101, Sec. 2, Kuang Fu Rd.
Hsinchu
Taiwan 30043
Contact: Hsiao-chin Hsieh

The Women's Committee of the United Nations
Association of the Republic of China
101 Ning Po West Street
Taipei, Taiwan
Telephone: 3121378, 2104565
Contact: Helen H C. Yeh Lee, Chairperson

The Women's Committee is a nongovernmental organization established in 1950 by a group of lawmakers, university professors, writers, medical doctors, members of the National Assembly and other prominent women. The purpose of the committee is to conduct studies on issues relating to women and to create an international coalition of women working together toward the improvement of women's lives throughout the world. Field studies are arranged to research women's activities in China and abroad, primarily in the United States, the Middle East, and Asia, with much emphasis placed on gender issues.

Included in the committee's community outreach programs are public lectures and symposiums on women's development; group discussions arranged to exchange viewpoints on current women's problems; and social gatherings for women of different nations.

The committee offers scholarships and grants to university graduates, school teachers, and other outstanding women workers in different fields who wish to pursue advanced studies abroad.

Publications: The Women's Committee has various publications in both Chinese and English. The papers in Chinese include: "Women's Status in the Past Seven Decades," by Titania C.T. Chien, "Women's Involvement in the Economic Development of the Republic of China," by Wan Jung Kuo, a handbook on the law for women compiled by UNAROC, and others. The papers in English are: "Women's Achievements during the Mid-Decade of the 1980s," focusing on equality, development, and peace; the "Report for UN Nairobi Forum '85" on women's status and contributions toward development in the Republic of China and "The Chinese Family" by Helen Hsieh Ching Yeh Lee; and "Asian Women and World Peace" by Ya Chuan Wang. All publications are available free of charge.

Women's Research Program
Population Studies Center
National Taiwan University
Taipei, Taiwan
Telephone: 3930097 or 3510231 Ext. 2595
Contact: Elaine Tsui, Coordinator

Following the first research conference on women in Taiwan held at the Population Studies Center, the Women's Research Program was established in September 1985 by four researchers representing four different disciplines. The program's major goals are to promote research on women and gender, to promote awareness in the public about women's changing roles and contributions to development, and to network with other women's organizations in Taiwan. Its activities center on research, publication, and the provision of resource materials.

Recently, research has focused on the quality of life for women who work in industrial and nonindustrial jobs; women's health; women's social supports and life satisfaction; and social roles, stress, and depression in urban communities.

Numerous lectures are held each year, as well as informal discussions involving local and foreign professors or researchers. A women's research team was organized in 1987, in connection with the National Research Council's Social Science Division, to coordinate research on gender. Panel discussions were held jointly with universities outside of Taipei. A summer seminar on gender studies and a conference on gender roles and changing society have been held. The program has a small grant project that enables two professors and twenty-one students to carry out research related to women and gender.

The program maintains a library containing books in English, Chinese, Japanese, and Korean and journals, research papers, conference reports, and other documents on women's organizations from a large number of countries. This is the largest collection of books and papers on women from Taiwan. It is open to people from various academic backgrounds and institutional bases; in Taiwan, library visits are customarily limited to university faculty and students.

The program was started with full funding for three years by the Asia Foundation. It continued to develop through partial support from the university, the Asia Foundation, the Hsu Yuan Chi Foundation, and established women's organizations. It is hoped that the university will increase its financial support, and that contributions can be obtained from other institutions in the future to ensure the continuation of the program.

Publications: The program publishes a monograph series, an occasional paper series, a quarterly *Bulletin,* and conference reports. Some of these are in English; most are in Chinese with English abstracts. The program also publishes the *Bibliography of Literature on Women in Taiwan,* 2nd ed., and the annual *Journal of Women and Gender Studies* in Chinese and English.

REPUBLIC OF KOREA

Korean Women's Development Institute
San 42-4, Bulkwang-don
Eunpyung-ku, Seoul 122-040
Telephone: 356-0070
Contact: Hyung-Deok Kim, President

The Korean Women's Development Institute (KWDI) was established on April 21, 1983 as a national focal point for women of the Republic of Korea to carry out comprehensive studies of women's issues and to reflect its findings in government policies. The major functions of KWDI are: research and study on women's issues; education and training to fully develop women's capacities; to promote effective utilization of women's resources; and collection and distribution of information on women. It is fully subsidized by the government and has a staff of 160.

Research is conducted in the following areas: law, policy, and programs that directly relate to improving the status of women; measures to develop women's skills; the mobilization of women's resources; and support systems for family life and women's well-being. Current projects focus on child care in low-income areas; women's employment and vocational training; home-based work; women employees in the service sector; welfare of fatherless families; factors in attitudes toward women's issues.

The institute runs a Women's Volunteer Bank and a vocational information and counseling center. Joint projects with women's organizations are conducted that include seminars and discussion meetings on promoting the status of women.

KWDI provides vocational training courses for low-income women and leadership training programs aimed at raising consciousness on women's issues and fostering proficiency. It produces audiovisual educational materials for use by women's or other groups.

Internships are available for undergraduate and graduate students who are majoring in women's studies, social welfare, or sociology.

Publications: Women's Development News (Korean monthly); *Korean Women Today* (English quarterly); *Women's Studies* (Korean quarterly); *Women's Studies Forum* (English annual); *KWDI Annual Reports* and *Research Activity Reports* (Korean).

Korean Women's Institute
EWHA Women's University
Seoul
Contact: Sei-Wha Chung, Director

Research Institute for Christian Women
32-1106 Hyundai Apt.
Abkujundong
Seoul
Contact: Ahn Sangnim

Research Center for Asian Women
Sookmyung Women's University
No. 53-12, 2-Ka Chungpa-Dong
Yongsan-Ku
Seoul
Contact: Young Hai Park

SENEGAL

Association of African Women for Research and Development
B.P. 3304
Dakar
Telephone: 23-02-11
Contact: Ivy Matsepe-Casaburi, President

The Association of African Women for Research and Development (AAWORD) is a pan-African nongovernmental association founded in 1977. Its secretariat is hosted by the Council for the Development of Economic and Social Research in Africa (CODESRIA) in Dakar. AAWORD is governed by its General Assembly, Executive Committee, and Editorial Committee. Its major objectives are: 1) to undertake research that calls for the participation of women and emphasizes their presence in all political, economic, social, and cultural processes of change; 2) to create networks among African women researchers and those concerned with development; 3) to identify resources that facilitate research by members; 4) to encourage formation of national research working groups in conjunction with national research centers.

AAWORD is an advocate for the recognition of the important roles of African women in their societies. Through active networking in national, regional, and international forums, it provides a major input in the formulation of African and Third World positions related to women. AAWORD has been at the forefront of demands to include gender as a major analytical category of social science research in Africa, in part through organizing seminars on women in development, rural development, women in communication, the impact of the African crisis on women, women and reproduction, women and the media in Africa, and other topics. The organization is currently taking steps to make its research accessible to a wider group of nongovernmental organizations, activists, and advocacy groups.

AAWORD receives financial support from research foundation organizations and collaborates closely with like-minded nongovernmental organizations.

Publications: AAWORD publishes *Echo,* a bilingual quarterly; *The AAWORD Journal;* proceedings of AAWORD seminars, including *Women and Rural Development in Africa, Research on African Women: What Type of Methodology,* and *AAWORD in Nairobi: Forum 1985;* and a series of annotated bibliographies on research themes of AAWORD working groups.

ENDA Third World
B.P. 3370, Dakar
Telephone: 21-60-27 and 22-42-23
Contact: Marie Helene Mottin-Sylla

The Environment Development Action in the Third World (ENDA) is an international nongovernmental organization that was established in 1972. Its headquarters is in Dakar, Senegal, and affiliates are located in Colombia, Dominican Republic, Zimbabwe, Mauritius, Morocco, and India. ENDA works with grassroots groups to supply research, documentation, publications, and training (courses and seminars) for any type of indigenous development.

The ENDA staff, including more than twenty-two nationalities, is organized in teams that focus on energy, fertilization and reforestation, consumption, health, appropriate technologies and popular creativity, urban and rural development, urbanization, biological agriculture, traditional practices affecting the health of women and children, and communication at the grassroots level. All of the areas addressed take into account the most deprived categories of the population, mainly women and children.

Some of the activities that are most directly concerned with women's issues are income-generating activities for women in rural and urban areas; technologies relieving the domestic chores of women; health and sanitation; nutrition and care for children; women's strategies for living; research and action on female circumcision and AIDS.

Internships and fellowships are available.

Publications: Among ENDA's publication series are *African Environment,* published in English and French; *ENDA Third World Documents,* leaflets on health, technology, communication, and medicinal plants, published in French, English, and Spanish; and occasional papers, published in French and English. ENDA also publishes *Vivre Autrement, le journal des consommateurs africains.* Special excerpts of ENDA publications dealing with women are available upon request.

SOUTH AFRICA

Center for Women's Studies
University of South Africa
P.O. Box 392
Pretoria 0001
Contact: Sylvia Viljoen, Head

SPAIN

Center for Research on the History of Women
Calle Brusi 61
Barcelona 08006
Telephone: 93-2004567, 2004389
Contact: Mary Nash, Director

The Center for Research on the History of Women was founded in 1982 and is an autonomous section of the Center for International Historical Studies at the University of Barcelona. It was created with the goal of promoting historical research in women's studies.

Areas of research are primarily women's history and the history of art and cinema. Current research projects focus on the history of birth control, maternity, nationalism, literature and language of women, education, work, everyday life, and sport; the center is also producing a thesaurus of nonsexist documentary language. The center offers a variety of teaching activities including postgraduate courses in women's history, a master's degree in women's studies, and seminars and conferences in women's studies.

Publications: Beyond Silence: Women in the History of Cataluna, Thesaurus of Women's Social History, and *The Modern Woman of the Twentieth Century: The New Woman in Cataluna,* all in Catalan.

Seminar on the Study of Women
Autonomous University of Madrid
Cantoblanco
Madrid 34
Contact: Maria Angeles Duran

Seminar of Women's Studies, University of the Basque Country
Triunfo
4 Bajo
20007 Donostia
Telephone: 943-468478
Contact: K. Vázquez, Sociologist

The Seminar of Women's Studies was started in 1981 with the goal of carrying out a collectively funded research project. Anthropology, sociology, psychology, and history are the main areas of research of the seminar. Fields of study include demography, space, art, images, socialization, and social change. Current research projects focus mainly on the role of women, sexual hierarchy, and attitudes toward gender in Basque society. A bibliography of literature on women is also being compiled.

Various seminars are held with open admission, and the seminar's documentation service is open to the community. A scholarship in history has been given for three years in support of a doctoral thesis on women's social and economic functions during the birth of Basque society.

Publications: Basque Women: Image and Reality, Ocean Cultures: Micronesia, Korrika: Language Rituals in Space, and *Women and Words* are a few titles of monographs published in connection with the activities of the seminar. Several articles have also been published as a result of research on Basque women.

SRI LANKA _____

Center for Women's Research
Sri Lanka Association for the Advancement of Science
120/10 Wijerama Mawatha
Colombo 7
Telephone: 502153
Contact: Swarna Jayaweera, Coordinator

The Center for Women's Research (CENWOR) was established in 1984 by a group of women researchers chiefly to undertake policy and action-oriented research on women's issues.

CENWOR has completed major research studies as part of the United Nations University Women's Work and Family Strategies international project, focusing on the contribution of women to industrial development in Sri Lanka and women in the Free Trade Zone. Among ongoing research activities are studies on export production villages, the economic needs of women in urban, low-income families, and subcontracting in industry.

Early in 1988, CENWOR established the Documentation Center and Library, a specialized reference center for women's studies. CENWOR produced a videotape for UNIDO on women in industry titled "Nimble Fingers: Image and Reality." Workshops held over the last few years have attempted to sensitize policy makers and administrators to gender issues in national, economic, and social development programs and to identify priorities for research and action. An internship program for young researchers was begun in early 1988 to help increase the number of researchers in women's studies.

CENWOR's current activities include follow-up action programs in research locations which promote support for preschools, three income-generating programs for women, a carpentry training-cum-production unit, a fish processing project, and home-based micro enterprises.

CENWOR's participation in national programs has increased through its role as the focal point for INSTRAW in Sri Lanka, and through the assistance it provides in developing and monitoring some of the women's programs funded by bilateral agencies. It hopes to expand its research and action programs to meet emerging needs and to promote women's studies in Sri Lanka.

Publications: CENWOR is the publisher of *UN Decade for Women: Progress and Achievements of Women in Sri Lanka,* in English and the two national languages, Sinhala and Tamil; *Bibliography on Women in Sri Lanka;* and a biannual newsletter.

Pacific Asian Women's Forum
623/27 Rajagiriya Gardens
Rajagiriya, Colombo
Contact: Sunila Abeyesekera

SUDAN

Ahfad University for Women
P.O. Box 167, Omdurman
Contact: Amna Rahama, Head of the School of Family Sciences

Ahfad University for women was established in 1966. It is composed of four schools: Family Sciences, Psychology and Preschool Education, Organization Management, and Rural Education and Development. Research focuses on areas that are relevant to rural development and women's studies: water supply and energy, appropriate technology, income generation by women, family planning, and the roles of women in different regions of the Sudan. Current research projects explore the development of women through family planning in rural Khartoum and Sennar (in cooperation with the Sudanese Family Planning Association); the role of women in water supply and sanitation in Aferi villages, Kordofan; women and energy development (including fuelwood development) and the impact of appropriate stoves; development of women farmers and credit facilities for them in the Darfur region. All the current research projects are linked to community outreach programs in different regions of the Sudan.

The university offers a four-year undergraduate program, as well as courses of three to six months for female village leaders working in the community outreach programs. Internships are provided by the rural village program for women of remote areas. Ahfad University also provides fellowships to the School of Rural and Educational Development for rural students and to other schools for disadvantaged students, especially those from southern Sudan.

Ahfad University plans to introduce a regional course in food and nutrition at the postgraduate level. A school of community medicine and an appropriate technology center will also be established.

Publications: The university publishes *The Ahfad Journal: Women and Change* (biannual); *Women,* a magazine of the Babiker Bedri Scientific Association for Women's Studies; and *El Nisif El Waid,* a student magazine in Arabic (both annual).

Sudan Women's Research and Development Organization
P.O. Box 208 I
Khartoum
Contact: Awartif Khalifa

The Sudan Women's Research and Development Organization is a non-profit association that attempts to improve the status of women by researching and documenting their roles and by promoting development. Its objectives are to function as a resource center, both for international agencies and within the Sudan; to act as a consultant body or to provide individual consultants to agencies or government; to establish a women's network; to plan and implement projects that improve the status of women; to instigate self-help projects in both rural and urban areas, and to act as advisor to such programs; to use grants to establish a revolving fund credit facility; and to conduct seminars to discuss issues and share information.

Publications: These include project reports and other materials assisting in the work of the organization.

SWEDEN

Center for Women Scholars and Research on Women
Uppsala University
Östra Ågatan 19 3r
S-753 22 Uppsala
Telephone: 018-182500
Contact: Mona Eliasson, Director

The Center for Women Scholars and Research on Women offers support to women researchers, particularly those conducting research on women. The research reflects the interest of the staff and is conducted in diverse areas including women and literature, psychological aspects of women's reproductive cycles, feminist theory, and feminist theology. Recent research projects include women writing in the 1880s, menarche and development, and the public's response to woman battering.

Although the main emphasis is on research and research related activities, the center offers a graduate course, "Feminist Theory in the Humanities and Social Sciences," and plans to develop more graduate courses to cope with increasing student demand. Recently, an undergraduate course was also introduced.

Temporary visiting scholar affiliation, including working space and library priviliges, can be arranged.

Publications: The center publishes an international series, *Uppsala Women's Studies in the Humanities;* and a newsletter, *Sofia,* which appears three times per year.

Center for Women Scholars and Research on Women
Stockholm University
S-106 91 Stockholm
Contact: Anita Dahlberg, Director

Swedish Network for Research and Gender Relations in the Third World
Population Participation Programs
Development Study Unit
Department of Social Anthropology
University of Stockholm
10691 Stockholm
Contact: Minou Fuglesang, Researcher

TANZANIA

Women in Development Program
Eastern and Southern African Management Institute (ESAMI)
P.O. Box 3030
Arusha
Phone: 2881/5
Telex: 42076 Arusha
Contact: Dr. Hilda Mary Tadria, Coordinator

Women's Research and Documentation Project
Box 35185
University of Dar es Salaam
Dar es Salaam
Contact: Betty Komba-Malekala

THAILAND

Women in Development Consortium
Thammasat University
Bangkok
Contact: Malee Pruekpongsawalee
For a description of this program, see pp. 238–47 in this volume. See also
Women in Development Consortium, York University, Canada, p. 279.

Women's Information Center and Foundation
P.O. Box 7-47
Bangkok 10700
Contact: Siriporn Skrobanek

Women's Research and Development Center
Prince of Songkla University
Faculty of Management Science
Head Yai 90112
Contact: Sirirat Taneerananon, Associate Dean

Women's Studies Program
Faculty of Social Sciences
Chiangmai University, Thailand
Telephone: (053) 221-699 ext. 3572
Contact: Virada Somswasdi, Chairperson

The Women's Studies Program of the Faculty of Social Studies was established in 1986 to encourage study, research, and the collection and distribution of information relating to women's issues, especially in the northern regions of Thailand. In addition, the program aims to create a liaison with other governmental and nongovernmental organizations working toward the development of women. These objectives arise from the need to provide an understanding of women's hidden contribution to all societies from a historical perspective; to develop a theoretical framework for the analysis of the root causes, forms, and dimensions of their subordination and exploitation in developing and developed societies; to promote a critical evaluation of existing development strategies at national and international levels from the point of view of their effects on women; and to search for alternative methods, policies, and strategies.

Research focuses on women and development in northern Thailand. A current project examines the impact of deforestation on the survival strategies of households through a case study of Pangkhum village.

The program conducts seminars, conferences, workshops, and lectures for various groups and is in the process of establishing undergraduate courses in women's studies at the Faculty of Social Sciences.

Future directions include a plan to set up a center of information and a data base on women's studies which can serve academicians, students, educational institutions and other organizations; to continue fostering the development and integration of women's studies into the curricula of all academic disciplines; and to strengthen liaisons with other women's organizations.

Publications: The program publishes newsletters, occasional papers, brochures and a book, *An Annotated Bibliography on Documents in Women's Studies of Northern Thailand.*

TRINIDAD AND TOBAGO _____

Caribbean Association for Feminist Research and Action (CAFRA)
P.O. Bag 442,
Tunapuna Post Office
Telephone: 809/ 663-8670
Contact: Rawida Balesh-Soodeen, Coordinator

The Caribbean Association for Feminist Research and Action (CAFRA) is an autonomous umbrella organization that was formed in response to the need for cooperation and networking among individual feminists and women's organizations in the Caribbean. It was founded on April 2, 1985 in Barbados and has members in nineteen Caribbean territories as well as associate members in Canada, the United Kingdom, the Netherlands, and the United States. Its secretariat is located in Trinidad and Tobago.

CAFRA's general aims include the development of an approach to women's problems that takes into account race and class as well as sex; the development of the feminist movement in the entire Caribbean region; and the promotion of the interrelationship between research and action. CAFRA has identified several priority areas for research and action, and is currently engaged in two such projects. These are "Women in Caribbean Agriculture" (WICA) in St. Vincent and the Grenadines and Dominica, and "Women's History" throughout the region. The first phase of the of the WICA project was recently completed, and the report of the community case studies (carried out in three communities in each island) will soon be available. The findings are now being taken back to the communities through workshops using popular education methodologies. The second phase may include national surveys. The "Women's History " project involves documentation of and assistance to groups in the region creatively involved in women's history research and education.

CAFRA provides support and solidarity to individual feminists; and provides members and other interested persons with updates on the projects with which CAFRA is involved.

Publications: CAFRA News, a quarterly newsletter. CAFRA has edited an anthology of Caribbean women's poetry called *Creation Fire,* published in conjunction with Sister Vision Press of Canada.

TUNISIA _____

All of Tunia Women for Research and Information on Women
7 Rue Sinan Pacha
Tunis

UNITED KINGDOM

Akina Mama wa Afrika
(Solidarity among African Women)
London Women's Center
Wesley House
4 Wild Court
London WC2B 5AU
England
Telephone: 01-430-1044 or 405-0678
Contact: Mabel Ikpoh

Akina Mama wa Afrika (AMWA) is an autonomous organization of African women living in Britain. It grew out of International Women's Day events held on March 8 and 9, 1985, and its purpose is to study the past, present, and future of African women, with two particular emphases: to address the problems created by the social, economic, political, and cultural environment faced by African women in Britain, and to encourage and support the struggles of peasant and working- class women who form the backbone of African economies. Full membership is open only to African women. All other interested people can join as friends, for a lower annual fee.

The objectives of the organization are to carry out research on African women; disseminate the results of such research and related publications; respond to and act as a pressure group on matters that affect African people, especially women; establish communication with grassroots women, workers, and peasants; represent the needs and opinions of the membership and be a link between the membership and black organizations, charitable trusts, other voluntary or public bodies, and government departments.

AMWA sponsors various activities for the community. Among these are workshops focusing on writing, publishing, children's concerns, and African women. The program sponsors fundraising activities for a variety of groups, including women's organizations in Africa, and talks on various subjects of interest to African women. Recent activities include an International Women's Day focus on uniting by, for, and about African women; research on the condition of African women in shelters and prisons, and on the status of their educational opportunities and welfare rights; and a conference on the effects of political upheavals on African women and children.

Publication: Focus on African Women

Centre for Cross-Cultural Research on Women
(formerly Oxford Women's Studies Committee)
Queen Elizabeth House
21 St. Giles
Oxford OX1 3LA
England
Telephone: 0865-273600
Contact: Shirley Ardener, Director

The Centre for Cross-Cultural Research on Women was established by a group of researchers to consolidate research and other activities that have been supported by the Queen Elizabeth House for more than fifteen years. Besides members of the Queen Elizabeth House, the center includes visiting fellows from many parts of the world in the fields of anthropology, economics, and history. Members have been engaged in a wide range of research topics, relating particularly to women of the Third World. This research has resulted in numerous articles, reports, and books.

A series of commemorative lectures honoring the late Audre Richards, Phyllis Kaberry, and Barbara E. Ward—all pioneers in cross-cultural research on women—have attracted large audiences and called attention to new work in the study of gender issues. In addition, the center sponsors guest lectures by visiting scholars.

The center supports the Oxford Women's Anthropology Seminar, which has been active since 1973, and from time to time convenes special seminar series on specific themes. It also sponsors relevant workshops, inviting participants from the United Kingdom and abroad. Although teaching has been secondary to research, some members undertake supervisory work at the center as well as outside teaching activities.

The center and its members individually have undertaken a number of consultancies, including written reports for various agencies, carrying out specific research projects, and supplying data for a film series.

While the center itself does not have funds to invite visiting scholars, it has helped to arrange financial sponsorship for some visiting fellows.

Individual members of the center have published more than thiry-five books and more than one hundred pamphlets and monographs. Beginning in 1975, the Oxford Women's Studies Committee published a series of books that came out of seminars, one of which was *Perceiving Women*, edited by Shirley Ardener (1975).

Centre for Research and Education on Gender
University of London Institute of Education
20 Bedford Way
London WC1H 0AL
England
Contact: Diana Leonard, Coordinator

Change
P.O. Box 823
London SE 24 9JS
England
Contact: Georgia Ashworth, Director

Feminist International Network of Resistance to Reproductive and Genetic Engineering
P.O. Box 583
London, NW3 1RQ
England
Telephone: 44-532-681109
Contact: Jalna Hanmer and Debbie Steinberg

The Feminist International Network of Resistance to Reproductive and Genetic Engineering (FINRRAGE) grew out of the Emergency Conference on New Reproductive Technologies that was held in Sweden in 1985 and attended by women from sixteen countries. The network now links more than seven hundred women from twenty-six countries. Research is conducted in several areas including international development of in vitro techniques, embryo transfer, sex predetermination, cloning, genetic engineering, contraception and population control, surrogacy, and infertility management. National and international conferences are held regularly.

Future goals of the network include establishing contacts with countries where none exist and expanding and properly funding the International Feminist Centre on Reproductive and Genetic Engineering.

Publications: FINRRAGE publishes national newsletters, international information packets, and *Reproductive and Genetic Engineering: Journal of International Feminist Analysis* (English). Publications are available in English, German, Dutch, French, and other languages; contact FINRRAGE for more information.

Institute of Development Studies
The University of Sussex
Brighton BN1 9RE
England
Telephone: 0273-606261
Contact: Naila Kabeer, Research Fellow
For a description of this program, see pp. 188–202 in this volume.

Women's Research and Resource Centre
Hungerford House
Victoria Embankment
London, England

Women and Technology Research Programme
University of Sussex
Science Policy Research Unit
Mantell Bldg., Falmer
Brighton, E. Sussex BN1 9RF
England
Contact: Felicity Henwood

UNITED STATES

Abigail Quigley McCarthy Center for Research on Women
2004 Randolph Ave.
College of St. Catherine
St. Paul, MN 55105
Telephone: 612-332-5521
Contact: Catherine Lupori

Alice Paul Center for the Study of Women
106 Logan Hall, CN
University of Pennsylvania
Philadelphia, PA 19104
Telephone: 215-898-8740
Contact: Janice Madden, Acting Director

American Association of University Women
Educational Foundation
2401 Virginia Ave., NW, 5th Floor
Washington, DC 20037
Telephone: 202-728-7603
Contact: Margaret Dunkle, Director

The Arthur and Elizabeth Schlesinger Library
Radcliffe College
10 Garden St.
Cambridge, MA 02138
Telephone: 617-495-8647
Contact: Patricia King, Director

The Barnard Center for Research on Women
3009 Broadway, Room 101 Barnard Hall
New York, NY 10027-6598
Telephone: 212-854-2067
Contact: Temma Kaplan, Director

Business and Professional Women's Foundation
2012 Massachusetts Ave., NW
Washington, DC 20036
Telephone: 202-293-1200
Contact: Linda Dorian, Director

Center for Advanced Feminist Studies
492 Ford Hall
224 Church Street, SE
University of Minnesota
Minneapolis, MN 55455
Telephone: 612-624-6310
Contact: Shirley Nelson Garner

Center for American Women and Politics
Eagleton Institute of Politics
Rutgers University
New Brunswick, NJ 08903
Telephone: 201-932-9384
Contact: Ruth B. Mandel, Director

Center for Education of Women
330 East Liberty St.
University of Michigan
Ann Arbor, MI 48104-2289
Telephone: 313-998-7080
Contact: Carol Hollenshead

Center for Research on Women
207 East Duke Bldg.
Duke University/University of North Carolina
Durham, NC 27708
Telephone: 919-684-6641
Contact: Christina Greene, Project Director

Center for Research on Women
College of Arts and Sciences
Memphis State University
Memphis, TN 38152
Telephone: 901-678-2770
Contact: Lynn Cannon, Director

Center for Research on Women
Wellesley College
828 Washington St.
Wellesley, MA 02181
Telephone: 617-431-1453
Contact: Susan Bailey, Director

Center for the Study of Women
236A Kinsey Hall
University of California, Los Angeles
Los Angeles, CA 90064
Telephone: 213-825-0590
Contact: Helen Astin, Acting Director

Center for the Study of Women and Society
33 West 42nd St.
CUNY Graduate School and University Center
New York, NY 10036
Telephone: 212-642-2954
Contact: Sue Rosenberg Zalk

Center fot the Study of Women in Society
636 Prince Lucien Campbell Hall
University of Oregon
Eugene, OR 97403
Telephone: 503-346-5015
Contact: Sandra Morgen, Director

Center for Women in Government
Draper Hall 302
1400 Washington Ave.
University at Albany
Albany, NY 12222
Telephone: 518-442-3900
Contact: Florence B. Bonner, Executive Director

Center for Women Policy Studies
2000 P Street, NW Suite 508
Washington, DC 20036
Telephone: 202-872-1770
Contact: Leslie R. Wolfe, Executive Director

Center for Women's Studies
Research and Resources Institute
University of Cincinnati
Cincinnati, OH 45221-0164
Telephone: 513-556-6657
Contact: M. Christine Andersen, Director

Center for Women's Studies
207 Dulles Hall
230 W. 17th Ave.
Ohio State University
Columbus, OH 43210-1311
Telephone: 614-292-1021
Contact: Susan Hartmann, Director
For a description of this program, see pp. 248–62 in this volume.

Center on Women and Public Policy
Humphrey Institute of Public Affairs
University of Minnesota
301 19th Ave S.
Minneapolis, MN 55455
Telephone: 612-625-2505
Contact: Barbara Nelson and Arvonne S. Fraser, Codirectors

The Council for INSTRAW
47-49 East 65th St.
New York, NY 10021
Telephone: 212-570-4335
Contact: Irene Tinker, President

Equity Policy Center
2000 P Street, NW
Suite 508
Washington, DC 20036
Telephone: 202-872-1770
Contact: Elizabeth Fox

Feminist Studies Focused Reseach Activity
Women's Studies
University of California, Santa Cruz
Santa Cruz, CA 95064
Telephone: 408-459-2781
Contact: Wendy Brown, Director

Graduate Group for Feminist Studies
527 O'Brian Hall
State University of New York, Buffalo
Buffalo, NY 14260
Telephone: 716-636-2549
Contact: Isabel Marcus

The Henry A. Murray Research Center of Radcliffe College
10 Garden St.
Cambridge, MA 02138
Telephone: 617-495-8140
Contact: Anne Colby, Director

Higher Education Research Institute
Department of Education
Moore Hall 322, 405 Hilgard Ave.
University of California at Los Angeles
Los Angeles, CA 90024-1521
Telephone: 213-825-2709
Contact: Helen S. Astin, Associate Director

Higher Education Resource Services, Mid-America
Colorado Women's College Campus
University of Denver
Denver, CO 80220
Telephone: 303-871-6866
Contact: Cynthia Secor, Director

Higher Education Resource Services, New England
Cheever House
Wellesley College
Wellesley, MA 02181
Telephone: 617-235-0320
Contact: Cynthia Secor, Director

Institute for Reseach on Women and Gender
Serra House, Serra St.
Stanford University
Stanford, CA 94305-8640
Telephone: 415-723-1994
Contact: Deborah Rhode, Director

Institute for Research on Women
State University of New York at Albany
Albany, NY 12222
Telephone: 518-442-4670
Contact: Christine E. Bose, Director

Institute for Research on Women
Rutgers University, Douglass College
New Brunswick, NJ 08903
Telephone: 201-932-9072
Contact: Carol H. Smith, Director

Institute for Research on Women and Gender
763 Schermerhorn
Columbia University
New York, NY 10027
Telephone: 212-854-3277
Contact: Martha Howell, Director

Institute for the Study of Women and Gender
417 Whitney Road
University of Connecticut
Storrs, CT 06268
Telephone: 203-486-2186
Contact: Patricia Carter, Director

Institute for the Study of Women and Men in Society
734 West Adams Blvd.
University of Southern California
Los Angeles, CA 90007
Telephone: 213-743-3683
Contact: Judith Glass, Director

Institute for Women and Gender Research
School of Natural Resources
Utah State University
Logan, UT 84322-5200
Telephone: 801-750-2580
Contact: Sharon Ohlhorst, Director

Institute for Women and Work
New York State School of Industrial and Labor Relations
Cornell University
15 E. 26 St.
New York, NY 10010
Telephone: 212-340-2800
Contact: Esta R. Bigler, Metropolitan District Director

Institute for Women's Policy Research
1400 20th St., NW, Suite 104
Washington, DC 20036
Telephone: 202-785-5100
Contact: Heidi Hartmann

International Center for Research on Women
1717 Massachusetts Ave. NW, Suite 501
Washington, DC 20036
Telephone: 202-797-0007
Contact: Mayra Buvinic, Director

International Women's Rights Action Watch
Humphrey Institute of Public Affairs
301 19th Ave. South
University of Minnesota
Minneapolis, MN 55455
Telephone: 612-625-2505
Contact: Arvonne S. Frazer, Senior Fellow

Mary Ingram Bunting Institute
Radcliffe Research and Study Center
Radcliffe College
34 Concord Ave.
Cambridge, MA 02138
Telephone: 617-495-8212
Contact: Florence Ladd, Director

National Association for Women Deans, Administrators,
and Counselors
1325 Eighteenth St., NW, Suite 210
Washington, DC 20036
Telephone: 202-659-9330
Contact: Patricia Reuckel

National Coalition for Women's Enterprise, Inc.
30 Irving Pl.
9th Floor
New York, NY 10003
Telephone: 212-505-2090
Contact: Marcia Cantarella, Executive Director

National Council for Research on Women
47-49 East 65th Street
New York, NY 10021
Telephone: 212-570-5001
Contact: Mariam Chamberlain

National Resource Center
Girls Clubs of America, Inc.
30 East 33 St.
New York, NY 10016
Telephone: 212-689-3700
Contact: Margaret Gates, Executive Director

National Women's Studies Association
University of Maryland, College Park
College Park, MD 20742
Telephone: 301-405-5573
Contact: Debbie Lewis, National Director

Northwest Center for Research on Women
Cunningham Hall
University of Washington
Seattle, WA 98195
Telephone: 206-543-9531
Contact: Angela Ginorio, Director

Office of Women in Higher Education
American Council on Education
One Dupont Circle
Washington, DC 20036-1193
Telephone: 202-939-9390
Contact: Donna Shavlik, Director

Pembroke Center for Teaching and Research on Women
Box 1958
Brown University
Providence, RI 02912
Telephone: 401-863-2643
Contact: Karen Newman, Director

Program of Policy Reseach on Women and Families
2100 M St., NW
Washington, DC 20037
Telephone: 202-833-7200
Contact: Elaine Sorenson, Senior Research Associate

Project on Equal Education Rights
NOW Legal Defense and Education Fund
99 Hudson St.
New York, NY 10013
Telephone: 212-925-6635
Contact: Helen Neubourne, Executive Director

Project on the Status and Education of Women
Association of American Colleges
1818 R St., NW
Washington, DC 20009
Telephone: 202-387-1300
Contact: Bernice Sandler, Director

The Project on the Study of Gender and Education
405 White Hall
Kent State University
Kent, OH 44242
Telephone: 216-672-2178
Contact: Averil McClelland, Director

Project on Women and Social Change
138 Elm St.
Smith College
Northamptom, MA 01063
Telephone: 413-584-2700
Contact: Susan C. Bourque, Director

Sojourner Center for Women's Studies
State University of New York at Binghampton
Binghampton, NY 13901
Telephone: 607-777-2815
Contact: Jane Collins, Carole Davies, and Susan Sterett, Codirectors

Southwest Institute for Research on Women
Douglass Bldg. 102
Tuscon, AZ 85721
Telephone: 602-621-7338
Contact: Karen Anderson, Acting Director

Women and International Development Group
c/o Harvard Institute for International Development
One Eliot St.,
Cambridge, MA 02138
Telephone: 617-495-4249

Women in Agricultural Development
Institute of Food and Agricultural Sciences
3028 McCarty Hall
University of Florida
Gainesville, FL 32611
Telephone: 904-392-1965
Contact: Marilyn M. Swisher, Assistant Director

Women in International Development Program
Office of International Research and Development
Oregon State University, Snell 400
Corvallis, OR 97331-1641
Telephone: 503-754-2228
Contact: Revathi Balakrishnan, Director

Women's Interart Center
549 West 52nd St.
New York, NY 10019
Telephone: 212-246-1050
Contact: Margot Lewitin, Artistic Director

The Women's Research and Education Institute
1700 18th St., NW
#400
Washington, DC 20009
Telephone: 202-328-7070
Contact: Betty Parsons Dooley, Executive Director

Women's Research and Resource Center
Box 362
Spelman College
Atlanta, GA 30314
Telephone: 404-681-3643, Ext. 360
Contact: Beverly Guy-Sheftall, Director

Women's Research Institute
50 Elizabeth St.
Hartford College for Women
Hartford CT 06105
Telephone: 203-233-5662
Contact: Sharon Toffey Shepela, Director

Women's Research Institute
Virginia Polytechnic Institute and State University
Blacksburg, VA 24061-0338
Telephone: 703-231-7615
Director: Carol J. Burger

Women's Resource Center
Higher Education Resource Services, West
293 Olpin Union
University of Utah
Salt Lake City, UT 84112
Telephone: 801-581-3745
Contact: Katherine Brooks, Director

Women's Resources and Research Center
10 Lower Freeborn Hall
University of California, Davis
Davis, CA 95616
Telephone: 916-752-3372
Contact: Linda Morris

Women's Studies
College of Liberal Arts
Arizona State University
Tempe, AZ 85287
Telephone: 602-965-2358
Director: Nancy Russo

Women's Studies Program and Policy Center
Stuart Hall, Rm. 203
George Washington University
Washington, DC 20052
Telephone: 202-944-6942
Contact: Roberta Spalter-Roth, Director

Women's Studies Research Center
209 North Brooks St.
University of Wisconsin
Madison, WI 53715
Telephone: 608-263-2053 or 608-263-4703
Contact: Cyrena Pondrom, Director

Young Women's Christian Association, USA
726 Broadway
New York, NY 10003
Telephone: 212-614-2700
Contact: Gwendolyn C. Baker, Executive Director

URUGUAY

Grupo Estudio la Condicion de la Mujer en Uruguay (GRECMU)
(Group for the Study of Women in Uruguay)
Juan Pamillier 1174
Montevideo
Contact: Isabel Miranda

U.S.S.R. ————————————————————————————

Center for Gender Studies
Institute for Socioeconomic Studies of Population
U.S.S.R. Academy of Sciences
Krasikova Str. 27
Moscow 117218
Telephone: 125-73-02, 129-04-00
Contact: Anastasiya Posadskaya, Director

VIETNAM ————————————————————————————

Research Center on Women
6 Qinh Cong Trang
Hanoi
Contact: Le Thi Nham Tuyet

ZIMBABWE ————————————————————————————

Women in Development Research Unit
Centre for Inter-racial Studies
Box M.P. 167
Mount Pleasant
Salisbury
Contact: Olivia D. Muchena

New and Forthcoming Books from The Feminist Press

The Captive Imagination: A Casebook on The Yellow Wallpaper, edited and
with an introduction by Catherine Golden. $35.00 cloth, $14.95 paper.

Eva/Ave: Women in Renaissance and Baroque Prints, by H. Diane Russell.
$59.95 cloth, $29.95 paper.

Here's to the Women: 100 Songs for and about American Women, by Hilda
Wenner and Elizabeth Freilicher. Foreword by Pete Seeger. $49.95 cloth,
$24.95 paper.

I Dwell in Possibility, a memoir by Toni McNaron. $35.00 cloth, $12.95 paper.

Intimate Warriors: Portraits of a Modern Marriage, 1899–1944, selected works
by Neith Boyce and Hutchins Hapgood, edited by Ellen Kay Trimberger.
Afterword by Shari Benstock. $35.00 cloth, $12.95 paper.

Lion Woman's Legacy: An Armenian-American Memoir, by Arlene Avakian.
$35.00 cloth, $12.95 paper.

Long Walks and Intimate Talks. Stories and poems by Grace Paley. Paintings
by Vera B. Williams. $29.95 cloth, $12.95 paper.

Margaret Howth: A Story of Today, a novel by Rebecca Harding Davis.
Afterword by Jean Fagan Yellin. $35.00 cloth, $11.95 paper.

The Mer-Child: A Legend for Children and Other Adults, by Robin Morgan.
Illustrations by Amy Zerner and Jesse Spicer Zerner. $17.95 cloth,
$8.95 paper.

Now in November, a novel by Josephine Johnson. Afterword by Nancy
Hoffman. $29.95 cloth, $10.95 paper.

On Peace, War, and Gender: A Challenge to Genetic Explanations, edited by
Anne E. Hunter. Catherine M. Flamenbaum and Suzanne R. Sunday,
Associate Editors. (Volume VI, Genes and Gender Series, edited by Betty
Rosoff and Ethel Tobach.) $35.00 cloth, $12.95 paper.

Women's Studies International: Nairobi and Beyond, edited by Aruna Rao.
$35.00 cloth, $15.95 paper.

Women Writing in India: 600 B.C. to the Present, edited by Susie Tharu and
K. Lalita. Vol. I: 600 B.C. to the Early Twentieth Century. Vol. II: The
Twentieth Century. Each volume $59.95 cloth, $29.95 paper.

For a free catalog, write to The Feminist Press at The City University of New York,
311 East 94 Street, New York, NY 10128. Send book orders to The Talman Company, 150 Fifth Avenue, New York, NY 10011. Please include $3.00 postage/
handling for one book, $.75 for each additional.